Georgia's Landmarks, Memorials and Legends

COMPLETE IN TWO VOLUMES
VOLUME II
(ILLUSTRATED)

By
LUCIAN LAMAR KNIGHT
(A.B., Georgia; M.A., Princeton)

COMPILER OF THE STATE RECORDS OF GEORGIA

Author of "Reminiscences of Famous Georgians," in two volumes;
"A Biographical Dictionary of Southern Authors";
"Historical Side-Lights"; Etc.

Part 2

PELICAN PUBLISHING COMPANY
Gretna 2006

Printed in the United States of America

Published by Pelican Publishing Company, Inc.
1000 Burmaster Street, Gretna, Louisiana 70053

CANDLER

Metter. On July 17, 1914, Governor Slaton approved a bill creating by Constitutional amendment the new County of Candler. It is to be carved out of territory formerly embraced within three contiguous counties, to-wit.: Tattnall, Bulloch and Emanuel. Metter, a wideawake little town, on a branch line of the Central of Georgia, will be the new county seat. There was practically no opposition to the measure at this session of the Legislature, as the various counties affected by the proposed legislation were friendly to the bill; but in former years the champions of the measure have waged a losing fight against bitter opposition. Since the creation of the new county involves an amendment to the Constitution, it is first necessary to submit the same to popular vote for ratification; but the result can be safely foreshadowed. The new county is named for Governor Allen D. Candler, one of Georgia's most distinguished sons. On the field of battle, in the halls of Congress, in the chair of Governor, in the office of Secretary of State, and, last but not least, as Compiler of State Records, he was called upon to serve the State in many distinguished capacities; but in not one of these high stations did he fail to approve himself a statesman and a man.

Says the Atlanta *Constitution*: "Governor Slaton on Friday signed the bill creating the new county of Candler, and thus ends one of the most determined fights waged in the Legislature. The effort of the people of Metter to secure the creation of the county of Candler is only equaled by that of the people of Winder, who succeeded some days ago in passing the bill to create the county of Barrow. The first bill to create Candler County was introduced ten years ago. For ten sessions the people of Metter have been knocking at the doors of the General Assembly, and finally they have been successful. This success is largely due to F. H. Sills, editor of the Metter *Advertiser*, and Dr. W. D. Kennedy, who helped finance the project. Dr. Kennedy was the first to conceive the idea of a new county. Three years ago Mr. Sills was put in charge of the campaign, and during that time he has given the legislature no rest. Governor Slaton signed the bill with a special fountain pen, which the people of Metter presented to Mr. Sills in recognition of his services. Candler County will have a population of 12,725; tax values of $2,729,000, and an area of 361 square miles.''

CARROLL

The Murder of General McIntosh. On the west side of the Chattahoochee River, within the borders of the present County of Carroll, stood the old home of General William McIntosh, the famous chief of the Cowetas or Lower Creeks. The unfriendly Indians, piqued by the relinquishment of the Georgia lands, were bent upon the death of the brave chief, at whose door lay the responsibility for the treaty at Indian Springs. He was accordingly condemned in general council, under color of what was claimed to be an unwritten law, exacting the forfeiture of life for the offence in question. Quite a party of Indians, numbering in the aggregate one hundred and seventy, undertook to execute the sentence; and, proceeding furtively to the home of General McIntosh, they concealed themselves under cover of the woods until just before dawn, on May 1, 1825. They were provided with light-wood knots, for the purpose of setting fire to the house, and they were also well armed.

Before emerging from ambush, they first sent an interpreter, James Hutton, along with two Indians, to ascertain, without arousing suspicion, what temporary sojourners the McIntosh abode sheltered. In an out-house in the yard, which was usually allotted to guests, the chief's son, Chilly McIntosh, was found, sharing the apartment with an old peddler. But the spies barely put foot upon the doorstep before the young man, guided by instinct, scented danger, and leaped at one bound through the open window. Fire was opened upon him, but the shots failed to overtake the mercurial youth.

And now the entire body of Indians surrounded the house in which General McIntosh slept, and began to light the fagots underneath the doors and windows. The sti-fling smoke awoke the brave chief, only to greet him with the crackling flames and to show him in the funeral glare of the red torches what deadly peril surrounded him. It was the most lurid dawn upon which he ever looked; and, fully comprehending the awful horror of the wild scene, he realized that he was now to perish amid the blazing rafters of his home. But the proud old Indian spirit within him nerved his sinews for the ordeal. He was determined to die game; and, though denied the honors of equal battle, he could at least greet the shades of his ancestors with the war-cry upon his lips.

Behind barricaded doors, with the aid of an Indian friend who was the only other occupant of the building at the time, he returned for several moments the blasting fire which came from the red belt. But an entrance was soon forced; and, hurling himself upon the invaders who now rushed in, the faithful ally was the first to fall, rid-dled with bullets. General McIntosh, retreating up the stairway in the suffocating smoke, fired shot after shot as he went, making the foul murderers pay heavy cost for the life which they were now about to take. But at last the brave chief lay prostrate upon the floor bleeding from countless wounds. And now the fiendish glee of the red devils filled the air with the most infernal music of pandemonium. They sang and danced and shouted about the mutilated body while the flames underneath and around roared and seethed. It was like the glimpse which one might get at hell-gate.

Still the brutal instincts of the savages were not yet fully gorged. The brave chief was next dragged by the heels into the yard, and while his lips yet breathed the challenge of an unsubdued old warrior, the bloody knife was plunged into his heart. It straightway ended the death struggles, and, lifting his mangled face to the fading dawn stars, William McIntosh, chief of the Cowetas, bravest of the brave, Georgia's true and tried friend, slept the heavy sleep of his fathers.

Rapine was next added to the measure of revenge which included already murder and arson. Everything of value about the place, which they were not able to carry off, they ruthlessly destroyed, like the savage hordes of Attilla. The devastation was made complete, and the rising sun found the home of the brave chief a mass of ruins. Georgia has always felt some twinge of conscience over the sad fate of McIntosh. It is said, on good authority, that the Indian chief, realizing the imminence of danger, had sent to Milledgeville for armed protection, and though it was readily promised, it was never received. General McIntosh was at all times the staunch friend of Georgia. In the War of 1812 he had resisted the most tempting overtures of the British emissaries; and, espousing the American cause, he had earned the rank of Brigadier-General. Later he had fought under General Jackson, in the campaign against the Seminole Indians in Florida. He was ever marked by an unswerving integrity of character, and to the famous Highland clan, of which he was a member, he brought new laurels. General Lachlan McIntosh, of the Revolution, was a kinsman. Governor George M. Troup, then Governor of the State, was a cousin. The latter's mother was a McIntosh, an own sister to the General's father. Though Governor Troup himself could boast no Indian blood in his veins, he possessed both the grim determination and the courage of his kinsman. The crisis which he was now called upon to face was well calculated to test the metal of the man in the executive chair.

Carrollton. When the County of Carroll was organized in 1826 out of lands acquired from the Creeks, under a treaty which cost the brave McIntosh his life, it extended from the borders of the Cherokee nation on the north, to the Alabama line, at what is now West Point, on the south. It was called the "Free State of Carroll," partly on account of its magnitude, and partly for the reason that it boasted at this time comparatively few slaves. The county-site was first located at what is today known as Old Carrollton, a point eight miles northeast of the present town. But in 1829 the site of public buildings was changed to a locality better adapted to the purpose, but the original name was still retained. Both the county and the county-site were named for Charles Carroll, of Carrollton, who lived to be the last survivor of the immortal group of patriots who signed the Declaration of Independence. On December 22, 1829, an Act was approved, making New Carrollton the permanent site for public buildings, and incorporating the town with the following commissioners: Henry Curtis, Hiram Sharp, William Bryce, George Gibson and Giles S. Boggess.* Carrollton is a wideawake business community, with a splendid body of citizens, numerous solid mercantile establishments, several strong banks, and many beautiful homes. The present public school system was established in 1886.

Unmarked Grave of General McIntosh. Overlooking the Chattahoochee River, on the famous McIntosh Reserve, within the present borders of Carroll, is the grave of General William McIntosh, unmarked, except for a pile of flint rocks, in a thicket of underbrush. As the result of his friendship for Georgia, several millions of acres were acquired by the State, under what is known as the second treaty of Indian Springs. But his own brave life was forfeited; and

*Acts, 1823, p. 201.

there will rest a foul blot upon Georgia's escutcheon until she marks with an appropriate memorial the last resting place of her true and tried friend: the martyred chief of the Cowetas.

CHARLTON

Folkston. In 1854, Charlton County was organized out of Camden,[1] and named for Judge R. M. Charlton, of Savannah. The commissioners to choose a county-seat were: Thomas Hilliard, A. J. Bessant, Thomas D. Hawkins, and Robert King.[2] Folkston is only a small village, named for an old family then resident in this neighborhood. Since the building of the A. B. & A. Railroad, on which the town is located, its growth has received a fresh impetus.

Center Village.   Volume I.

CHATHAM

**Savannah
Founded 1733.**   Volume I, Pages 378-380.

**First Jury Em-
paneled in Georgia.** One of the chief concerns of Oglethorpe, after fixing the site of the town, was the erection of a courthouse, for the administration of justice in the settlement. Though a somewhat rude affair, the building, which was speedily raised for this purpose, also met the religious needs of the colony for several years. The following persons composed the first jury ever empanelled in Georgia: Samuel Parker, Thomas Young, Joseph Cole, John Wright, John West, Timothy Bowling, John Milledge,

[1] Not out of Wayne and Appling, as inadvertently stated in Vol. I.
[2] Acts, 1853-1854, p. 290.

Henry Close, Walter Fox, John Grady, James Carwell, and Richard Cannon. The recorder was Noble Jones. His constables were Richard Cannon and Joseph Cole, while his bailiffs were George Symes, Richard Hodges and Francis Scott. The first tax collectors, or tithing-men, were Francis Magridge and Thomas Young. The following prominent citizens were made conservators of the peace: Peter Gordon, William Waterland, Thomas Causton, Thomas Christie, George Symes, Richard Hodges, Francis Scott and Noble Jones.[1]

Georgia: the Only Free-Soil Colony. Under the laws enacted by the Trustees slavery was forbidden in Georgia. It is an interesting fact that at this time the institution was elsewhere unchecked. There were slaves in Massachusetts and Rhode Island, as well as in Virginia and South Carolina. The earliest prohibitive legislation upon the subject emanated from the Trustees of Georgia; and the first of the English colonies in America to outlaw slavery was the colony founded by Oglethorpe.*

Other enactments of the Trustees made it impossible either to sell or to mortgage lands in Georgia. They excluded rum from the colony, and sought to encourage the manufacture of wine and silk. Such restrictions were ill-adapted to meet the demands of competition. The colony began to languish. Discontent became widespread, and finally these measures were repealed.[2]

First Commercial House in Georgia. James Habersham, in association with Charles Harris, established in Savannah in 1744 the first commercial house in Georgia. The firm was known as Harris and Haber-

---

[1] Jones, Stevens, McCall, Lee and Agnew.
[2] Bancroft's History of U. S., Vol. 2, p. 287; 1, 513, 572; 2, 268-280; also McCall, Jones, Stevens, etc.

sham. It gave great encouragement to planters, from whom were purchased deerskins, poultry, lumber, and other wares, a cargo of which, valued at $10,000, was shipped to England in 1749. This was the beginning of the foreign trade relations through the port of Savannah. The establishment of Habersham and Harris was located near the water's edge, in the rear of where the commission house of Robert Habersham afterwards stood.[1]

The Jews in Georgia: Volume I, Pages 97-103.

Georgia's First Barbecue. "On the Sunday morning before leaving South Carolina, the colonists held a special thanksgiving service, after which Oglethorpe, at his own expense, gave a grand dining, to which, in the name of the colonists, he invited the soldiers from the barracks, besides a number of citizens. More than three hundred people partook of the feast, at which was served, so we are told by one who was present, four fat hogs, two fine English beeves, eight turkeys, one hundred chickens and ducks, a hogshead of rum punch, a hogshead of beer, and a barrel of wine. Notwithstanding the large quantity of liquor consumed, not a man became intoxicated, and perfect order was preserved. This was the first Georgia barbecue; for, though spread in South Carolina, it was given by the first Georgian, and was served in the abundant and generous way which has since made Georgia barbecues the most famous of feasts."[2]

Traditions of Sir Walter Raleigh. "In ascending the Savannah River, Oglethorpe is said to have carried with him the Journal of Sir Walter Raleigh. From the general characteristics of the place, from the latitude which it occupied, and especially from the traditions of the Indians, he was led to believe that the celebrated English explorer had landed at Yamacraw bluff and had conversed with the natives. In fact, a grave-mound, distant some half a mile from the

---

[1] Lee and Agnew, Jones, Stevens, McCall, etc.
[2] J. Harris Chappell, in Stories of Georgia.

spot, was pointed out by the Indians, who informed the founder of the colony of Georgia that the king who then talked with Raleigh was there interred.''*

Christ Church.   Volume I, Pages 77-80.

The Wesleys: When Oglethorpe returned to Geor-
John and Charles. gia, in 1736, after a sojourn of several
months in England, there sailed with
him to Savannah two young religious enthusiasts, whose
names were destined to become household words throughout the whole of Christendom: John and Charles Wesley.
It was the founder's anxiety for the spiritual welfare
of the colony which induced him to make overtures to
these devout men. On the other hand, it was the somewhat ascetic creed of self-denial embraced by the Wesleys which induced them to exchange the luxurious life
of an English country-side for the privations of an un-
explored wilderness beyond the Atlantic. Reared under
the pious roof of old Samuel Wesley, who, for more than
forty years, was rector of the church at Epworth, both
heredity and environment impelled them toward the pulpit. However, it was not until they became students at
Oxford that they acquired the austere habits of life which
set them peculiarly apart; and here, in association with
congenial spirits, few in number but kindred in character, they formed a club, which drew upon them no small
amount of ridicule and abuse. They were regarded in
the light of pietists. The name which finally stuck—
Methodists—seems to have been given to them by a
fellow of Merton College. At first John Wesley declined
the offer of Oglethorpe. His father was recently deceased and his mother was old. The latter, however,
rallied him with mild rebuke. ''Had I twenty sons,'' said
she, ''I should rejoice that they were all so employed,

---

*Chas. C. Jones, Jr., in History of Georgia, Vol. I.

though I should never see them more.'' Thus admonished, he waived his scruples and agreed to accompany Oglethorpe to Georgia, his special desire being for missionary work among the Indians; and for this purpose he came with full religious ordination. But Charles engaged himself in the capacity of private secretary to Oglethorpe; and his acceptance of purely secular work in preference to holy orders is said to have given offense to John, whose paramount reason for sailing to Georgia was ''to save his soul.'' But Charles, almost from the outset, felt himself to be a misfit. It was at the expense of the Society for the Propagation of the Gospel in Foreign Parts that John embarked upon the expedition. At first he refused to receive the stipend of fifty pounds per annum, but he afterwards agreed to take it. Another of the Oxford band who joined the brothers was Benjamin Ingham, a man of parts, who later joined the Moravian brethren, married a titled lady, and became the head of a sect called the Inghamites.

It was late in the fall of the year when two vessels, the Symond and the London Merchant, each of 220 tons burden, quit the English docks, bearing three hundred emigrants to Georgia. The Wesleys traveled in the former. Among the passengers were twenty-six Moravians, whose demeanor during the progress of a somewhat stormy voyage made an extraordinary impression upon the Oxford men; and such was John Wesley's eager desire to converse with them that he immediately began the study of German and acquired no little familiarity with the language before reaching port. The piety of these devout Moravians moved him to admiration. Indeed, he questioned the genuineness of his conversion prior to meeting them. In his mission to the new world he was destined to meet with little apparent success, but he needed just the mental and spiritual discipline which it gave him. To quote Dr. J. W. Lee: ''The John Wesley who went out to Georgia was still in a crysallis condition; he had yet to learn how to expand his wings. It is not true that his career in Georgia was the utter failure it has been represented to be in many treatises. It is true, however, that it was hampered by the uncertain condition of will which is apt to precede some great spiritual change." On the 14th of February, 1736, which proved to be the Sabbath, the vessels anchored in one of the coves of an island, probably Cockspur. The day was calm and beautiful. Early in the morning the voyagers went ashore, and there, on a rising knoll, with his fellow voyagers around him, John Wesley lifted his voice in prayer for the first time in the new world, where the present generation sees his followers numbered by millions. Soon after reaching Savannah, John Wesley was designated to succeed Samuel Quincy, in charge of the religious affairs of the settlement, while Charles, in company with Oglethorpe, journeyed still further to Frederica.

**The Grave of
Tomo-Chi-Chi.**   Volume I, Pages 85-87.

Bethesda.   Volume I, Pages 80-85.

**The Cradle of
Methodism.** "Through John and Charles Wesley, the early life of Savannah and of the Colony of Georgia is linked with one of the most powerful religious movements of the eighteenth century. John Wesley himself says: 'The first rise of Methodism was in 1729, when four of us met together at Oxford. The second was at Savannah in 1736, when twenty or thirty persons met at my house. The last was at London, on this day, May first, 1738, when forty or fifty of us agreed to meet together every Wednesday evening.' Of the four young men who met together at Oxford, all visited Savannah, John and Charles Wesley, Benjamin Ingraham and George Whitefield, three of them having the charge of churches in the colony. Verily, Savannah has every right to be a stronghold of Methodism. But a mistaken notion has somehow caught the popular credence regarding the Wesleys and Whitefield.

They were all Church of England men, and were appointed as such to be chaplains in Savannah. Their methods of life gained them the name of Methodists; applied at first simply to those who performed rigid outward observance of devotional duties; and it gradually acquired and embodied the doctrines peculiar to Wesley as they were unfolded.

"Another event which lends luster to the small settlement on the banks of the Savannah River was the establishment of a Sunday-school in the parish of Christ Church by Reverend John Wesley, nearly fifty years before Robert Raikes began his system of Sunday instruction in Gloucester, Eng., and eighty years before the first Sunday-school in America, modeled after his plan, was established in New York. . . . This Sunday-school begun by Wesley, was perpetuated by Whitefield at Bethesda, and has continued until the present—constituting the oldest Sunday-school in the world. Nor does this end the claim of Savannah upon John Wesley. Here in Savannah was his first book of hymns written, though it was published in Charleston, in 1737. But one copy is known to be in existence, discovered in England in 1878. Rare as any Shakespeare, this hymnal escaped the search of both English and American collectors; no biographer of John Wesley so much as dreaming of its existence. It is also interesting as an early-printed American book, apart from its interest as a hymnal and a portrayal of Wesley's mind during his eventful visit to Georgia. The volume is a small octavo volume of seventy-four pages, the title page of which reads: 'A Collection of Psalms and Hymns—Charleston. Printed by Timothy Lewis, 1737.' "*

John Wesley Quits Savannah: His Love Affair. Says Dr. James W. Lee, in narrating the circumstances under which the great founder of Methodism left Savannah, in 1736:

"During his stay at Ebenezer, Wesley opened his heart to Spanenberg on a matter which was weighing heavily upon his mind; and he has placed on record his approval of the good pastor's advice. On his return to Savannah the affair was to assume a very serious aspect, and to bring to an abrupt termination his career in the settlement. The chief man at Savannah was a certain Thomas Causton, who began his career as the com-

---

*Adelaide Wilson, in Historic and Picturesque Savannah. Consult also: James W. Lee, in Illustrated History of Methodism.

*Though Savannah has been called the "cradle of Methodism," it was not until 1807, nearly three-quarters of a century after the Wesleys returned to England, that this new religious denomination succeeded in obtaining a foothold in Savannah. Rev. Hope Hull, in 1790, undertook to hold a series of meetings in a chairmaker's shop, but, according to Dr. White, his preaching aroused mob violence, and his success was small—White's "Historical Collections of Georgia," under Chatham.

pany's storekeeper, and was successful in securing the good will of Oglethorpe. This led to rapid advancement, which, however, was undeserved;
for, some years later, he was detected in a course of fraudulent dealing and
was summarily cashiered.

"There was living in his household at this time an attractive young
lady, named Sophia Christina Hopkey, or Hopkins, his niece, who showed
herself a devoted attendant at church services, and most receptive to the ministrations of the handsome young pastor. Desirous of learning French, she
found in him an excellent teacher. Wesley's London friend, Delamotte,
however, who regarded Miss Sophia as sly and designing, and doubted the
sincerity of her professions, warned John Wesley against her. Wesley
seems also to have discussed the matter of her sincerity—or rather of her
fitness to be a clergyman's wife—with the excellent Moravians. The advice which they gave him coincided with Delamotte's, and the result was
a distinct coolness in his manner toward the young lady. She resented
the change, and, understanding its significance, accepted the advances of
a less scrupulous suitor named Wilkinson, a man by no means conspicuous
for piety. As her spiritual adviser, Wesley still continued to visit Mrs.
Wilkinson.

"At length, believing that he perceived in the lady's conduct distinct
marks of spiritual degeneracy, he deemed it his duty to repel her from
holy communion. This summary and injudicious step was naturally in-
terpreted in an unpleasant way. The husband and uncle of the lady sued
him in the civil court for defamation of character; and, in the squabble
which followed, the people took part against Wesley. Holding peculiar
views respecting the limited jurisdiction possessed by civil courts over cler-
gymen, Wesley refused to enter into the necessary recognizances, and a
warrant for his arrest was accordingly issued. To avoid further trouble, he
determined to fly, like Paul from Damascus. He left the place secretly by
night, in the company of a bankrupt constable, a ne'er-do-well wife-beater
named Gough, and a defaulting barber. They rowed up the river in a
boat to the Swiss settlement at Purysburg, and proceeded thence on foot
to Beaufort; but, misdirected by an old man, they lost the way, wandered
about in a swamp, and, for a whole day, had no food but a piece of ginger-
bread. Finally they arrived at Beaufort, where Delamotte joined them, and
thence they took boat to Charleston. Here Wesley preached again 'to this
careless people,' and four days later took leave of America, embarking on
board the 'Samuel,' Captain Percy.

"On the voyage, which was a stormy and unpleasant one, he devoted
himself to ministering to the spiritual wants of those on board. In the
solitude of his cabin he gave himself up to deep heart-searching. He felt
that the want of success which attended his work in America was due to
some lack of real devotion in himself. As he expressed it very tersely in
a note to one of the entries in his journal: 'I had even then the faith of
a servant, though not of a son.'

"Meanwhile, George Whitfield, to whom he had sent a pressing invitation to join him in Georgia, had embarked on his journey; and, the two vessels, as it happened, the one outward bound, bearing Whitfield, all aglow with missionary enthusiasm, the other about to enter port, carrying the disappointed Wesley, met at the mouth of the Thames. The question whether Whitfield should proceed or return weighed heavily on the mind of the older man, who seems to have thought that the decision rested with him. At length, having cast lots—a Biblical practice shared by him with the Moravians—he sent word to Whitfield that he had better return. But Whitfield did not highly esteem this method of coming to a practical decision, resolved to continue on his voyage; and, in due time, he landed at Savannah.''*

Wesley's Georgia Diary and Hymn-book. ''Bishop E. R. Hendrix had the good fortune, while on a visit to England in 1900 as the fraternal delegate of the Methodist Episcopal Church, South, to the British Wesleyan Conferences, to come into possession of the original diary kept by John Wesley during his stay in Georgia. This rare manuscript journal has been in the hands of only two families since it was given, in 1817, by the Rev. Henry Moore to Miss Elizabeth Taylor, of Caermarthen. She left it by will, in 1847, to the Rev. John Gould Avery, a Wesleyan preacher, who valued it so highly that it was retained in the possession of himself and his only daughter, Mrs. Norton Bell, the wife of a London architect, until bought, in 1897, by Mr. R. Thursfield Smith, J. P., of Whitechurch, Shropshire, a retired engineer and iron manufacturer.

''The book is a small duodecimo, bound in leather, and contains one hundred and eighty-six pages, all but eleven of which are numbered, and are filled with Wesley's handwriting. Each of the numbered pages is devoted to the doings of a single day, and each line to the work of a single hour, except on one or two occasions when the writer was traveling. The whole, therefore, contains a minute account of the way in which Wesley spent every hour of every day during the time embraced in the record. The first entry is dated Saturday, May 1, 1736 [Old Style]; the last is dated February 11, 1737. Wesley relates in his printed journal that he 'first set foot on American ground,' Friday, February 6, 1736, entering upon his ministry in Savannah on Sunday, March 7, of the same year; and on Friday, December 2, 1737, he continued, 'I shook off the dust of my feet and left Georgia, after having preached the gospel there—not as I ought but as I was able—one year and nearly nine months.' He took his final leave of America on the twenty-second. This record therefore relates to the greater part of the time spent by him as a missionary in Georgia.

''In the journal, the entries for the day begin at four o'clock in the

---

*Rev. James W. Lee, D. D., in Illustrated History of Methodism.

morning, and end at nine o'clock at night; and also every hour of the day is inserted, whether the writer was on land or sea. The dates are given at the head of each page with the utmost exactness. The handwriting is neat and clear, and resembles that found in Wesley's later manuscripts. It was all written with a quill pen, on good paper, and with durable ink. The book is stained with oil or sea water, for he carried it with him on his voyages during his stay in America, several of such voyages being mentioned in the book. In one passage he uses the shorthand of Byrom's system, which he learned as early as 1731. The book shows that he was often attacked by ailments which ordinary mortals would have regarded as severe. Again and again he is seized with 'cholick,' which he sometimes spells with and sometimes without the 'k.' The first registered attack was on May 5th. It was on this date he met with trouble by declining to baptize a child because the mother refused to have it dipped. Wesley dined there, and 'took a glass of spirit and water to cure me of the cholick.' He abstained from spirituous liquors, 'unless in cases of extreme necessity' or 'at a wedding feast.'

"On one occasion he suffered from an attack of 'St. Anthony's fire,' which 'smarted much.' He was also attacked by 'shocking headaches,' intermittent fever, violent and protracted nausea, dysentery, and boils. He was also occasionally deprived of sleep by the attacks of nocturnal insects. He had often to take 'physick,' and was frequently 'in pain' or 'sick.' The only robust exercise he took was 'walking' or 'felling trees,' or 'nailing pales.' References are made to different places about Savannah, such as Frederica and Thunderbolt, and to the different people whom he chanced to meet. He speaks of Tomo-chi-chi and the Indians. While in Savannah, Mr. Wesley acquired German, Spanish and Italian. He prepared while there a small volume of seventy-four pages, with the title-page: 'A Collection of Psalms and Hymns. Charles-town: printed by Lewis Timothy.' This was the first Methodist hymn-book ever published."*

Wormsloe.   Volume I, Pages 87-90.

Brampton.   Volume I, Pages 93-97.

Georgia's First Se-   "Memorable in the political annals
cession Convention.   of the colony were the proceedings
of the Provincial Congress, which
assembled at Savannah on the 4th of July, 1775. Every
parish was represented, and the delegates were fitting

---

*James W. Lee, D. D., in Illustrated History of Methodism, Appendix A.

exponents of the intelligence, the dominant hopes, and the material interests of the communities from which they respectively came. This was Georgia's first secession convention. It placed the province in active sympathy and confederated alliance with the other twelve American colonies, practically annulled within her limits the operation of the obnoxious acts of Parliament, questioned the supremacy of the realm, and inaugurated measures calculated to accomplish the independence of the plantation and its erection into the dignity of Statehood.''

The following members submitted proper credentials and came together at Tondee's Long Room:

TOWN AND DISTRICT OF SAVANNAH.—Archibald Bulloch, Noble Wymberley Jones, Joseph Habersham, Jonathan Bryan, Ambrose Wright, William Young, John Glen, Samuel Elbert, John Houstoun, Oliver Bowen, John McClure, Edward Telfair, Thomas Lee, George Houstoun, Joseph Reynolds, John Smith, William Ewen, John Martin, Dr. Zubly, William Bryan, Philip Box, Philip Allman, William O'Bryan, Joseph Clay, Seth John Cuthbert.

DISTRICT OF VERNONBURGH.—Joseph Butler [declined to take his seat], Andrew Elton Wells, Matthew Roche, Jr.

DISTRICT OF ACTON—David Zubly, Basil Cowper, William Gibbons.

SEA ISLAND DISTRICT.—Colonel Deveaugh, Colonel Delegall, James Bulloch, John Morel, John Bohun Girardeau, John Barnard, Robert Gibson.

DISTRICT OF LITTLE OGEECHEE.—Francis Henry Harris, Joseph Gibbons, James Robertson [declined to take his seat].

PARISH OF ST. MATTHEW.—John Stirk, John Adam Treutlen, George Walton, Edward Jones, Jacob Wauldhauer, Philip Howell, Isaac Young, Jenkin Davis, John Morel, John Flert, Charles McCay, Christopher Cramer.

PARISH OF ST. PHILIP.—Colonel Butler, William LeConte, William Maxwell, James Maxwell, Stephen Drayton, Adam Fowler Brisbane, Luke Mann, Hugh Bryan.

PARISH OF ST. GEORGE.—Henry Jones, John Green, Thomas Burton, William Lord, David Lewis, James Pugh, John Fulton.

PARISH OF ST. ANDREW.—Jonathan Cochran, William Jones, Peter Tarlin, Lachlan McIntosh, William McIntosh, George Threadcraft, John Wereat, Roderick McIntosh, John Witherspoon, George McIntosh, Allan Stewart, John McIntosh, Raymond Demere.

PARISH OF ST. DAVID—John Cuthbert Seth, William Williams, Sr.

PARISH OF ST. MARY.—Daniel Ryan.

PARISH OF ST. THOMAS.—John Roberts.

PARISH OF ST. PAUL.—John Walton, Joseph Maddock [declined to take his seat], Andrew Burns, Robert Rae, James Rae, Andrew Moore, Andrew Burney, Leonard Marbury.

PARISH OF ST. JOHN.—James Screven, Nathan Brownson, Daniel Roberts, John Baker, Sr., John Bacon, Sr., James Maxwell, Edward Ball, William Baker, Sr., William Bacon, Jr., John Stevens, John Winn, Sr.

The congress was organized by the election of Archibald Bulloch as president and of George Walton as secretary. Both these officers were unanimously chosen. Its organization having been perfected, the body adjourned to the meeting-house of the Rev. John J. Zubly, who preached a sermon on the alarming state of American affairs.*

--- --

Bonaventure. Volume I, Pages 90-93; also Volume II, Historic Church-Yards, etc.

--- --

Georgia's First Among other important changes made
General Assembly. by the Trustees, a Colonial Assembly
was authorized, consisting of sixteen members, proportioned to the population of the different parishes or districts, writs of election were issued, and the members were required to convene at Savannah, on the 15th of January, 1751. The Assembly met on the day appointed. Francis Harris was chosen speaker, and Noble Jones and Pickering Robinson were appointed a committee to prepare a report on the state of the colony, said report to furnish the basis of discussion. Oaths of allegiance and abjuration were administered to members on the day following. The gentlemen who constituted the first General Assembly of Georgia were:

SAVANNAH DISTRICT.—Francis Harris, Speaker; John Milledge, William Francis, William Russell.

AUGUSTA DISTRICT.—George Catogan, David Douglass.

EBENEZER DISTRICT.—Christian Reidlesperger, Theobald Keiffer.

ABERCORN AND GOSHEN DISTRICTS.—William Ewen.

JOSEPH TOWN DISTRICT.—Charles Watson.

VEGNONBOURGH DISTRICT.—Patrick Hountoun.

---

*Charles C. Jones, Jr., in History of Georgia, Vol. 2.

ACTON DISTRICT.—Peter Morell.
LITTLE OGEECHEE DISTRICT.—Joseph Summers.
SKIDAWAY DISTRICT.—John Barnard.
MIDWAY DISTRICT.—Audley Maxwell.
DARIEN DISTRICT.—John Mackintosh, B.

It appears that the powers of the Assembly amounted to little more than those of a grand jury, in making a presentment of grievances to be redressed. Several articles were laid before the president, but the members were powerless to enact laws, and the business of the Assembly being finished, the house adjourned, after a session of twenty-two days.[1]

According to the basis of representation fixed by the Trustees, every town or district, which numbered ten families, was entitled to one deputy; and wherever thirty families were settled, they were entitled to two deputies. Savannah, being much the largest town in the province, was allowed a representation of four deputies; but Ebenezer and Augusta were restricted to two. For some reason, Frederica was not represented in the first general assembly at Savannah. Doubtless the town had commenced to decline; but two delegates were apportioned to Frederica, provided the settlement at this place could muster thirty families.

Some of the qualifications for future membership in the assembly possess an amusing interest. In the first place, it was provided that after June 24, 1751, no person could be chosen a deputy who had not one hundred mulberry trees planted and fenced upon every fifty acres he possessed; and in the next place, it was provided that after June 24, 1753, no person could be chosen a deputy who owned an excess of negro slaves ,beyond the fixed proportion, who had not at least one female in the family who was well instructed in the art of reeling silk, and who did not produce fifteen pounds of silk upon every acre of land.[2]

One of the recommendations of the first General Assembly was that the militia be organized, and President Parker, immediately after his appointment, proceeded to carry out this recommendation. General Oglethorpe's regiment having disbanded, the colony was left almost without protection against the Indians, whose friendship was uncertain. Those citizens who owned as many as three hundred acres of land were ordered to appear at Savannah at a certain time on horseback, to be organized as cavalry, and all who owned less land were to be organized as infantry. The first general muster or gathering of the militia was held in Savannah in

---

[1] Capt. Hugh McCall, in History of Georgia, Vol. I.
[2] Condensed from History of Georgia, by Wm. Bacon Stevens, M. D., D. D.

June, 1751, when about two hundred and twenty men paraded under Captain Noble Jones.*

First Rally On July 14, 1774, there appeared in the **of Patriots.** Georgia *Gazette,* a card calling upon the friends of liberty to meet at Tondee's Tavern on the 27th day of the same month. It was signed by Noble Wymberley Jones, Archibald Bulloch, John Houstoun, and John Walton, the last a brother of the signer. At the appointed time and place a number of patriots assembled, but some of the parishes were not represented. Another meeting was, therefore, set for August 10, and, notwithstanding the Governor's proclamation of warning, it was well attended. Strong resolutions were passed; and, though it was thought best not to send delegates to the Continental Congress, the action of the assemblage was unequivocal. Thus the youngest of the original thirteen colonies and the most loyal to England of the entire sisterhood was at last aroused; and nothing save the most strenuous activities of Governor Wright prevented the most radical steps from being taken.

Some of the more radical members, in protest against the conservative action of the body, met and chose Noble Wymberley Jones, Archibald Bulloch and John Houstoun to represent the province in the Continental Congress. However, since they lacked the proper credentials they did not repair to Philadelphia; they simply addressed a letter to John Hancock, expressing the sympathetic attitude of Georgia. The Puritans of the Midway settlement alone went to the full limit of protest. They dispatched Lyman Hall to Philadelphia, single-handed and alone, to represent the Parish of St. John. It was not until after the battle of Lexington, in 1775, that the tie of allegiance to England was formally severed by a famous convocation held at Tondee's Tavern.

*Lawton B. Evans, in School History of Georgia.

Tondee's Tavern.   Volume I, Pages 385-386.

Georgia's First   Twelve years prior to the battle of Lex-
Newspaper: ington, the earliest printing-press was
"The Gazette."   installed in Savannah; and on April 7,
                      1763, appeared the initial number of
the *Georgia Gazette,* edited by James Johnson. It was
the eighth newspaper to be published in the colonies.
Beyond the announcement of vital statistics, the arrival
and departure of vessels in the harbor, and items relating
to traffic, the little weekly sheet contained no local news.
According to one authority, Savannah and Charleston
exchanged brieflets in regard to each other: the Charleston editor would gather information about Savannah
from visitors who came to trade in Charleston; and this
he would publish in the Charleston paper. Two weeks
later it would appear in the *Georgia Gazette,* and vice
versa.

But the local column was soon developed. The spirit
of resistance to the oppressive measures of the British
Parliament bore fruit in news items, which were published at first hand. The earliest bugle call for the
patriots to assemble in Savannah was sounded through
the columns of the *Georgia Gazette,* on July 14, 1774.
They were requested to meet at the Liberty Pole, in
front of Tondee's Tavern, on July 27 following, and
the card was signed by the famous quartette of liberty:
Noble Wymberley Jones, Archibald Bulloch, John Houstoun and John Walton, the brother of the signer. Though
a large number responded at the appointed time, the
Province at large was not represented, and another call
was issued for August 10, 1774. At this time, in spite
of the Governor's solemn edict of warning, also published in the *Gazette,* they met together and took conservative but firm action. The strong influence of the
Governor and the effective opposition of such pronounced Loyalists as James Habersham and Noble Jones

alone kept the assemblage from sending delegates at this time to the Continental Congress in Philadelphia.

Among the patriots who responded to the earliest summons were: John Glen, Joseph Clay, Noble Wymberley Jones, John Houstoun, Lyman Hall, John Smith, William Young, Edward Telfair, Samuel Farley, John Walton, George Walton, Joseph Habersham, Jonathan Bryan, Jonathan Cochrane, George McIntosh, William Gibbons, Benjamin Andrew, John Winn, John Stirk, David Zoubly, H. L. Bourquin, Elisha Butler, William Baker, Parmenus Way, John Baker, John Stacy, John Morel and others.

Other Historic Sheets of Savannah. In 1796, some three years before the suspension of the *Georgia Gazette,* arose the *Columbian Museum and Savannah Advertiser,* a periodical which appeared semi-weekly, on Tuesdays and Fridays. It finally merged into the *Museum and Gazette.* On January 1, 1802, appeared the first number of the *Georgia Republican,* also a semi-weekly, owned and edited by John F. Everett. Later it became a tri-weekly, appeared in the afternoon, and also underwent a change of name, styling itself the *Georgia Republican and Savannah Evening Ledger.''* On October 17, 1817, it became a daily during the fall and winter months. Espousing the Whig principles, it adopted, in 1840, this motto: "The Union of the Whigs for the Sake of the Union." Among the men of talent who were associated with the editorial columns of this influential paper were P. W. Alexander and James R. Sneed. It ran for seventy years, covering twenty-four changes of management.

With the advent of the Christmas holidays of 1818 appeared the first issue of the *Georgian,* edited by John M. Harney, an erratic genius, whose "Farewell to Savannah" still abides among the local traditions. Written in clever verse, it calls down the direst maledictions of heaven upon the city, whose dust he was preparing to shake from his shoes. One of his earliest successors was Israel K. Tafft, a name fragrant in Savannah. Later R. D. Arnold and William H. Bulloch became joint editors and proprietors, and, in 1849, Henry R. Jackson, fresh from the fields of Mexico, brought martial honors, as well as literary gifts, to the editorial helm. Successive changes occurred; and finally, in 1859, on the eve of the Civil War, it ceased to exist. The gifted Albert R. Lamar also at one time edited the *Georgian.* In 1852 came the *Evening Journal,* founded by J. B. Cubbege, and from time to time other sheets appeared.

But the newspaper most conspicuously and brilliantly identified with Savannah entered the lists in 1850: the *Savannah Morning News.* It was founded in 1850 by John M. Cooper, in association with the famous humorist, William T. Thompson. The latter's pen for more than thirty years flashed from the editorial page. Under him the paper became one of the most powerful dailies of the State; and, though proprietors came and went, he remained steadfastly at his post. Joel Chandler Harris was also at one time on the editorial staff.

Upon the Federal occupation of Savannah, S. W. Mason took possession of the plant, and began the publication of the *Savannah Herald,* subsequently settling the claims of the former proprietors, which were submitted to arbitration. It then became the *Savannah News and Herald,* but in 1867 Mr. John H. Estill purchased an interest in the paper, and, buying his partner's stock some time later, he resumed the original name: the *Savannah Morning News.* The business sagacity of Colonel Estill, who was one of Georgia's ablest financiers, soon retrieved the disasters of the paper, enlarged its area of circulation and made its influence felt more potentially than ever upon the political life of the Commonwealth.

Gazaway Hartridge, one of the most brilliant young men of his day in Georgia, edited an afternoon paper in Savannah at one time; but accepting a position in New York he removed to the metropolis, where he soon afterwards died. On Novemebr 19, 1891, under the management of Pleasant A. Stovall, proprietor and editor, was launched the *Savannah Evening Press,* one of the most powerful and popular dailies of the State. In the recent election for United States Senator, Mr. Stovall was one of the strongest minority candidates.* Since the election of Woodrow Wilson, whose nomination he was among the first to advocate, Mr. Stovall has been appointed U. S. Minister to Switzerland.

Mulberry Grove.	Volume I, Pages 108-113.

Savannah's Revolutionary Monuments.	Volume I, Pages 103-108.

Roman Catholic Diocese of Savannah: Cathedral of St. John.	Right Reverend Benjamin J. Keiley, Bishop of Savannah, contributes the following outline sketch of the Roman Catholic Church in Georgia. Says Bishop Keiley:

''The present diocese of Savannah, embracing the entire State of Georgia, was, at first, subject to the spiritual jurisdiction of the Bishop of Baltimore, Rt. Rev. John Carroll, who was appointed in 1790. The impossibility of caring for such an extended territory was soon evident, and thirty years afterwards the three States of North Carolina, South Carolina and Georgia were separated from the jurisdiction of Baltimore and a See established in Charleston, to which Rev. John England, an Irish priest, was appointed. Bishop England was consecrated in Cork, in September, 1820, and, sailing from Belfast, arrived in Charleston December 30 of the same year. He labored in his diocese for twenty-two years. He was in all probability the ablest man that the hierarchy in these States has pro-

---

*Authorities: History of Georgia, 1850-1881, by Isaac W. Avery; Historic and Picturesque Savannah, by Adelaide Wilson.

duced. A man of great learning, untiring zeal, and striking force, he wielded a great influence outside his fold. Bishop England found about 1,000 Catholics in his diocese, and left more than 12,000, besides 16 churches, 21 priests and 2 convents. He was the founder of the institution of the Sisters of Mercy, to which Savannah and Charleston are indebted for devoted work during the yellow fever epidemics.

"The great obstacle which confronted Bishop England was the unreasoning and un-Christian prejudice against Catholics. It was during his episcopate that North Carolina repealed her Constitutional enactment, whereby civil rights were denied Catholics. Nor was the feeling in Georgia less decided. One of the striking anomalies of human nature is shown when men who ostensibly leave home to escape persecution for religion's sake, no sooner establish themselves under new conditions, than they set up a system of exclusion and persecution. It was not confined to the meddlesome and intolerant Puritans to justify the accusation of 'falling first on their knees and then on the aborigines.'

"Reasons similar to those which induced the creation of the See of Charleston demanded the erection of the See of Savannah, and on November 10, 1850, Rev. F. X. Gartland, V. G., of Philadelphia, was consecrated the first bishop of the See of Savannah. Bishop Gartland had as priests in his new diocese Fathers Whelan, Barry, Jerry O'Neill, Sr., Jerry O'Neill, Jr., Kirby, Duggar, Quigley and James O'Neill. He died of the fever in 1854, and his successor, Father Barry, was not consecrated until August, 1857. After Bishop Barry came Bishop Verot, who died Bishop of St. Augustine, having been transferred in 1870. Bishop Persico came next in succession, but his health failing he resigned, and Bishop W. H. Gross became the fifth bishop of Savannah. The latter was transferred to Oregon, and Bishop Becker, of Wilmington, Del., was selected by the Holy See as the sixth incumbent of the Savannah diocese. Bishop Becker died July 29, 1899, and the present bishop was appointed as his successor and consecrated at Richmond, Va., June 3, 1900.

"The records of the church in Georgia, however, antedate the coming of Bishop England.

"From the records of our Cathedral, I find, under the date of Saturday, October 15. 1796, the following entry: 'Today the funeral service was supplied in the cemetery of Savannah, at the grave of the venerable and zealous man, John Le Moyne, parish priest of the city of Marly le Roi, in France, who died on the 16th. day of November 1794; by me, a priest and canon regular of the Order of St. Augustine in France, in the presence of Messrs. Charles Pardeilles, M. D. and Thomas Decheneaux, a merchant of Savannah, who have attested this with their signatures.

"'LE MERCIER, Canon Regular.
" 'CHARLES PARDEILLES, M. D.
" 'THOMAS DECHENEAUX.'

"Father Le Mercier appears to have served the few Catholics in Savannah (mostly from San Domingo and Ireland) until 1804, when Rev.

Anthony Carle seems to have been the pastor of the Church of St. John the Baptist; a small chapel having been built near where St. Patrick's school-house now stands. Father Carle's name continues as rector until December, 1819, when a vacancy existed for some time. During the period of these two rectors there are found entries signed by Rev. Felix McCarthy. Father Le Mercier was here in 1806, but his name appears as rector of the church in Charleston.

"On the 21st of January, 1821, our records contain the following notice, in the well-known hand of Bishop England:

" 'The See of Charleston has been created on the 11th. of July 1820, and I having been consecrated first bishop thereof, on the 19th. day of January 1821, I visited this city and appointed the Rev. Robert Brown, of the Order of Hermits, of St. Augustine, to discharge the pastoral duties therein.

" 'JOHN, Bishop of Charleston.'

"Bishop England found only one resident pastor when he came, viz., the one at Augusta."

"Father Brown remained as rector of the Church of St. John the Baptist until 1825, when he was succeeded by Rev. Francis Boland, whose name does not occur on the record after August 15, 1826. There are found the names of Rev. J. W. McEncroe during the rest of 1826 and of Rev. John McGinnis until December, 1827. After that date Rev. Joseph Stokes is signed to the records as pastor of Savannah. During a portion of his incumbency, Father McGinnis seems to have acted as assistant. The last entry made by Father Stokes is under date of October 22, 1833, and on November 23, there is the record of a baptism performed by Rev. John Barry, and on November 21, there is a marriage performed by J. F. O'Neill (Father Jerry O'Neill, whose memory and name are held in benediction in Georgia wherever his ministry called him), who for nearly forty years lived in Savannah. Father Jerry was a devoted friend of the South. His death took place some twenty years ago. He brought the Sisters of Mercy to Savannah in 1845, where they yet carry on institutions of education and charity. One of the original colony, Mother Agnes, only died a few years ago. During Father O'Neill's pastorate a new church was erected in Savannah, as the number of Catholics had increased. Other names, dear to the older Catholics, are found on our registers: Fathers Peter Whelan, J. F. Kirby, P. J. Kirby, Edward Quigley, C. C. Prendergast, P. Dufau, V. Van Roosbroeck, W. J. Hamilton, Patrick, Aloysius, John (the last three being companions of Bishop Persico), J. B. Langlois and M. Cullinan.

In 1877, I find the first entry of a baptism performed by the late revered Father Cafferty. Savannah now has three churches for white and one for colored Catholics, an infirmary, a home for the aged poor, under the charge of the Little Sisters of the Poor, an orphan asylum for the white and one for the colored children, and a Catholic population of about

7,000. The Sacred Heart Church has been recently erected, with a fine college for boys, in charge of the Benedictine Fathers.

The magnificent cathedral of St. John the Baptist, in Savannah, was destroyed by fire on Sunday night, February 6, 1898. On the following Tuesday, the bishop called a meeting of prominent Catholic gentlemen of the parish, and it was unanimously resolved to build the cathedral in a handsome and more substantial manner than before. The first contribution received for the rebuilding fund was from Master Fitzhugh White, son of Rev. Robb White, then rector of the Protestant Episcopal Church (Christ's), who of his own accord gave $5 in gold. Tenders of temporary quarters came from the Savannah Guards, the Young Men's Hebrew Association and Rev. Charles H. Strong, of St. John's Protestant Episcopal Church, who at once offered the parish hall. Letters of sympathy also came from the session of the Independent Presbyterian Church and the wardens and vestrymen of Christ Church, as well as from the rector of St. Stephen's Protestant Episcopal Church (colored). Rev. Isaac P. Mendes, the respected rabbi of Temple Mickva Israel, was one of the earliest contributors to the cathedral fund.''

The Old Masonic Hall: an Historic Rookery. From an old copy of the *Savannah Morning News*, dated March 28, 1888, is condensed the following item in regard to one of the old landmarks of Savannah:

"The two-story wooden building on a brick basement, fronting on President Street, was erected by the members of Solomon's Lodge, in 1799, and was used by the Masonic fraternity until 1858, when they removed to the building on the northeast corner of Bull and Broughton streets, having sold the old site to the city in 1856. Together with this particular piece of property, the city also bought the lot adjoining on the west, which was at one time the residence of General Lachlan McIntosh, of the Revolutionary Army, intending to erect thereon a guard-house or police station; but the people in the neighborhood objected, and it was sold to the late John J. Kelly for $1,000. He afterwards bequeathed it to the Union Society. The workmen yesterday pulled down the partitions which divided the old lodge-room into bedrooms,· and it once more assumed the appearance of a meeting-place of the brethren. It was here that Hon. William Stephens, General James Jackson, Governor Josiah Tattnall and other illustrious Georgians and Masons met in the early days; and here it was also that the young Cuban patriot, General Lopez, who was soon afterward garroted in Havana, was made a Mason in 1850. The Whitefield Building, a noble structure, will succeed the old hall, and the site is virtually a Masonic contribution; for not only was the land itself the gift of the late John J. Kelly, but the money for the erection of the new structure is part of the bequest of the late William F. Holland, to the Union Society; and both of these public benefactors were Masons of high rank. The building will be an appropriate memorial to George Whitefield, the founder of the Bethesda Orphan House, and to John J. Kelly and William F. Holland, two members of the society, whose timely beneficence has added this property to the assets from which is to be derived an income for the support of the orphans of the Union Society, the present guardian of White-field's sacred trust to the people of Savannah.''

''Concerning the origin of the first Masonic Lodge in Georgia there is an interesting tradition to the effect that in 1733 a number of Masons under the leadership of General Oglethorpe, while at Sunbury, then a small settlement on Medway River, organized, under an immense live oak, a lodge which was afterwards known as Savannah Lodge. However, the authentic records begin with an organization which was chartered in 1735 as Solomon's Lodge. This is the Mother-Lodge of Georgia. From the old tree under which the first shrine is supposed to have been erected, a relic of precious value has been carved in the form of a chair, which ornaments the lodge-room of the Masonic Hall. After the year 1800, Union, L'Esper-ance, Hiram and Oglethorpe lodges were instituted. During the Morgan excitement, these were broken up, however, and only Solomon's Lodge remained. The first hall erected for the meetings of the brotherhood was the two-story building on President Street, to which reference has been made in the above newspaper extract. The present hall is an elegant brick structure on the northeast corner of Bull and Broughton.''

Chatham Academy: Savannah's Pioneer School. It was not until 1812 that work commenced in the erection of Chatham Academy; but the enterprise derived its legal beginning from an Act of the Georgia Legislature, passed on February 1, 1788, in the city of Augusta, when the following trustees were appointed: Messrs. John Houstoun, John Habersham, William Gibbons, Sr., William Stephens, Richard Wylly, James Houstoun, Samuel Elbert, Seth John Cuthbert and Joseph Clay, Jr. By the same Act the proporety of Bethesdo College, or Orphane House, was vested in Selina, Countess of Huntington, in obedience to the trust of the late George Whitefield. The Academy was thus from its inception associated with Bethesda College. These were sister institutions. The one, the property of George Whitefield, bequeathed by him to Lady Huntington, in trust for literary and benevolent purposes; the other the property of Bartholomew Zouberbuhler, devised by him for benevolent purposes. The Legislature proposed to make practical use of the latter's

---

*Lee and Agnew, in Historical Record of Savannah.

gift by placing it in the hands of the trustees for the projected academy, with the proviso that nothing therein should bar the claim of any legal heir to the property of the said Zouberbuhler. But trouble arose, and, on December 8, 1791, the Legislature passed an Act to quiet the heirs. They were required, however, to pay an annuity of one hundred pounds, for the ensuing four years, to be applied to the support of the Academy; and, on failure to do so, the trustees were authorized to recover same in the courts.

Still the matter dragged. Finally, on December 23, 1808, the Legislature passed an Act providing for the sale of the property of Bethesda, both real and personal, in order that the purposes of the institution might be more effectively served. It was stipulated that the debts of the institution should be paid first; and then, of what remained, one-fifth was to be given to the Savannah Poor-House and Hospital. The rest was to be divided equally between Chatham Academy and Bethesda Orphanage; and in connection with this donation the former institution was directed to educate, without cost, at least five orphan children.

Funds having accumulated sufficient to warrant the building of an academy, the City Council, in 1810, on the joint application of the trustees of Chatham Academy and the president of the Union Society, passed an ordinance granting five lots in Brown Ward as a site for a structure to be erected by the two institutions for educational purposes. The work was put in charge of a committee of the two organizations, of which Mr. John Bolton was chairman. The basement walls were laid with heavy rock ballast, probably brought from abroad in the vessels coming to Savannah. On January 5, 1813, at noon, the completed structure as formally opened for the reception of scholars. Dr. Henry Kollock delivered an eloquent address, and two hundred and nineteen pupils were enrolled. At a meeting of the Union Society, on May 7, 1813, it was decided to sell to Chatham Academy the interest of Bethesda Orphanage in the common property, an exception being made of the western wing. This was used for a number of years as a hotel. However, in 1887, it was purchased by the trustees of Chatham Academy and converted into class-rooms. This handsome addition was christened Hunter Hall, in honor of Mr. William Hunter, for many years president of the board. At the present time, Chatham Academy occupies the entire building, one of the most substantial and elegant structures in Savannah, with the main entrance on Bull Street.*

General Lafayette Arrives on Georgia Soil. This happy event took place on Saturday, March 19, 1825. Up to the last hour almost, the time for the arrival of our venerated guest was but conjectural, opinions were various as to the moment at which he might be expected. The stages and packets were crowded with passengers, particularly from the South. The Light Dra-

---

*Adelaide Wilson, in Historic and Picturesque Savannah.

goons from Liberty County, under the command of Captain W. M. Maxwell and the Darien Hussars, commanded by Captain Charles West, had reached town on the preceding Tuesday. At half past five o'clock on Saturday morning, by a signal from the Chatham Artillery, the various organizations were warned to repair to the several parade grounds. The line was formed at eight o'clock, after which, there being no appearance of the boat, arms were stacked and the troops dismissed until the arrival. The first tidings of the welcome vessel were announced by the Exchange Bell, and almost at the same moment the volumes of smoke which accompanied her was perceived over the land; she was then about twelve or fifteen miles off, but rapidly approaching. The troops were immediately formed and marched to the lower part of Bay Street, where they were placed in position on the green in front of the avenue of trees. It proved to be an ideal day. About nine o'clock the mists dispersed, the skies became clear, and a gentle breeze arose, blowing directly up the river, as if to add speed to the vessel which was to land the distinguished visitors upon our shores.

As the steamboat passed Fort Jackson she was boarded by the Committee of Reception, and the General was addressed by the chairman, George Jones, Esq. The boat now approached in gallant style, firing, by the way, while a full band of music on board played the Marseillaise Hymn and other favorite French and American airs. At the anchorage a salute was fired by the Revenue Cutter Gallatin, under the command of Captain Matthews, and General Lafayette was assisted to the first barge, accompanied by the committee, the other boats being occupied by the remainder of the suite. At the docks were assembled the leading dignitaries and officials of the State; deputations from the Hibernian, St. Andrew's and Agricultural Societies, all bedecked with badges; besides a multitude of citizens. The Savannah Volunteer Guard, in honor of the Nation's guest, wore the Revolutionary cockade. As the General placed his foot upon the landing place, a salute was fired by the Chatham Artillery, in line on the bluff, with four brass field pieces, one of which was captured at Yorktown. He was here received by William C. Daniel, Esq., Mayor of the city, amid cheers from the assembled spectators.

On arriving at the top of the bluff, he was presented to Governor Troup, by whom, in the most cordial manner, he was welcomed to the soil of Georgia. Lafayette replied in feeling terms, and was then introduced to several Revolutionary soldiers, among whom were General Stewart, Colonel Shellman, Eb. Jackson, Sheftall Sheftall and Captain Rees. The eyes of the old General sparkled. He remembered Captain Rees, who proceeded to narrate some incident. "I remember," said Lafayette, taking the captain's hand between both of his own, and, with tear-filled eyes, the two men stood for a moment, absorbed in the recollection of youthful days. The officers of the brigade and of the regiment were then introduced, after which the procession moved as prescribed in the arrangements of the day, and about half-past five o'clock in the afternoon he arrived at the lodgings assigned to him, at Mrs. Maxwell's, where Governor Troup also was lodged. During the passage of the procession, windows and doors everywhere were crowded to excess; and the expression of feeling displayed by all was most enthusiastic, from the highest to the lowest. He was saluted by the ladies with the waving of handkerchiefs; which he returned by the repeated and continued inclination of the head in acknowledgment. At sundown, another salute was fired by the Marine Volunteer Corps.*

Savannah's Con- One of the artistic features of For-
federate Monument. syth Park, where it stands upon a
high mound overlooking a beautiful expanse of velvet green, is Savannah's handsome monument to the Confederate dead. It is a structure of Gothic design, massive in proportions. The corner-stone was laid on June 19, 1874, at which time Captain George A. Mercer delivered the address, while the city council, the military, and the Masonic orders took part. The unveiling occurred on May 24, 1875, when Hon. Julian Hartridge, then a member of Congress, delivered the address. At the urgent request of the Savannah Memorial Association, General Joseph E. Johnston acted as grand marshal. Surmounting the handsome pile stands the bronze figure of a Confederate soldier at parade rest. This, together with the iron railing which surrounds the lot, was the gift of Mr. G. W. J. DeRenne, of Wormslow.

Memorial Arch: On February 14, 1914, the handsome
Colonial Park. memorial arch which forms an exquisite
gateway of stone to Colonial Park, was formally unveiled by Savannah Chapter, of the D. A. R., in the presence of a large concourse of people. Georgia's

---

*Accompanying General Lafayette from Charleston were several distinguished South Carolinians, including the Governor; but, according to the laws of the Palmetto State, her Chief Magistrate was not allowed to cross the border, and he, therefore, returned, after making the proper apologies. However, two of the escort, Colonel Huger and Major Hamilton, remained and participated in the exercises.

Chief-Executive, Hon. John M. Slaton, was an honored guest of the occasion and took a prominent part in the exercises. There is not a burial ground in the State whose soil is consecrated by the ashes of a greater number of Revolutionary patriots, and the monument was reared to commemorate the heroism of these brave men. Here sleep the Habershams, the Clays, the Cuthberts, the Wyllys, the Bullochs, the McIntoshes, and scores of others identified with the heroic struggle of independence. The following detailed report of the ceremonies of unveiling is reproduced from a newspaper account:*

With fitting ceremonies the beautiful memorial arch erected at the main entrance to Colonial Cemetery by the Savannah Chapter, Daughters of the American Revolution, was unveiled Thursday morning, Georgia Day, and formally presented to the city, in memory of the soldiers of the Revolution whose remains are interred there.

The occasion was an inspiring one. A number of distinguished guests, including Governor Slaton, were on the speakers' platform, and soldiers, including the coast artillery corps from Fort Screven and the National Guard of Georgia, in their bright uniforms, were on every hand. The unveiling was preceded by a parade of the military.

When the time came for the unveiling of the monument Otis Ashmore, master of the ceremonies, and Mrs. John S. Wood, regent of the Savannah chapter, descended from the speakers' platform and walked to the first row of chairs in front of the arch, where were seated Miss Rosalind Wood, daughter of the regent, and Miss Susie Cole Winburn, daughter of a former regent, who were to act as sponsors.

As the two young women were escorted to their stations, the band began playing ''To the Flag,'' and at this signal the two immense American flags that had previously hidden the memorial from view were drawn slowly back, disyplaying the beautiful design. As the arch came into view the heads of the men in the gathering were bared, and the soldiers stood at ''salute.''

The parade formed in front of the City Hall. The line of march was headed by the band from Fort Screven, followed by squads from six companies of regulars stationed there. Then came a picked company from the First Georgia Regiment, Captain Morgan in command, and the rear was Georgia Hussars, Captain Frank P. McIntire commanding. The military formed a square about the monument.

In front of the arch and to the left of the speakers' platform were seated the members of the Savannah Chapter, Daughters of the American

---

*Savannah Morning News.

Revolution, the hostesses of the occasion, and their guests. Behind these were as many people as could crowd into the limited space, and the streets were blocked for some distance on either side.

The Right Rev. F. F. Reese, Bishop of the Episcopal Diocese of Georgia, pronounced the invocation. The dedicatory address was delivered by Judge Walter G. Charlton, of the Superior Court of Chatham County, who presented the arch to the city in perpetuity. John Rourke, Jr., in the absence of Mayor Richard J. Davant, accepted the gift on behalf of the city.

CHATTAHOOCHEE

Cusseta. On February 13, 1854, an Act was approved creating out of the two counties of Muscogee and Marion a new county, to be called Chattahoochee, after the river which formed its western border. The following commissioners were empowered by this Act to choose a county-site and to negotiate a purchase of land on which to erect public buildings, viz., James R. Love, William Bagby, David M. Glenn, William Wooldridge and Joshua M. Cook. Near the center of the county a site was chosen, to which, in honor of a tribe of the Lower Creek Indians, was given the name Cusseta. The town was incorporated in 1855. Since obtaining railway connections, Cusseta has commenced to bristle with new life and to enter upon a new era of development. The Cusseta Institute was chartered in 1897, with the following board of trustees: J. M. Leightner, Dr. C. N. Howard, W. F. Cook, J. J. Hickey, C. C. Wilkinson, John Stephens, J. C. F. McCook, D. J. Fussell, J. S. Brewer, and C. W. F. King.*

CHATTOOGA

Summerville. Within a few months after Chattooga County was created in 1838 from Walker and Floyd, an Act was approved by Governor Charles J. McDonald, making the site for public buildings per-

*Acts, 1897, p. 182.

manent in the town of Summerville.[1] During the same
year a charter was granted to the Summerville Academy, the original trustees of which institution were: John
Hunter, Robert Bailey, John T. Story, Edwin Sturdi-
vant, and Middleton Hill.[2] Three years later five new
trustees were added to this number: Charles A. Heard,
Charles Price, S. E. Burnett, D. C. Hunter and R. W.
Jones. The Summerville Male and Female Academy
was chartered in 1856. It is said that the name of this
town was suggested by its peculiar charm of environment, in a picturesque open valley of the mountains. Sequoya, the modern Cadmus, who invented an alphabet
for the Cherokee language, lived at one time near Al-
pine, on the borders of Chattooga. Two famous Indian
villages of frontier days in this county were: Broom
Town and Island Town. Judge John W. Maddox, at one
time a member of Congress, and Hon. William C. Glenn,
a former Attorney-General of Georgia, were natives of
Chattooga.

CHEROKEE.

Canton. Originally the name of this historic town was
        Etowah, so called from the river which divides
the county into two almost equal parts. Soon after the
county was erected out of lands then recently acquired
from the Cherokees, Etowah was chartered by an Act
of the Legislature, approved December 24, 1833, at which
time the following residents were named as commissioners: Howell Cobb, Philip Croft, M. J. Camden, James
Burns and William Gresham.[3] These gentlemen were
also made trustees of the town academy, with the exception of Mr. Camden, in whose place William Lay was
chosen. But Etowah did not suit the people for some
reason, and on December 18, 1834, the name was changed

[1] Acts, 1839, p. 210.
[2] Acts, 1839, p. 6.
[3] Acts, 1833, p. 331.

to Canton.[2]   Early in the forties, one of Georgia's most illustrious sons, Joseph E. Brown, afterwards Governor, Chief Justice and United States Senator, chose this town as his future home; and late in the fifties the County of Cherokee became the birth-place of another Governor, Joseph M. Brown.   Canton was for years the home of Dr. John W. Lewis, a Senator of the Confederate States, and here, at a green old age, resides Judge James R. Brown, a noted jurist and a brother of Georgia's war Governor.

History of the Famous "Joe Brown Pike."   There are few people living in Georgia who have not heard of the famous weapon of defence devised by Georgia's war Governor to meet the exigencies of a very grave situation in this State during the late civil conflict. It was known as the "Joe Brown Pike."   But while the name of this hostile instrument may be a familiar one to the ear there is not one man in a hundred who knows what the "Joe Brown Pike" resembled or where and how it was manufactured.   The following article on the subject from the pen of Clark Howell, Jr., appeared in the *Atlanta Constitution* of July 14, 1912.   Says Mr. Howell:

"Half a century ago, when the Civil War was well under way and the Union forces were making their dreaded invasion of the Southland, when all the gun factories and practically everything in a manufacturing line was owned by the North, Georgia's famous war Governor. Joseph E. Brown, issued an official call to the mechanics of Georgia, urging them to produce the so-called 'Joe Brown Pike.'   The South was short on weapons or defence and the Governor adopted this as a dernier resort.

"The call was issued from the executive department of the old State Capitol at Milledgeville, February 20, 1862.   Along with the call there was sent to every mechanic and blacksmith in the State a letter urging him personally to help in the general work of aiding the Confederacy in its dire troubles by making pikes.   If the receiver of one of these letters notified the Governor that he was favorably disposed he was sent full in-

---

[2] Acts, 1834, p. 263.

structions as to how to manufacture the implements, as well as 'a sample pike.

"The pikes were made with a long white oak or hickory stick with an iron head. The wooden part of the pike was 6 feet 7 inches long and was bound by four iron bands, the blade being 18 inches long and reminding one of the two-edged swords of the Crusaders. The blade, when not in use, could be lowered into the stock, which was about twice the size of an ordinary broom handle, but could readily be placed in position for defence or attack by releasing a spring, which pushed the blade into position, where it was held by the upper bands. In the same way it was dropped and caught by the lower bands.

"The celebrated order of Georgia's war Governor is here produced:

" 'Executive Department, Milledgeville, Ga., February 20, 1862.

" 'To the Mechanics of Georgia:

"The late reverses which have attended our armies show the absolute necessity of renewed energy and determination on our part. We are left to choose between freedom at the end of a desperate and heroic struggle and submission to tyranny, followed by the most abject and degraded slavery to which a patriotic and generous people were ever exposed. Surely we cannot hesitate. Independence or death should be the watchword and reply of every free-born son of the South.

" 'Our enemies have vastly superior numbers and greatly the advantage in the quantity and quality of their arms. Including those, however, which have been and will be imported, in spite of the blockade, we have guns enough in the Confederacy to arm a very large force, but not enough for all the troops which have been and must be called to the field. What shall be done in this emergency? I answer: use the 'Georgia pike,' with a side knife, 18-inch blade, weighing about 3 pounds. Let every army have a large reserve, armed with a good pike and a long knife, to be brought upon the field, with a shout for victory, when contending forces are much exhausted or when the time comes for the charge of bayonets. When the advance columns come in reach of the balls let them move in double quick time and rush with terrific impetuosity into the lines of the enemy. Hand-to-hand the pike has vastly the advantage of the bayonet, which is itself but a crooked pike with a shorter staff, and must retreat before it. When the retreat commences let the pursuit be rapid, and if the enemy throw down their guns and are likely to outrun us, if need be, throw down the pike and keep close to their heels with the knife, till each man has hewn down at least one of his adversary.

" 'Had five thousand reserves, thus armed, and well trained to the use of these terrible weapons, been brought to charge at the proper time, who can say that the victory would not have been ours at Fort Donaldson? But it is probably unimportant that I state here the use to be made of that which I want you to manufacture. I have already a considerable number of pikes and knives, but desire within the next month ten thousand more of each. I must have them, and appeal to you, as one of the most patriotic classes of our fellow citizens, to make them for us immediately.

" 'I trust that every mechanic who has the means of turning them out rapidly and the owner of every machine shop in this State will at once lay aside all other business and appropriate a month or two to the relief of the country in this emergency. Each workman who has the means of turning them out in large numbers without delay will be supplied with a proper pattern by application to the ordinance department at Milledgeville. Appealing to your patriotism as a class and to your interest as citizens, whose all is at stake in this great contest in which you are engaged, I ask an immediate response.

" 'In ancient times that nation, it is said, usually extended its conquests further whose arms were shortest. Long range guns sometimes fail to fire and waste a hundred balls to one that takes effect, but the short range pike and the terrible knife (as they can be almost in a moment) wielded by a stalwart patriot's arm, never fail to fire and never waste a single load.

" 'I am, very respectfully,

" 'Your fellow citizen,

" 'JOSEPH E. BROWN.'

"In addition to the pikes made by the free men of Georgia, in response to the Governor's call, two or three thousand were made by the convicts in the State penitentiary at Milledgeville. These were crated in coffin-like boxes, a hundred to the box, and sent to Savannah, where they were to be usd in the defence of Fort Pulaski. There was never occasion to use them in actual fighting, although several battalions were well drilled in the use of the pike and knife.

"After the war a large number of these pikes were stored in the arsenal at Augusta, where they remained until ten years' ago, when they were sold at public auction by the Government. There were four different patterns of the knives. The sale was avertised by the Government, and people came from Maine to California to buy the curious war implements."

CLARKE

Oldest State University in America. Franklin College: Volume I, Pages 139-146, 425-436.

Historic Homes of Athens.   Unrivalled among the cities of Georgia for its majestic old Southern mansions of the ante-bellum type, Athens, even at the present day, pictures to the imagination what life in

DR. CRAWFORD W. LONG'S OLD HOME, ATHENS, GA.

Dixie was before the war; for while commercially a town of the most progressive pattern, it is nevertheless, in its domestic ideals, still charmingly reminiscent of the Old South's palmiest days and best traditions. Several years before the war, Colonel John T. Grant, one of the wealthiest citizens of the State, erected on Prince Avenue a magnificent home, which is still one of the glories of Athens. Its graceful Corinthian columns, its wide porticos, its lofty arches, make it still the finest specimen extant of the classic style of architecture, peculiar to the ante-bellum period. This stately old mansion is a beautiful monument within itself to the civilization which produced it: proud, aristocratic, ample, elegant. It was built by Colonel Grant soon after his marriage to Miss Martha Cobb Jackson, a granddaughter of the peerless old Governor who fought the Yazoo fraud; but on his removal to Atlanta at the close of the war Colonel Grant sold his splendid old home in Athens to Hon. Benjamin H. Hill, afterwards a United States Senator, who located in Athens mainly for the purpose of educating his two boys, Ben and Charlie. When Mr. Hill removed to Atlanta in 1875 this handsome property was purchased by Mr. James White, its present owner and occupant.

Scarcely inferior to the old Grant home, either in stateliness of proportions or in simple elegance of design is the fine old Joseph H. Lumpkin mansion, on Prince Avenue. It was built by the great Chief Justice soon after his removal to Athens from his former home in Lexington; and, when first built, it occupied an eminence some distance from the avenue which it overlooked. Rising out of a wealth of evergreens, it presented a semi-regal aspect, and, due to its elevation, it made a more impressive picture to the eye than did the Grant home, which was built on a level with the street, with a smaller area of ground in front. Here the famous Home School was taught for a number of years by the Sosnowskis. The handsome old mansion is today occupied by Mr. W. L. Childs, and is owned by himself and his sister, Mrs. David C. Barrow, wife of the Chancellor.

What is known as the Tom Cobb place, a stately old mansion on the same avenue, was built by Mr. Charles McKinley and sold by him to Judge Joseph Henry Lumpkin, who gave it to his daughter, Mrs. T. R. R. Cobb. It is now owned and occupied by Mr. A. M. Dobbs. On the opposite side of the street stands the Camak home, one of the oldest landmarks in Athens. It was built by James Camak, Esq., shortly after his removal to Athens in 1817, and here for the remainder of his days this pioneer railway builder and financier resided. It is today owned and occupied by his son's widow, Mrs. M. W. Camak. The old Dearing home, on Milledge Avenue, a handsome specimen of Colonial architecture, was built by Mr. Albon Dearing, whose son of the same name is its present owner and occupant. The old Hull home, a stately mansion of the best ante-bellum type, is still one of the ornaments of Milledge Avenue. It was formerly owned by Colonel Benjamin C. Yancey, and later acquired by the Hulls.

On Prince Avenue, at the intersection of Grady Street, stands the majestic old mansion in which the South's great orator journalist spent his boyhood days and to which he feelingly referred in his famous New England speech. It was built by Colonel Robert Taylor, who sold it early in the fifties to Major William S. Grady, a wealthy business man of Athens, who fell at Petersburg, in 1863. The Grady home is now owned and occupied by Mrs. L. D. DuBose. Standing some distance back from this same avenue, near the intersection of Barber Street, looms an impressive old land-mark: the Thomas home. It was built by General Howell Cobb and sold by him to Mrs. Nina Thomas. The stately old residence is now owned and occupied by Mr. W. I. Abney. The handsome old home on Milledge Avenue, now the property of Judge Strickland, was built by Dr. Jones Long, a brother of Dr. Crawford W. Long.

General Howell Cobb built the handsome old home on Hill Street, which continued to be his home for a number of years, and where his son, Judge Howell Cobb,

BOYHOOD HOME OF HENRY W. GRADY, ATHENS, GA.
From an original sketch by Miss Garland Smith.

afterwards resided. It is now the home of Mr. I. W. Richardson. On Pulaski Street, a fine old Colonial mansion, was built by Mr. Blanton Hill, whose daughter, Mrs. Augusta Noble, occupied it for a number of years after his death. It is today the property of Mr. John D. Moss. On this same street, a stately old home was also built by Mr. Stevens Thomas, a wealthy antebellum citizen of Athens. It is now used by the Y. W. C. A. as a home for working girls, and faces on Hancock Avenue.

The old Lucas home, at the south end of Jackson Street, was built by a Mr. Hopping. Afterwards, for a while it became the home of Hon. Eugenius A. Nisbet, and still later the home of Mr. F. W. Lucas, who occupied it for years. It is now owned by the University of Georgia and used for the time being as a dormitory for students. The home of the late Mr. Stephen C. Upson, on Prince Avenue, was built by Hon. Henry G. Lamar, the marriage of whose daughter to Hon. O. A. Lochrane, afterwards Chief Justice, was here solemnized. The Chancellor's home on the University campus was built for Dr. Alonzo Church when he was president of Franklin College. The Crawford W. Long home, on Prince Avenue, an attractive structure of the modern type, became in after years the boyhood home of Judge Peyton L. Wade, of the State Court of Appeals. Cedar Hill, the famous old home of Governor Wilson Lumpkin, on an eminence overlooking the Oconee River in the immediate environs of Athens, was inherited by his daughter, Mrs. Martha Lumpkin Compton, from whom the place subsequently became known as Compton Hill. It is now owned by the University of Georgia. The old home has recently been removed to one side, in order to make room for the new agricultural building, and some of the students now reside here during the college sessions. The old Hamilton home, built by Dr. James S. Hamilton, is now owned and occupied by Mr. E. R. Hodgson, Jr. Dr.

E. S. Lynden's home, at the north end of Jackson Street, was built by Dr. Edward Ware.*

The Lucy Cobb
Institute.   Volume I, Pages 437-438.

John Howard
Payne's Georgia
Sweetheart.   Volume II, Pages 62-71.

Origin of the
Southern Cross
of   Honor.   Volume I, Pages 222-224.

James Camak. One of the earliest pioneer residents of Athens was James Camak, Esq., whose name was inadvertently omitted from a list of settlers in Volume I of this work. But no history of Athens can be written without some account of this eminent citizen of the ante-bellum period, who, coming to Athens from Milledgeville, in 1817, built the stately old mansion on Prince Avenue, still owned by the family, perhaps the oldest surviving landmark of a community famed for its historic homes. With far-sighted ken, Mr. Camak was quick to see and prompt to grasp the possibilities of the Iron Horse. He became one of the builders of the Georgia Railroad, a corporation with whose directorate he was identified until the hour of his death. The town of Camak, an important station on the main line, today commemorates the part played by this wise builder in the railway development of his State. Mr. Camak, in 1834, organized in Athens the famous old Branch Bank of the State of Georgia, a financial institution of which he became the first executive head. He married Helen Finley,

*Authority: Miss Garland Smith, Athens, Ga.

the daughter of an early president of Franklin College; and for years was an honored trustee of the oldest State University in America.

———

Where the Geor- To quote a distinguished local histor-
gia Railroad   ian: "The Georgia Railroad, one of
Originated.   the most important enterprises in the
                  State, had its inception in Athens. The
first meeting was held here in June, 1833, with Mr. As-bury Hull as chairman, and later, during the same year, he introduced in the Legislature a bill for its incorpora-tion. Here for years the annual meetings of the road were held, and all its directors were Athens men until the line was completed. The board of directors in 1835 was composed as follows: James Camak, William Will-iams, John A. Cobb, Elizur L. Newton, Alexander B. Linton, James Shannon, W. M. Morton, and W. R. Cun-ningham. The road was originally intended to run be-tween Augusta and Athens, while a branch line to Greensboro was contemplated. Subsequently the Greens-boro branch became the main stem, extending to Atlanta, after which Athens was left on the branch road."*

———

The Cobbs. Dr. Henry Hull, one of the most distin-
            guished of the ante-bellum residents of
Athens, has left us the following unique comparison be-tween the two famous brothers, Howell and Thomas R. R. Cobb. It was written soon after the close of hos-tilities, when Dr. Hull was quite an old man. Though both of the Cobbs were distinguished soldiers, the title which he gives the former is "Governor," while the latter he calls "General." Says Dr. Hull:

"The question has often been asked, Which was the more talented of the two. One may as well inquire which is the greater genius, a great painter or a great philosopher? There is no unit of measurement with

———

*A. L. Hull, Annals of Athens, p. 100.

which to compare them. So of these two brothers—their minds were of different structure. The Governor controlled men by unequalled management and tact; the General by the irresistible force of argument. The Governor was the greater politician, the General the greater lawyer. While the wonderful talents of both commanded respect, the social qualities, the genial bon homme, the generous open-heartedness of the Governor secured your love; the commanding power of intellect in all the General said or did excited the admiration. The Governor would, in commercial language, look at the sum total of an account, without regard to the items, or grasp the conclusion of a proposition without examining each step by the demonstration. The General received nothing as true which could not be proven, and submitted every question to the crucible of reason before he pronounced upon its absolute truth.

"I do not speak of the public acts of these brothers, but remember them only as boys, students, and fellow-citizens. The Governor was generous and liberal, almost to prodigality. When his father, from a reckless disregard of economy and mismanagement of his affairs, had allowed his debts to accumulate to an amount which could not be paid by the sale of his property, the Governor devoted the whole of a handsome estate—left him by an uncle, Howell Cobb, for whom he was named—to the liquidation of the remaining liabilities, so that no man should say that he had been injured by his father. With a hand open as day to melting charity, he gave to those who asked of him, and from those who would borrow of him he turned not away. And many were the cases of a princely generosity and charity of which this world never heard, but which were elsewhere recorded. The General gave as much, or perhaps more, in proportion to his means than the Governor, but in a different way. His benefactions were governed by the dictates of reason, rather than by the impulses of feeling. All plans suggested for the promotion of the public good received his efficient and hearty support. He took a lively interest in everything connected with the prosperity of the town, including the University, the schools and the churches. He was the founder of the Lucy Cobb Institute, and contributed more of his time, influence and money to insure its success than did any half dozen men put together.

"General Cobb was prominent in every association of which he was a member. He was a man of the most wonderful versatility of talent, and would concentrate the power of his wonderful mind on the propriety and necessity of secession, on some intricate and abstruse point of law, on the best manner of conducting a Sunday-school, or on any subject which men thought of and talked about, with equal facility, and as if the matter under discussion was the only one he had ever studied, and with a rapidity of transition from one to another, which was almost startling, even where the topics were totally dissimilar. The patient and long-continued investigation of the most abstruse subject was pastime to him, and after such labor he would meet you with a cheerful smile on the brightest face, and crack his jokes as if he did nothing else all his life. He was surely the most remarkable man of his day.''

To the foregoing parallelism it may be added that General Cobb took no active part in politics until the election of Mr. Lincoln. He then fairly electrified the State with his eloquence, advocating immediate and unconditional surrender. The suddenness of his appearance upon the hustings and the popular enthusiasm which he aroused over Georgia caused Mr. Stephens to liken him to Peter the Hermit, a comparison which was peculiarly apposite, in view of Mr. Cobb's intensely religious nature. He was one of the most pious of men. With reference to his capacity for labor, Judge Richard H. Clark, who was associated with him in the first codification of the laws of Georgia, states that at the close of each day's work his mind was invariably fresh and buoyant. He was an absolute stranger to mental weariness, though he performed the labors of Hercules. At the age of 36 he wrote Cobb on Slavery, a masterpiece of legal literature. As chairman of the Judiciary Committee of the Provisional Congress, he also drafted the Constitution of the Confederate States. The original document, in General Cobb's own handwriting, is still preserved in the family of his daughter, Mrs. A. L. Hull.

The Lumpkins: Mr. Augustus L. Hull, of Athens, Ga., who possessed an intimate personal acquaintance with the Lumpkins, has given us the following pen-picture of the famous brothers, Wilson and Joseph Henry Lumpkin, both of whom were long residents of Athens:

''The one, the eldest, the other, the youngest, of eight children, they were as dissimilar as brothers could be. One a shrewd politician, the other abhorring politics; one commanding by his ability, the other persuading by his eloquence; one robust in his aggressiveness, the other fond of study; one a Baptist, the other a Presbyterian; one an adherent of Clark, the other of Troup; one a Democrat, the other a Whig; one tall, the other short in stature; but both men of striking presence, and both of great abilities.

"Wilson Lumpkin was Congressman, United States Senator and Governor of Georgia. During his administration the State road was built, and he devoted his energies to the material development of the State. Governor Lumpkin was long the president of the Board of Trustees of the University of Georgia. As he headed the procession to the chapel on commencement occasions, with a tall, commanding presence, erect and dignified, with long hair brushed back from his head and falling over his shoulders in gray curls, he seemed one of the most impressive men I have ever seen. He was thrice married, and built the old stone house, now in the campus extension, in which he lived for many years, and where he died in the closing days of 1870. One of his children, a very bright and attractive boy of six or seven years, wandered one afternoon away from the house and lost his way in the woods along the river. Though search was made all night, he was not found till next morning, exhausted with wandering and wild with terror. The horrors of the darkness of that night destroyed his mind, and though he grew to be a man of fine proportions and pleasing countenance, mentally he was never any older than on the morning when he was found, and forty years afterward, as though he recalled that dreadful night, he wandered again into the woods and was drowned in the river, not far from the place where they found him before.

"Judge Lumpkin was a learned jurist and a finished scholar. He loved study, and was a great reader. His speeches, of which no record now remains, were full of pathos, and the fire of eloquence, and his decisions while on the Supreme bench are models of clearness and elegant composition. A natural teacher, for many years he imparted instruction to the young men in his office and in the Lumpkin Law School, charming them alike by the elegance of his language and the thoroughness of his knowlegde. He was a great temperance advocate, and his voice, always heard on the side of righteousness, was a power for good.

"Judge Lumpkin was the first Chief Justice of Georgia; and one of his successors in office, Chief Justice Bleckley, said of him: 'His literary power was in vocal utterance. In the spoken word he was a literary genius, far surpassing any other Georgian, living or dead, I have ever known. Indeed, from no other mortal lips have I ever heard such harmonies and sweet-sounding sentences as came from his. Those who never saw and heard him cannot be made to realize what a great master he was.' Judge Lumpkin died June 4, 1867, from a stroke of paralysis."

One of Washington's Men. In an old cemetery, near the historic site of Cherokee Corner, lie the mortal remains of Charles Strong, Sr., a Revolutionary soldier, who served under the immediate command of General Nelson. His commission was issued by William Lochren, January 18, 1781. He was present when Cornwallis surrendered to Washington at York- town, in Virginia, after which he removed from his old home in Goochland County, Va., to a plantation in Clarke County, Ga., near Cherokee Corner, where he died Octo- ber 15, 1848. There are numerous descendants in Geor- gia of this revered soldier and patriot.*

CLAY

Fort Gaines. During the Creek Indian War there was built near the site of the present town of Fort Gaines, on the Chattahoochee River, a stronghold to protect the extreme western frontier of Georgia. It was named for General Edmond P. Gaines, an officer of the United States Army, and a prominent figure in the military operations of this period against the Creeks. We find from the records that by an Act approved De- cember 14, 1830, the town of Fort Gaines was chartered, with the following named commissioners, to wit: Gabriel Johnson, John Dill, Edward Deloney, George W. Pres- cott and James V. Robinson.[1] One year later, the old Fort Gaines Academy was chartered, at which time Messrs. Samuel Johnson, Thomas B. Patterson, Sr., Leonard P. McCollom, Ira Cushman and James Buch- anan were named as trustees.[2] But one school was not enough. Though on the frontier, Fort Gaines was edu- cationally wideawake, and, on December 31, 1838, an Act of the Legislature was approved, granting a charter to the Fort Gaines Female Institute, one of the earliest pioneer schools for young ladies. The management of this school was entrusted to the following trustees: John Dill, Simon Green, Samuel Gainer, James P. Holmes,

*Authority: Mrs. W. C. Clarke, Covington, Ga.
[1] Acts, 1830, p. 217.
[2] Acts, 1831, p. 17.

and William Mount.[1] When Clay County was organized from Randolph and Early in 1854, the county-seat of the new county was made permanent at Fort Gaines. Clay's first representative in the Legislature was L. B. Dozier. Others who followed him were: Peter Lee, F. T. Cullens, John L. Brown, W. A. Graham, S. R. Weaver, R. A. Turnipseed and John B. Johnson.

CLAYTON

Jonesboro. On the site of the present town of Jonesboro, there was formerly a village known as Leaksville, an academy for which was chartered as early as December 22, 1823, with the following pioneer residents named as trustees:[2] Thomas Wilburn, Robert Leak, John Chislum, Jack Wilburn and Columbus Watson. When the Central of Georgia reached this point, imparting new life to the town and giving rise to visions of civic importance, the name of Leaksville was discarded, and, in compliment to one of the civil engineers who surveyed the line, Mr. Samuel G. Jones, the town was called Jonesboro. Mr. Jones was the father of the late Governor Thomas G. Jones, of Alabama, afterwards a District Judge of the United States. When the County of Clayton was organized in 1858, Jonesboro was made the county-site of the new county; and by an Act of the Legislature, approved December 13, 1859, the town was incorporated with the following-named commissioners: James B. Key, Sanford D. Johnson, G. L. Warren, Joshua J. Harris, W. H. Sharp, R. K. Holliday and James Alford.[3] One of the strongest advocates of the measure creating Clayton County was Judge George Hillyer, a member of the present Railroad Commission.

[1] Acts, 1838, p. 4.
[2] Acts, 1823, p. 15.
[3] Acts, 1859, p. 175.

Judge Hillyer was then just entering public life, and he made a host of warm friends by his plendid work for the bill.

Pioneer Settlers. As gathered from the oldest records extant, some of the pioneer settlers of Clayton were as follows: James B. Key, John M. Huie, Stephen G. Dorsey, R. E. Morrow, Philip Fitzgerald, Abner Camp, James Davis, J. B. Tanner, N. C. Adamson, G. W. Adamson, A. Y. Adamson, Andrew L. Huie, A. J. Mundy, Joshua J. Hanes, James Daniel, W. W. Camp, Thomas Moore, John Stanley, Elijah Glass, Hilliard Starr, W. Y. Conine, James McConnell, Luke Johnson, Reuben Wallis, James F. Johnson, Thomas Johnson, James S. Cook, William Cater, Moab Stephens, James H. Chapman, Thomas Byrne, Zachariah Mann, Patrick H. Allen, Peter Y. Ward, and others. James F. Johnson was the first State Senator and Elijah Glass the first Representative, both elected in 1859.

CLINCH.

Homerville. Homerville, the county-seat of Clinch County, was founded in the year 1859 by Dr. John Homer Mattox. The public buildings were first located at Magnolia, but the need of a central location and the desire to be on a railroad brought about the removal of the court-house to Homerville in 1862. As soon as the Atlantic and Gulf Line was completed to this point, Dr. Mattox saw a bright future for a town in this neighborhood. Accordingly, he began to lay off some of his land into town lots. This property was first acquired, in 1842, by his father, Elijah Mattox, and, at the latter's death, was inherited by Dr. Mattox.

The new town was first called "Station Number 11." However, in a few years the name was changed to Homerville, in honor of Homer Mattox. At this time, a group of homes, a small store and a shed designed for the railroad station, marked the beginning of the future county-seat. Today Homerville possesses a bank, two handsome church buildings, several stores, and some of the most attractive homes in this part of Georgia. Waterworks and electric light plants have recently been installed, while a telephone system has been in use for several years. The Bank of Homerville has a capital stock of $25,000, with a surplus equal to half this amount. Its officials are: President, R. G. Dickerson, a former State Senator and one of the State's foremost men; Vice-President, W. T. Dickerson, also formerly State Senator and a prominent lawyer; and Cashier, G. A. Gibbs.

Among the prominent citizens of Homerville, in addition to the bank officials mentioned, are Judge John T. Dame, the Ordinary; his brother, George M. Dame, a strong factor in county and town affairs; S. L. Drawdy, Judge of the County Court of Clinch, and a former Representative; his brother, Charlton C. Drawdy; J. F. Barnhill and J. H. Ferdon, two prominent naval stores men; W. V. Musgrove, and many others. Homerville was first incorporated in 1869. In the western part of the town is the handsome new school-house, DuBignon Institute, named in honor of the late Fleming G. DuBignon, one of Georgia's most gifted sons. The original building was destroyed by fire in 1909, but on the same site the present structure was completed the following year.*

COBB

Marietta: A Brief Sketch. Nestling almost within the shadow of Kennesaw Mountain, the little city of Marietta is identified with some of the most heroic memories of the Civil War. On either side of the town there are beautiful cemeteries consecrated to the ashes

---

*Authority: Mr. Folks Huxford, Homerville, Ga.

of the gallant dead, most of whom fell in fiercely contested battles around Marietta, in the campaign of 1864. The Federal Cemetery, a magnificently wooded area, to the east of the town, contains the graves of 12,000 Federal soldiers; while over 3,000 wearers of the gray uniform sleep in the beautiful enclosure of ground, known as the Confederate Cemetery, just to the west of the State Road.

But the history of Marietta antedates by more than a generation the titanic death grapple between North and South. It came into existence when Cobb County was erected out of a part of the territory wrested from the Cherokee Indians, and was made the permanent county-site by an Act of the Legislature, approved December 19, 1834, at which time the following pioneer citizens were named as commissioners: Leonard Simpson, Washington Winters, James Anderson, George W. Cupp and Lemma Kerkly.* As a health resort, Marietta enjoyed from the start a peculiar prestige among the towns of the Georgia uplands. It furnished a delightful retreat in summer for scores of families from the coast and developed excellent schools, which made it a seat of culture and a center of refinement, long before the Civil War.

John Heyward Glover. Perhaps the pioneer citizen to whose constructive leadership the city of Marietta owes its largest debt of gratitude was Colonel John Heyward Glover, a native of Beaufort District, S. C. Settling at Marietta, in 1848, he became at once a dominant factor in the affairs of the town and was the first citizen to hold the office of mayor. He donated the land for the present court-house and public square; while his widow, in after years, donated the tract today known as the Confederate Cemetery, but used for general purposes of burial. He was one of

---

*Acts, 1834, p. 252.

Marietta's earliest captains of industry; and his tire-
less energies supplied an impetus from which much of
the subsequent growth of Marietta has resulted. He
died in the prime of life, on March 28, 1859, and his untimely death was made the subject of resolutions adopted
by the town council of Marietta and by the local Bar, at
a meeting over which Judge George D. Rice presided.

Some Early   But there were many other men of note
Pioneers.   connected with the beginnings of Marietta.
Captain Arnoldus V. Brumby, who founded
the Georgia Military Academy, famous in war times as
our Georgia West Point, came to Marietta in the early
fifties. He was followed, in 1858, by his brother, Prof.
Richard T. Brumby, at one time a partner of the noted
William C. Preston, of South Carolina, in the practice
of law, and afterwards an educator of eminent distinction. Dr. Isaac Watts Waddell, an early pastor of the
Presbyterian Church, was one of the tall landmarks of
his denomination in Georgia. Mrs. Lizzie Waddell
Setze, his daughter, has lived in Marietta continuously
since 1842. Dr. Scott, the first rector of St. James, afterwards became a Bishop. On the present site of the
Episcopal Church, John R. Winters helped to build the
first house in Marietta. General A. J. Hansell built the
handsome old home where Miss Sarah Camp now lives,
on Kennesaw Avenue. Governor Charles J. McDonald
was a pioneer resident of Marietta, and a part of his
original home place is today owned and occupied by
Governor Joseph M. Brown. Judge George D. Anderson, Colonel George N. Lester, Colonel James D. Waddell, Colonel James W. Robertson, afterwards Adjutant-
General of Georgia; Judge David Irwin, one of the original codifiers of the law of Georgia; General William
Phillips, who commanded a noted legion of cavalry during the Civil War; his brother, Colonel Charles D. Phil-

lips, Hon. William Y. Hansell and many other men of note were identified with Marietta's early days.

The Georgia Military Institute. On December 8, 1851, an Act was approved, chartering the famous Georgia Military Institute at Marietta, as a private enterprise, under the control of certain well-known citizens, to wit: David Irwin, Andrew J. Hansell, William P. Young, John H. Glover, Martin G. Slaughter, David Dobbs, John Jones, Charles J. McDonald, William Harris, Mordecai Myers and James Brannon.[1] Some few years later it became an institution of the State. Colonel A. V. Brumby was the first superintendent. He was the father of the gallant officer of Dewey's flagship, Lieutenant Thomas M. Brumby, who raised the first United States flag at Manila.

The first commandant was Colonel James W. Robertson. In the wake of Sherman's march to the sea, the Georgia Military Institute became a blackened ruin; but during the fourteen short years in which it existed as an institution, it literally sowed the dragon's teeth from which an army of trained warriors was destined to spring. As a feeder for the Confederate ranks, it became famous throughout the land, and there must have been a thrill of peculiar satisfaction in the breast of the great Federal commander when he applied the torch to an institution which was the dread and terror of Yankeedom. The following account of the origin of this school is condensed from White.[2] Says he: "Its first session opened on July 10, 1851, with only seven cadets; but before the close of the term the number was increased to twenty-eight. Since then the number has steadily and rapidly increased at each session until the present time; and now, having completed but two years

---

[1] Acts, 1851-1852, pp. 298-299.
[2] White's Statistics.

of its history, it numbers one hundred and twenty cadets, five professors and one assistant professor. It was incorporated by the Legislature as a college, during the session of 1851-1852. At the same time, the Governor was directed to make requisition upon the government of the United States for arms and accoutrements. These have been received. The government and discipline of the Institute are strict. The course of study is thoroughly scientific and practical, and the whole is modeled after the United States Military Academy at West Point.''

With the approach of General Sherman towards Marietta, in 1864, the cadets were organized into a battalion, under the command of Major, afterwards Bridgadier-General, F. W. Capers, and there were no better fighters in Johnston's army than these beardless boys.

They served from May 10, 1864, to May 20, 1865. Scores of them were wounded in battle. Not a few of them were killed outright. In every action they gave a brave account of themselves; and, according to Judge Robert L. Rodgers, one of the gallant band, they constituted the last organized body of Confederate soldiers on duty east of the Mississippi River. Under an order from General Lafayette McLaws, dated May 1, 1865, after both Lee and Johnston had surrendered, they rendered service to the Confederate government by guarding the military stores at Augusta, until relieved by a garrison of Federal soldiers, who came to take possession.

Thus it was reserved for these cadets of the Georgia Military Institute to obey the last orders of a Confederate officer during the war between the States.

————

Where Two Governors Have Lived: An Historic Home. The town of Marietta has given the State two Governors who occupied the same home site: Charles J. McDonald and Joseph M. Brown. The latter, when an employee of the Western & Atlantic

Railroad, in the capacity of traffic manager, with little thought of what the future held in store for him, purchased the old McDonald place at Marietta, and after his marriage, on February 12, 1889, to Miss Cora McCord, made this his home for the future. He purchased the property from General Henry R. Jackson, of Savannah, from whose name it borrows an added wealth of associations, and here, surrounded by stately forest oaks, he has since spent the greater part of his time, in the enjoyment of an ideal home life, semi-rural in character. The site was happily chosen by Governor McDonald during the early ante-bellum period. It included originally quite a large portion of the present town, and something like 110 acres were embraced in the tract conveyed to Governor Brown. The old residence, which was built and occupied by Governor McDonald, was burned to the ground by General Serman. But the comparatively new residence of the present Governor was built only a stone's throw from the old chimney piles which survived the general wreck.

The present Governor's father was a warm admirer of Governor McDonald. It is said that the former, after drafting his first inaugural address, submitted the manuscript to Governor McDonald for approval and was more than gratified by the fact that the old Governor could suggest nothing in the way of improvement or correction. As a further proof of the friendship which existed between them, one of the sons of Georgia's war Governor was named for Governor McDonald. They were both men of positive convictions, and were both trained in the Jeffersonian school of politics.

Governor McDonald was born in Charleston, S. C., but his sturdy virtues were cast in the rugged molds of the Scottish Highlands. He came to Georgia when a lad and lived for a while in Hancock. At the age of twenty-eight he was elected Judge of the Flint Circuit and two years later was made Brigadier-General of the State militia. From 1839 to 1843 he held the high office

of Governor, and from 1855 to 1859 he wore the ermine
of the Supreme Court of Georgia. He was an ardent
advocate of State rights, a strict Constructionist of the
Federal Constitution, and a devoted patriot. Due to his
extreme views upon questions of the day, he was defeated
by Howell Cobb for Governor in 1850, but scarcely more
than a decade passed before the State came to his way
of thinking and adopted the ordinance of secession. He
died in Marietta, on the eve of the Civil War, at the age
of sixty-eight.

Governor Brown was first elected to the office of Governor in 1908. He had previously been a member of
the State Railroad Commission, an office to which he
was appointed by reason of his familiarity with railroad
matters. But he took a position in regard to port rates
at variance with the views held by Governor Smith, in
consequence of which there occurred an open rupture
between them. The Commissioner's resignation was
demanded. To vindicate himself before the people, Mr.
Brown became a candidate for the office of Governor, and
in the ensuing election was victorious at the polls. There
is a story told to the effect that Mr. Brown had sent a
communication to Governor Smith voluntarily relinquishing his office as commissioner, but that Governor Smith
had refused to open it, thereby hurling a fire-brand into
Georgia politics, which ultimately compassed his defeat.
It is certain that Mr. Brown sent a letter to Governor
Smith, which the latter returned to him with the seal
unbroken; but what it contained has never been divulged.

The whole State was divided into Brown and Smith
camps, and the political feud between Clark and Crawford was re-enacted upon a wider stage of politics.
Though Governor Brown was successful in the first election, Governor Smith opposed him in the second campaign, and was again elected to the office of Governor.
But, during his term of office, the Legislature elected him
to fill the unexpired term of Senator Clay, a race in
which he defeated Hon. Joseph M. Terrell, who was tem-

porarily filling the vacancy under an appointment by Governor Brown. Thus the fight was still on. Upon the election of Governor Smith to the United States Senate, the friends of Governor Brown urged him to re-enter the field for Governor. He did so; and, on December 7, 1911, was re-elected. The interval of sixty days between the retirement of Governor Smith and the inauguration of Governor Brown was filled by the President of the State Senate, Hon. John M. Slaton, who became ad interim Governor of Georgia. The only instance on record in the history of the State, where father and son have held the office of Governor, is furnished by the Browns. The library of the present Governor contains a number of rare books, and is particularly rich in works which deal with early American antiquities. Several years ago, he published a romance, entitled ''Astyanax,'' in which he portrays the ancient civilization of Mexico. Though not an orator in the forensic sense, he wields an effective pen, and is characterized by much of his father's far-sightedness of vision. Besides the home place at Marietta, Governor Brown cultivates an extensive plantation in Cherokee.

———

Governor Charles J. McDonald: An Episode of His Career. Judge Spencer R. Atkinson, a grandson of Governor Charles J. McDonald, and himself a Georgian of distinguished attainments, has preserved the following dramatic incident in the life of the illustrious statesman. Says he:

''Governor McDonald came into office under trying circumstances. The State treasury was empty. The evil effects of the great panic of 1837 were still pressing upon the people, like a nightmare. The great work of building the Western and Atlantic Railroad was languishing. The public debt had been increased to one million dollars—an enormous sum in those days. Worst of all, the State credit was at a low ebb, because of the protest of an obligation of three hundred thousand dollars, which had been contracted by the Central Bank under authority of the General Assembly of Georgia. Commerce and business generally were paralyzed. In 1837 the Legislature had passed an act allowing the counties of the State to retain the general tax, the same to be applied by the inferior courts to county purposes. As might have been expected, the counties frittered away the money. The bank was nearly destroyed by putting upon it a burden which did not belong to it, and the State was left without resource or credit.

"Governor McDonald had inherited from his Scotch ancestors a hard head and a sound judgment. Never did he need his inherent qualities more than he did in the situation which then confronted him. He first recommended that the State resume the entire amount of the State tax which had been given to the counties, with but little benefit to them and greatly to the injury of the State. This recommendation prevailed, and a law was enacted ordering the State tax to be turned into the treasury. Almost immediately following this necessary action, the Legislature, in 1841, passed an Act reducing the taxes of the State twenty per cent. This Act Governor McDonald promptly vetoed, with an argument, brief and pointed, and a statement which made his veto message unanswerable. He had been re-elected in 1841 and, on November 8, 1842, in his annual message urging upon the Legislature the only effective remedy for relieving the State from its difficulties, he used these words: 'The difficulty should be met at once. Had there been no Central Bank the expense of the government must have been met by taxation. These expenses have been paid by the Central Bank and have become a legitimate charge upon taxation. This must be the resort, or the government is inevitably dishonored. The public faith must be maintained, and to pause to discuss the question of preferences between taxation and dishonor would be to cast a reflection upon the character of the people, whose servants we are.'

"The issue was joined. The Legislature had rejected a measure calling for additional taxation to meet these just claims. The session was near its close. It was evident that unless some drastic action was taken the Legislature would adjourn, leaving an obligation of one hundred thousand dollars unmet. Governor McDonald acted with firmness and promptness. He shut the doors of the treasury in the face of the members of the General Assembly of Georgia. Great excitement followed. The members of the Legislature denounced him as a tyrant worse than Andrew Jackson, who had gone beyond the limits of reason. Even his political friends, alarmed at the storm which had been raised, urged him to recede from his position and to rescind his order to the Treasurer. He resolutely refused. As a result, the necessary bill was finally passed, and at the next session he was able to report an improved condition of the finances and a revival of confidence in the Central Bank. It was without doubt a most fortunate thing for Georgia at this critical period in the history of the State that a man of Governor McDonald's firmness, prudence, and business sagacity was at the head of affairs.'

Governor McDonald is buried in the Episcopal Cemetery, at Marietta: The grave is handsomely marked by a monument of marble, which consists of a solid column surmounted by an urn, the whole resting upon a pedestal of granite. The coat of arms of Georgia is chiselled into the column, while above the device is inscribed "McDonald." Underneath appears the following epitaph:

> "Sacred to the memory of Charles James McDonald. Born July 9, 1793. Died December 16, 1860. Aged 67 years, 5 months, and 7 days. 'Come, behold the works of the Lord, what desolation He hath made in the earth.'"

Cobb in the Mexican War. In 1845, when hostilities with Mexico began, a company of soldiers was dispatched from Cobb to the seat of war. It was called the Kennesaw Rangers, and was annexed to the Georgia Regiment of Volunteers, in command of Colonel Henry R. Jackson, of Savannah. Its officers were as follows: Captain, A. Nelson; First Lieutenant, James M. Dobbs; Second Lieutenant, W. J. Manahan; Sergeants, J. H. Mehaffey, H. Trotter, Andrew B. Reed and Joseph H. Winters; Corporals, S. M. Anderson, William D. Neal, William D. Gray and William H. Craft. Ninety-two members enrolled.

The Little Brass Cannon. There stands in the Confederate Cemetery, at Marietta, a little brass cannon, concerning which there is a story of dramatic interest. During the year 1852, the Georgia Military Institute, at Marietta, was presented by the State with four six-pounder guns, made of brass, to be used in the artillery drills. On the occasion of the inauguration of Governor Herschel V. Johnson, at Milledgeville, in 1856, the cadets were present. They took with them two of the guns, to be used in the inaugural ceremonies; but while a cadet was loading one of them it fired prematurely, mutilating an arm of the gunner. The disastrous affair occurred on the Capitol grounds. Two years later the cadets witnessed the induction into office of Governor Joseph E. Brown, on which occasion they again took two of the guns with them; but fortunately this time there was no mishap.

When the Institute was closed, in 1864, by reason of the imminence of hostilities, due to the approach of General Sherman, a battalion of cadets was formed. As the boys, however, were armed with Belgian rifles and were enlisted as infantrymen, they did not need the heavy guns. So the six-pounders were left on the parade grounds at the Institute. At the close of the war they were not to be found in Marietta.

Judge Robert L. Rodgers is of the opinion that they were brought to Atlanta, in the wake of Johnston's army, and that in the battles around the beleaguered citadel of the Confederacy, the guns fell into the hands of the Federals. At any rate, they were captured by the enemy, whether at one place or at another.

Years elapsed without bringing any word in regard to the missing guns. Finally, in 1909, Governor Joseph M. Brown, who was then in office, was notified by the War Department at Washington that in the arsenal at Watervliet, N. Y., there was a little brass cannon having on it the inscription: "Georgia Military Institute, 1851." At the same time it was stated that the trophy of war could be purchased for the sum of $150. In proportion to the sentimental value of the old relic, the amount was nominal. But Governor Brown was not authorized to pay the money out of the treasury of the State. Moreover, the ex-cadets were scattered throughout the Union—the few who still survived the flight of fifty years. So the Governor referred the matter to the Ladies' Memorial Association, at Marietta. These patriotic women immediately went to work. They enlisted the co-operation of Senators Bacon and Clay and of Congressman Gordon Lee, the latter of whom represented the district. Together, they induced the Government to donate the cannon to the Ladies' Memorial Association, of Marietta. It was a generous act on the part of the Federal authorities, especially in view of the partisan role which such an engine of war is supposed to have played, but the cannon was never fired by the cadets against the United States flag.

Soon after the matter was thus happily settled the cannon arrived. In due time it was installed upon a pedestal of granite and placed in the Confederate Cemetery, at Marietta, within sight of Kennesaw Mountain, to guard the heroic dust which here sleeps. On April 26, 1910, it was formally unveiled with impressive ceremonies. Judge Robert L. Rodgers, of Atlanta, welcomed the little cannon back home in an eloquent speech, while the veil was drawn by Miss Annie Coryell, the charming little granddaughter of Colonel James W. Robertson, the first commandant of the Institute. There were a number of the old cadets present, besides a host of distinguished visitors, including his excellency, Governor Joseph M. Brown. The site of the famous old school is in the immediate neighborhood of the spot where the little cannon keeps vigil.

Kennesaw Mountain.   Volume I, Pages 208-211.

Cheatham's Hill: On June 27, 1914—fifty years after the
The Illinois battle of Kennesaw Mountain—a superb
Monument. perb monument of Georgia marble was
formally unveiled by the State of Illinois, at Cheatham's Hill, a part of the historic battle ground, near Marietta. Governor E. F. Dunne, representing the State of Illinois, accompanied by a special delegation from the General Assembly of his State, and Governor John M. Slaton, representing the State of Georgia, with a special committee from the Georgia House and Senate, took part in the impressive exercises. One of the features of the day was a basket-dinner served by two of Mari-

etta's patariotic organizations: Kennesaw Chapter, U. D. C., and Fielding Lewis Chapter, D. A. R. The monument is built of silver gray Georgia marble, twenty-six feet in height and nineteen feet wide at the base. It carries a bronze statue of a soldier, seven feet in height, interposed between two allegorical figures, and the total cost of the structure was $20,000, which amount was appropriated by the Legislature of Illinois. Miss Sara Sadely, eleven years, old, of Anderson, Ind., a little granddaughter of W. A. Payton, of Danville, Ill., the supervising architect, who constructed the monument, drew the cord which unloosed the veil from the handsome structure. Both of the chief executives delivered eloquent speeches, full of the spirit of reconciliation. Governor Dunne, in a beautiful word picture, paid tribute to the soldiers of the two great armies who here struggled for mastery; to the followers of Johnston, as well as to the men under Sherman; and he closed his splendid address by quoting the following stanza from Finch's great poem:

> "Under the sod and the dew,
> Waiting the judgment day;
> Love and tears for the Blue,
> Tears and love for the Gray."

Lieutenant Brumby Raises the American Flag at Manila. During the war with Spain, in 1898, it was reserved for an American sailor, whose boyhood was spent in Marietta, to achieve signal distinction. This was Lieutenant Thomas M. Brumby, whose father, Colonel A. V. Brumby, was the first superintendent of the Georgia Military Institute at Marietta, a soldier who followed the Stars and Bars, and a gentleman who was universally esteemed. "Tom" Brumby was a lieutenant on board the famous "Olympia," the flagship of Admiral Dewey. He is credited by one of the war correspondents, Mr. E. W. Harden, of the *Chicago Tribune,* with having suggested the plan of the battle, and

since the Spanish fleet was completely annihilated by
this exploit, while not an American boat was injured
nor an American sailor killed, it is no slight honor to
have planned such an engagement. However, there are
other things to the credit of this gallant officer which
cannot be questioned. It devolved upon him to hoist the
American flag over the surrendered citadel, an act which
not only announced the formal occupation of the Philip-
pine Islands by the United States government, but also
proclaimed a radical change of national policy, which,
reversing the precedents of one hundred years, elected to
keep the American flag afloat upon the land-breezes of
the Orient.

Returning home, some few weeks later, Lieutenant
Brumby was the hero of the hour in Georgia. The most
enthusiastic demonstration was planned in honor of the
brave officer; and on the Capitol grounds, in Atlanta,
before an audience which numbered thousands of people
he was awarded an elegant sword. Hon. Clark Howell,
President of the State Senate, introduced Governor
Allen D. Candler, who, in turn, made the speech of presentation. Sea-fighter though he was, Tom Brumby
faced the great concourse of people like an embarrassed
school girl. He felt more at home when riding over the
perilous torpedoes, but he managed to stammer his simple thanks and to tell the audience that he merely did
his duty as a sailor. Unobserved by many in the vast
throng, whose eyes were riveted upon the hero, there
quietly sat in the background an old lady, who was bent
with the weight of fourscore years. It was Tom Brumby's mother. Thus was the master touch added to a
scene which lacked none of the elements of impressive-
ness. But the irony of fate was there, too; for ere many
weeks had softened the echoes of applause, the brave
lieutenant was dead. The spectacle presented on the
grounds of Georgia's State Capitol was only the first
part of the hero's Welcome Home.

Roswell.   Volume II, Pages 215-222.

Dr. Francis
R. Goulding.   Volume II, Pages 222-225.

The Grave of In the little burial-ground of the Pres-
Dr. Goulding. byterian Cemetery, at Roswell, lies the
dust of the famous author, whose tale of
"The Young Marooners" has endeared him to the heart
of childhood in two hemispheres. The grave is unmarked
by any towering shaft. Only the simplest pieces of marble, one at the head and one at the foot—neither of them
six inches above the ground—tell where the great author
sleeps. There is a peculiarity about the inscription which
I have never witnessed in any other burial-place of the
dead. It consists of his name alone; but scant as the
epitaph is, it is divided between the two stones. The
one at the head spells "Rev. Francis R." The one at
the foot reads "Goulding." Unless the visitor is guided
to the spot by the caretaker of the little grave-yard, he
is apt to miss it, so dwarfed are the simple markers beside the splendid piles which rise in the immediate neighborhood. Perhaps the lowly grave is in keeping with the
modest life which Dr. Goulding lived. He was only an
humble shepherd of Zion, whose duty it was to feed the
lambs of the Master. He preached in obscure places.
He walked in wayside paths. But the whole world today
is filled with the fame of Dr. Goulding. The author of
"The Young Marooners" is one of the immortals; and
if the children whose fancies he has charmed could only
build him a monument by each contributing a mite it
would overtop the tallest pine at Roswell.

The Tomb of It was the wish of Roswell King to be
Roswell King. buried near the factory which he built
in the little town which bears his name.
Consequently, when the old pioneer died he was laid to

rest on a hill overlooking the busy theatre of his labors. Perhaps he imagined that the whir of the spindles might lull him to peaceful dreams. At any rate, his dying request was fulfilled; and on the spot where he was buried a monument of massive proportions was afterwards reared. It bears the following inscription:

"In memory of Roswell King, born at Windsor, Conn., May 3, 1765, and died at Roswell, Cobb County, Ga., February 15, 1844. Aged 78 years, 9 months, and 12 days. He was the founder of the village which bears his name, etc."

Though somewhat soiled by the touch of time the shaft is well preserved. The interment of Roswell King at this place caused a grave-yard for public use to be opened on the hill, and today it goes by the name of the "Old Presbyterian Cemetery," others more recent having superceded this pioneer burial-ground. Barrington King, who succeeded his father as president of the factory, sleeps in the "New Presbyterian Cemetery," not far removed from Dr. Goulding, where his grave is handsomely marked. There is still another cemetery in Roswell, which is owned by the Methodists; and in view of the fact that the population of the little town has rarely exceeded one thousand inhabitants it has been lavishly supplied with facilities for leaving the world.

Where an Ex-President's Grandfather Sleeps. Less than fifty feet distant from the tomb of Roswell King is the grave of Major James S. Bulloch, the grandfather of ex-President Theodore Roosevelt. It is marked by a slab somewhat dingy with age, on which, however, the lettering is quite distinct. The inscription reads:

"James S. Bulloch. Died in Roswell, February 18, 1849, in the 56th. year of his age. There are no partings in heaven."

Major Bulloch was an exceedingly devout man. He was superintendent of the little Presbyterian Sunday-school at Roswell, and one day, when intent upon his duties in this capacity, he was stricken with paralysis and summoned from his useful work to his crown of reward.

COFFEE

Douglas. Coffee County was organized in 1854 out of four other counties: Clinch, Ware, Telfair and Irwin, and was named in honor of General John Coffee, a distinguished soldier and civilian of this State. The place selected as a county-seat was called Douglas, in honor of the noted Stephen A. Douglas, styled the "Little Giant." For years the growth of the town was slow; but, with the coming of railway facilities, it has forged rapidly to the front. Douglas was chartered as a town in 1895 and as a city in 1897.

COLQUITT

Recollections of Walter T. Colquitt. Major Stephen F. Miller, in his Bench and Bar of Georgia, speaking of Walter T. Colquitt, says:

"It made no difference how many speakers of note were assembled on the platform at a mass-meeting, whether from other States or from Georgia, whether ex-Governors or ex-members of the Cabinet, he towered above them all in energy of declamation and in power to sway the multitude. His was an eye which could look any man or any peril in the face, without blanching, as an eagle is said to gaze upon the sun.

"Judge Colquitt imitated no model. He grasped the hand of a poor man as cordially and treated him with as much respect as if he had been the richest in the land; and if his attentions to either varied, it was only to show more kindness to the humble, to ward off any appearance of neglect. As an advocate, he stood alone in Georgia, perhaps in the whole South. No man could equal him in brilliancy and vigor where the passions of the jury were to be led. In criminal cases, where life or liberty was at stake, he swept everything before him. No heart could resist his appeals, no eye withhold its tears, on such occasions. He has been known to get down upon his knees and to implore jurors by name to save the husband, the father, the son; not to break anxious hearts at home, not to stamp disgrace upon innocent kindred. At other times he would go up to certain members of the jury and address them: 'My Baptist brother,' 'My Methodist brother,' 'My young brother,' 'My venerable brother,' applying suitable expressions to each one as the facts might authorize, and, with a look and a prayer to heaven, which impressed the greatest awe, would stir the soul to its very depths. Many examples of the kind might be given, as the author has been informed by eye-witnesses: he never heard Judge Colquitt make a speech in court, but has heard him in other places. It is said that he rarely failed to obtain verdicts in favor of his clients when the occasion called forth his energies. Delivery, gesticulation, pathos, ridicule, scorn, mimicry, anecdote, the tone of his voice, the motion of his features—all acted a part, all assisted in the incantation. No wizard could have been more potent in exercising his charms. In all this exhibition there was much to offend particular schools of acting; but it was nothing more than holding a mirror up to nature—nature in a tempest.

"Nor was Judge Colquitt at a loss for other methods. He could be as gentle as a zephyr when it suited his purpose, when there were pictures of bereavement or sorrow to press home to the jury. Then the sweet, plaintive tones of his voice, the melting sadness of the heart, and the glistening pearl-drops from the eye, would dissolve all opposition. He would take a poor, fainting mortal in his arms, and softly as an angel he would lay him down to repose amid the flowers of Eden.''*

Moultrie.   Volume I.

The Colquitt   Judge Walter T. Colquitt was three times married.
Family Record.   His first wife, whom he married February 23, 1823,
                           was Nancy H. Lane, daughter of Joseph Lane,
Esq., for many years a Representative in the Legislature from Newton.
Six children were the result of this union, four of them reaching mature
years. Alfred H. Colquitt became a Major-General in the Confederate
Army, Governor of the State, and United States Senator from Georgia, fill-
ing the chair once occupied by his distinguished father in the upper national arena. Peyton H. Colquitt became a Colonel in the Confederate
Army and was killed at the head of his regiment in the battle of Chickamauga. Emma married Samuel M. Carter, son of Colonel Farish Carter,

*Stephen F. Miller, in Bench and Bar of Georgia, Vol. I.

and himself an eminent planter; while another daughter married Hon. O. B. Ficklin, of Illinois, at the time a Representative in Congress.

The second marriage of Judge Colquitt was in 1841 to Mrs. Alphia B. Fauntleroy, formerly Miss Todd, sister of the late H. W. Todd, Esq., of West Point, and aunt of Dr. J. Scott Todd, of Atlanta. She lived only a few months.

Judge Colquitt was united in marriage the third time to Harriet M. Ross, daughter of Luke Ross, and sister of the late well-known merchants J. B. and W. A. Ross, of Macon. Four children were born of this union, among them Hugh Haralson Colquitt.

The father of Judge Colquitt was Henry Colquitt, a native of Virginia, who emigranted to Georgia and settled in Wilkes. His mother was Nancy Holt. Related to him, on the maternal side, were Judge William W. Holt, of Augusta; Judge Thaddeus G. and General William S. Holt, of Macon; Hon. Hines Holt, of Columbus, and Mrs. Judge N. L. Hutchins, of Lawrenceville, mother of the late Judge Hutchins. After the death of her first husband, the widow Colquitt married the father of the late General Hartwell H. Tarver, of Twiggs.

The Colquitts: A Parellelism.   During the memorial exercises, held in the United States Senate Chamber, on January 8, 1895, in honor of Alfred H. Colquitt, United States Senator from Georgia, General John B. Gordon, his colleague and life-long friend, delivered an address, in the course of which he drew the following comparison between the two Colquitts, both of whom became United States Senators. Said he:

"Walter T. Colquitt—the father—was one of the most brilliant Georgians of his day. He filled many positions of responsibility and trust, and illustrated them all. As an advocate before a jury he had no superior and few peers. As a lawyer or political debater there was scarcely a limit to his mental activity, to his capacity for grasping facts analyzing arguments, and forcing his convictions upon others. In the court-house, legal technicalities and even venerated precedents went down before his fiery eloquence, the impetuosity of his assaults, and the blighting effects of his withering sarcasm. His form and face, eye and voice, all reflected the action of his brain and the rapture of his spirit; and when greatly aroused there was not an emotion or passion or sensibility that he did not touch and master. He was preacher, judge, general of militia, member of the House of Representatives, and Senator. The versatility of his genius and the power of his endurance, both physical and mental, were almost phenomenal. It is a tradition of his early career that he united a couple in marriage, drilled his brigade of militia, tried a man for his life, sentenced him to be hung, and preached a great sermon, all on the same day.

"Alfred H. Colquitt, my long-cherished friend and recent associate in this Chamber, whose death we mourn, was the eldest son of this remarkable man. The two, father and son, possessed traits and characteristics in common; but in many particulars they widely differed. Both were possessed of the keenest insight into human nature. Both were emphatically men of the people. Both had in them the martial instinct and the spirit of command. Both were members of the House of Representatives and of the Senate. Both were devoted and prominent communicants of the Methodist Church; and both were accustomed, while engaged in other avocations, to minister at its altars and teach from its pulpits.

"These two distinguished men differed widely, however, in the method and manner of presenting truth, whether from rostrum, hustings, or pulpit. The elder as a public speaker was fervid, lucid, rapid, impetuous. The younger Colquitt was perhaps less emotional, but more logical; less passionate, but more persuasive. The elder was more the natural orator than his gifted son, with a more intense nature and electric style. He was greatest when confronting a multitude differing from him in opinion. On such occasions he was almost matchless. When in the whirlwind of political debate, his words came in a tempest of invective against supposed personal wrongs or injustice to his party and people. The younger Colquitt excelled, however, in the more orderly and logical, if not more forceful presentation of his arguments and convictions, in pathos and persuasive power, and in the enduring hold upon the hearts and control over the actions of men. . . . It is no exaggeration to say of him, Mr. President, that few men with a career so long and brilliant have lived a life so pure and blameless, and left a legacy so rich and inspiring to the young men of the country. He died as he had livel, beloved by his people anl accepted of God. In the bosom of his native State we have laid him, and on his chosen hillside, where the music of Ocmulgee's waters and the weird songs of the pines will chant above him their everlasting anthem of praise and benediction."

COLUMBIA

Old Kiokee: Daniel Marshall's Arrest. While Planting the Baptist Standard in Georgia. On the first day of January, 1771, Daniel Marshall, an ordained Baptist minister, sixty-five years of age, moved from Horse Creek, S. C., and settled with his family on Kiokee Creek, about twenty miles northwest of Augusta. He had been residing for some time in South Carolina, where he had organized two churches, and while living at Horse Creek had made frequent evangelistic tours into Georgia, preaching with wonderful fervor in houses and groves.

We will gaze upon him as he conducts religious services. The scene is in a sylvan grove, and Daniel Marshall is on his knees, engaged in prayer. While he beseeches the Throne of Grace, a hand is laid upon his shoulder, and he hears a voice say:

" 'You are my prisoner!'

"Rising to his feet, the earnest-minded man of God finds himself confronted by an officer of the law. He is astonished at being arrested under such circumstances, for preaching the gospel in the Parish of St. Paul; but he has violated the legislative enactment of 1758, which established religious worship in the colony according to the rites and ceremoneis of the Church of England. He is made to give security for his appearance in Augusta on the following Monday, and is then allowed to continue the services. But to the surprise of every one present, the indigation which swells the bosom of Mr. Marshall finds vent through the lips of his wife, who has witnessed the whole scene. With the solemnity of the prophets of old, she denounces the law under which her husband has been apprehended, and to sustain her position she quotes many passages from the Holy Scriptures, with a force which carries conviction.

"One of the most interested listeners to her exposition was the constable, Mr. Samuel Cartledge, who was so deeply convinced by the inspired words of exhortation which fell from her lips that his conversion was the result; and, in 1777, he was baptized by the very man whom he then held under arrest. After the interruption caused by the incident above described, Mr. Marshall preached a sermon of great power, and before the meeting was over he baptized, in the neighboring creek, two converts, who proved to be relatives of the very man who stood security for his appearance at court. On the day appointed Mr. Marshall went to Augusta, and after standing a trial was ordered to desist; but he boldly replied in the language of the Apostles, spoken under similar circumstances:

" 'Whether it be right to obey God or man, judge ye.'

"It is interesting to note that the magistrate who tried him, Colonel Barnard, was also afterwards converted. Though never immersed, he was strongly tinctured with Baptist doctrines, and often exhorted sinners to flee from the wrath to come. He lived and died in the Church of England. Following this dramatic episode, Mr. Marshall does not seem to have met with further trouble; but the outbreak of the Revolution soon suspended religious activities."

"Daniel Marshall was born at Windsor, Conn., in 1706, of Presbyterian parents. He was a man of great natural ardor and holy zeal. For three years he buried himself in the wilderness and preached to the Mohawk Indians near the head waters of the Susquehanna River. War among the savage tribes led him to remove ultimately to Virginia, where he became a convert to Baptist views. He was immersed at the age of forty-eight, his wife submitting to the ordinance at the same time; and then, after preaching for several years in the two Carolinas, he came to Georgia, settling on Kiokee Creek at the time above mentioned.

"Though neither learned nor eloquent, he possessed the rugged strength of mind which fitted him for pioneer work, and he knew the Scriptures. From his headquarters on Kiokee Creek he went forth preaching the Gospel with great power. By uniting those whom he had baptized in the neighborhood with other Baptists who lived on both sides of the Savannah River, he formed and organized Kiokee Baptist Church, in the spring of 1722; and this was the first Baptist Church ever constituted within the limits of Georgia.

"The Act incorporating the Kiokee Baptist Church was signed by Edward Telfair, Governor; Seaboard Jones, Speaker of the House, and Nathan Brownson, President of the Senate. It is dated December 23, 1789, seventeen years subsequent to the actual time of organization. The first meeting house was built where the town of Appling now stands. Daniel Marshall became the pastor. He served in this capacity until November 2, 1784, when he died in his seventy-eighth year. Abraham Marshall, his son, continued his work.

"When this pioneer minister moved into the State, he was the only ordained Baptist clergyman within its bounds; but he lived to preside at the organization of the Georgia Association, in the fall of 1784, when there were half a dozen churches in the State, hundreds of converts, and quite a number of preachers. His grave lies a few rods south of Appling Court House, on the side of the road leading to Augusta. He sleeps neither forgotten nor unsung, for every child in the neighborhood can lead the stranger to Daniel Marshall's grave.''*

On December 23, 1789, the pioneer Baptist church in Georgia was incorporated by an Act of the Legislature, under the name of the "Anabaptist Church on the Kioka," with the following trustees: Abraham Marshall, William Willingham, Edmond Cartledge, John Landers, James Simms, Joseph Ray and Lewis Gardner.*

*Condensed from History of the Baptist Denomination in Georgia. Compiled by the Christian Index.
*Marbury and Crawford's Digest, p. 143.

Peter Craw-
ford's Tomb.
Some time ago, while engaged in making certain researches in Columbia County, Prof. Alfred Akerman, of the State University, stumbled upon an old burial-ground, almost completely overrun by weeds and briars. Even the inscriptions upon the tombs were so blurred that he could hardly decipher them; but he finally managed to trace the letters. One of these tombs contained the following epitaph:

> In memory of PETER CRAWFORD, a native of Virginia. He became early in life a citizen of Georgia. Highly gifted mentally and physically, he closed a long life of distinguished usefulness. As clerk of the Superior Court and Senator of the County in the Legislature of the State, during nearly the whole period of his manhood, these records attest the value of his services. Under a sense of right he was inflexible. His social virtues were marked by an expansive hospitality and benevolence. The widow and the orphan gratefully bestowed on him the honorable title: Their Friend. Born February 7, 1765. Died October 16, 1830. My father.

Peter Crawford was a power in Georgia politics. For years he voted the Whig ticket; and during the latter part of his life became involved in a controversy the outcome of which was a duel fought between his son, Hon. George W. Crawford, and a talented young lawyer of Appling, Hon. Thomas E. Burnside. Gov. Crawford manfully espoused his father's side in this quarrel, since the latter was then an old man, and jeopardized his own life in order to avenge his father's honor. His filial devotion is further shown in the erection of this monument, for which he probably wrote the epitah. On a neighboring tomb, this record is inscribed, no doubt also from the pen of Governor Crawford:

In memory of MARY ANN, wife of PETER CRAW-FORD. A cherished wife, she was the mother of a large family. For many years the survivor of her partner, she was the center and light of a large social circle. A Christion, she bestowed her charities with the gentleness of her sex. A woman, she was steadfast to her sterner duties. Her four-score years only weakened the tie which binds life to the body; all else was clear and calm. Born May 9, 1769. Died January 22, 1852.

Pioneer Senators and Representatives. During the early ante-bellum period of the State's history, Columbia was represented in the General Assembly of Georgia by a brilliant galaxy of men. Some of her pioneer Senators included: James O'Neil, Thomas Carr, John Foster, William Wilkins, Peter Crawford, Archer Avary, Abner P. Robertson, William B. Tankersley and Thomas H. Dawson. On the list of Representatives we find: Walter Drane, James Simms, Benjamin Williams, John Foster, Hugh Blair, John Hardin, Solomon Marshall, William B. Tankersley, Thomas Carr, Archer Avary, George Carey, Arthur Foster, Thomas E. Burnside, Turner Clanton, Nathaniel F. Collins, Nathan Crawford, Thomas N. Hamilton, John Cartledge, Moody Burt, and Robert M. Gunby.*

Duels Fought by the Crawfords. Volume II. Under the Code Duello.

CRAWFORD.

Fort Lawrence. This stronghold was built to protect the old Creek Indian Agency on the Flint River, and was located on the east bank of the stream, occupying an eminence not far from where the Flint River is crossed by the main highway running from Macon to Columbus. The last vestige of the ancient fort has long since disappeared; but it was probably a stockade fort built after the fashion common in pioneer days. If con-structed by Col. Hawkins, who resided here for sixteen years as agent among the Creek Indians, it was probably

*See Vol. I of this work, pp. 34-39.

not unlike the defensive structure at Fort Hawkins, a stronghold built under his immediate supervision.

Survivor of Goliad Massacre. Few of Fannin's men escaped the brutal massacre at Goliad, in the war for Texan independence, in 1836, but one of these was a former resident of Crawford: Mr. John T. Spillers. Surviving the frightful holocaust, Mr. Spillers returned to his old home in Georgia, where his last days were spent. He probably joined the company organized in Macon by Colonel William A. Ward. This company passed through Knoxville, Ga., en route to Texas, where it was annexed to Fannin's command. While passing through Knoxville, a flag of white silk bearing a lone star of blue was presented to the company by Miss Joanna E. Troutman—afterwards Mrs. Vinson—who designed with her own hands this unique and beautiful emblem, which afterwards received adoption as the national flag of Texas.* During the year 1913, the body of Mrs. Vinson was exhumed from its former resting place at Knoxville and re-interred with official honors in the State cemetery at Austin, Texas.

Most of the gallant men to whose keeping this historic flag was entrusted by its fair designer, met an ignominious death at the hands of the treacherous Mexicans; but Mr. Spiller escaped. How he managed to do so is explained in an affidavit given to his attorney, Mr. William I. Walker, of Crawford, in 1874, when the latter was seeking to obtain for him a pension from the State of Texas.

Mr. Spillers was at this time quite an old man, as nearly forty years had elapsed since the Goliad massacre; and he was probably also in reduced circumstances. The old soldier states in this affidavit that he is entitled to a

---

*Documents in the possession of Mrs. E. T. Nettingham, of Thomaston, Georgia.

pension "by reason of his having served as a volunteer
in the army of Texas, under Colonel Fannin, in the Texas
revolutions, in the years 1835 and 1836, having escaped
the massacre of Fannin's command by reason of being
kept a prisoner and laborer by the Mexicans."* Mr. Walker believed implicitly in the justice of the old soldier's
claim, to secure which he made a special trip to Texas,
bearing a letter of introduction from Governor James
M. Smith.

Anecdote of   Joseph Beckham Cobb narrates the fol-
Mr. Crawford's   lowing incident of Mr. Crawford's
School-Days.   school-days at Mount Carmel:

"It was determined by himself and some of the elder school boys to
enliven the annual public examinations by representing a play. They selected Addison's Cato; and, in forming the cast of characters, that of
the Roman Senator was of course, assigned to the usher. Crawford was
a man of extraordinary height and large limbs, and was always ungraceful
and awkward, besides being constitutionally unfitted, in every way, to act
any character but his own. However, he cheerfully consented to play
Cato. It was a matter of great sport, even during rehearsal as his companions beheld the huge, unsightly usher, with giant strides and stentorian
tones, go through with the representation of the stern, precise old Roman.
But, on the night of the exhibition, an accident, eminently characteristic
of the counterfeit Cato, occurred, which effectually broke up the denoue-
ment of the tragedy. Crawford had conducted the Senate scene with
tolerable success, though rather boisterously for so solemn an occasion, and
had even managed to struggle through with the apostrophe to the soul;
but, when the dying scene behind the curtain came to be acted, Cato's
groan of agony was bellowed out with such hearty good earnest as totally
to scare away the tragic muse, and set prompter, players and audience in
a general, unrestrained fit of laughter. This was, we believe, the future
statesman's first and last theatrical attempt.'"*

Knoxville. Four counties of Georgia were organized by
an act approved December 23, 1822, viz.,
DeKalb, Bibb, Pike and Crawford; and, for the last

---

*Joseph Beckham Cobb, in Leisure Hours.

named of these counties, the site of public buildings was fixed at a convenient place called Knoxville, in honor of Gen. Henry Knox, of the Revolution. The town was incorporated on December 24, 1825, with the following pioneer residents named as commissioners: John Harvey, John Vance, Frank Williamson, Jesse Stone, Martin T. Ellis.[1] At the same time a charter was granted to the Knoxville Academy, with Messrs. James Lloyd, Coleman M. Roberts, Edward Barker, Levi Stanford, and Wm. Lockett as trustees.[2] Miss Joanna E. Troutman, who designed the Lone Star flag of Texas, was a resident of Knoxville, where she was living when the war for Texan independence began in 1836.

COWETA.

Bullsboro.   Volume 1. pp. 484-486.

Newnan.   Newnan, the county-seat of Coweta County, has already been treated at some length in the former volume of this work, as the successor of old Bullsboro, a town out of which it grew, and the site of which is today marked by an old pecan tree which stands some two miles to the north-east of the present court-house. During the past few years the growth of Newnan has been marked. Its cotton mills employ an army of operatives and produce annually an enormous output of the best fabrics. As a commercial center, with fine railway facilities, the town supplies an extensive trade, while the surrounding country is rich in agricultural products. There is a briskness, a vim, and a stir about the city of Newnan, an evidence of thrift on its streets and in its market-places, the like of which can be found in few communities of its size; and with the impetus acquired from its re-

[1] Acts, 1825, p. 183.
[2] Acts, 1825, p. 9.

cent growth, it will eventually become one of the largest towns of the State. Its per capita of wealth is already considerably above the average. Many of its homes are palatial; its schools afford the very best educational advantages; and its local affairs are controlled by men of intelligence, of character, and of enthusiasm for the public weal. Long before the war it was widely known as a seat of learning on account of the prestige of its noted Temple College. Some of Georgia's best families have long been identified with Newnan, such as the Dents, the Berrys, the Bigbys, the Norths, the Pinsons, the Kirbys, the Halls, the Wrights, the Thompsons, the McLendons, the McKinleys, the Calhouns, the Hills, the Rays, the Caldwells, the Coles, the Hardaways, the Nimmonses, the Orrs, the Robinsons, and the Powells. From its professional and business ranks have come some of the most distinguished men of Georgia, such as Hon. W. B. W. Dent, Judge Hugh Buchanan and Judge John S. Bigby, all of whom were members of Congress; Gov. Wm. Y. Atkinson, former Attorney-General, Hewlette A. Hall, Dr. A. B. Calhoun, whose son, the renowned specialist, lately deceased, Dr. A. W. Calhoun, spent his boyhood days in Newnan; Hon. Peter Francisco Smith, a distinguished legal scholar, writer, and man of affairs; Judge Dennis F. Hammond, Judge L. H. Featherstone, Judge Owen H. Kenan, Judge John D. Berry, Judge R. W. Freeman, Dr. James Stacy, for more than forty years pastor of the Presbyterian church, a scholar and a historian; Prof. M. P. Kellogg, a noted educator; Carlisle McKinley, a gifted poet and journalist; Hon. Ezekiel McKinley; Hon. J. J. McClendon, and a host of others.

Oak Hill. Historic Church-yards and Burial-Grounds.

College Temple. One of the most noted institutions of learning in Georgia during the last half of the Nineteenth Century was "College Temple," at Newnan, a college for women, and the first to grant the higher degree, for in a printed address by the president, Prof. Kellogg, given on the twenty-fifth anniversary of the school he refers to "that maiden commencement (in 1855). when the degree—Magistra in Artibus (M. A.)—was conferred the *first* time by a female college in America."

The college was the life work of Prof. Moses Payson Kellogg, the sole proprietor and president. Prof. Kellogg was born in Richford, Vt., on May 19th, 1823. He graduated at the University of Vermont, at Burlington, and came to Georgia about 1843. His first school was at Rock Springs Academy, in Coweta County; and his success there attracted the attention of the trustees of the Newnan Academy, who invited him to take charge of that institution. This he did in 1849.

Prof. Kellogg was a very scholarly man, splendidly educated, with a wonderful amount of executive ability. He kept fully abreast of the times and introduced into his school many useful aids for imparting knowledge. When teaching at the academy he had a telegraph instrument with wires encircling the building, and brought to the town a daguerreotype artist with his newly invented instrument.

In December, 1851, Miss Harriet Robie Baker came from Weare, N. H., where she was born, August 14th, 1825, to teach at the Academy under Prof. Kellogg. They were married the following August 4th. Throughout, his wife was his counsellor and chief assistant, always at his side.

Prof. Kellogg believed thoroughly in the higher education of girls as an important factor toward improving the men of the future, and he conceived the idea of founding in Newnan, a college for women only. This he located on a plot of ground on the east side of the present Temple Avenue between Clark and College Streets. The corner stone of the first building of "College Temple" was laid on May 19th, 1852, and the first term of the school was opened on Sept. 7th, 1853. The college was chartered by an act of the State Legislature on Feb. 11th, 1854, and the first graduating class of eight girls received their M. A. degree in June, 1855.

The school buildings were three in number, all of attractive architecture, designed by Prof. Kellogg. These were located on extensive grounds laid out in artistic style with long hedges and walks, and groups of trees and shrubs. The dormitory was a large square three-story building, entirely surrounded by an upper and lower veranda. The main building, known as Arcade Hall, contained a large auditorium, school assembly hall, class rooms and library. This library was one of the interesting features of the school and held several hundred volumes of reference books, classics and high class fiction, besides numerous globes, charts, astronomical and geometrical maps and maps on physical geography. Many specimens of gold and other minerals were used in the study of mineralogy. The third building, the Laboratory, was well equipped with instruments for experiments in chemistry, electricity and physics.

The "Fly Leaf," the school paper, made its first appearance in 1855, and continued many years. It was edited by the senior class, and after the first few years, set up and printed by them at the college. The school contained a primary and a collegiate department, with a large corps of teachers. In the collegiate department besides Greek and Latin, the German, French and Italian languages were taught.

Important to note is the fact that this was the first school for girls in the state to teach industrial work, typography and telegraphy having been taught almost from the beginning. Cooking and sewing were taught also at this period, but left to the choice of the pupil. The students came from Georgia and the surrounding states, and a few from New England and the West. No pupil was turned away for lack of money, and hundreds of girls were educated free by this good man. In these Prof. Kellogg took great pride. The annual commencements lasted several days, and attracted large crowds.

In 1864 the school session was discontinued for several months, and the 7 buildings occupied by hospitals for wounded and sick Confederate soldiers. The senior class was, however, graduated that year as usual. The school continued without other interruption until the last class received its diplomas in June, 1889.

Owing to Prof. Kellogg's advanced age and the establishment of the public school system in Newnan in 1888, the college was discontinued. All the buildings were destroyed in 1904, except the Laboratory, which was made into a dwelling. There is a large marble shaft in the Newnan cemetery erected to Prof. Kellogg by his loving pupils, which recalls the past of this noble institution, and the work of this good man.*

CRISP.

Fort Early. Some twelve miles to the south of the present town of Cordele was located a stronghold which, in pioneer days, played an important part in defending our exposed frontier: Fort Early. It was named for a distinguished Governor of this State who occupied the executive chair when the fort was built during the war of 1812. It was constructed by Gen. David Blackshear, a noted Indian fighter, and afterwards used by Gen. E. P. Gaines and Gen. Andrew Jackson. As to the character of the fort, little is known, but it was probably a stockade fort like Fort Hawkins, designed especially for Indian warfare on the border. Between Fort Early

---

*Authority: Miss Ruby Felder Ray, State Editor, D. A. R. Atlanta, Ga.

and Cordele runs a little branch known as Cedar Creek, where the last attack made by the Creek Indians upon the whites in this section of Georgia was successfully repelled, on January 22, 1818. Two gallant American soldiers, Capt. Leigh, and a private, Samuel Loftis, perished at this place while trying to find a safe passage across the swollen stream for a portion of Jackson's army. They were shot by the savages from ambush.

Cordele.   Vol. I. pp. 499-501.

DADE.

Trenton.   On December 25, 1837, an Act was approved by Gov. George R. Gilmer, creating the county of Dade out of lands formerly included in Walker. The place chosen as a county-site was first called Salem. But there were a number of localities throughout the State, including not a few old churches and camp-grounds, which bore this name. Consequently, in 1840, it was changed to Trenton.[1] On February 18, 1854, the town was incorporated with the following named commissioners: James M. Hill, Robert L. Hawkins, Horace Lindsay, Wm. C. Shanock, and Manoes Morgan.[2]

---

[1] Acts, 1840, p. 36.
[2] Acts, 1854, p. 251.

DAWSON

Dawsonville. Dawson County was formed from Lumpkin, in 1858, and named for the distinguished Wm. C. Dawson, a United States Senator from Georgia, then lately deceased. The site chosen for public buildings was called Dawsonville; and, on Dec. 10, 1859, the town was incorporated with the following named commissioners: Dr. John Hockinhull, J. M. Bishop, Lawson Hope, Samuel C. Johnson, and Wm. Barrett.*

Recollections of William C. Dawson. In a letter to Major Stephen F. Miller, Judge Dawson's son, Edgar G. Dawson, writes thus concerning the distinguished statesman and jurist:

"I see that the Masonic Fraternity is preparing to raise a monument to his memory and to establish a 'Dawson Professorship' in the Masonic Female College.

"My father was very liberal in his donations to such institutions. He was always active in the cause of education. As you are aware, he was eminently social—remarkably fond of the chase—always kept a fine pack of fox-hounds, the fleetest in the country, for he spared no expense in procuring them. He was the best horseman I ever saw, surpassing all his companions in his exploits upon the field. I have frequently seen him from day-break until night in the chase of the red fox, and then return home and work in his office until twelve or one o'clock. I think he was one of the most industrious men I ever knew.

"He made companions of his children, and never failed to have them with him, when not inconvenient to do so—upon the circuit, at Washington, in his travels, on the plantation. He seemed delighted in the chase to see his sons well mounted, contesting with him the palm of horsemanship, in leaping fences and ditches, and in keeping nearest the hounds in full pursuit through woods and fields.

*   *   *   *   *   *   *

"Just a few months prior to his death he wrote me: 'I shall return to the practice in the spring, and, having naught to draw my attention from it, I shall expect to be pointed at by the people and to hear them say: 'There is a rising and promising young man who will soon make his mark

---

*Acts, 1859, p. 152.

at the bar.' He always contended that he was never over thirty years of age, and in fact, he was as able and active at fifty-eight as he was at thirty-eight.''

DECATUR

Bainbridge. Under an Act, approved December 19, 1823, organizing the county of Decatur, the following named commissioners were chosen to select a county-seat to superintend the erection of public buildings thereon, to-wit: Duncan Ray, Wm. Hawthorn, Philip Pittman, John Sanders, and Martin Hardin[1] The site chosen was a point of land overlooking the Flint River, within a mile of Fort Hughes. It was called Bainbridge, in honor of the gallant naval officer, William Bainbridge, who commanded the celebrated frigate "Constitution." The county itself was named for the illustrious American Commodore Stephen Decatur. On December 22, 1829, the town was chartered with the following named commissioners: Peter Cohen, Daniel Belcher, Jethro W. Kieth, Matthew R. Moore, and Jeremiah H. Taylor.[2] The old Decatur Academy was chartered on December 19, 1829, with Messrs. Alexander McGowan, Wm. Whiddon, John DeGraffenreid, Wm. Williams, Wm. Powell, and Thomas King as trustees.[3] In 1840 a female seminary was chartered. Bainbridge is today one of the most important commercial centers of the State, with extensive railway and steamboat connections. It is also the center of a territory rich in agricultural resources. See Vol. 1. for additional facts in regard to Bainbridge.

[1] Acts, 1823, p. 58.
[2] Acts, 1829, p. 186.
[3] Acts, 1829, p. 10.

Fort Hughes   Volume 1. Page 504.
(Bainbridge).

Fort Scott. This stronghold was built during one of
the campaigns against the Seminole Indians
in Florida. It was located on the west bank of the Flint
River, a stream then called by the Indians "Thronateeska." The Fort was named for Gen. Winfield Scott,
a distinguished officer of the United States Army, under
whose leadership the campaign was conducted. Nothing
is known at this time concerning the character of the fort,
which was probably little more than an earthwork, enclosed by a stockade.

Distinguished Res-
idents of Decatur.   Volume I. Pages 506-507.

Attapulgus. Attapulgus, a town on the Southern & Florida line, in
the lower part of the county, is one of the oldest communities in Decatur, founded some time in the eighteen-thirties. The
Pleasant Grove Academy, located at this place, was chartered in 1836, but
three years later the name of the school was changed to the Attapulgus
Academy, and at this time the following trustees were chosen. to-wit.:
Thomas. Hines, William Williams, Daniel T. Lane, John Durham, Asa
Hutchings and Hiram King.[1] Five new trustees were added in 1841, as
follows: James E. Martin, Edmond Smart, William Martin, Joshua Grant
and Isaac M. Griffin.[2] In 1849, John H. Gibson, Daniel McKinnis and
Robert J. Smallwood were added to the board.[3] On January 22, 1852, a
charter was granted for a female school, with the following named trus-
tees, to-wit.: James Gibson, Andrew McElroy, Emery Lassiter, William
Smith, Thomas R. Smith, Charles J. Munnerlyn and John P. Dickinson,
to be styled "Trustees of the Female Amademy of Attapulgus.'"[4] The
town was incorporated December 21, 1866, with Messrs. Emery Lasseter,
George W. Donalson, Thomas R. Smith, W. A. B. Lasseter and L. H.
Peacock named as commissioners.

---

[1] Acts, 1839, p. 6.
[2] Acts, 1841, p. 10.
[3] Acts, 1849-1850, p. 22.
[4] Acts, 1851-1852, p. 329.

DEKALB

Decatur. DeKalb County was organized in 1822 from Henry and Fayette counties and was named for ;the celebrated Baron DeKalb, of Revolutionary distinction. The county-site was called Decatur, for the famous American Commodore, Stephen Decatur, whose brilliant naval exploits were then still fresh in the public mind. Decatur was formally incorporated as a town, on December 10, 1823, with the following named commissioners: Reuben Cone, Wm. Morris, Wm. Gresham, James White, and Thos. A. Dobbs.[1] The DeKalb County Academy was chartered on December 18, 1825, but the charter was amended one year later, at which time the following trustees were named: Samuel T. Bailey, Zachariah Holloway, Wm. Ezzard, Joseph Morris, Joseph D. Shoemate, Reuben Cone, James Blackstocks, Wm. Towns, Merrill Collier, Samuel Prewett, and James M. C. Montgomery.[2] Decatur is one of the strongest Presbyterian communities of the State, outside of the large cities. The church of this denomination here is the mother church of this section of Georgia.

Agnes Scott College, one of the most noted schools of the country for the education of young ladies, is located here, under Presbyterian control. Decatur was the home of the famous poet and painter, Dr. Thomas Holley Chivers. Hon. Charles Murphey and Hon. Milton A. Candler, both members of Congress, also lived in Decatur. This wideawake community has recently organized a Chamber of Commerce, whose enterprising activities have been the wonder of the State resulting locally in a rapid increase in the town's volume of business, besides arousing the emulation of other communities.

---

[1] Acts, 1823, p. 169.
[2] Acts, 1825, p. 5.

DODGE

Eastman. On October 26, 1870, an Act was approved creating the new county of Dodge out of lands formerly included in three large counties of this section: Montgomery, Telfair and Pulaski. Under the terms of this same Act, the county seat was fixed at Eastman, otherwise known as station number 13, on what was then the Macon and Brunswick Railroad.[1] The town was chartered in a separate Act approved on the day following, at which time Messrs. John L. Parker, David M. Buchan, J. J. Rozar, E. E. Lee, and John F. Livingston were named commissioners.[2] The county was named for William E. Dodge, of New York, a wealthy merchant, whose lumber interests in this immediate section were extensive, in addition to large holdings on St. Simon's Island. The town was named for Mr. W. P. Eastman, a native of New England, who organized the Dodge Land Company, a syndicate largely instrumental in developing this part of Georgia. The present public school system of the town was established in 1894. Eastman is the center of a rich agricultural section and is one of the most progressive trade centers in Georgia, possessing several strong banks, a number of solid business establishments, and many elegant homes.

The Eastman Riot. Eastman, the capital of Dodge County, in what is known as Middle South Georgia, has an unusual record. Here a hanging occurred in 1882, in which four men and a woman suffered the penalty of death. This is believed to be the largest

---

[1] Acts, 1870, p. 18.
[2] Acts, 1870, p. 186.

number of people ever legally executed at the same time in any place in the United States. The hanging was the culmination of what was known as the Eastman Riot, and to the credit of the town, although it was only in its teens, the law was allowed to take its course, and Judge Lynch was kept in the background. It is an interesting story and deserves to go down in history as one of the bloody chapters of the Black Belt.

On Sunday, August 6, 1882 a big negro camp meeting began in Eastman. The town at that time was only a small village. Fully three thousand negroes from the surrounding country came in on several special excursion trains. Provisions were made for a few white people, and among them was Jim Harwood, a boy about eighteen years old from Cochran, who came to visit relatives. In Eastman at that time there were nine drug stores, most of them being places opened for the sale of whiskey and calling themselves drug stores to keep within the law. Into these places many of the negroes, both men and women, went to fill up on fire-water, and soon they had reached the danger line.

One negro stole a watch of another and was detected. He was arrested and taken in charge by two town marshals, A. P. Harrell and B. A. Buchan. They started with him toward the calaboose. but he had been drinking enough to make him obstreperous, and he began an attack on the officers. He succeeded in freeing himself and ran. Buchan, thinking to frighten him, fired at him. The ball hit him just where his suspenders were crossed in the back, and he fell dead.

Great 'excitement followed among the negroes, most of whom were half drunk, and they gathered themselves into a howling mob not less than a thousand strong, and pursued the officers, both of whom managed to escape. As the mob turned a corner, young Harwood saw them coming, and ran. Thinking he was one of the officers, the negroes, like a pack of wolves, followed. He ran to the home of Mr. Wright Harrell and crawled under the house. The family was at dinner, and young Harwood ran into the back room and hid under the bed. The negroes stormed the house, and Mr. Harrell begged them to leave, assuring them that their man was not there. Brushing him aside, they broke into the house and soon found the unfortunate youth. They dragged him out. beating him with clubs and pistols. As they came out with him an old negro, who had been a slave of his father, forced his way through the crowd, and throwing his arms about the young man's neck, begged that his life be spared. He was beaten into insensibility, and then the boy was shot and beaten to death with pickets snatched from the fence by the members of the bloodthirsty mob. As Harwood was being dragged into the house, Ella Moore, a negro woman, ran up and made several desperate efforts to cut his throat.

The death of the boy seemed to arouse the negroes to a sense of their danger, and rushing to the trains they compelled the trainmen, at the point of revolvers, to pull out of town. Many of the negroes were left, and soon they were fleeing in all directions.

In about an hour fifty or more farmers, armed to the teeth, rode into Eastman. They were organized and began a systematic search for the rioters. The jail was soon filled with prisoners, and there was a strong sentiment to lynch the whole crowd. This was strengthened when it was learned that three people who had been sick had died from the shock they had sustained when they had heard of the riot. There were conservative men enough in the town to let the law take its course, and soon there were twenty-two prisoners in the jail, with evidence enough against them to convict.

Many of them had been arrested on the testimony of reputable witnesses in the neighboring towns, who had heard them boasting of what they had done.

Five of the twenty-two, Simon O'Gwin, Joe King, Bob Donaldson, Reddick Powell and Ella Moore, were tried before Judge A. C. Pate, Tom Eason being the solicitor-general. They were convicted of murder, and all five of them dropped to death at the same moment in the court-house yard on the 20th of October, 1882. Seventeen of the others were found guilty, but recommended to mercy, and were sent to the penitentiary for life. Many of the witnesses of the deeds of this dark and bloody Sunday are still living at Eastman.*

DOOLY

Vienna. The original county-seat of Dooly was a little town on the Flint River called Berrien. It was selected, under an Act of 1823, by a board of five commissioners, to wit: Blassingame Pollet, Wm. Hilliard, Thomas E. Ward, Thomas Cobb, and Littleberry Richardson.[1] In 1833, the name of the town was changed from Berrien to Drayton, due presumably to a protest felt in this section against some of the unpopular views of Judge Berrien, who held that a United States Senator was not to be governed, on every question, by the wishes of his constitutents.[2] But the new county-site failed to give satisfaction. On December 23, 1839, an Act was approved, appointing Wm. Smith, David Scarboro, Joel Dorsey, James Oliver, Thomas Cobb, and John Crumpler, to select a new site for public buildings. At the same time,

---

*Authority: Rev. Alex. W. Bealer, of Eastman, Ga.
[1] Acts, 1823, p. 190.
[2] Acts, 1833, p. 322.

provision was made to compensate the owners of property in the town of Drayton.[1] Meanwhile, another town, named for Judge Berrien, seems to have arisen; and, on December 11, 1841, an Act was approved providing that, when a sufficient quantity of land was donated at Berrien, the new county-site should be located at said place; but there is nothing in the records to show that a removal was ever made.[2] Finally, however, in the late forties, the county-seat was changed to Vienna; and, on February 18, 1854, the new county-seat was incorporated as a town with the following commissioners: Chas. H. Everett, Seth Kellum, Lemuel M. Lasseter, John Brown and Stephen B. Stovall.[3] With two railway connections, Vienna is today quite a thriving center of trade; notwithstanding its proximity to Cordele, a town whose growth has been phenomenal.

DOUGHERTY

Albany.   In Volume I, of this work, will be found a brief outline sketch of Albany, to which it may be added that, under an Act approved December 27, 1833, the following pioneer residents were named town commissioners: Herman Mercer, Samuel Clayton, Mordecai Alexander, Nelson Tift, and Jeptha C. Harris. In this same Act, Nelson Tift, Jeptha C. Harris, and Tomlinson Fort were given a permit for constructing a bridge across the Flint River at this point. When Dougherty County was formed in 1853, from Baker, the town of Albany became the new county-seat.

Dougherty's Distinguished Residents.

---

[1] Acts, 1839, p. 213.
[2] Acts, 1841, p. 70.
[3] Acts, 1854, p. 273.

EARLY

Blakely. On December 15, 1818, Early County was created by an Act of the Legislature, out of treaty lands acquired from the Creek Indians. However, it was not until 1825, that the county was completely organized. It was originally one of the largest counties in the State, but portions of it were given to other counties to somewhat equalize them in size. The first settler near the town of Blakely was Wesley Sheffield, whose descendants in the country are still numerous. About the year 1821, Mr. Benjamin Collier donated four acres of land to be used for the site of public buildings, an offer which the commissioners accepted, calling the town Blakely, after Capt. Johnson Blakely, a distinguished naval officer in the war of 1812. The local historian who records this interesting fact adds that if Earlytown had been chosen as the name of the capital of Early County, it would have saved much ink, paper, time, and temper to postmasters and others.

Mr. Collier erected the first dwelling house in Blakely on what is today known as the old Fleming place, on South Main Street. Blakely, no doubt, began to make history at an early date, but the first notice taken of her by the historian was in 1829, when the town contained eight private dwellings, a school house, a court house, and a jail. The first Clerk of the Court was N. M. McBride, Esq. Judge Benjamin Hodges was an early Justice of the Peace, and John Floyd was the first Sheriff. According to Deed Book, Vol. C., County Records, the earliest known settlers in Blakely were Benjamin Collier, Joel Perry, James T. Bush, F. Mercier, A. M. Watson, and Robert Grimsley. From 1821 to 1829 these names appear: J. H. Bush, A. D. Smith, Joseph Miller, Willis Dobbs, David D. Smith, John Floyd, Isaac Livingston, J. W. Mann, James W. Alexander, John B. Applewhite, Wm. Phillips, and A. O. Daniels. About 1830 records are found of Peter Howard, A. M. Freeman, Miller Garrett Freeman, Aaron Goolsby, Anthony Hutchins, James Buchanan, John Hays, Joel Crawford, and others.

To visitors, an object of much interest in the neighborhood of Blakely, is an Indian mound, some three miles distant which is supposed to have been formerly a trading post and rendezvous of the Indians. Blakely is today a progressive city, of 3,000 inhabitants. Many handsome homes, public buildings, churches, and banks, testify to her growth in recent years. All the religious denominations have lately erected beautiful temples of worship. Last year the city completed an up-to-date school building, at a cost of $25,000. The Club Women of Blakely are engaged in active work. There are two patriotic societies—the Blakely Chapter, U. D. C., and the Peter Early Chapter, D. A. R.; also a splendid Public Library Association, and a Woman's Civic Club. The local camp of Confederate Veterans is Camp Doster, named for Dr. B. R. Doster, a brave Early County soldier. The erection of a granite boulder to mark the Jackson Trail is contemplated at an early date by the D. A. R. chapter.*

Flag-Pole and Monument. On the beautiful court house grounds, at Blakely, there stands a landmark of unique historic interest: the old Confederate Flag Pole. It looks today just as it did in the sixties when it floated the Stars and Bars, high above surrounding objects. This hallowed reminder was erected in the spring of 1861, and no other section of the South today is known to boast one of these emblems of liberty. It was manufactured from a huge pine tree, the stump of which stands a short distance south of Blakely. During a cyclone several years ago, the flag-pole was broken off near the base, but by request of the President of the U. D. C., of Blakely, it was bound together with strong brass bands and iron clamps painted white and re-erected

*Authority: Mrs. Walter Thomas, Regent Peter Early Chapter, D. A. R., and first president Blakely Chapter, U. D. C.

by the city electrician. The flag-pole towers nearly to the court house dome, commanding an outlook upon the horizon for miles in every direction—a cherished relic of the Civil War.

Close to the flag-pole stands the Confederate monument, a handsome structure of solid granite, dedicated to the heroes of the Lost Cause, by the local U. D. C. chapter. The shaft rises 30 feet and is 18 feet wide at the base. It rests upon a green mound charmingly ornamented with plants and flowers. The monument was unveiled on April 26, 1909, at which time, Judge Arthur G. Powell, a native of Blakely, then Judge of the Court of Appeals delivered the oration. Lettered upon the monument are the following inscriptions:

> East Face: "Erected by Blakely Chapter, U. D. C. Lest We Forget." West Face: "A tribute to the noble Confederate soldiers who cheerfully offered their lives in defence of local and self-government. To those who fought and survived." North Face: "1861—1865." Flags furled. South Race: Crossed Sabers.*

Recollections of Peter Early.

"In court, Judge Early knew no parties, but maintained his office with the sternest proprieties, and measured out justice with an even balance. There was a peculiarity about the corners of his mouth which I never saw in any other man's. His lips were always conpressed and firm. I never saw him smile. His countenance reflected more of sadness than of cheer, yet indicated the deepest reflection. Seated on the bench, he was erect and commanding, with his arm usually folded across his breast, and one knee thrown over the other. He seldom altered this posture. He looked severe and haughty; yet he was dignified without the least affectation. His mind was in perfect correspondence with his body; it never hesitated or faltered, but comprehended instantly whatever was presentd to it. Having drawn his inferences with the sound judgment for which he was distinguished, he rarely saw cause to change his opinion. He possessed the highest degree

---

*Authority: Mrs. Walter Thomas, who unveiled the monument.

of self-respect, and knew how to respect others. He met promptly and decided positively all points of law brought before him. There was nothing negative or vacillating in the character of Judge Early. In every respect, he was a model judge and a perfect specimen of man.''*

ECHOLS

Statesville. Statesville, the county-seat of Echols, was incorporated on December 13, 1859, with the following commissioners: Jesse P. Prescott, John T. Allen, R. W. McAlhaney, Benj. Statsvey, and James S. Carter.[1]

EFFINGHAM

Springfield. On February 7, 1799, an Act was passed by the Legislature at Louisville, appointing five commissioners, viz., David Hall, Joshua Loper, Samuel Ryals, Dodhelf Smith, and Druries Garrison, to lay out a tract of land for a county-site, and to superintend the erection of public buildings thereon. This was the beginning of the present town of Effingham. The town academy was chartered by an Act approved December 1, 1809, with Messrs. Thomas Polhill, Sr., John Kogker, Christian Treutlen, Wm. Bird, and George S. Newland, as trustees.[2] Springfield was incorporated on December 31, 1838, with the following commissioners: John Charlton, J. W. Exley, S. Bourquine, J. M. Shellman, and W. W. Wilson.[3] The town was re-incorporated in 1850.

Elberton. The county-seat of Effingham, from 1787 to 1796, was Elberton, a small town located near Indian Bluff, on the north side of the great Ogeechee River, and named for General Elbert.

---

*Dr. John G. Slappey, in a letter to Major Stephen F. Miller.
[1] Acts, 1859, p. 200.
[2] Clayton's Compendium, p. 518.
[3] Acts, 1838, p. 130.

Tuckasee-King. Under an Act of the Legislature of Georgia, dated February 26, 1784, this place was designated as the first county-seat of Effingham. It was located near the present line of Screven. The site, however, proved to be unsatisfactory, necessitating a change to Elberton.

The Salzburgers. Pages 179-193.

ELBERT

Old Ruckersville: Whoever writes of old Ruckersville **A Rural Community.** —the Ruckersville of ante-bellum days—to write intelligently, must speak of a whole community! Not those alone who lived within the confines of a small incorporated village of some 200 souls, but of the many who resided along the banks of the Savannah River in the southeastern belt of Elbert County, Georgia. Socially, politically, and in all matters of religion, they were one large family; and it may be doubted if there existed, anywhere, just previous to the great Civil War, a people so hardy, so independent, or with such lofty ideals of right living. When it is pointed out that in their business activities they were almost wholly agricultural, the volume of their prosperity is truly amazing.

It was the fixed habit of these people to practice the Golden Rule. Obedience to the law of the land was rigidly enjoined; and a man's word was his bond. To take advantage of another was regarded as beneath good morals, to get into lawsuits was to a man's discredit, and while the annals of the village reveal that here lived the Preacher and the School Master, the Banker and the Doctor, the Merchant and the Tailor, the Wheelwright and the Surveyor, yet no lawyer ever had the hardihood to hang out his shingle in Ruckersville, and when Ruckersville furnished a member of the Legislature for the County, he went from the ranks of those employed in agriculture.

Just here it may be noted, that, it was this same member of the Legislature who introduced and caused to be passed the first Homestead bill in the South, giving to the wife and children $50.00 worth of household and kitchen furniture. Of politics there was a plenty—truly educative and of absorbing moment. It was not a question of which party was the most honest or economical, but a question of men's lives and fortunes. In Ruckersville the old line Whig had been supreme—Henry Clay was the idol to be worshipped; and when Toombs and Stephens thundered in the village grove beneath the giant oaks, dangerous and ominous was the new democracy to that people. "'Tis true tis pity, and pity tis tis true"—that the Whig did not prevail!

How the Village Began: Joseph Rucker. Many of the most familiar names in Middle Georgia may be traced back to Virginia, and to that tide of immigration which about 1786, began to flow southward from the Old Dominion, and, hence, it came to pass that Ruckersville, Virginia, and Ruckersville, Georgia, were both founded by members of the same family. When Peter Rucker, planter of St. Mark's Parish, Orange County, Virginia, died in 1742, he left a large off-spring. The Virginia village was named in honor of this family, and it fell to the lot of his great grandson, through Thomas, and Cornelius, and John, to name a village in Georgia, Ruckersville! This great grandson was Joseph, the son of John Rucker, and Elizabeth Tinsley, born on January 12, 1788. In his young manhood, he was fortunate enough to win the affections of Margaret Houston Speer, daughter of William Speer, who lived at Cherokee Falls, on the Savannah River. They were married in January, 1812, and settled on the head waters of Van's Creek. Early in life, Joseph evinced the strength of character, which marked him a leader among men. In later years

Joseph Rucker

Planter and Financier, Who Stamped His Impress Upon Ante-Bellum Georgia.

(Reproduced from an old daguerreotype.)

he often said that he owed everything to his mother to whom he was a devoted son.

In 1822, the village of Ruckersville was incorporated, but no boundaries were fixed, and from that day until this, the name has been applied not so much to a town as to a large neighborhood. In 1827 Sherwood's Gazateer described it as containing 10 houses, 6 stores and shops, an academy, and a house of worship for the Baptists. In 1849 it had 200 souls. This paragraph, quoted from a sketch of Joseph Rucker in the Cyclopedia of Georgia, will help us to form a picture of Ruckersville:*

"From our present standpoint there was little in the locality to commend it as a center of influence, or as the seat of a great estate. The land was young, roads were bad, markets there were none, and it was a four days journey to Augusta, the nearest approach to a city. And yet, in that secluded locality, remote from marts and markets, Joseph Rucker not only created a fortune great for his day and generation, but displayed such wisdom and executive ability and manifested such high traits of character as marked him as an extraordinary man."

Plantation Management on a Colossal Scale. In this day of subdivided labor, it is difficult to appreciate the kind and variety of talent then required in the successful management and development of great landed estates at points distant from centers of trade and according to present standards, practically inaccessible for want of highways, railroads, and means of transportation. The successful agriculturist in every stage of the country's history has needed the highest order of judgment and forethought, and has necessarily been a man of affairs. But the successful planter at the early ante-bellum period required in the Southern States at least, a combination of talent, which would

Vol. III, p. 222.

now thoroughly equip the master minds who control the colossal enterprises of the Twentieth Century. For such a planter had not only to be an agriculturist, but a manufacturer and a financier; and, above all, he had to know how to manage, care for, and develop men. In all these departments Joseph Rucker was conspicuous. The cotton industry was in its infancy, but even in this he made a marvelous success. Stock of all kinds, horses, mules, cows, goats and sheep, were raised. The cotton was to be ginned, and the ginnery and the press were supplemented by the spinning of yarn and wool, and the weaving of cloth. There were blacksmiths, wheelwrights, and carpenters, besides saw-mills to make the lumber for the Quarters. This prince of planters had his own tan-yard, and tanners, his harness-makers and shoe-makers. Immense crops of wheat and corn were raised. Corn cribs abounded. There were also mills for converting grain into meal and flour. The management of these separate and various industries was not the most difficult task. There were the slaves themselves, a large and heterogeneous body, a wholly irresponsible people, whose ancestors had only recently come from Africa. These had to be trained and taught, and how humanely and well this was done, by the old time planter, is shown by the conduct of these same slaves, when, during the war, discipline was necessarily relaxed and control partially suspended.

Joseph Rucker: A Pen Picture. Joseph Rucker lived the typical life of the Southern planter. Self-centered and independent, he lived at home. He had little to buy and always something to sell, and his great crops of cotton were shipped in Petersburg boats down the Savannah to Augusta. The neighboring community was unusually prosperous. The Harpers, the Martins, the Heards, the Whites, the Maddoxes, the Clarks, the Adamses, and a host of others, made a neighborhood ideal in its social and domestic charms. Joseph Rucker's home especially, was the scene of a wide and generous hospitality—a social center which made its impress upon its inmates, and the memory of which abides to the third and fourth generation. He was pre-eminently a good neighbor, counsellor, and friend, for he gave needed help at the right moment. Extremely dignified, grave and reticent, he was also open-handed and generous. In politics, a Whig, he was one of the chosen friends, counsellors, and advisers of the great leaders of the Party in that District so noted in State and National Politics. He never sought political preferment, though always taking an interest in the questions of profound importance which then agitated the South.

Living at a time when the country was experimenting with Bank laws, he organized, and, as President, managed, with phenomenal success, the Bank of Ruckersville, under circumstances which would now provoke a smile. We cannot think of a bank, a moneyed institution, with hardly a human habitation in sight, surrounded by original forests. This institution was operated in a small, unpretentious frame building. Its doors and shutters were studded with nails at close and regular intervals to guard against the burglars' axe. It had a safe without time lock, opened with a key carried by the President. The furniture was of the plainest, but it issued bills which passed current par throughout the State. It throve and prospered, and with the assistance of the wealthy planters in the neighborhood, became a strong financial institution, contributing to the development and prosperity of that part of the State. In his old age, Joseph Rucker was a man of striking appearance, ruddy cheeks, snow-white hair, clear blue eyes. Dressed in the prevailing style, black broadcloth coat, cutaway to the waist line at the front, beaver hat, turn down collar and stock, and gold fob, he might have posed for the portrait of the antebellum planter, one of those who made the old South.

His son-in-law, the late Rev. James S. Lamar, of Augusta, in an unpublished manuscript, has left us the following graphic pen picture of Joseph Rucker:

"In manner and bearing Squire Rucker was simple and unpretentious, and by nature thoughtful, quiet and dignified. He enjoyed a good anecdote or story. and possessed a rich store of personal reminiscence, from which he was fond of drawing for the entertainment of others. He told his stories well, and, of course, like all genuine reconteurs, he sometimes repeated himself. It was his custom to go to Elberton on the first Tuesday in every month, when the principal men of the county would assemble in a sort of general meeting together, to attend the sheriff sales, to transact business with each other, to laugh and talk and crack jokes, and especially to save the country by discussing politics. Among the leading citizens of the town or county at that time were such influential men as Major Hester, Major Jones, Mr. Pverton Tate, Mr. Lofton, the Mattoxes, the Harpers and the Burches, Judge W. W. Thomas, and (during court week) Alexander H. Stephens, Robert Toombs and Judge William M. Reese. All of them were squire Rucker's friends.

"Squire Rucker's judgment was never known to fail him. Violently opposed to secession, when the final act came at Milledgeville, he said, pointing to one of his slaves: 'See that fellow. A year ago he was worth $1,500.00; today he isn't worth a silver thrip.' But he accepted the situation—helped to equip a company—took $30,000 of the first issue of Confederate bonds, at par. These bonds were lying in the old Bank of Athens, in the care of the late Albin Dearing, when the war was over; not a coupon had ever been clipped.''

"The house was approached through a long avenue of cedars and box planted by Margaret, from which the place became known as Cedar Grove. The fine oll trees, the office, the flower garden, the kitchen garden, the well-house, the smoke-house, the kitchen, the buildings for house servants, and, not far off, the barns, the carraige houses, the quarters, presentd a typical picture of the life of the ante-bellum planter who lived at home, making on his own acres all that was needed for those dependent upon him. For there, as in so many other similar places throughout the State, the tannery, the blacksmith-shop, the corn-mill, the flour-mill, the cotton gin, the spinning wheels, the looms and the wheelwright were an essential part of the plantation. It was a hive of industry, and it is not surprising that in time a name should be given to the little center, nor is it strange that it should have been named after the village in Orange County, Virginia, from which John Rucker had come in 1785.

"He was always called Squire Rucker. I well remember the first time I saw him. It was in the summer of 1856. He was dressed in the old-fashioned suit of broadcloth, a vest also of cloth, and a coat of the same material in the style called shad-belly—somewhat like the cutaways of the present day. He wore it unbattoned—a watch chain with a heavy seal

HOME OF JOSEPH RUCKER, AT OLD RUCKERSVILLE, GA.

hanging from a fob, or watch, pocket. His neckcloth was then and always pure white. It was not a simple tie, but a sort of folded handkerchief, put on by laying the middle part against the throat, leading the ends back and crossing them, then bringing them to the throat to be tied together. The knot was plain. I am not sure that there was even a bow. .

"He was polite, but very reserved. He seemed to be studying me. His conversation, so far as it was directed to me, was mainly questions—chiefly about men and women and things in Augusta—Mrs. Tubman, the Cummings, the Claytons, the Gardiners, and Mr. Metcalfe—then about cotton and business and prospects; but no human being could have told from any expression of his face what effect my answers had upon him, or what inference as to me he drew from them. Considering the time of the year and the purpose of my visit, I must say it was a little chilly. Presently supper came on—such a supper as only the Ruckers could get up—and the conversation took a somewhat wider range. The family were book people—Dickens was the rage then, and I had read Dickens and Thackery, and had dipped into Cousin and various philosophers; and at that period of my life I could talk—an art which I have unfortunately lost. So that when the old gentleman found that I could hold my own with Elbert and others, and that all the family treated me with sincere respect and consideration, he seemed to thaw, little by little, concluding, I suppose, that I might turn out to be something in my way, if I was nothing in his."

Personal Sketches. Col. L. H. O. Martin, a native of Elbert County, was one of the most prominent and successful planters of his day—essentially a man of affairs, of striking appearance and fascinating manners, he numbered his friends by the hundreds. In early life he married the daughter of Col. Thomas Heard, who lived near Savannah River. He was the bosom friend of Joseph Rucker and of his son, Tinsley Rucker, and rarely a day passed that there was not mutual visits between the families. He was the most delightful of talkers, and a safe counsellor in all matters of weighty importance. He was among the foremost of that brilliant coterie of men that made social life so pleasing to the planters of the day. During the Civil War he served upon the staff of General Toombs.

Colonel James Loftin was the fountain head of all knowledge to be gained from books for the rising generation, for many years at Ruckersville. A ripe scholar of vast information, he successfully taught the classics, philosophies, and mathematics in his school for young men. He had a most charming family, and one of his sons, John Loftin, was a leading member of the Macon Bar for many years after the War.

———

Peter W. Alexander, born in Ruckersville, in 1823, graduated from the University of Georgia in 1844. From his early youth his tastes were literary—of magnificent frame and courtly bearing, he was a splendid type of a Southerner. Removing to Columbus, Ga., he entered Journalism, and soon became a writer of note. The outbreak of the Civil War found him in Savannah, owner and editor of the Savannah "Republican." His opinions in political life were eagerly sought, and as war correspondent for his paper, he was the most noted of all Southern correspondents.

His love for his old home and associates at Ruckersville has kept green his memory in the hearts of many to this day.

———

Overton Tate, a planter of large means, married Rebecca Clark, a niece of Joseph Rucker. His home was always the center of large entertainment and social enjoyment. His wife, still living, at the age of ninety years, surrounded by loving and accomplished children and grandchildren, is one of the noblest specimens of womanhood that ever graced the life of any community.

———

Dr. Richard Banks, of Ruckersville, was a noted physician, for whom Banks County was named. He was the beloved good Samaritan of his day, and it was said of him that his charities were only bounded by his opportunities for doing good unto others.

———

Tinsley White Rucker was the oldest son of Joseph Rucker. Born at Ruckersville, in 1813, he graduated at the University of Georgia in 1833, and soon married Sarah Elizabeth Harris, the daughter of General Jeptha V. Harris, of Farm Hill. He represented Elbert County in the State Legislature in 1836. A man of lofty ideals and of high purposes, his life was without fear and without blemish. Farm Hill, his home, previous to the Civil War, was one of the best known and one of the most beautiful estates in Georgia.

———

Elbert M. Rucker, another of Squire Rucker's sons, was a man of great learning and of rare oratorical powers. So vast was his information, that General Toombs once declared it to be more varied and extensive than any other living man's. But no sketch of Ruckersville is complete that fails to mention the fact that one of the most noted of present-day novelists was born in this village: Mrs. Corra White Harris, who wrote "The Circuit Rider's Wife." It was also the birth-place of Associate-Justice Joseph R. Lamar, of the Supreme Court of the United States.

———

Petersburg: An Old Forgotten Tobacco Market. On a peninsula which the Broad and Savannah Rivers unite to form, in the extreme southeast corner of Elbert, there once stood an important town, which, until the tobacco trade was abandoned by the planters, was one of the foremost commercial centers of Georgia—old Petersburg. But even this ancient town stood upon the ruins of one much older still. During the Colonial period there was located here a settlement which was called Dartmouth. It was named in honor of the Earl, to whose influence was due the concessions enjoyed by a band of colonists engaged at this point in trade with the Indians. The area in question was known as the New Purchase, and to defend it against assault there was erected in the angle between the two rivers a stronghold called Fort James.

But the little settlement failed to realize the expectations of those who planted it, and, after struggling somewhat feebly for existence, it met an early death. The second effort to settle the place was more successful. On February 3, 1786,[1] for the convenience of planters in the immediate neighborhood, an Act was passed by the Legislature at Augusta, authorizing Dionysius Oliver to erect on his land a warehouse, to be used for the inspection and storage of tobacco; and from this circumstance dates the commencement of the town of Petersburg. The cultivation of tobacco was just beginning to attract the attention of planters. On the coast, both the production of silk and the cultivation of indigo were languishing. Cotton was little grown at this time, because it lacked the stimulus of the cotton gin. Many of the early settlers in this particular neighborhood, according to Colonel Jones,[2] were from Virginia, and, besides bringing with them to Georgia a love of the weed, they also possessed a high appreciation of tobacco as an article of prime commercial value. Since the lands in this locality were well adapted to the culture of the plant, it soon became the market crop of the farmers; and to comply with the law which forbade the exportation of tobacco, without previous inspection, together with the payment also of certain fees, it was necessary to establish warehouses at convenient points.

Under the invigorating spell of the tobacco trade, Petersburg began to grow. The area was divided into town lots, with convenient streets intersecting each other at right angles. The warehouse was located near the point of confluence between the two streams, but far enough removed from the water's edge to escape an overflow. In the course of time others were built in the same neighborhood, including one by William Watkins, who secured Legislative permission in 1797.[3] The intellectual character of the residents is attested by the fact that in 1802 eighteen of the principal citizens of the town organized themselves into a union, the avowed purpose of which was the diffusion of knowledge and the alleviation of want. Its membership was as follows: Shaler Hillyer, president; John Williams Walker, secretary; Memorable Walker, Oliver White, James Sanders Walker, John A. Casey, Thomas Casey, Robert Watkins, William Jones, Albert Bruxe, Robert H. Watkins, Rigual N. Groves, Nicholas Pope, Andrew Greene Semmes, James Coulter, William Wyatt Bibb, Garland T. Watkins and Thomas Bibb. Dr. W. W. Bibb became a United States Senator. He was also the first Territorial Governor of Alabama, an office in which he was succeeded by his brother, Thomas Bibb. The town was governed by commissioners, who were first chosen by the Legislature and afterwards by the local citizenship.

---

[1] Watkin's Digest, p. 325.
[2] Dead Towns of Georgia, p. 234, Savannah, 1878.
[3] Watkin's Digest, p. 658.

It is of record that on December 1, 1802,[4] Robert Thompson, Leroy Pope, Richard Easter, Samuel Watkins and John Ragland were appointed commissioners of the town of Petersburg and were charged with its "Better regulation and government." In the zenith of its prosperity, the town numbered between seven and eight hundred souls, and was considered second in importance only to Augusta. As long as the tobacco trade continued, the town flourished; but with the rise of the cotton plant it began to decline. The residents gradually moved to other localities. Only a few remained to people the little grave-yard of this deserted village; and today sunken wells and moss-covered mounds, with an occasional loose brick from some ancient chimney pile, survive to tell the wayfarer where Petersburg once stood in the forgotten long ago.

Rose Hill. Reminiscent of the best days of the old regime and famous throughout the whole length and breadth of the South, is one of the fine old ancestral homes of Elbert: Rose Hill. The original structure, built in the early part of the last century by Thomas Jefferson Heard, still constitutes the main part of the present establishment; but wings have since been added on either side, giving it a much more regal appearance than it wore in the days of its first owner. The oldest building is known as Middlesex; while the two annexes are called respectively, Essex and Wessex. The estate itself is called Rose Hill, a name whose appropriateness is well maintained by the scene which greets the visitor's eye, on approaching this magnificent home. Acres of roses, rising terrace upon terrace, furnish a mountain of fragrance, out of which loom the stately parapets of the old mansion.

Rose Hill is today the home of Mr. and Mrs. Eugene B. Heard, the fame of whose hospitality has long since crystalized into a proverb. Mr. Heard acquired Rose Hill by inheritance from his grandfather; but the estate has lost none of the splendor of the old days in his possession. Peaches are cultivated on a vast scale. The cotton acreage is something enormous, and scores of la-

---

[4] Clayton Digest, p. 92.

borers are employed; but there is not a negro on the plantation whose welfare is not an object of constant solicitude to the humane owners of Rose Hill. Mrs. Heard is one of Georgia's most gifted women, an acknowledged leader in not a few of the great forward movements of her time; and here, in this beautiful home of the Old South, some of the most beneficent and helpful reforms of the new era, have found an inspirational beginning. Here originated the Traveling Library of the South, and here the first Federated Woman's Club in Georgia was organized. To give our readers a better acquaintance with Rose Hill, we quote from a well-known writer the following descriptive paragraphs:*

Box and cedar hedges border both sides of the walks. Large magnolia and crepe myrtle trees, gnarled and spotted from old age, envelop the home in their green foliage; ivy from Kenilworth Castle covers Middlesex windows and walls, and the sparrows and jay-birds make merry all day long, hiding in its deep branches. Purple iris and small, old-fashioned gladioli planted by the owner's grandmother, bloom in reckless masses over the green lawn. Roses climb to the second-story balconies, their petals blowing out over the air as a soft summer breeze would sway the graceful stems.

Roses everywhere, a wealth of bloom and variety from stock bought of famous collections or given by friends from some distant place, their own kind they name for the favorite guests. A bright red rose is the Josie S., called for the dark-haired, bright-cheeked girl who would come down from the city with her lovers to see if they were as nice in the quiet of the country as on the more diverting streets of town. Another, a pale yellow bud, fragrant as a tea rose, is the Kitty T., its namesake a tall blonde girl with a wealth of golden hair and twinkling gray eyes.

Stone gates lead out into the ''park,'' and tall cedar hedges follow the drive to the outer entrance on the main highway. A garage has been built for their automobile, but it has been so hidden by shrubs and vines that it looks almost as old as the ''outbuildings'' which were on the ''street'' in slave time, where were the cabins of those negroes working about the yard.

Telephones and an ample water supply bring the city comforts to them, and the library tables are covered with magazines and newspapers. But the pride of the owners are the old English prints of 1803 and the colonial mirrors in empire style of gold and mahogany that have been in the family for more than half a century. Tall colonial mantels, hand-

---

*Miss Nita Black, in the Atlanta Journal.

carved, are just as they were in the days of their ancestors. Candles are used almost entirely, and for these there are tall, old-time brass holders. In Middlesex are the general living rooms, two libraries with heavily laden book shelves, the dining-room and the breakfast-room. Upstairs are the several guest-rooms. "Little Miss," the only daughter, is now married and lives in Essex, while her father and mother reside in Wessex."

Elberton. In 1790, Elbert County was formed out of Wilkes, and named for Governor Samuel Elbert, in whose honor the county-seat was likewise named. It is said that a bold spring of excellent water settled the location of the future seat of government. Elberton was incorporated by an Act approved December 10, 1793, the preface to which contains this insignificant sentence: "Whereas the town of Elberton requires regulation." The commissioners of the town named in this Act were: Middleton Woods, Reuben Lindsay, Doctor John T. Gilmer, Beckham Dye, and James Alston. Only Beckham Dye is represented by the present population. Elberton made little progress for many years. The wealthy pioneers were planters who resided mainly along the Savannah River. Ruckersville and Petersburg were the centers of local commerce.

But the early residents must have believed in education, as indicated by Legislative Acts incorporating Philomathia Academy in 1823; Eudisco Academy in 1823, and Elberton Female Academy in 1826. The Elberton Female Academy continued without change even in name until it was superseded by the public schools of the present time. The Elberton Male Academy was incorporated later. It closed during the Civil War, and small boys were received into the Female Academy. Methodist and Baptist churches were built soon after the town was established. The Presbyterians built many years later.

The leading representative citizens between 1825 and 1860 were: Major Alfred Hammond, Robert McMillan, Esq., Thomas Jones, William Nelms, Zachariah Smith,

W. A. Swift, Amos Vail, J. A. Trenchard, Young J. Harris, Dr. Henry J. Bowman, Dr. Calhoun Wilhite, Simeon Hall, Robert Hester, Esq., Doctor M. P. Deadwyler, Dr. D. A. Mathews and Major John H. Jones. Robert McMillan and Robert Hester were brilliant lawyers. Dr. Deadwyler was the leading physician, a courteous gentleman, loved by everyone. He died without children, leaving as sole heir to his liberal fortune, a wife who generously and wisely distributes it to worthy causes. The present handsome Baptist Church, one half of which she donated, stands as his memorial.

But Elberton owes her chief debt of gratitude to Major John H. Jones. He was born in Elberton in 1814, and here he died in 1899. In 1873, Elberton was thirty miles from any railroad. Many times its citizens had tried to build a railroad and failed. Major Jones then took up the fight. For six years he gave to this work his time and brains and character. The Elberton Air Line Railroad from Elberton to Toccoa, Ga., was the result. It was completed December 5, 1878, and Elberton, now 8,000 population, dates its progress from its completion.

Major Jones married Lavonia, daughter of Major Alfred Hammond. The splendid city of Lavonia was named in her honor. They reared a large family of children and their children and grandchildren are among the people most prominent in business, social, educational and church work. Major Jones graduated from the State University in 1838. He was refined, courteous, affectionate, good. Upon every public question, he stood for the progressive and the moral. The present Elberton is his most enduring monument.

———

Tomb of Hon. Within a stone's throw of the town cen-
Wiley Thompson. ter, on property owned and occupied by one of the leading business men of Elberton, is the tomb of Hon. Wiley Thompson, a distin-

---

*Authority: Judge Geo. C. Grogan.

guished statesman, who represented Georgia in Congress for several successive terms during the early ante-bellum period. He met his death at the hands of Seminole Indians in Florida. The inscription on this distinguished Georgian's monument reads as follows:

> WILEY THOMPSON. Born Sept. 23, 1781. Murdered at Fort King, Florida, by the Seminole Indians, Dec. 28, 1837. Aged 56 years, 3 mos. and five days. "Blessed is the man that loveth the Lord and delighteth in his commandments."

EMANUEL

Swainsboro. On November 18, 1814, an Act was approved by Gov. Early, designating as a site for public buildings in the new county of Emanuel, a locality within one mile of the place pointed out by one Jesse Mezzle, as the center of the county.[1] The commissioners to choose a site and to superintend the erection of public buildings were named in the original Act of 1812, creating the new county, to wit: Edward Lane, Francis Pugh, Needham Cox, Eli Whitdon, and Uriah Anderson.[2] To these were subsequently added, Jesse Mezzle and Archibald Culbreth. The site agreed upon for the county-seat was made permanent by an Act approved December 6, 1822, and the name of the town—as this Act informs us—was to be Swainsboro.

To Paris and Back. Thirty years later an effort was made to change the name of the town to Paris; and by an Act approved February 18, 1854, this name was formally bestowed upon the town.[3] At the same time Paris was to be retained as the county-seat, and the following commissioners were appointed to put into effect the terms of this act, viz., Elam B. Lewis, Joshua J. Arnold, Berry Stroup, Nathan

---

[1] Lamar's Digest, p. 210.
[2] Lamar's Digest, p. 197.
[3] Acts, 1853-1854, p. 269.

Stephens and D. B. Smith. But Paris was short-lived; and eventually Swainsboro reappeared. Since railway facilities were obtained, the growth of the town has been marked. Swainsboro was named for an influential family of pioneer settlers from the State of North Carolina. Stephen Swain represented Emanuel in the Senate of Georgia almost continuously from 1813 to 1836, after which, according to the records, Ethelred Swain was frequently returned.

EVANS

Claxton. On August 14, 1914, an Act was approved creating by Constitutional amendment the new County of Evans out of lands formerly included in Tattnall and Bulloch; and if this amendment is ratified at the polls it will give Georgia one-hundred and fifty-two counties. Claxton, the new county-seat, was originally known as Hendrix. But there was already a post-office in Georgia by this name; consequently the postal authorities at Washington requested the ladies of the communities to select a new name for the town, which they did, selecting the name of Claxton. Situated on the Seaboard Air Line, the growth of the town of late years has been exceedingly rapid.

Gen. Clement A. Evans. Gen. Clement A. Evans, whose services to the State are memorialized in this Act of the Legislature, was a gallant Confederate officer, who, at Appomattox, commanded Gordon's famous division. Some time after the surrender had taken place, there was heard the noise of rapid firing in a remote part of the field. On investigation, it was found that Gen. Evans, ignorant of affairs at headquarters, was leading a victorious charge upon the enemy's breastworks. Subsequent to the war, Gen. Evans became a devout minister of the gospel and served a number of Methodist churches; but he also gave much of his time to public affairs. In 1894, he was a popular candidate for Governor of Georgia, but retired from the race prior to the date of election, on account of a physical inability to meet the demands of a strenuous campaign. Ten years later, he was elected by his old war comrades to succeed Gen. Stephen D. Lee as Commander-in-Chief of the United Confederate Veterans. As a member of the State Board of Prison Commissioners, he rendered the State an important service in his old age. Two great orations were delivered by Gen. Evans during the last

years of his life: one on the unveiling of an equestrian statue to Gen.
John B. Gordon, on the capitol grounds, in Atlanta; and the other on the
dedication of the famous monument in Richmond, Va., to his revered
chieftain: Jefferson Davis.

FANNIN

Morganton. In the Act creating Fannin County, in 1853, judges of the Inferior Court were empowered to select a county-seat, near the center of the county; and, in pursuance of this Act, a locality was chosen to which was given the name of Morganton. The town was incorporated by an Act approved March 5, 1856, with the following town commissioners, to wit: James H. Morris, Wm. B. Brown, Thomas M. Alston, Wm. Franklin, and Madison Casady. The charter was afterwards several times ameneded.

Massacre of   Pages 115-121.
Fannin's Men.

Blue Ridge. Blue Ridge, the present county-seat of Fannin, was incorporated as a town on October 24, 1887, at which time Hon. J. W. Gray was designated to fill the office of mayor, and Messrs. M. McKinney, F. H. Walton, W. T. Buchanan, Wm. Taylor, E. L. Rickets, and W. B. Wuce were named to serve as aldermen pending the first regular election. The corporate limits of the town were fixed at one mile in every direction from the depot of the Marietta and North Georgia Railroad; but, in 1890, this area proving too large for immediate purposes, was diminished.* On August 13, 1895, the county-seat of Fannin was changed to Blue Ridge, as the result of an election for which due and legal notice was given.* The present public school system of Blue Ridge was established in 1899.

*Acts, 1855-6, p. 353.

FAYETTE

Fayetteville. In 1822, Fayette County was organized out
of lands recently acquired from the Creeks,
under the first treaty of Indian Springs. By an Act approved December 20, 1823, Fayetteville was made the
permanent site for public buildings. At the same time
a charter of incorporation was granted, with the following residents named as commissioners: Jordan Gay, Simeon L. Smith, Wm. Harkins, John Hamilton, and Tandy
D. King.* The Fayette County Academy was chartered
in 1840. Both the town and the county were named for
the great palladin of liberty, General LaFayette, who
made his last visit to Georgia in 1825.

————

FLOYD

Rome. In 1832, Floyd County was organized out of lands
then recently acquired from the Cherokees, and
named for Gen. John Floyd, a noted Indian fighter of
Georgia. The first county-site chosen by the Inferior
Court judges was Livingston; but in 1838, the seat of
government was transferred to Rome, at the head of the
Coosa River. The Rome Academy was chartered in
1837; the Cherokee College of Georgia in 1850; the Cher-
okee Wesleyan Institute in 1854, and the Rome Female
College in 1857. As a seat of culture, Rome gradually
forged ahead of Cassville, for years an educational cen-
ter of Cherokee Georgia. Some of the early pioneers of
Rome were: Daniel R. Mitchell, Philip W. Hemphill,
Judge John H. Lumpkin, Judge Wm. H. Underwood, Ma-
jor Chas. H. Smith, Andrew J. Liddell, Zachariah B.
Hargrove, Wm. Smith, A. T. Hardin, Wm. T. Trammell,
Alfred Shorter, Judge John W. Hooper, Dr. H. V. M.
Miller, Simpson Fouche, Thomas Hamilton, T. J. Ste-

———

*Acts, 1823, p. 179.

phens, Nathan Bass, Judge Augustus R. Wright, W. S. Cothran and many others.

————

Historic Third Ave- The following article from a local
nue: The Girlhood contributor recently appeared in one
Home of Mrs. of the newspapers:
Woodrow Wilson.

"Third Avenue, of this city, since the election of Woodrow Wilson, is now considered more historic ground than ever. On the north, the avenue is bounded by the Oostanaula River, and extending in the far distance is Lavender range of mountains, at whose base Generals Hood and Sevier marched. DeSoto, the famous discoverer, is said to have camped over the river opposite Third Avenue on his way to the Mississppi. At the eastern end of the avenue, where runs the Etowah River, is a little island that marks the site where Revolutionary soldiers once camped.

"At the foot of Third Avenue runs the first of Rome railroads. On the street was once the Shelton manse, on whose campus once camped Federal soldiers. When peace was restored and years rolled by, Shorter College was built on this site by Alfred Shorter, as a gift to one of his daughters. Across the street from the Presbyterian Church is a house where Henry W. Grady brought his bride from Athens. Near the First Methodist Church, on this same street, is the old home of Bill Arp. The brick cottage, now "Rosemont," was once the home of Mrs. John J. Seay, a kinswoman of Secretary Bayard. Mrs. Seay's sister was bridesmaid to Miss Mittie Bullock, Theodore Roosevelt's mother.

"Just below the brow of the hill there stands an old garden, and just beyond it a low white cottage. Some of the shrubs and flowers were planted by Rev. S. E. Axson, when this was the girlhood home of Ella Lou Axson, the first lady of the land and the wife of President-elect Woodrow Wilson. In that little white house her big brown eyes looked wonderingly out toward the future. What were her girlish dreams, her hopes, her ambitions? She lived with her books and her paintings, among the Southern flowers; and here with her gentle mother and sainted father she spent many of her girlhood days."

————

Prehistoric Memor- The region of country between the
ials: The Mound- Oostanaula and the Etowah Rivers
Builders. is rich in antiquities. Besides an un-
written body of traditions, there are numerous relics which testify to the former existence in this locality of a race of inhabitants older than the Cher-

okees.   We quote from an account written by Colonel
Charles C. Jones, Jr., in 1861.   Says he:*

"The organic traces of the Mound-Builders are frequent in this neighborhood. Just where the rivers meet, there once stood upon the point of
land, whos base is washed by these streams, an interesting mound, circular
in shape, some twelve or fifteen feet in height and, at the base, not less
than fifty feet in diameter. The earth and clay which composd this tumulus
have been almost entirely removed, the same having been employed in level-
ing the streets of Rome and in making a landing place for the ferry-boats.
From this mound silver ornaments and heads of gold were taken. It was
found to contain numerous skeletons, pots, vases, stone axes, arrowheads,
spearheads, shell ornaments, pipes, copper beads, mortars, circular stones,
carefully rounded and polished, besides other relics of a less interesting
character. Along the banks of the two rivers are numerous traces of inhumation. This spot appears to have been consecrated to the purposes of
burial. The swollen tides never wash the shore, without bringing to light
new proofs of this fact. In the immediate neighborhood were several
other mounds of smaller dimensions, all of which seem to have been devoted to the purposes of sepulture. They are now nearly level with
the plain. Upon the very spot occupied by at least two of them have
been erected the dwellings and work-shops of another and a nobler race.
The contents of these were all similar. They were composed of the blue
clay and alluvial soil of the valley, interspersed with stones and muscle
shells taken from the beds of the confluent streams."

But the Cherokees possessed no information concerning these mounds.
They knew nothing whatever of the race of people by whom they were
built. Says Colonel Jones:* "When questioned by the whites who first
located here, they replied by saying that they retained not even a tradition
of those who constructed them." The story is shrouded in oblivion. With
respect to the physical characteristics of the environment, Colonel Jones
waxes eloquent. Says he: "Beautiful in all its features is this necropolis
of a departed race. Standing upon the almost obliterated traces of the
larger mound, whose base is washed by the confluent waves of the Etowah
and the Oostanaula, the eye, gladdened by the joyful meeting, watches the
stranger wavelets, now friends, as in joyous companionship they leap along
the current of the softly gliding Coosa. . . . The dark green foliage
which crowns the left bank grows darker still as the shadow of the opposite
hill—almost a mountain—settles upon the river; while the trees on the
other side are joyously waving their beautiful branches in the soft sunlight
which rests upon the valley beyond. On the right, hill succeeds hill in gentle
undulation. Behind, stretches the valley of the Etowah, beautiful in its

---

*Monumental Remains of Georgia, by Charles C. Jones, Jr., pp. 82-83,
Savannah, 1861.
*Ibid., p. 83.

foliage, attractive in its graceful windings, as it bends over to guard in its accustomed channel, the stream which imparts its life and verdure. Upon the adjacent eminences, sits the village of Rome. The stately trees have fallen before the stroke of the woodsman. Broad bridges span the waters. The steamboat, freighted with the products of intelligent husbandry, stem their currents. Through the echoing valley of the Etowah, are heard the shrill whistle and the rapid march of the locomotive. On every side are seen the traces of a new, a superior, and an advancing civilization. How changed since the time when the Mound-Builder fixed here his home, and above the remains of his family and friends, heaped these memorials of his sorrow—these tributes to the memory of the departed.''

Indian Antiquities. ''Some eight miles above Rome, in a bend of the Oostanaula River, known as Pope's Bend, is a mount, at present some five or six feet in height and, at the base, some eighty feet in diameter. It stands in the middle of a field, which is said to have been cleared and cultivated by the Indians. Circular in form, its central portion is considerably depressed. In consequence of the exposure of this tumulus to the immediate action of wind and tempest and due to its having been for years cultivated, its present proportions do not realize its original size. The walls of this mound must at first have been raised several feet above its central portion. In this respect, it seems quite unique. Now, however, the outer rim has an elevation of not more' than two feet. It is composed entirely of the sand and soil of the valley. Upon its surface were found broken fragments of pottery, a stone axe, a pipe, a soapstone ornament, broken clay utensils and numerous fragments of human bones. This was, without doubt, a burial mound. Just across the river, and upon a neck of land formed by the confluence of Armurchee Creek and the Oostanaula, is still another. The surface of the ground for several acres here is covered with pieces of pottery, and a great varity of spear and arrow-heads. From this mound were taken a mortar of beautiful proportions, pestles, stone axes, etc. We are inclined to refer these last tumuli to an Indian origin. Certain it is that many of the remains found in and about them are purely Indian in character. It will be observed, however, that the same locality sometimes, and in fact not unfrequently, indicates the existence of remains peculiar both to the Mound-Builders and to a later period.

''. . . From the best authority it appears that the Cherokees of this region did not, as a general rule, erect mounds over the dead. The usual custom was to hide the body in some rocky fissure, covering it with bark, despositing with it the bow and arrow, pots, stone axes, and other articles, the property of the deceased, and then close securely the entrance. Often the hut of the deceased was burnt, and with it many articles used by the late owner. Sometimes they interred beneath the floor of the cabin, subsequently setting fire to the walls and roof, thus obliterating every trace of the inhumation.

"Again, they buried by placing the body underneath a ledge of rocks, or upon the slope of a hill in some unfrequented spot, heaping above it a pile of stones. Subsequently they adopted the plan of digging a grave some three feet or more in depth, into which the corpse was lowered. Above it was heaped a small tumulus, some six or eight feet in length and two or three feet in height. Upon the range of hills running to the south of Rome are several graves of this latter description. They lie north and south and are generally located in the vicinity of large trees. On the right bank of the Etowah River, near Rome, at a point known as 'Old Bridge,' a heavy ledge of rocks, projecting from the side of the hill, overhung the river. It was necessary to remove this, in order to construct the track of the Rome Railway. When forced from its position by the blast, the fissures in the ledge were found to be filled with the skeletons of Indians. By many they were supposed to have been the dead killed in a battle fought but a short distance from this spot, and here secreted by those who survived. Upon the hill opposite Rome, known as 'Cemetery Hill,' many bodies have been discovered securely lodged in the inequalities of the hillsides, carefully covered and with utensils of the chase, of war, and of domstic use, buried with them. Scattered throughout these valleys, however, there are mounds of moderate dimensions, circular or ovoidal in form, which are doubtless to be referred to an Indian origin. Judging from the internal evidence, we are inclined to regard them as the oldest organic remains of the Cherokees. Elevated spaces, perfectly level at the top, are still to be seen. These were formerly used by the Cherokees for the purposes of sport, dancing, ball playing, and quoit rolling. In one locality, not far from the village of Rome, was pointed out a track, some quarter of a mile or more in extant, which tradition designates as an Indian race-course. All traces of the dwellings have, of course, disappeared, with the exception of some of the more modern buildings—such as the ruins of the house formerly occupied by John Ross, the chief of the national, beautifully situated upon a gentle elevation, on the edge of the Coosa Valley, near the inception of the river; and the former residence of Major Ridge, which still remains in good preservation [1861], upon the left bank of the Oostanaula River, some two miles from Rome. These, however, are modern in character and belong to the semi-civilized Indian, as modified in his tastes and habits by association with the white race.'"*

The aboriginal remains of these valleys may be divided into three classes: 1. Those which are to be referred

---

*Charles C. Jones, Jr., in Monumental Remains of Georgia, pp. 82-93. Savannah: 1861.

to the Mound-Builders.   2. Such as are purely Indian in
character.   3'. Those which, although the work of Indians, were modified by intercourse and contact with
Whites or Europeans.   Authorities: Jones, Adair, Bar-
tram.

——— ——

Base-Ball: A Game There is little room for doubt that
of Indian Origin. the most typical as well as the most
popular of American games, viz.,
base-ball, originated among the North American Indians.
As played by them the game was, of course, crude, and
in some respects was not unlike the game of foot-ball.
It is only by an evolutionary sort of process that the
favorite sport of the modern college athlete can be traced
to the primitive play-grounds of the savage wilderness,
but the essential principles of the game were undoubtedly
derived from the aboriginal inhabitants of the continent.
Throughout the whole of upper Georgia, there are traditions without number concerning important issues,
such as boundary line disputes, which were settled by the
game; traces of the old fields can still be found on which
the famous contests occurred; and in Cherokee County,
not far from the town of Canton, is a village which com-
memoratively bears the name of Ball Ground. To James
Adair, the celebrated annalist of the North American savage, are we indebted for the following description of
this favorite pastime of the Indian:

"The ball is made of a piece of scraped deer-skin, moistened and
stuffed with deer's hair, and strongly sewed with deer' sinews. The ball
sticks are about two feet long, the lower end somewhat resembling the
palm of a hand. They are worked with deer-skin thongs. Between these
they catch the ball and are enabled to throw it a great distance, when
not prevented by the opposite party, whose effort it is to intercept its
passage. The goal is some five hundred yards in extent. At each end of
it, they fix into the ground two long, bending poles, which are three yards
apart at the bottom, but reach much farther outward at the top. The
party who succeeds in throwing the ball over these, scores one; but if the
ball goes underneath, it is cast back and played for as usual. The game-
sters were equal in number on both sides; and at the beginning of every

course of the ball they throw it high in the center of the ground and in a direct line between the two goals. When the crowd of players prevents the one who catches the ball from throwing it directly in front, he commonly sends it in the right course by an artful, sharp twirl. They are so exceedingly expert in this manly exercise that, between the goals, the ball is mostly flying the different ways, by the force of the playing-sticks, without falling to the ground; for they are not allowed to catch it with the hand. In the heat and excitement of the game, the arms and legs of the players are sometimes broken. The celebration of this game is preceded by fastings and night-watches, by those who are about to engage in it. They turn out to the ball-ground, in a long row, painted white, and whooping as if Pluto's prisoners had all broken loose. The leader then begins a religious invocation, which is joined in by his companions. Each party strives to gain the twentieth ball, which they esteem a favorite divine gift.'' From the foregoing description it will be observed that while the modern game of base-ball differs materially from the primitive game played by the North American Indians, the equally popular game of foot-ball preserves many of the savage characteristics of its original prototype.'"

FORSYTH

Cumming. The county of Forsyth was organized in 1832 out of a part of the Cherokee lands named for the Hon. John Forsyth of Georgia. The county-site was called Cumming, in honor of a gallant officer of the war of 1812, Col. Wm. Cumming, of Augusta. Cumming was incorporated by an Act approved December 22, 1834, with the following commissioners: John Jolly, Daniel McCoy, John H. Russell, Daniel Smith, and Wm. Martin.[2]

Recollections of John Forsyth. "In the great Anti-Tariff Convention, at Milledgeville, in 1832, Mr. Berrien, who led the movement, was forced to grapple with the best off-hand debater in the world. Burke may have been more philosophical and ornate, Fox more logical and comprehensive, Sheridan more brilliant in repartee, and Pitt, in stately grandeur of eloquence, may have surpassed him, but not one of these was the polemic gladiator, the ever-buoyant and ready master of

----

[1] Charles C. Jones, Jr., in Monumental Remains of Georgia, pp. 91-93; also James Adair, in the History of the Indian Tribes, etc.
[2] Acts, 1834, p. 255.

elocution that Mr. Forsyth was, with look and gesture, inflection of voice, and all the qualities of a high-bred soul gushing for victory. He was a perfect model of eloquence, without having copied any man or any rules. By some happy method, accidental or otherwise, he had accommodated his organs of speech to the capacity of the lungs for respiration. He was never out of breath; his voice was always clear and resonant, always pleasing to the ear in its high or low keys and in its grand or simple modulations. There was no hurry, no discord, no break, in the constant stream of pure vocalization. The listener had no dread of failure. . . . His very looks accomplished a great deal. A glance of the eye, a motion of the finger, a wave of the hand, a curl of the lip, a twitch of the Roman nose, could kill or cripple at the will of the speaker. The person of Mr. Forsyth was exceedingly handsome. His form was classical. He was neither too light nor too heavy for grace of manner. No orator in the United States possessed such a fine command of the keys and modulations whereby the heart is subdued at the will of the orator. His supply of the best words was inexhaustible. In this respect, he very much resembled Lord Erskine. Had he been less a man of the world, less indoctrinated in the etiquette and levity of courts, less inclined to the heartless formalities of fashion, he would have been more of a public benefactor and more deeply entwined in the affections of men. His instincts were not with the masses. He was faithful to his trusts, because it was impossible for him to do a mean or base act. He was always courteous and obliging in his personal relations; still there was a diplomatic element in which he loved to revel, and from which he derived his chief enjoyment. Beyond this, life was measurably insipid; nor is it certain that the philosophy of Bolingbroke or the morals of Chesterfield contributed to his happiness. But if Mr. Forsyth had his defects—and he would be more than mortal to be exempt— let it be remembered that the sun has spots which do not mar its brilliance. It may be centuries before such a man shall again exist.''[*]

''The late John Forsyth was one of the most accomplished men of his time. As an impromptu debater, to bring on an action or to cover a retreat, he never had his superior. He was acute, witty, full of resources, and ever prompt—impetuous as Murat in a charge, adroit as Soult when flanked and out numbered. He was haughty in the presence of enemis, genial and winning among friends. His manners were courtly and diplomatic. In the times of Louis the XIV, he would have rivalled the most celebrated courtiers; under the dynasty of Napoleon he would have won the baton of France. He never failed to command the confidence of his party; he never feared any odds against it; and, at one time, was almost its sole support

---

[*]Stephen H. Miller, in Bench and Bar of Georgia, Vol. II.

in the Senate against the most brilliant and powerful opposition ever organized against an administration.''*

FRANKLIN

Carnesville.   In 1784, the Legislature of Georgia created two large counties: Franklin and Washington, out of lands obtained from the Indians, under the treaties of 1783, negotiated at Augusta. These were the first counties created after the war for independence, and most of the lands in these counties were given in bounty warrants to Revolutionary soldiers. Due to conditions on the frontier, several years elapsed before there was any permanent county organization. But Carnesville, as a mountain village, doubtless arose soon after the Revolution. It was made the permanent site for public buildings in the county of Franklin, by an Act approved November 29, 1806, at which time the following commissioners were appointed: James Terrell, Obadiah Hooper, Joseph Chandler, Frederick Beal, and James King.[1] The town was incorporated on December 7, 1809, by an Act entrusting its better regulation to the following board of commissioners: Frederick Beall, Samson Lane, Benjamin Dorsey, Dudley Jones, and Andy Williamson.[2] The town was named for Judge Thomas P. Carnes, a noted Congressman and jurist of the early days.

FULTON

Atlanta.   As stated in Volume I, of this work, Atlanta was the offspring of railways, and was first called Terminus, afterwards, Marthasville. The latter town was incorporated by an Act approved December 23, 1843, with the following commissioners: L. V. Gannon, John

---

*J. F. H. Claiborne, in The Cabinet—Past and Present.
[1] Clayton's Compendium, p. 309.
[2] Clayton's Compendium, p. 320.

Bailey, Willis Carlisle, John Kile, Sr., and Patrick Quinn.[1] Later on, the name of the town was changed to Atlanta, and under this name was incorporated as a city by an Act approved December 29, 1847, with provision for its government by a mayor and councilmanic board, consisting of four members. Moses W. Formwalt was the first mayor. It is commonly understood that Atlanta's original charter was drawn by the late Judge John Collier. Until 1853, Atlanta was in DeKalb County; but, when the new county of Fulton was organized under an Act approved December 20, 1853, out of DeKalb and Henry Counties, Atlanta was chosen as the new county-site. The First Baptist church, chartered on January 26, 1850, was the earliest church incorporated. The trustees were: David G. Daniel, Ira O. McDaniel, Fred Kicklighter, Alfred W. Woodin, and James S. Baker.[2] Next came the First Presbyterian church, whose charter was granted on February 10, 1854, with the following board of trustees: John Glenn, Oswald Houston, Julius A. Hayden, James Davis, Joel Kelsey, George Robinson, and Wm. Markham.[3] There is no record of a charter for the Methodists, but they were here in the very beginning and afterwards acquired the property which was at first jointly owned by the several denominations in common, on the site of the present Candler building, where the First Methodist church long stood. The present school system of Atlanta was established in 1872.

"Gate City": When the Sobriquet was First Used. At a meeting of some of the early pioneers, held at the Kimball House, on the evening of April 24, 1871, soon after the original structure was completed, quite a number of spicy reminiscences of the ante-bellum days were revived. To the fund of

---

[1] Acts, 1843, p. 83.
[2] Acts, 1849-1850, p. 76.
[3] Acts, 1853-1854, p. 274.

anecdotes, the following contribution was made by Judge
William Ezzard, an ex-Mayor. Said he:

"The name of the Gate City was first given to Atlanta in Charleston
in 1856, and it came about in this way. When the road was completed
between Charleston and Memphis, the people of Charleston put a hogshead
of water on the car, together with a fire-engine, and accompanied them to
Memphis for the purpose of mingling the waters of the Atlantic with the
waters of the Mississippi. In the year 1857 the Mayor of Memphis, with
quite a number of ladies in the party, came to Atlanta, en route to Charleston, carrying water from the Mississippi, and they also carried a fire-
engine for the purpose of mingling the waters of the Mississippi with the
waters of the Atlantic. They arrived about 12 o'clock. I was then Mayor
of Atlanta, and we gave them a reception and prepared a handsome colla-
tion for them. The next morning they left for Charleston. I went with
them. There were also several others in the party from Atlanta. We arrived in Charleston, and had a grand time there. We paraded the streets,
marched down to the bay, and then went through the ceremony of pumping
this water from the Mississippi into the ocean. There were a great many
people present on this occasion; they came from all parts of Georgia and
from all parts of South Carolina; and a grand banquet was given by the
people of Charleston. Everything was well arranged. There was a toast
drafted for Savannah, one for Macon, one for Augusta, and one for Atlanta, and so on. The toast prepared and given for Atlanta was: 'The
Gate City—the only tribute which she requires of those who pass through
her boundaries is that they stop long enough to partake of the hospitality
of her citizens.' This was the substance of the toast. I may not recall the
exact language. After that Atlanta was always called the Gate City, and it
was never known as that before. I responded to this toast for Atlanta. It
was given, I suppose, from the fact that this railroad had just been constructed through the mountains, for the purpose of connecting the West
with the Atlantic seaboard, and there was no way to get to either place
except to pass through Atlanta.' "*

"Peachtree:"   There is little room for doubt concerning
Its Derivation.   the source from which the name of At-
                      lanta's thoroughfare was derived. In the
early days of the last century, an Indian village, called
the standing Peachtree, stood just to the North of the

History of Atlanta and Its Pioneers, published by the Pioneer Citizens
Society, p. 210.

city's present site. The stream which meandered near the village was called Peachtree Creek, while the path which led to it through the forest was called Peachtree Trail. With the influx of population, the path was eventually widened into Peachtree Road, a thoroughfare which is today lined with some of the most palatial and elegant homes to be found south of Baltimore.

To cite authorities: Dr. Abiel Sherwood, in his quaint little work entitled "Sherwood's Gazeteer," published in 1830, states, on page 103, that the town of Decatur was then "95 miles northwest of Milledgeville, 25 miles southwest of Lawrenceville, 9 miles southwest of Rock Mountain, and 12 miles east of the Standing Peachtree on the Chattahoochee." The author prints the words "Standing Peachtree" in capitals, just as in the case of the towns mentioned. Moreover, since the various roads entering Atlanta, viz., the Roswell, the Marietta, the Decatur, the McDonough, were each named for the towns to which they led, the same, especially in the light of other evidence, must be inferentially true of Peachtree.

But there is still another witness. At the outbreak of the War of 1812, Governor George R. Gilmer, who was then barely of age, received a lieutenant's commission; and as soon as enough recruits were collected an order was issued for them to be put in charge of an officer, and sent into the Indian country, where active hostilities were going on against the Creeks. Says Gov. Gilmer:[*]

"I asked for the command and received it. I marched with twenty-two recruits, having no arms, except refuse drill muskets, a small quantity of loose powder, and some unmolded lead. My appointed station was on the banks of the Chattahoochee, about thirty or forty miles beyond the frontier, near an Indian town, not far from where the Georgia Railroad [meaning Western and Atlantic], now crosses the Chattahoochee River." It was an awkward business for one who had only seen a militia muster and who had never fired a musket. I was ordered to build a fort. I had never seen a fort, and had no means of knowing how to obey the order but what I could get from Duane's Tactics. I went to work and succeeded very well, so far as I know, as the strength and fitness of my fortification was never tested. Some few days after my arrival at the standing peachtree, a rough Indian fellow came into the camp with some fine catfish for sale. I had supplied myself with hook and line for catching cat in the Chattahoochee before I left home, and had bated and hung them from limbs

---

[*]Gilmer's "Georgians."

into the water. I had noticed this fellow the day before gliding stealthily along near the bank of the river, in a small canoe, where the lines with baited hooks were hung. I intimated to him that the fish he was offering to sell were taken from my hooks. With demoniac looks of hatred and revenge, he drew his knife from his belt, and holding it for a moment in the position for striking, turned the edge to his own throat, and drew it across; expressing thus more forcibly than he could have done by words his desire to cut my throat. I never saw him afterwards.'"

The Atlanta Campaign.   When Grant was made commander-in-chief of the armies of the United States, Sherman succeeded him in the chief command at the West, and, under Sherman, were three armies with three superb commanders: the Army of Tennessee, under McPherson; the Army of the Cumberland, under Thomas, and the Army of the Ohio, formerly under Burnside, but now commanded by Schofield. At the beginning of May, 1864, this triple army covered a line about twenty miles in length, a little south of Chattanooga: McPherson on the right, with 25,000 men; Thomas in the center, with 60,000, and Schofield on the left, with 15,000; in all, 100,000 men, with 260 guns. Opposed to this force was a Confederate army, under command of Joseph E. Johnston, who, among the Southern generals, ranked next in ability to Lee. It was generally understood by the public that Sherman's grand object in this campaign was the capture of Atlanta, the principal city of Georgia between the mountains and the sea-coast. But Grant and Sherman well knew that an even more important object was the destruction or capture of Johnston's army, and this was likely to be no light task. Johnston was a master of Fabian strategy, whom it was next to impossible to bring to battle unless he saw a good chance of winnuing.'"

Hood Supersedes Johnston.   Despite the masterful tactics of Johnston, in opposing the march of Sherman from Dalton to Atlanta, there was great dissatisfaction over what seemed to be the failure of the former to accomplish definite results, notwithstanding the heavy odds which confronted him. With President Davis he had never been a favorite; and, on July 17, 1864, when the two hostile armies stood before

---

[1] On page 257, the same authority speaks of a meeting of the chiefs of the Standing Peachtree with two or three chiefs of the neighboring villages.
[2] The Mississippi Valley in the Civil War, by John Fiske, pp. 324-325.

Atlanta, the President felt constrained to relieve him of the command, appointing in his stead an intrepid soldier: John B. Hood, who was expected to conduct an aggressive campaign. His reputation as a fighter was well established and his appointment carried with it the understanding that defensive tactics were to be abandoned. It is said that Sherman, on hearing of the change, made this remark: "Heretofore, the fighting has been as Johnston pleased, but hereafter it shall be as I please." When the news reached the Union army, it undoubtedly formed the subject of some conversation between Sherman and McPherson, as they sat on the steps of the porch of a country house. In allusion to the incident, Sherman himself says in his "Memoirs": We agreed that we ought to be unusually cautious and prepared for hard fighting, because Hood, though not deemed much of a scholar, or of great mental capacity, was undoubtedly a brave, determined, and rash man." General O. O. Howard in "Battles and Leaders of the Civil War," comments thus: "Just at this time, much to our comfort and to his surprise, Johnston was removed and Hood put in command of the Confederate army." In the light of subsequent events, the judgment of Mr. Davis in making the change, is at least open to criticism; and, to quote the language of Henry R. Goetchius, a distinguished student of the campaign: "Who knows but what the history of the Confederate States of America might have been written differently had not the criticism of the rash, the thoughtless and the ignorant been allowed to lead to a substitution of the Confederate Fabius with a brave, but impetuous Varro."*

The Battles Around Atlanta. On July 20, 1864, Hood attacked the Federal army at Peachtree Creek, near Atlanta, and then began the struggle for the prize of war. There followed a week of desul-

*Sherman's Memoirs, Vol. II, p. 75; Battles and Leaders of the Civil War, Vol. IV, p. 313; Johnston's Narrative, etc.

tory fighting, in which he lost perhaps 8,000 men and accomplished nothing. Says Professor Derry: "Through bad management the attack was not made as promptly as Hood desired, nor with as good results; for the Confederates were repulsed with heavy loss." For the defence of the city over 10,000 State troops had been placed in the trenches, cannon had been obtained, and supplies made ready for the anticipated assault. Major-General Gustavus J. Smith commanded the State militia and General Toombs, at this time, was on his staff. The four brigades of State troops were commanded by the following officers: R. W. Carswell, P. J. Phillips, C. D. Anderson, and H. K. McCay. Besides these, there were several Georgia regiments in the Confederate army under General Hood, and they served throughout the campaign. Quite a number of Georgians, with the rank of Brigadier-General, participated in the battles around Atlanta, among them, Alfred Iverson, Jr., Hugh W. Mercer, M. A. Stovall, John K. Jackson, Alfred Cumming, Claudius C. Wilson, Robert H. Anderson, Henry R. Jackson, and B. M. Thomas. Lieutenant-Generals Joseph Wheeler and William J. Hardee were both in these engagements; and Major-General W. H. T. Walker. On July 22, occurred one of the most terrific engagements of the entire war. Both sides fought with grim determination. It was Hood's plan to drive Sherman back toward the Tennessee line, but at the close of the day he was still where the morning found him.

Walker and McPherson Killed: Battle-Field Memorials. Two of the ablest commanding officers of the Civil War fell, on July 22, in the heat of this renowned engagement. Major-General James B. McPherson was killed while making a reconnoisance near the skirmish line of the Confederates. He was ordered to surrender; but, raising his hand as if to salute, he wheeled about and galloped off. Instantly a volley of muskets was discharged, and the brave officer fell from his horse to the ground, bleeding from several wounds. Both Sherman and Grant placed the highest estimate upon his abilities.

The other distinguished soldier who was numbered among the slain was Major-General Wm. H. T. Walker, a Georgian. He was gallantly leading an attack upon the Federals, who occupied the crest of a hill, when he was shot in the thigh. As he fell to the ground, he was caught by an officer, who, in the act of leaning toward him, was shot in the head. The body of General Walker was sent to Augusta, for burial; but the spot on which he fell, about two miles east of Atlanta, has been appropriately marked. The memorial consists of a cannon mounted upon a pedestal of granite and surrounded by an iron railing. At each corner of the base is a pyramid of cannon-balls. On the south side is this inscription:

In Memory of
MAJOR-GENERAL WM. H. T. WALKER,
C. S. A.

On the north side is inscribed the following:

Born, November 26, 1816
Killed on this spot
July 22, 1864.

The monument was erected some few years ago, by the veterans of Camp Walker. In like manner, the place where General McPherson fell has been marked. It is half a mile distant on the same tragic field. This monument was erected by the United States Government. In honor of the same gallant officer, the local military post bears the name of Fort McPherson. Lieutenant-Colonel John M. Brown, a brother of Georgia's war Governor, was also among the victims, while Brigadier-General Hugh W. Mercer was severely wounded.

Applying the Torch to Atlanta: A Metropolis in Flames. When Hood left the fated city, on the night of September 1, 1864, he started toward the Tennessee line, his object being to force Sherman to quit Georgia, in order to protect his base of supplies. It was an unexpected development. The wily commander was somewhat perplexed; but instead of starting in pursuit, he ordered Thomas to follow Hood, while he kept his clutch upon Atlanta. Then it was that the idea of continuing his triumphant march to the ocean front fired his brain; and, after receiving Grant's permission to undertake the movement, provided Thomas was left sufficiently strong to cope with Hood in Tennessee, he began to make preparations. The city's destruction was resolved upon; and, on September 4, an order was issued requiring the departure of all citizens, save such as were in the employ of the Federal government. Those who did not choose to go South, were sent North. Only the smallest amount of personal property could be taken away. This ruthless expulsion of over twelve thousand people, some of whom were entirely without means, worked the most grievous hardships; and, though Mayor Calhoun urged a revocation of the order, his appeal was fruitless.

Then began the fiendish work of incendiarism. The torch was remorselessly applied. To quote Colonel Clarke: "What could not be consumed by fire was blown up, torn down, or otherwise destroyed. No city during the war was so nearly annihilated. The central part or business locality was an entire mass of ruins, there being only a solitary structure standing on our main street, Whitehall, between its extreme commercial limits. At least three-fourths of the buildings in the city were destroyed, the remainder consisting chiefly of dwelling houses. Father O'Reilly was instrumental in saving the Catholic and several Protestant churches, and also the City Hall. The Medical College was saved through the efforts of Dr. N. D'Alvigny. Atlanta was left a scene of charred and desolate ruins, the home of half-starved and half-wild dogs, who, with the carrion crows, feasted upon the refuse, together with the decaying carcasses of animals.''[1]

Sherman's March to the Sea Begins. On November 15, 1864, with sixty thousand men, Sherman left the smouldering ruins of Atlanta behind and started upon his devastating march to the sea. The port of Savannah became his objective point. Cutting a swath forty miles wide, his army marched like a pestilence through Georgia, destroying what could not be utilized for food. Crops were laid waste, farmhouses burned, and whole villages wrecked. Horses were seized; and cows and hogs were either used for food or left dead in the field. Thieves who followed the army, or belonged to its lowest elements, reveled in the plunder of silver chests or other receptacles in which valuables were stored. The track of desolation was three hundred miles in length; and Sherman, in his report, said: ''I estimate the damage done to the State of Georgia at one hundred million dollars.''[2]

Atlanta Becomes the State Capital. During the war period, Atlanta was an important depot of supplies. Its destruction by General Sherman emphasized its value not only from the strategic but equally from the commercial point of view; and, furthermore, under the regime of reconstruction, it was the chief abode of the military power. Between the two oceans there was scarcely a point on the map which was better known in newspaper circles.

Consequently, when the Constitutional Convention of 1868 assembled in Atlanta, the city again sued for the coveted boon. The council agreed to furnish the necessary buildings, well equipped for the purpose, and without cost to the State for ten years; these to include a residence for the Governor, a receptacle for the State Library, and convenient quarters for the executive, leg-

---

[1] E. Y. Clarke, in Illustrated History of Atlanta; Wallace P. Reed, T. H. Martin, etc.; also John Fiske in the The Mississippi Valley in the Civil War.

[2] Lawton B. Evans, in History of Georgia for Schools: Isaac W. Avery, in History of Georgia, 1850-1881.

islative, and judicial departments. The fullest protection was also guaranteed for the safety of important State documents and papers. The council agreed further to donate the old fair grounds, containing twenty-five acres, on which to erect the new capitol building, or in lieu thereof, any unoccupied ten acres within the city limits which the General Assembly might prefer. By resolution adopted on February 27, 1868, the convention accepted the city's offer; and, in the Constitution, which was subsequently ratified at the polls, an article was inserted making Atlanta the seat of government. Thus the battle was won.

In 1889, the new capitol building, a structure of magnificent proportions in every respect, worthy of the great commonwealth, was completed on the south side of the town and on the site of the old City Hall Park, for years the seat of legislation in local affairs. The ground is somewhat elevated at this point, giving to the lordly dome, which crowns the massive pile, an appropriate setting. It is to be regretted that the building is not constructed entirely of Georgia stone, the quarries of this State having become so famous that many public building throughout the Union have made use of our home products. But the vast marble and granite resources of Georgia were not sufficiently developed at this time to meet competition. Hence oolitic limestone was substituted; an excellent material of great durability and strength, obtained from Indiana. However, the interior finish of the building shows the exquisite beauty of ornamentation which belongs to Georgia marble. The magnitude of the building is such that the demands for space can be met for years to come, however great the increase in the volume of official business. The labor of construction occupied five years. But so care-

Unbesmirched by Graft: Georgia's Capitol a Monument to Official Integrity.

fully was the work supervised by the men to whom this important responsibility was entrusted, that the structure was not only built within the figures of the original appropriation, but an unexpended residue of several thousand dollars was left in the treasury, to challenge the admiration of an age of graft. Thus an object-lesson is presented to New York, to Pennsylvania, and to other States, in which similar enterprises have furnished the opportunity for unlimited corruption. The following distinguished Georgians constituted the commission: Governor Henry D. McDaniel, General Philip Cook, General E. P. Alexander, Captain Evan P. Howell, Hon. W. W. Thomas, and Judge A. L. Miller. The cornerstone of the building was laid with masonic ceremonies in 1884, and the oration was delivered by the polished and eloquent General Alexander R. Lawton, of Savannah. Carpeted with grass and ornamented with shrubs and plants the area surrounding the capitol building has been made very attractive, at small expense, by the exercise of good taste and judgment, together with watchful attention.

Atlanta's Great Newspapers. There will be no one to question the statement that much of Atlanta's phenomenal growth since the Civil War has been due to her great newspapers. These have proven an effective supplement to her railroads; for they have not only been king-makers in the world of politics, but powerful factors in the sphere of industrial economics. They have fostered great civic movements; they have embodied progressive ideals; they have set the pace for newspapers in other parts of the South, and while seeking primarily to build up Atlanta, they have stimulated the forces of development throughout the entire Piedmont region.

But the Gate City of the South was long a death-trap for journalistic experiments.

It is needless to go behind the Civil War period in search of testimony to support this statement. However, there are not a few items of interest to be found in the ante-bellum regime of newspaperdom. Atlanta's earliest

---

Isaac W. Avery, in History of Georgia, 1850-1861; Lawton B. Evans, in History of Georgia for Schools; E. Y. Clarke, in Illustrated Atlanta; Wallace P. Reed, Thos. H. Martin, newspaper files, etc.

sheet—published in 1845—was the *Luminary,* a somewhat crude affair, of which the Reverend Joseph Baker was the editor, and he used in printing it a small hand press. But the beams of this pioneer beacon were soon extinguished. Its successors were legion, but they were uniformly short-lived. Atlanta for years became a sort of infirmary for sick newspapers and a grave-yard for dead ones. Even the *Southern Miscellany,* brought to Atlanta from Madison and edited by the afterwards famous William T. Thompson, proceeded almost instanter to give up the ghost—though an artistic success. *The Intelligencer,* a newspaper founded in the early fifties and edited for quite awhile by J. I. Whitaker, managed to weather successfully the storm of Civil War, but went down under the incubus of Reconstruction. It was on this paper that Colonel John H. Seals—who afterwards edited *The Sunny South*—earned his journalistic spurs. The Southern Confederacy, another war-time sheet, acquired wide note. It was often printed on brown paper, but was read throughout the Confederate lines. Colonel George W. Adair and Mr. J. Henly Smith were the owners, On its editorial staff was the present world-renowned dean of American newspaperdom, Henry Watterson—then a youthful novitiate, serving his apprenticeship to the pen. Two of Atlanta's most prominent business men —John H. James and B. B. Crew—first began to show the metal which was in them on this famous paper. It also possessed a poet of no mean gifts in the well-known A. R. Watson.

But it died.

History repeated itself after the war. There was no decline for years in the number of newspaper obsequies and interments. Even the first journalistic effort of the brilliant Grady—who undertook to launch the *Herald*—proved to be a tragic disaster. His associate, Robert A. Alston, a man of gifts, who scathingly denounced the convict-lease system, was afterwards killed in the State Capitol by Captain Ed. Cox. It was when the *Herald's* last issue appeared that Mr. Grady penned his famous epigram: ''General Toombs loaned like a Prince and collected like a shylark.'' In 1872 Alexander H. Stephens entered the local arena. He acquired from Judge Cincinnatus Peeples the famous Atlanta *Sun,* in order to fight the election of Horace Greeley; but straightway the orb began to set. It is no exaggeration to say that at least a score of newspapers have been decently buried in Atlanta since Sherman's visit. The first daily publication to take vigorous root and to acquire permanent lodgings above ground was the *Constitution.*

This famous old daily was founded in the summer of 1868. Its first editor was Carey W. Styles, while W. A. Hemphill and J. H. Anderson managed the business interests. Colonel Hemphill retained his connection with the paper for more than three decades. J. R. Barrick, I. W. Avery, and E. Y. Clarke, each in succession, directed the editorial policy of the paper for the first eight years. Major Barrick was a Kentuckian by birth and a poet by grace. In 1876 Captain Evan P. Howell acquired Colonel Clarke's interest and became editor-in-chief. With his wonderful insight into men, Captain Howell soon gathered about him a galaxy of gifted writers. It was at this time that Joel Chandler Harris, refugeeing from Savannah to escape the ravages of yellow fever, came to Atlanta, where he was soon annexed to the staff and began to write the name of Uncle Remus the famous dialect stories which were destined to carry his name around the globe. Henry W. Grady and Samuel W. Small were also discovered by this keen-eyed man of affairs; and it was not long before P. J. Moran was added to the group. In 1889 came one with a song, in the person of the gifted Frank L. Stanton, who still edits his famous column—"Just from Georgia."

Not long after the paper was launched N. P. T. Finch bought an interest and became associate editor; but eventually he left Atlanta for the West, selling his interest to Mr. S. M. Inman—ever a friend to Atlanta's great undertakings. In 1880, Henry W. Grady, who had been a space-writer, acquired an interest and became managing editor, a position which he held until his death; and it was largely under the leadership of this journalistic Napoleon that the *Constitution* became a power in newspaperdom. His feats of journalistic enterprise established new precedents, while his editorials—like blasts from a silvery bugle—thrilled and electrified the State. He was succeeded at the helm by Clarke Howell, the present superbly-equipped editor-in-chief. Captain E. P. Howell eventually retired, and Hugh T. Inman then acquired an interest, which, in turn, passed to the Bunnigan estate. In 1902 Colonel Hemphill's interest was purchased by Clark Howell, in association with Roby Robinson, the latter becoming business manager. Ten years later, Mr. Robinson relinquished this office, retaining, however, his interest; and Mr. James R. Holiday was duly installed as his successor.

In 1883 rose the *Atlanta Journal*, founded as an afternoon paper by Colonel E. F. Hoge, a prominent member of the local bar. But Colonel Hoge's health failed. The ownership then passed to John Paul Jones, who two years later sold it to a syndicate, including Hoke Smith, H. H. Cabaniss, Charles A. Collier, Jacob Haas and others. Josiah Carter was made managing editor, and the brilliant F. H. Richardson also began at this time his long connection with the paper as its chief editorial writer. Mr. Smith became president of the corporation and Mr. Cabaniss the business manager. It is due to the powerful leverage which the *Journal* developed in the Presidential campaign of 1892 that Mr. Smith—who directed the policy of the paper—was invited to enter the Cabinet of Mr. Cleveland as Secretary of the Interior. This was the beginning of his distinguished career in national politics. Twice after this he became Governor of Georgia, and on the first Monday in December, 1911, he took his seat in the Senate of the United States. In 1900 both Mr. Smith and Mr. Cabaniss retired. The paper was then sold to H. M. Atkinson, Morris Brandon and James R. Gray, after which other changes followed; but Mr. Gray still remains at the helm as editor and president.

In 1906 the *Georgian* was founded as an afternoon paper by Mr. F. L. Seely, who associated with him Colonel John Temple Graves as editor. The latter—equally famed for his versatile pen and for his rare eloquence on the platform—was soon coveted by the metropolis of the nation, and in 1908 resigned his chair to become editor of the *New York American*, the greatest of the Hearst papers. Soon after the *Georgian* was founded, Mr. Seely acquired by purchase the *Atlanta News*, of which Colonel Graves had formerly been the editor; and the two papers were then combined. It must be said to the credit of this latest entry in the newspaper lists that in a number of battles for reform it led a victorious and splendid fight, including the crusade for the overthrow of the convict lease system and the campaign for State-wide prohibition. In 1912, Mr. Seely sold the *Georgian* to William Randolph Hearst, of New York. It was on the *Southern Temperance Crusader,* a weekly journal founded in 1858, that gifted novelist and poet, Mrs. Mary E. Bryan, made her bow to the public. She afterwards became a contributor to the columns of the *Sunny South,* a weekly periodical founded by Colonel John H. Seals in 1875 and purchased by the *Constitution* some quarter of a century later. This paper was long a fireside companion throughout the South. During the late sixties, *The Christian Index,* Georgia's pioneer religious journal, came from Penfield to Atlanta, where it is still edited; and in 1906 Joel Chandler Harris founded the *Uncle Remus Magazine,* for some time edited and published by his eldest son, Julian Harris, who inherits in no small degree the paternal genius.

Atlanta's First Memorial Day. Atlanta's first Memorial Day was observed on April 26, 1866, just one year after Gen. Johnston's surrender. The moving spirit in this pioneer celebration was Mrs. Joseph H. Morgan, a gentle lady whose whole life has been unselfishly devoted to good deeds. Mrs. Morgan has seen nearly fifty recurring aniversaries of Memorial Day, but her heart is still young in its beautiful enthusiasm for a Lost Cause, while her labor of love for the boys in gray has never known a moment's languor or weariness. As Miss Eugenia Goode, she was for three years secretary of the Atlanta Hospital Association, a relief society of which the beloved Mrs. Isaac Winship was president. On April 15, 1866, inspired by a letter from the pen of Mrs. Charles J. Williams, of Columbus, advocating a Memorial Day, Mrs. Morgan requested Mrs. W. W. Clayton, with her two daughters, Julia and Sallie, afterwards Mrs. Hoge and Mrs. Crane, to unite with her in calling the ladies of Atlanta together. Accordingly a meeting was held at which initial steps were taken.

Re-enforced by Mrs. John N. Simmons, the above named ladies, within two days, raised $350 out of a poverty-stricken town with which to put the cemetery in order and to meet necessary expenses. Mrs. Morgan, with her father and mother, Major and Mrs. Hamilton Goode, the Misses Clayton, and others, went day after day to the cemetery, often taking a light lunch with them; and in person directed the hired labor until they had cleared the ground where the known Confederate dead were buried. Cedar, out of which to make wreathes, was brought from Stone Mountain to Atlanta, free of charge, by the Georgia Railroad. Both of the local papers espoused the movement and urged the merchants of Atlanta to observe the day by a general closing of stores. There was no formal oration at the cemetery, due to positive orders from the Federal officers. But Col. E. F. Hoge, in a few well-chosen words, introduced the chaplain of the occasion, Rev. Robert Q. Mallard, pastor of the Central Presbyterian church, who offered a most eloquent prayer, prefaced by a few opening remarks.

As the immediate result of this simple service over the graves of the dead, there was formed in Atlanta, within the next few days a Memorial Association constituted as follows: President, Dr. J. P. Logan; 1st Vice-President, Mrs. Joseph H. Morgan; 2nd Vice-President, Mrs. E. B. Walker; 3rd Vice-President, Mrs. J. N. Simmons. Besides, there was chosen a board of directors, with the following members, to wit: Gen. G. T. Anderson, Col. John S. Prather, Col. E. F. Hoge, Major Austin Leyden, Capt. W. M. Williams, Dr. J. G. Westmoreland, Mrs. R.

Bass, Mrs. J. M. Johnson, and Mrs. W. F. Westmoreland.
Dr. J. P. Logan promptly declined the executive honors.
whereupon Mrs. Joseph H. Morgan was elected president, an office which she filled for two years.   In the
spring of 1868, she relinquished her official duties on account of a contemplated absence from the city for an
indefinite length of time, but she had given the work its
initial impetus.   On returning to Atlanta, she resumed
her place in the ranks, where she has ever since been tire-
less in her manifold activities.   Mrs. Morgan's successors in office have been as follows: Mrs. John B. Gordon,
Mrs. J. M. Johnson, Mrs. W. W. Clayton, Mrs. John
Milledge, and Mrs. W. D. Ellis.   The last named lady has
now been president of the Memorial Association for
nearly twenty years.   One whose name does not appear
in the above list, but who, until her removal to Chattanooga was an unwearied worker in the ranks was Mrs.
George T. Fry.   Though still open to some dispute, Atlanta's Memorial Association was probably the first one
organized as such in the Southern States.

Re-Interring   During Mrs. Morgan's tenure of office, the
the Dead.   building of a monument was first projected.   But the most imperative obligation
at this time binding upon them was the re-interment of
the dead soldiers then lying in the trenches around Atlanta.   Accordingly, a petition was made to the city
council for an additional area of ground in which to re-
inter the dead bodies.   This request was granted.   But
due to a lack of funds the work of removal was postponed
for another year.   In the meantime, Major Joseph H.
Morgan painted and lettered five hundred head-boards
with which to mark the graves of his fallen comrades.
When the task of removing the dead bodies from the
trenches around the city was at last undertaken, Mrs.
John M. Johnson became the most conspicuous figure in
the activities of this period.   Mrs. Johnson was the wife

of a much-beloved physician of Atlanta and a sister of
two noted Confederate Generals: Howell and Thomas R.
R. Cobb. With a spirit which never once flagged, Mrs.
Johnson superintended in her own person the work of removing the dead bodies. The sphere of her operations
covered an area of ten miles around Atlanta. There was
hardly a square foot of ground which she left unvisited.
In some of the trenches, Mrs. Johnson found as many as
eighty or a hundred soldiers, wrapped in war-blank-
ets, with their hands crossed and with their caps over
their faces. Lumber was needed for boxes; and since
none was to be obtained at this time in Atlanta, Mrs.
Johnson went to Stone Mountain, where she succeeded
in obtaining supplies. She then supervised the making
of boxes into which, first and last, some three thousand
Confederate soldiers were reverently gathered and given
the rites of Christian burial. When the dead bodies were
re-interred, council granted the ladies permission to sub-
divide the unoccupied ground into lots and to offer the
same for sale. Out of the proceeds arising from this
source, they were enabled to place marble head-stones
over the graves, to unveil the Lion of Lucerne as a memorial to the unknown dead and to make other needed improvements without calling upon the public for aid.

———

Atlanta's Con- On April 26, 1874, the magnificent
federate Monuments. granite shaft in Oakland Cemetery
was unveiled to the memory of the
Confederate dead. Hon. Thomas Hardeman, Jr., of Macon, was the orator of the occasion, introduced to the assemblage by Col. Robt. A. Alston; while the prayer of invocation was offered by Gen. Clement A. Evans. The
monument is sixty-five feet in height. It is Romanesque
in style, resting upon a base twenty feet square, from
which it rises in a series of six gradations, is built of

Stone Mountain granite, devoid of ornamentation, and contains only this inscription:

> OUR CONFEDERATE DEAD—1873.

From base to apex, it represents a free-will offering to the South's heroic dead. The granite was donated by the Stone Mountain Granite Company and transported free of charge by the Georgia Railroad. Mr. Wm. Gay, the designer, donated both the tablet and the inscription. Dr. Amos Fox assumed the contract for its erection and Mr. Calvin Fay gave his services as supervising architect. The total cost of the monument was only $8,000 though it represented a minimum value of little less than $20,000. Concerts, teas, suppers, charades, moon-light picnics—these were some of the ways in which the money was realized. The corner-stone of the monument was laid on the day of Gen. Lee's funeral, at which time the oration was delivered by one of his greatest lieutenants—Gen. John B. Gordon. Some of the men of Atlanta who were unremitting in the help which they gave to the Ladies' Memorial Association were: Major Tom Williams, Capt. Wm. Williams, Mr. Charles Herbst, Mr. A. R. Watson, Col. E. Y. Clarke, Col. John S. Prather, Major Austin Leyden, Col. George W. Adair, Col. Thomas C. Howard, Mr. Neil Robson, Major Hamilton Goode, Judge W. W. Clayton, Major Joseph H. Morgan, Dr. Amos Fox, Gen. Wm. S. Walker, Col. E. F. Hoge, Mr. B. A. Pratte, Major W. D. Luckie, Mr. Anthony Murphy, and others. These names deserve to be embalmed in Atlanta's grateful remembrance. Two other Confederate monuments typifying the love of Georgia's capital city for the wearers of the gray are the Lion of Lucerne, unveiled to the Unknown Dead, in Oakland cemetery, and the handsome monument erected by the Confederate veterans to the private soldier of the South, in Westview.

Miss Junia McKin- To be honored with a bronze memor-
ley: Her D. A. R. ial tablet in the capitol of a great
Memorial. State is a goal of ambition which few
can ever hope to attain; but such is
the tribute which an appreciative public sentiment has
paid to one of the noblest of Georgia's gentle women:
Miss Junia McKinley. On December 2, 1909, Piedmont
Continental Chapter, D. A. R., by special permission of
the State authorities, placed this handsome tablet on
the walls of the State Library, near its main entrance.
Inscribed upon the tablet, in beautiful raised letters, is
the following record:

> In grateful remembrance of our beloved founder,
> MISS JUNIA McKINLEY. 1854-1907. One of the
> foremost genealogists, Daughters of the American Revo-
> lution organizers, educators and patriotic relief workers
> in the Spanish-American War.
>
> ───────────
>
> This tablet is erected by Piedmont Continental Chap-
> ter, Daughters of the American Revolution, Atlanta,
> December, 1909.

But the wording of this memorial is entirely too brief
to be more than merely suggestive. When the tablet was
unveiled by Piedmont Continental Chapter, Governor Joseph M. Brown made the speech of acceptance for the
State, while Hon. Hugh V. Washington, of Macon, Ga.,
made the speech of presentation. Mrs. Lewis D. Lowe,
Regent of the Chapter, and Mrs. William Lawson Peel,
Honorary State Regent, also delivered short addresses,
rich in tender memories. There was a large assemblage
present, completely filling the spacious hall.

These exercises constituted an extraordinary tribute,
but one fully deserved. In the ranks of her patriotic
order, Miss McKinley was a pioneer. She founded Atlanta Chapter, the oldest in the State, organized on the
same day which witnessed the birth of the chapter in
New York. When the movement was in its infancy she
cherished it, loved it, brought to it her own marvelous

resources of strength. When others faltered, she stood firm; when hope flickered in other hearts, her own enthusiasm blazed the brighter. If she did not foresee its future destiny, she at least realized its inherent claims, its manifold possibilities. For months she united in her own person the various offices of her chapter and carried upon her willing shoulders the weight of its combined activities; but she found her reward in the joy of service and at the time of her death was honorary State Regent of the D. A. R.

Miss McKinley was also a gifted educator. At the age of sixteen she organized a private school which she conducted most successfully for more than twenty years. Her work was always along constructive lines. During the Spanish-American War—impelled by the spirit of Florence Nightingale—she established the D. A. R. Hospital Corps of Atlanta Chapter, becoming its vice-president. She gave her entire time to relief work at Fort McPherson and under the auspices of the American Red Cross, opened a diet kitchen for the invalid soldiers. In recognition of her work she received the appreciative thanks of a grateful government, engraved upon parchment. Miss McKinley was a kinswoman of the great President whose life, like her own, went out ere it registered its maturest powers. Her day was brief—too brief; but, from dawn to dusk, it was full of the summer's radiance, its precious moments were garnered, its golden opportunities were met, and it ended calmly, with the white promise of the stars.

Woodrow Wilson:
An Incident in His
Career as a Lawyer.
Woodrow Wilson, the twenty-eighth President of the United States, began his career as a lawyer in Georgia's State capital. He was formally admitted to the bar in 1882; and his license to practice law in the courts of this State bears the signature of Hon. George Hillyer, Judge of the Atlanta

Circuit. Entering into a legal partnership with a brilliant young barrister like himself, Edward J. Renick, the professional shingle of the new firm was displayed from a modest office on the second floor of the old Hulsey building, on the corner of Broad and Marietta Streets. But there was no immediate rush of clients, and becoming discouraged as weeks lengthened into months without materially swelling the bank account of either, they decided to dissolve the partnership agreement and to set out in quest of new pastures.

Mr. Renick became in after years assistant Secretary of State under President Cleveland. Still later he was made special representative of the great banking house of Coudert Brothers. He died in the city of Paris while on a very important mission concerning the Gould interests, and his death was deplored on both sides of the water. Mr. Wilson went to Baltimore, to pursue a special course of study at Johns Hopkins. He was then called to an adjunct professorship of history at Bryn Mawr; thence in 1888 he went to Wesleyan University, at Middletown, Conn., where he taught political science; and two years later accepted the chair of jurisprudence and politics at Princeton, relinquishing this chair in 1902, to become President of the Institution. The policy of his administration was to make this great seat of learning a Democracy. On account of a disagreement with his board of trustees touching a matter which he considered too vital to admit of compromise or surrender, he resigned the helm of affairs, only to be tendered the Democratic nomination for Governor of New Jersey.

Since his entry into politics, the career of President Wilson has been an open book. The following incident of his sojourn in Atlanta is taken from the files of the Constitution, under date of November 6, 1912:

"Two years after his arrival here the tariff commission appointed by President Hayes to visit the various sections of the country and report of the tariffs workings came to Atlanta and sent out invitations asking any one interested to meet with them and ;point' out unjust discriminations as they saw them. John W. H. Underwood was the Georgia member of the commission. When the board assembled in the convention hall of the Kimball House they were greeted by a single man, come to talk over the tariff. For two hours or more he fired question after question at the tariff experts, turned the 'evidence meeting' into a debate between himself and the board and showed those gentlemen just what the situation was in the South, says Henry Peeples, one of Atlanta's best-known attorneys, in recalling the scene:

" 'What is your name?'' asked the commission of the young man.

" 'I am Woodrow Wilson, a lawyer,' he answered.''

Though a native of Virginia, where he was born at Staunton, in the renowned Valley, the greater part of the President's boyhood was spent in Georgia. His father, Dr. Joseph R. Wilson, was a noted Presbyterian minister, who was for years pastor of a church in Augusta. Here the future president received his elementary education, and one of his teachers at this time was Professor Joseph T. Derry, the famous historian and educator, now of Atlanta. It was in the town of Rome, at the residence of a cousin, that he first met and courted his future wife, then Miss Ellen Louise Axson. The marriage occurred, in 1885, at Savannah, the home of the bride's grand-parents, with whom Miss Axson was then living. Two of his children were born in the town of Gainesville, at the home of an aunt, Mrs. Brown, the mother of Colonel Edward T. Brown, of Atlanta. From this somewhat rapid biographical survey, his complete indentification with Georgia is made apparent, and there is no section of the State which the career of this foremost citizen of the nation has not touched. Illustrious both in politics and in letters, he has written a score of standard books and received the doctor's degree from a dozen world renowned institutions.

Dedicated by a Woman. At a cost considerably in excess of $1,000,000, Fulton County has just completed a magnificent court-house, which will doubtless meet the demands of expansion for the next one hundred years. It is a massive structure of granite, the walls of which will often ring with eloquent appeals from gifted lawyers. But an interesting fact to be noted by the future historian is that the first speech ever made in Fulton County's temple of justice was made by a woman: Mrs. Richard P. Brooks, of Forsyth. On December 9, 1913, when the roof of the building was completed, there was a flag-raising under the auspices of Piedmont Continental Chapter, D. A. R., at which time Georgia's State flag was presented to the State of Georgia, to the County of Fulton, and to the city of Atlanta, by this patriotic organization. General Clifford L. Anderson, chairman of the Board of County Commissioners, presided. The ceremonies were held in the court-house basement, and the programme rendered was as follows:

Address of Presentation, by Mrs. Richard P. Brooks, Regent Piedmont Continental Chapter, D. A. R.

Speech of Acceptance for the city of Atlanta, by Mayor James G. Woodward.

Speech of Acceptance for the County of Fulton and for the State of Georgia, by State Historian, Lucian Lamar Knight.

Remarks, by Mrs. Sheppard W. Foster, State Regent, D. A. R.

Two Great Universities: Oglethorpe and Candler. Besides acquiring one of the twelve regional banks, under the new currency system of the Wilson administration, an achievement which in itself makes Atlanta one of the recognized financial capitals of the land, this favored metropolis has, during the current year, 1914, secured two great educational institutions—Oglethorpe University, a school endowed by the Presbyterians, and Candler University, a school founded by the Methodists. Oglethorpe University was formerly located at Midway, near Milledgeville, Ga.; but, after giving the immortal Sidney Lanier to American literature and educating a future Governor in the person of Joseph M. Brown, it perished amid the wreckage entailed by the great Civil War. During the present year, chiefly through the splendid initiative of one man, Rev. Thornwell Jacobs, D. D., who has made this magnificent project his dream and his passion, Oglethorpe University has been revived in Atlanta, with an endowment, aggregating in small subscriptions, over $1,000,000, besides an extensive campus, at Silver Lake, on Peachtree Road, generously donated by a syndicate owning this beautiful tract of land. It is fully expected that Oglethorpe will become a $5,000,000 plant before a decade has passed.

When the Southern Methodists, in the spring of this year, relinquished Vanderbilt, at Nashville, Tenn., it was decided by the General Conference of the Church to establish two great universities in the South, one on either side of the Mississippi River. Through the munificent liberality of Col. Asa G. Candler, who subscribed $1,000,-000 to the fund—thus making the largest individual gift ever made to education by a Southern man, during his lifetime—Atlanta has secured one of these great schools, while the other one is to be located at Dallas, Tex. Col. Candler's letter, accompanying his gift, thrilled and electrified the whole Christian commonwealth. Its deep religious note and its true ring of piety make it an extraordinary document—one to be treasured in the archives of the Church; but aside from these characteristics its significance is historic. Local pledges have already swelled the subscription to something beyond $2,000,000 and when the canvass of the South-eastern States is completed it will doubtless result in a grand total of $5,000,-000 for this colossal plant. Bishop Warren A. Candler has been placed temporarily at the head of the institution and will doubtless be made its permanent chancellor. As this work goes to press, the choice of a name for the proposed school has not yet been made; but throughout the bounds of the South there is only one voice and one sentiment; and if what seems to be the universal desire of the Church prevails it will bear a name illustrious in Southern Methodism; Candler.

The Burns Memorial Cottage. One of the most unique memorials in existence is located on the outskirts of Atlanta, near the terminus of the Confederate Soldier's Home car line, just half an hour's ride from the town center. It is an exact reproduction in granite of the Ayrshire Cottage, in which the immortal bard of Scotland—humanity's best-loved poet—first saw the light of day. In 1907 the Burns Club, of Atlanta,

THE BURNS MEMORIAL COTTAGE, ATLANTA, GA.

purchased in this neighborhood a tract of thirteen acres, luxuriantly wooded with forest trees, and selling in 1910 a fractional part of this property for a sum equal to three times the cost of the entire original tract of land, a fund was thus provided for erecting the Burns Cottage and for beautifying the adjacent grounds. The corner-stone of the cottage was laid on November 5, 1910, by the Grand Lodge of Georgia Masons, at which time Hon. J. H. Lumpkin, of the Supreme Court of Georgia, paid an eloquent tribute to the memory of the great bard. Three months later, on the evening of January 25, 1911, the cottage was formally dedicated with a dinner, every detail of which was most elaborately planned. The literary address on this occasion was delivered by Lucian Lamar Knight, Esq., in addition to which feature of the program speeches were delivered by the following well-known Georgians, in response to toasts: Hon. John M. Graham, president of the Burns Club; Judge Marcus W. Beck, Judge Richard B. Russell, Judge Arthur G. Powell, Dr. Joseph Jacobs, Dr. E. S. Lynden and others. Two streets, called Ayr Place and Alloway Place, have been opened to the Burns Cottage.

GILMER

Ellijay. On the site of an old Indian village of this name arose the present town of Ellijay. When the new county of Gilmer was created out of the Cherokee lands in 1832, and named for Governor George R. Gilmer, it was found that the center of the county was not far from this Indian village, and accordingly Elljay was made the county-seat. It was incorporated by an Act approved December 20, 1834, with the following commissioners: Wm. P. King, Henry K. Quillian, B. L. Goodman, Nathan Smith, and Joshua Bourn.*
The Gilmer County Academy was incorporated in 1833.

*Acts, 1834, p. 247.

GLASCOCK

Gibson. On December 19, 1857, an Act was approved organizing the new county of Glascock out of lands formerly included in Warren. It was called Glascock in honor of a distinguished soldier and civilian, then recently deceased, Gen. Thomas Glascock, whose father of the same name, was a gallant officer of the Revolution but unfortunately for his reputation, a Yazooist. The new county-seat was called Gibson, in honor of Judge William Gibson, of the Middle Circuit, who gave $500 toward the erection of the court-house.

GLYNN

Brunswick.　　　　　　　　　　　　　　Volume I.

Brunswick's   On November 10, 1906, under the auspices
Liberty Tree.   of Brunswick Chapter, D. A. R., Mrs. E.
F. Coney, regent, there was planted a Liberty Tree, upon which the eyes of the nation have since been fixed with absorbed interest. The soil to nurture the roots of the tree came from every section of the United States and the occasion was one replete with such interest not only from a spectacular but from a patriotic point of view that other localities have since followed the example set by Brunswick, with the result that a new era has been marked in national patriotism. To make the occasion a success the Governors of the various States gladly co-operated in the matter, not only furnishing soil but writing letters of encouragement; and in addition to these letters there were scores of telegrams and messages received by the local chapter. Young ladies from the Brunswick schools were chosen to represent the different States. Dressed in the national colors, Columbia, with her thirteen maids of honor, representing the original colonies, came first, under a military escort,

followed by the band. Then came forty-nine girls, each
bearing a flag and a hand full of soil from the State
which she represented; and passing down the line, to the
music of "America," deposited the soil at the roots of
the Tree. There is a handsome bronze tablet to further
mark this historic spot in the heart of Brunswick, the
significance of which is to remind the youth of our country that sectional estrangement no longer exists and
that in place of it we have today—

> A Union of lakes and a Union of lands,
> A Union of States none can sever;
> A Union of hearts and a Union of hands,
> And the flag of our Union forever!

Memorial of   During the summer of 1913, the historic
Bloody Marsh.   battle-field of Bloody Marsh, on St. Si-
                          mon's Island, was marked by a handsome
granite memorial, unveiled under the auspices of two patriotic organizations: the Georgia Society of Colonial
Dames of America, and the Georgia Society of Colonial
Wars. Hon. Richard D. Meader, of Brunswick, Chancellor of the latter society, delivered the principal address, in which he discussed the far-reaching significance
of this decisive battle, on the Georgia coast. Said he,
among other things:

"The entire population of Georgia in 1750, eight years after Bloody
Marsh, was only 5,000, whereas South Carolina at the same time had 68,000,
North Carolina 80,000 and Virginia 275,000. In 1742 Georgia probably
did not number more than 4,000 inhabitants, so that we have the spectacle
of a small army of 650 men, less than a modern regiment, defending more
than 300,000 people against the attack of a powerful enemy without any
assistance from those people. Assuming that Georgia's population was
4,000 in 1742, it is not probable that the adult male population was more
than one-third that number, so that we see another unusual spectacle, that
of one-half the entire male population being engaged in one force, a proportion which I doubt has ever been equalled in the world's history. Had
this small army of 650 men been killed or captured by the Spaniards, there
could have been no effective resistance from the other parts of the colony,

and Georgia as an English colony would have ceased to exist, while South Carolina and the more northern colonies would have had to fight for their existence.

"Oglethorpe, knowing the overpowering strength of the Spanish and his own weakness, realized the desperate straits he was in and made repeated but fruitless calls for additional troops upon the more northern colonies. Finally realizing that he must rely upon what force he had, in the face of great and impending danger he wrote those brave and memorable words which appear above his name on the monument that we are dedicating today.''

Embedded in the monument is a neat tablet of bronze on which the following inscription is lettered:

> "We are resolved not to suffer defeat. We will rather die like Leonidas and his Spartans, if we but protect Georgia and the Carolinas and the rest of the Americans from desolation."—Oglethorpe.
>
> Erected on the battlefield of Bloody Marsh—by the Georgia Society of Colonel Dames of America and the Georgia Society of Colonial Wars in memory of the great victory won over the Spaniards on this spot July 7, 1742.

The Story of the Dodge Millions.   When William E. Dodge, the great lumber baron who founded the town of St. Simon's, died in the city of New York, he left an estate, the value of which was expressed in eight figures. To share this splendid property there were several children, two of whom were Anson Phelps and Norman B. Dodge. To the first of these was born a son, Anson Phelps, Jr., and to the latter a daughter, who, wedding her first cousin, Anson Phelps, Jr., was the possessor at the time of her marriage, in her own right, of a fortune estimated at not less than three millions. Before many years had elapsed Anson P. Dodge, Jr., who was educated for the Episcopal priesthood, began to feel the lure of the foreign field. The spirit of the missionary became so powerful within him that he finally embarked upon the high seas for India, taking with him his young wife, who was by no means loath to share his lot in distant lands and among alien peoples. On the eve of her departure, however, she made her will, the contents of which she kept a secret, even from her husband, acquainting him only with the fact that he was to be her sole executor. The sultry climate of India proved to be too drastic for the frail American girl, whose delicate organism had been attuned to gentler conditions of life in her far-away home. She fell an early victim to the Indian fever; and, having her body embalmed, the disconsolate husband brought the remains back to the United States and interred underneath the chapel of Christ Church, on St. Simon's Island, near the old town of Frederica. On breaking the seal of his wife's will,

Mr. Dodge found that she had made him merely the trustee of the estate, barring a nominal support for himself. The bulk of the property was to be devoted to religious and benevolent ends. He cheerfully assumed the responsibilities which were thus put upon him; and besides helping hundreds of churches and institutions, he established at Frederica the Dodge Orphanage, for the proper care and maintainance of indigent children. He also revived and enlarged the work of Christ Church Parish, an organization whose beginning dated back to the days of Oglethorpe; and by his faithful ministrations as an undershepherd he sought the spiritual betterment and uplift in his island home. The waves of influence which went forth from the old town of Frederica touched the remotest confines of Christendom. In the meantime he married Miss Annie Gould, who entered sympathetically and helpfully into his plans and who, since the death of her husband, several years ago, has continued his great work, infused and infilled by no little of his spirit. On the walls of Christ Church there are marble tablets commemorating the unselfish lives of the saintly pair, who, under divine guidance, sought to make the wisest and best use of the Dodge millions.

The Tomb of Thomas Butler King. In the historic old burial-ground appurtenant to Christ church at Frederica, lie the mortal ashes of the far-sighted Georgian who first conceived the idea of a transcontinental railway line to connect the two oceans—Thomas Butler King. He was a member of Congress, a wealthy sea island cotton planter, and a special envoy of the United State government to Europe. The grave of Mr. King is in the rear of the church and is marked by a handsome block of marble, on which the following epitaph is inscribed:

> THOMAS BUTLER KING. 1800-1860. A profound statesman who faithfully labored for the public good, a man gentle and true, a devoted husband and father, a kind master.

His wife is buried beside him. Here also rests the celebrated scientist and planter, John Couper; his equally distinguished son, James Hamilton Couper; the noted Thomas Spalding, for whom Spalding county was named; Captain Alexander Campbell Wylly, a Captain in the Royal Army during the Revolution, afterwards Governor

of New Providence; Major Pierce Butler, and members
of other prominent Georgia families, including the Pages,
and the Postells.

Oglethorpe's   Whatever may be said to the disparagment
Regiment.   of Georgia as a Colony of indigent debtors
                and of impecunious exiles, there was not
to be found in the service of the King of England a body
of soldiers whose family connections were superior to
those of the men who composed Oglethorpe's Regiment.
The story of how he gathered them is thus told by Colonel Jones.* Says he:

"Oglethorpe's regiment was limited to six companies of one hundred
men each, exclusive of non-commissioned officers and drummers. To it a
grenadier company was subsequently attached. Disdaining to 'make a
market of the service' by selling commissions, the General secured the appointment, as officers, only of such persons as were gentlemen of family
and character in their respective communities. He also engaged about
twenty young gentlemen of no fortunte to serve as cadets. These he subsequently promoted as vacancies occurred. So far from deriving any
pecuniary benefit from these appointments, the General, in some cases, from
his private fortune advanced the fees requisite to procure commissions, and
provided moneys for the purchase of uniforms. At his own expense he
engaged the servics of forty supernumeraries—'a circumstance,' says a
contemporary writer, 'very extraordinary in our armies, especially in our
plantations.' In order to engender in the hearts of the enlisted men an
attachment for and an interest in the Colony which they were to defend
and also to induce them to become settlers, permission was granted to each
to take a wife with him, for the support of whom additional pay and
rations were provided. So carefully was this regiment recruited and of-
ficered that it constituted one of the best military organizations in the
service of the King.''

As gathered by Mr. G. W. J. DeRenne, from the Book
of Army Commissions, from 1728 to 1841, in the Record
Office in London, some of the members of Oglethorpe's
Regiment are given below. The list is fragmentary, but
a more complete one is probably not in existence. These
names are as follows:

----

*Dead Towns of Georgia, pp. 66-67.

James Oglethorpe, Colonel of a regiment of foot.
James Cochran, Lieut.-Colonel.
Wm. Cook, Major.
Hugh Mackay, Captain.
Richard Norbury, Captain.
Alex. Herron, Captain.
Albert Desbrisay, Captain.
Philip Delegall, Senior Lieutenant.
Philip Delegall, Junior Lieutenant.
Raymond Demere, Lieutenant.
George Morgan, rank not stated.

George Dunbar, rank not stated.
Will Horton, Ensign.
James Mackay, Ensign.
Wm. Folsom, Ensign.
John Tanner, Ensign.
John Leman, Ensign.
Sandford Mace, Ensign.
Hugh Mackay, Adjutant.
Edward Dyson, Clerk and Chaplain.
Thomas Hawkins, Surgeon.
Edward Wansall, Quartermaster.

GORDON

Oothcaloga. The great valley lying between the Cohutta Mountains on the east and the Chattoogatas on the west forms a natural gateway between the North and the South, and important highways have led through this valley since the earliest prehistoric times. Gordon County lies across this valley; and, long before the coming of white men, its territory was threaded by great Indian trails connecting the regions of the Great Lakes and the Canadian woods with the waters of the South Atlantic and the Mexican Gulf. At the confluence of the Coosawattee and the Connasuaga Rivers stood New Echota, the last capital of the Eastern Cherokees. Some four miles west of this site, one or more Indian trails crossed the Oostanaula River, at a place where ancient mounds still mark the location of a once populous town of the red men; and, on this spot in after years grew the present county-seat of Gordon County: Calhoun.

But the earliest name by which the settlement at this place was known to civilization was Oothcaloga. The first whites who came into the country followed the Indian trails which, in time, they converted into roads. Still later, great lines of railway were built along the routes fixed by these ancient Indian highways. Traders camped at the river crossing, and as soon as conditions called for a place in which to hold court a log cabin was constructed in the grove nearby and called Oothcaloga court ground. Mrs. W. J. Hall, one of the oldest residents of Calhoun, thus describes the appearance of the settlement at this remote time. Says Mrs. Hall:

"We lived just down the Oothcaloga valley, and as my brother had to go to the river for a load of sand my sister and I went with him. We drove along a dim road through the woods, passing several deserted Indian houses and at one place a number of Indian graves covered with basketwork. This basket work had been made of canes, some of which had been buried in mud and made black, and these, woven in with the white canes, made various stripes. We saw a large herd of deer feeding in the woods

near the new court-house, which had just been built. We had never seen
a court-house of any kind, and in our childish minds wondered what it
would be like. My brother drove up to the door, which was tightly closed,
and we got out of the wagon and looked through the cracks between the
logs, but saw no one anywhere.''

With the coming of the Western and Atlantic railroad, the little station
of Oothcaloga grew in importance. A trader named Dawson established
a store here and played an important part in the life of the community,
giving his name to the place which ceased to be known as Oothcaloga and
became Dawsonville.

Calhoun. It was soon apparent that a new county must
be formed out of the northern portion of Cass
and the adjacent counties of Floyd and Murray, and spec-
ulation became rife as to the location of the new county-
seat. Judge John P. King of Augusta, who had been a
heavy investor in lands along the line of the new railroad, bought a large amount of real estate at Dawsonville
and exerted his influence to make that place the capital
of the county. He erected a large hotel and offered to
give lots for all public buildings. In this way Calhoun
became the owner of several handsome parks.

After the formation of Gordon County, a spirited
election was held at a place called Center, now known as
Big Spring, to determine the location of the county-seat.
Two places were voted for, ''Center,'' and ''Railroad.''
A large crowd assembled at Center and remained all
night to learn the result. ''Railroad'' won and preparations went rapidly forward to convert the thriving village of Dawsonville into the county capital which was
soon named in honor of South Carolina's immortal son,
John C. Calhoun.

Among the leading. spirits of the new town were
Dennis Johnson, who assisted in making the survey of
streets and parks; David G. Law, who soon became a
prosperous merchant; Dr. Wall, whose name is preserved in one of the leading streets of the town; and William H. Dabney, a young lawyer who came seeking a location in the new county. He afterwards became one of

the leading jurists of northwest Georgia. As the territory around Calhoun developed its population and business grew. It became a large grain and live stock market, and the nearby town of New Echota which had prospered as a trade center after the removal of the Cherokees gradually died and its site is now a cultivated farm.

Calhoun was almost totally destroyed by Sherman's army in 1864, but after the war it rapidly regained its former prosperity. It is now not only one of the most beautiful towns in the State, but one of the most prosperous. Calhoun was the boyhood home of Maurice Thompson, the well-known author. His brother, Will H. Thompson, who wrote "The High Tide at Gettysburg," was also born and reared here.*

The Nelson Monument. On the court-house square at Calhoun stands a monument to General Charles Haney Nelson, a distinguished soldier of the ante-bellum period. General Nelson won his spurs as a soldier in the war with the Seminoles, after which he became a conspicuous figure in the military operations around New Echota, incident to the removal of the Cherokees. He was not a native of this section of Georgia, but falling in love with the mountainous country he bought a plantation at Big Springs, some nine miles from the present town of Calhoun. There, on what is still known as the Nelson farm, he lies buried. At the outbreak of the Mexican War, in 1845, he went to the front, bore an important part in the struggle, and returned home with the rank of Brigadier-General. But enfeebled by exposure to a tropical climate, he survived for only a few months. The inscription on his monument reads as follows:

> Dedicated by the Surviving Officers, Soldiers and Friends to the Memory of Gen. Charles Haney Nelson. Born in Wilkes County, Ga., Nov. 2, 1796. Died Sept. 30, 1848.

*Mr. J. A. Hall, formerly of Calhoun, now of Decatur, Ga.

GRADY

Cairo.   On August 17, 1905, an Act was approved creating the new county of Grady out of lands formerly included with Decatur and Thomas, and designating Cairo, a progressive and wideawake town on the Atlantic Coast Line, as the new county-seat. The town was incorporated by an Act of the Legislature, approved October 28, 1870, at which time the following commissioners were designated to hold office until the election of a mayor and councilmen as prescribed by law. These commissioners were: Milton White, Dr. J. W. Clements, and J. M. Lawrence.* During the past few years the growth of Cairo has been rapid, due to the agricultural wealth of the surrounding country, and to the public enterprise of a united citizenship.

GREENE

Greensboro.   Greensboro was made the county-seat of Greene County, when the county was first created in 1786, and was named in honor of the illustrious soldier who ranked next to Washington as a commander in the Revolution: Major-General Nathanael Greene. The town was incorporated by an Act approved December 10, 1803, providing for its better regulation; and at this time the following residents were named as commissioners: Jonas Fouche, Henry Carlton, Wm. W. Strain, John McAllister, John Armour, and Fields Kennedy.* There was a strong sentiment at one time in favor of making Greensboro the seat of the University of Georgia. It has always been a center of refinement and culture as well as a conservative business town, op-

*Acts, 1870, p. 175.
*Clayton's Compendium, p. 149.

erating upon safe and sound principles. The Greensboro
Female Academy, a noted ante-bellum school, was char-
tered in 1853. On the court-house square stands a handsome Confederate monument erected by the Greensboro
women. Included among the men of eminence who have
resided here may be mentioned: Hon. Thomas W. Cobb
and Hon. Wm. C. Dawson, both United States Senators;
Hon. Thomas F. Foster, a member of Congress; Dr.
Francis Cummins, an early pioneer of Presbyterianism;
Judge Thomas Stocks, one of the founders of Mercer
University; Judge Francis H. Cone, an eminent jurist;
Judge Henry T. Lewis, of the State Supreme Court, and
a host of others. Gen. Hugh A. Haralson and Judge
Eugenius A. Nisbet, were natives of Greene. On the
banks of the Oconee River, in the upper part of the county, is the grave of Gov. Peter Early, whose ashes in the
near future will probably rest in the cemetery at Greensboro, where several of his kindred lie buried. Bishop
George F. Pierce was born on the old Foster place, three
miles from Greensboro.

**Penfield: The Cradle
of Mercer University.** Seven miles to the north of Greensboro, in a part of the county today
remote from the main highway of
travel, there is located an obscure village within whose
quiet precincts much of the history of the Baptist Church
in Georgia has been written. Here the famous university
of the Georgia Baptists was founded and here the great
Jesse Mercer sleeps on the old college campus. The atmosphere of the locality is rich in fragrant associations.
Nor is it any small part in the drama of events which
the little town of Penfield has played.

In 1829, when the Georgia Baptist Convention met
at Milledgeville, it was announced to the body that Josiah Penfield, of Savannah, a deacon in the church, had

bequeathed to the convention, the sum of $2,500 as a fund for education, on condition that an equal amount be raised. The following committee was named to suggest a plan of action in regard to the matter: Thomas Stocks, Thomas Cooper, H. O. Wyer and J. H. T. Kilpatrick. They made a report at once, suggesting that the requisite sum be subscribed; and accordingly, within fifteen minutes, the amount of money necessary to secure the gift was pledged in *bona fide* notes, given to Dr. Adiel Sherwood, clerk and treasurer of the Georgia Baptist Convention. The loyal pioneer Baptists, whose generosity helped to lay the foundations of Mercer, are numerated below, together with the amounts subscribed:

Jesse Mercer	$250	Adiel Sherwood	$125
Cullen Battle	200	Thomas Cooper	110
James Shannon	100	William Flournoy	100
Armstead Richardson	75	James Armstrong	50
James Davis	50	J. H. T. Kilpatrick	100
H. O. Wyer	150	Joshua Key	100
I. L. Brooks	100	Andrew Battle	50
James Boykin	125	R. C. Shorter	50
Barnabas Strickland	36	Jonathan Davis	150
William Walker	100	Thomas Stocks	50
B. M. Sanders	150	Jabez P. Marshall	100
Robert C. Brown	50	Edmund Shackelford	150
Peter Walton	25	J. Whitefield, Cash	10

Due authority having been given, a committee purchased from James Rudd, a tract of land, seven miles to the north of Greensboro containing 450 acres. Dr. Billington M. Sanders, then a young man just entering upon the work of the ministry, but well-educated and well equipped, was engaged to act as principal. Under him the wilderness was cleared, temporary quarters were provided, and, on the second Monday in January, 1833, a manual school at Penfield was formally opened. Associated with Dr. Sanders, the first corps of instructors, were, Iro O. McDaniel, J. F. Hillyer, J. W. Attaway, W. D. Cowdry, A. Williams, and S. P. Sanford. John Lumpkin, the father of Governor Wilson Lumpkin, was a mem-

ber of the executive committee under whose oversight
the school was established.

Penfield was the name given to the locality in honor
of Josiah Penfield, from whose estate came the original
bequest; but the school itself was named for Jesse Mercer, then the most influential Baptist divine in Georgia.
Mr. Mercer, throughout his long life, constantly befriended the institution and at his death it became the
principal beneficiary under his will. At the start, it was
quite an unpretentious affair. Mercer Institute was the
name which was first given to the modest educational
plant at Penfield. In the course of time there developed
around it an important town; but with the building of the
Georgia Railroad it began to yield prestige to Greensboro, a town on the main line and settled by an enterprising community of well-to-do planters.

However, the Institute prospered. The students were
required to perform a definite amount of work each day,
for which they were paid at the rate of six cents per hour.
They were also put through a course of study which was
somewhat exacting. Dr. Sanders remained at the head
of the school for six years. He was most successful in
organizing the work upon solid foundations, partly because of his experimental acquaintance with agriculture
and partly because of his exceptional qualifications as
a disciplinarian. But he was none too sanguine at first
in regard to the educational outlook in Georgia. He was
somewhat apprehensive of failure, due to certain adverse
conditions which he feared could not be successfully overcome. To illustrate his attitude, it was found that before the school could be organized an additional sum of
$1,500 was needed. Dr. Sanders was asked, among others
to be one of thirty to raise this amount. He replied
to the effect that he was willing to be the thirtieth man
to contribute, a statement which either implied some
doubt in regard to the ultimate outcome, or else an an-

xiety on the part of Dr. Sanders to make the Baptists of Georgia exert themselves.

But the sum was raised. Moreover, this wise and good man was placed at the head of the school. Under him, the command to halt was never once sounded. The Institution moved steadily forward. But, after six years, he relinquished the helm. Possibly for the reason that his successors were men of books, who knew comparatively little of practical agriculture, there followed a laxity in the management of affairs. Dissatisfaction arose, and in the course of time the manual school feature was abandoned.

In 1837, the name of the school was changed from Mercer Institute to Mercer University; a charter was obtained from the Legislature; and a fund of $100,000 was raised among the Georgia Baptists with which to give it a permanent and substantial endowment. The first graduating exercises were held in the summer of 1841, when diplomas were awarded to three young men. Richard Malcolm Johnston, who became one of the foremost educators and authors of his day; Benjamin F. Thorpe, afterwards an eminent divine; and Dr. A. R. Wellborn, a successful practitioner of medicine, received degrees on this occasion. In 1840 the Theological Department was added; and Dr. Adiel Sherwood was put at the head of the newly organized school of the prophets. The name of this stalwart, and sturdy old pioneer is still fragrant in the annals of Georgia.

At the outbreak of the Civil War, the senior classmen at Penfield entered the Confederate Army almost to a man, and there were few better soldiers. Though the college did not formally suspend until 1865, it maintained an existence which was purely nominal. Most of the trustees were at the front. Widespread demoralization prevailed. So, after the invasion of the State by Sherman, the faculty with great reluctance closed the doors. Professors Sanford and Willet, the two senior members of the faculty, opened a school in the college building and held a quasi-commencement, but the lamp of learning could not be rescued from extinction. It flickered dimly, amid the ruins, enough to reveal the chaotic conditions; and then expired in darkness.

For seven years after the war there came a break in the academic life of Mercer. The work of rehabilitation was slow, due to the utter prostation of the State, during the period of Reconstruction. Finally when the Institution again arose it was upon the heights of Macon where it today stands. Prior to the war two separate efforts were made by Griffin to secure Mercer, but without success. The various presidents of Mercer University, in the order of service, have been as follows:

Rev. Billington M. Sanders, Principal and President.
Rev. Otis Smith.
Rev. John L. Dagg, D. D.
Rev. Nathaniel M. Crawford, D.D.
Rev. H. H. Tucker, D.D.
Rev. Archibald J. Battle, D.D.
Rev. G. A. Nunnally, D.D.
Pinckney D. Pollock, LL.D.
Rev. S. Y. Jameson, D.D.

Some of these executive heads have been amongst the most eminent theologians and educators of the South.

Dr. Patrick H. Mell, afterwards Chancellor of the University of Georgia; Dr. Shaler G. Hillyer, Professor William G. Woodfin and others, also taught for a while at Mercer. Perhaps the most distinguished laymen who have occupied chairs in the Institution were Professor S. P. Sanford and Professor J. E. Willet. The former headed the department of mathematics. The latter taught the natural sciences. Both were identified with the Institution for something like fifty years and both were men of broad scholarship. The text-books on mathematics compiled by Professor Sanford are still extensively used. Though Penfield has not felt the awakening touch of Prospero's wand since the removal of Mercer University to Macon, it possesses an excellent high school. The people of this historic little town do not put the emphasis of life upon material things. With a population of less than one thousand inhabitants, the old village of Penfield may create no ripple in the great world of commerce. But who can measure the influence which it still exerts upon thought and character? The pulsating waves of intellectual and moral energy put in motion fifty years ago have not ceased; and, be the future of the town what it may, the memories of Penfield are immortal.

The Methodist Schism of 1844: How it Originated.   Says Dr. George F. Smith:

"Before Bishop Andrew went to the West, he had made an engagement to marry Mrs. Leonora Greenwood, of Greensboro, Ga. The condition of his family, and his long absences from home, made this a necessary act; so, without undue haste, and, with great discretion, he had selected a second companion. She was very attractive in person, beautiful in manners, gentle in spirit, and deeply though undemonstratively pious. After the marriage he conveyed to his wife, in due form of law, all the rights in her property which the fact of marriage had given him as her husband. When Mrs. Andrews died, in 1854, the law re-invested him with rights in this same property, but he promptly dispossessed himself the second time, and turned it all over to her children. Bishop Andrews did not expect trouble from this marriage, and there were good reasons why he did not; for he himself had been a slaveholder for several years prior to this, in the very same way that he was now—through his wife.

"Dr. Olin, who was highly esteemed at the North and even in New England, had owned slaves and, having sold them, had the proceeds of the sales still in his possession. The General Conference appointed slave-holders, such men as Dr. Capers, to positions of distinction and trust; and only eight years before had strongly condemned the societies of Abolitionism; and many of the extreme men of New England had actually left the Church and formed another connection. Neither the spirit nor the letter of the law of the Church had been broken. On what ground, then, could he suppose that his marriage with an elegant and pious lady, who happened to own a few slaves, would call forth a tempest of such violence as to destroy the unity of the Church?

"The fact is, he did not dream of such a result. Nor was he aware of any excitement on the subject until he reached Baltimore in April, when on his way to the General Conference in New York in May. Here he learned of the intense excitement caused by the news that one of the Bishops of the Methodist Episcopal Church owned slaves, and received the first intimation that it would be a matter for investigation. He possessed a woman's delicacy of feeling, and to have his private affairs discussed by the General Conference was abhorent to his very soul. He resolved to resign, and so expressed himself, both in Baltimore and in New York. This resolution, however, he did not execute, for the reason that the Southern delegates demurred in formal resolutions and urged him not to do so, on the ground that it would inflict an incurable wound on the whole South, and inevitably lead to division.

"Resignation now became almost an impossibility; and when it was intimated that he had broken faith and must either resign or be deposed, then resignation was entirely out of the question. The issue had to come. The mass of the Northern preachers were opposed to slavery, but they were not abolitionists. They found themselves hard put to defend themselves; and when it was known that a Bishop was a slaveholder they felt that they were in a sad predicament. Accordingly, Alfred Griffith and John Davis, two members of the Baltimore Conference, were put forward to lead the attack. They introduced a resolution declaring, among other things, that Bishop Andrew was nominated by the slave-holding States in the Conference because he was not a slaveholder; and that, having become one,* 'Therefore be it Resolved, That James O. Andrew be affectionately requested to resign.'

"This precipitated the issue. The discussion was Christian in spirit and courteous in language, to which, however, there were some exceptions. To ask him to resign was so painful to many who did not wish a slaveholder in office that Mr. Finley, of Ohio, introduced his famous substitute, declaring that it was the sense of the General Conference that he desist from the exercise of the office of Bishop so long as the impediment remained. Mr. Finley was Bishop Andrew's personal friend and offered the substitute, believing it to be less offensive to the Southern delegates than the original resolution. But it was really more offensive, because, since it could not consistently remove the impediment, it amounted to permanent deposition. No man in the Conference was more strongly attached to Bishop Andrews, perhaps, than Dr. Olin. The night before he was to speak he visited the Bishop and told him the course he intended to take, and why he would take it. He would advocate the substitute; for if it were not passed New England would withdraw, and there would be division and disintegration everywhere in the North. But, if it were passed, the South would depart, and there would be union and peace throughout her borders.

---

*Several years previous an old lady of Augusta bequeathed to Bishop Andrew a mulatto girl in trust until she was nineteen, when, with her consent, she was to be deported to Liberia. But the girl refused to go or to accept freedom.

"The debate continued for several days. Among the Southern delegates who participated in the discussion were Dr. Winans, of Mississippi, Dr. Pierce and Judge Longstreet, of Georgia, and Dr. William Capers, of South Carolina. Others took part, but these were the giants. On the opposite side were also arrayed men of strong intellect, including Dr. Olin. Strong efforts were made to stay the tide, but all in vain. On the first of June the vote was taken on the substitute of Mr. Finley, and 111 were for, while only 69 were against it. This was virtual deposition. Grieved, but not surprised, Bishop Andrews left for his home in Georgia. One man from the North, who was a tower of strength, stood by him shoulder to shoulder in all this conflict. It was Joshua Soule, the senior Bishop of the Church. Born and reared in Maine, living in Ohio, never a slave-holder, nor a pro-slavery man, with every interest to bind him to the section in which he lived, he yet came to the South, because he believed the South was right.

"Before the General Conference adjourned the question of division was virtually settled; and with great unanimity the Annual Conference at the South appointed deelgates to meet in convention at Louisville the following May. The South did not really desire division, but after the course of the General Conference it was evident that separate organization was the only way of preserving Methodism in this section—the only way of holding the Master to the Church and of carrying the Gospel to the slave. It was division or death. At the appointed time the convention met. Bishop Andrew, Soule, and Morris were all there; action was unanimous; and a call was issued to elect delegates to a General Conference to meet in Petersburg, Va., the following May. No doctrine was changed, no policy altered, no usages, rites, or customs modified; and after this convention the Bishops of the Methodist Episcopal Church resolved to withdraw from the South and leave the whole territory to the new organization. Thus the Methodist Episcopal Church, South, came into existence; and the General Conference at Petersburg did but little more than adjust itself to the changed condition of affairs, elect an agent for its publishing interests, editors for its papers, and two additional Bishops, Robert Paine and William Capers.''*

*Condensed from Dr. George G. Smith's Life of James Osgood Andrew.

Gov. Early's Body to be Removed. On an eminence overlooking the Oconee River, in the upper part of Greene County, near Skull Shoals, the remains of Governor Peter Early have rested since 1817; but there is now a movement under way to remove the ashes of this illustrious Georgian to the cemetery at Greensboro, where several of his kindred lie entombed.

Originally the burial-ground formed a part of the old Early estate, one of the largest in Georgia. Today it occupies a corner of Mr. M. L. Bond's horse and cow lot; and, though enclosed by a wall, it is no longer a fit place for this great man's sepulchre. His widow, who afterwards married the famous Dr. Adiel Sherwood, sleeps beside him, together with an infant daughter; but the reader is referred to Volume I of this work for additional particulars in regard to the Early burial-ground. As a rule, it is best to let the ashes of the dead lie undisturbed. But until the body of Gov. Early is removed Georgia will owe an unfulfilled debt not only to the memory of an honored former chief-magistrate but to her own self respect. In the cemetery at Greensboro the old Governor's grave will not be an unvisited spot; and, what is more, it will always be guarded with sacred care and tenderness.

Joel Early: His Views on Slavery. Joel Early—the old Governor's father—was probably the first man in the United States to advocate a return of the negro race to Africa; and, notwithstanding the fact that he owned a great many slaves, he offered not only to release them from servitude, but to defray the expense of sending them back to Liberia. Early's Manor, before its destruction by fire, was perhaps the finest old country seat north of Savannah. Here, on his fertile acres, Joel Early lived the life of an English gentleman, surrounded by everything which could minister to his ease or contribute to his enjoyment. But he was an eccentric old man, full of queer whimsicalities. Eleazer Early, one of his sons, prepared and published the first map of Georgia.*

*Authority: Judge George Hillyer, of Atlanta.

Benjamin Weaver: A Revolutionary Patriot. One of the many soldiers of seventy-six, who acquired land in Greene County, Ga., was Benjamin Weaver. Enlisting as a youthful private in a North Carolina Regiment, he was an active participant in numerous engagements and carved a record for gallantry on the field of battle, which is today proudly cherished by his descendants. He married Elizabeth Daniel, a cultured lady, with distinguished connections in both Virginia and North Carolina. The late United States Senator John W. Daniel, of the former State, came of the same virile stock. Two sons were born to the Weavers, whose names respectively were: William Wiley Daniel Weaver, and Travis Archibald Daniel Weaver. The former remained in Greene, while the latter settled in Upson. Though not among the original settlers of Greene, the Weavers were prominent in the county for more than a hundred years. After the death of Judge William Weaver, in 1905, the old home was broken up. Among the many descendants of Benjamin Weaver, not a few of whom have been men of marked prominence, may be mentioned: Judge Howard E. W. Palmer, of Atlanta; Dr. J. C. Weaver, of the medical staff of the Federal Prison in Atlanta; Dr. Olin Weaver and Hudson Weaver, of Macon; Mrs. M. M. Burks, of the English Department of Wesleyan Female College, at Macon; Dr. W. W. Stewart, of Columbus; Stewart Ticknor, a grandson of the author of "Little Giffen;" Dr. J. A. Weaver, and W. T. Weaver, of Buena Vista; Rev. Rembert G. Smith, of Emory College, Oxford; Dr. Carrie Weaver Smith, of the Virginia K. Johnson Home, Dallas, Tex.; G. A. Weaver, Jr., president of the Thomaston Branch of the Central of Georgia; G. A. Weaver, Sr., president of the Weaver Merchandise Company, of Thomaston, Ga., and Prof. W. T. Weaver, for years a distinguished educator in the common schools of this State.*

---

*Information kindly furnished by Mrs. Kate Weaver Dallas, of Thomasville, Ga.

GWINNETT

Lawrenceville. Lawrenceville, the county-seat of Gwinnett County, was incorporated by an Act approved December 15, 1821, with the following town commissioners: James Wardlaw, Hugh B. Grenwood, James McClure, John Geddes, Sr., and Paschal Brooks.* It was chosen as the site for public buildings when the county was first organized in 1818, and named in honor of the gallant naval officer, Captain James Lawrence, of the "Chesapeake," whose last words as he fell mortally wounded were: "Don't give up the ship!" The county itself was named for one of the signers of the Declaration of Independence, Button Gwinnett. Two flourishing institutions of the town in pioneer days were: the Lawrenceville Academy, founded in 1825, and the Lawrenceville Female Institute, chartered in 1837. On the courthouse square in Lawrenceville stands a monument in honor of two Lawrenceville boys, who perished in the massacre at Fort Goliad, in 1836, Capt. James E. Winn, and Sergeant Anthony Bates, of the Texas Volunteers. It also commemorates the heroic death of eight Gwinnett County men, who were killed in the Creek Indian War of 1836. Major Charles H. Smith, better known as "Bill Arp," was born near Lawrenceville. This has also been the home of the famous Hutchins family, each generation of which has produced strong leaders; the home of the Simmons family, of which the distinguished Wm. E. Simmons, is a member; the home of the Peeples family, represented by the late Hon. Tyler M. Peeples. Here, too, at one time, resided Gen. Gilbert J. Wright, Col. L. P. Thomas, and Dr. James F. Alexander.

Buford. One of the most enterprising communities in this section of Georgia is the town of Buford, famed throughout the country for its splendid tanneries. The town was incorporated by an Act approved August 24, 1872, at which time Messrs. Adam Pool, A. C. Harris,

---

*Acts, 1821, p. 37.

John F. Espey, W. R. Chamblee, J. R. Stringer and J. A. Pattillo were designated to serve as commissioners, pending an election to be held on the first day of January, 1873. The corporate limits were fixed at one-half a mile in every direction from the depot of the Atlanta and Richmond Air Line, now a part of the Southern Railway system.* In 1891 intoxicants were prohibited. With a rapidly increasing population, Buford began to dream of larger possibilities; and on December 23, 1896, to meet the demands of growth, a new charter was granted by the Legislature conferring upon the "City of Buford" a municipal form of government, with greatly enlarged powers.

HABERSHAM

Clarkesville. On November 26, 1823, an Act was approved by Gov. Troup, making Clarkesville the permanent county-seat of the new county of Habersham, created out of lands then recently acquired from the Cherokee Indians. The following commissioners were named in the Act: Wm. Hamilton, Jehu Sterrett, John Bryant, Miles Davis, and H. A. Hill.* The present city charter was granted in 1900. Clarkesville was named for the illustrious General John Clarke, a soldier of the Revolution, an Indian fighter, and a Governor, twice honored with a seat in the executive chair. On account of its high altitude, in a beautiful mountainous region of the State, Clarkesville soon became a favorite resort for wealthy families of the coast, a large number coming from Savannah. Here lived Hon. Richard W. Habersham, and Hon. George W. Owens, both members of Congress; and Col. Garnett McMillan, a brilliant lawyer who defeated Ben Hill for Congress, but died soon after the election. It has also been the home of many noted families like the Erwins, the Woffords, the Wests, and others. The Clarkesville Academy was chartered on December 24. 1836, with the following trustees: George D. Phillips,

---

*Acts, 1823, p. 176.

George W. Owens, Richard W. Habersham, and John B. Matthews.*

Aleck's Mountain. In the neighborhood of Clarkesville there looms a peak of the Blue Ridge, locally known as Aleck's Mountain, on which to this day may be seen the remains of an old fortification, supposed to date back to the visit of DeSoto to North Georgia in 1540. According to our foremost antiquarian, Colonel Charles C. Jones, Jr., Xualla, one of the Indian towns at which the Spanish adventurer stopped in his quest for gold, was located in Nacoochee Valley; and, on this assumption, his march from the Savannah River westward toward what is now the city of Rome, lay directly across Aleck's Mountain, in the present county of Habersham. But aside from the ancient ruins to be found on this peak there are numerous relics in this part of the State which point to an occupancy in prehistoric times by civilized white men; if not by Spaniards, at least by Europeans.

Pioneer Senators and Representatives. Some of the leading men of the county in pioneer days may be obtained from a list of Habersham's early State Senators and Representatives, beginning with the creation of the county, in 1819, and coming on down to the outbreak of the Civil War. This list includes the following State Senators: Benjamin Cleveland, James Blair, William B. Wofford, William H. Steelman, Stephen Smith, John Trammell, John R. Stanford, Thomas Kimsey and George D. Phillips. During this same period the Representatives were: William B. Wofford, James Blair, Benjamin Chastain, Benjamin Cleveland, William H. Steelman, Absalom Holcomb, Kinchen Carr, Jesse Sanford, Thomas M. Kimsey, Elihu S. Barclay and Joseph Underwood.*

HALL

Gainesville. On April 21, 1821, an Act was approved by Gov. John Clark, chartering the town of Gainesville, selected as the county-site for the new county of Hall. In this same Act, the following pioneer citizens were named as commissioners: Stephen Reed, John

*Acts, 1836, p. 16.

Stringer, John Finch, Jesse Clayton, and Eli Sutherland.[1] As was the custom of the State, whenever a new
county was organized, an academy for the proper instruction of the young was invariably provided; and, on
Christmas Day, 1821, an Act was approved, chartering
the old Hall County Academy, with the following trustees, to wit: Stephen Reed, David H. McClesky, William
Cobb, John McConnell, Sr., and Bartimeus Reynolds.[2]
In 1832, the town was re-incorporated, with Messrs.
James W. Jones, James Law, Miner W. Brown, Larkin
Cleveland, and John W. McAfee, as commissioners.[3]
The town was not named for Gen. Edmond Gaines, as
some have supposed, but for an old pioneer family resi-
dent in this locality when the county-site was first chosen.

Gainesville, on account of its high altitude, has always enjoyed a splendid health record, and has been a
favorite resort for summer tourists and for invalids
seeking the magic balsam. As the seat of Brenau College
and Conservatory of Music, it is also widely known
throughout educational circles. The city of Gainesville
is located on the line of the Southern Railway, 53 miles
above Atlanta; and of late years its growth has been
substantial and rapid. Some of Georgia's most distinguished sons have been residents of this fine old town,
including Dr. Richard Banks, for whom a county was
named; Gen. James Longstreet, renowned as Lee's Old
War Horse; Gov. Allen D. Candler, Judge John B. Estes,
and a host of others. It is also the home of the present
Congressman from this district Hon. Thomas M. Bell.
Though never a resident of the town, Gov. James M.
Smith is here buried beside his last wife. Two of the
daughters of President Woodrow Wilson were born in
Gainesville, where an aunt was then living, Mrs. Brown.
The monumental features of the town include a handsome
Confederate shaft, on the town square, and a memorial

---

[1] Acts, 1821, p. 6.
[2] Acts, 1821, p. 125.
[3] Acts, 1832, p. 201.

fountain, near the post-office building, in honor of the late Col. C. C. Saunders, a much beloved citizen.

**State Rights:
The Hanging
of George Tassel.** During the administration of Governor George R. Gilmer, there occurred near Gainesville an incident which set at defiance the power of the United States Government, and which in an acute issue between State and Federal authorities, gave the victory to the State of Georgia. This was the execution of a Cherokee Indian named George Tassel. This was told by Professor J. Harris Chappell. The story runs thus:* In December, 1828, the Georgia Legislature passed a bill enacting that the Cherokee country should be put under the jurisdiction of the laws of Georgia. The Act was passed on the ground that, as the Cherokee country was part and parcel of the State of Georgia, it should be governed by the laws of Georgia; but the real object was to move the Cherokees from the State. In order to give them plenty of time, the Act was not to go into effect until June 1, 1830. The Cherokees felt deeply outraged, and they determined at the first opportunity to test the validity of this Act before the Supreme Court of the United States.

An opportunity soon occurred. In the summer of 1830, a half-breed Cherokee by the name of George Tassel committed a murder in the Cherokee country. He was arraigned before the Superior Court, then sitting in Hall County, and was duly tried, found guilty and sentenced to be hanged. His attorneys appealed the case to the United States Supreme Court, asking that the verdict be set aside, on the ground that the Act of the Legislature giving the State of Georgia jurisdiction over the Cherokee country was a violation of the Federal Constitution, and was therefore null and void. The case of George Tassel versus the State of Georgia was duly entered on the Supreme Court docket.

Governor Gilmer was officially notified of the action, and was instructed to appear before the court for Georgia, as defendant in the case. But the Governor replied with spirit that the United States Supreme Court lacked jurisdiction in the case, and that the State of Georgia would scorn to compromise itself by appearing before that tribunal as defendant, under these circumstances. It was a foregone conclusion that the case would be decided against Georgia. To prevent this he resorted to the extraordinary measure of dispatching a special messenger to the sheriff of Hall County, with instructions to hang George Tassel immediately, before the case could be reached on the Supreme Court docket. The sheriff obeyed the order promptly, so poor George Tassel was hanged while his case was pending in the Federal Supreme Court. Thus ended the case, an end which, we must admit, was brought about by a rather high-handed measure on the part of the State. Georgia's action was severely criticised in the halls of

---

*Georgia History Stories, p. 294.

Congress; it was furiously condemned by the Cherokees themselves, and it was violently censured by a large part of the people of the North. But these protests were without effect upon Georgia. The Cherokees struck no blow from the shoulder out, but they were determined at the first opportunity to appeal again to the Supreme Court of the United States.

———

Unveiling of the Candler Monument. On June 3, 1913, the grave of Ex-Governor Allen D. Candler, in Alta Vista Cemetery, at Gainesville, was most impressively marked by a handsome shaft of marble, the funds for which were contributed by the members of Governor Candler's official household. These included the various appointees commissioned by the lamented former chief-magistrate during his term of office as Governor. The Candler lot is in the center of the burial-ground. Near the Governor, sleeps his distinguished father, Capt. Daniel G. Candler; while, in the immediate neighborhood, repose Gen. Longstreet, Dr. Richard Banks, Gov. James Milton Smith, and a host of noted Georgians. Overhead a blue sky beamed upon the vast concourse of people gathered at the grave of Gov. Candler. The official of the city of Gainesville, the Candler Horse Guards, the Daughters of the Confederacy, and distinguished visitors from a distance participated in the program of exercises. When the hour arrived for the unveiling, Col. S. C. Dunlap introduced Pension Commissioner, Hon. J. W. Lindsey, marshal of the day, who, after a short address, called upon Rev. Luke Johnson to make the opening prayer. Judge Lindsey then introduced Hon. Hamilton McWhorter, of Athens, who formally presented the monument to Gov. Candler's family, to the city of Gainesville, and to the State of Georgia. Speeches of acceptance were then made as follows: by Judge John S. Candler, on behalf of the family; by Mayor P. E. B. Robertson, on behalf of the city; and by Compiler of Records, Lucian Lamar Knight, Esq., on behalf of the State, the last-named speaker representing Governor Joseph M. Brown, who was unavoidably ab-

sent. The inscription on Governor Candler's monument
read as follows:

"Placed to the memory of ALLEN DANIEL
CANDLER by his appointees to office and places of
honor while Governor of Georgia.
            "Nov. 4, 1834—Oct. 26, 1910.''
A Graduate of Mercer University in the Class of
1859. A Soldier and Colonel in the Army of the Confederate States, 1861-1865. A Member of the House
of Representatives of Georgia, 1873-1878. Senator, 1878-
1880. Member of the Congress of the United States,
1883-1891. Secretary of State, 1894-1898. Governor of
Georgia, 1898-1902. Compiler of State Records, 1902-
1910.
He was an upright man, a patriotic citizen, a true
soldier, and a faithful public servant, who, in peace and
in war, exemplified the virtues of incorruptible integrity,
fearless courage, and unselfish devotion to the welfare
of his country.

HANCOCK

Sparta. Sparta, the county-seat of Hancock County, was
named for the ancient capital of the Peloponnes-
sus. Nor was the name an inappropriate one for this
little frontier town on the exposed border, where the
ever-present dread of an Indian outbreak called for
Spartan virtues of the most pronounced type. As soon
as Hancock County was organized out of lands formerly
included in Washington and Greene counties, Sparta
was made the new seat of government. The town was
chartered on December 3, 1805, by an Act providing for
its better regulation, at which time the following commissioners were appointed: Thomas Lancaster, Archibald Martin, James H. Jones, Samuel Hall, and Willie
Abercrombie.[1] The Sparta Academy was chartered on
December 17, 1818, with trustees as follows: Wm. G.

---

[1] Clayton's Compendium, p. 232.

Springer, John Lucas, Nicholas Childers, Charles E. Haynes, and Thomas Haynes.[1] Two of the most noted academies in the State were located in Hancock, not far from the town of Sparta, viz., Powelton and Mount Zion. The Powelton Academy was chartered on November 13, 1815; the Mount Zion Academy on December 20, 1823. It was at Powelton that the Baptist State Convention of Georgia was organized, and here at one time lived Gov. Wm. Rabun and Rev. Jesse Mercer. The Baptist Church of Powell's Creek was chartered November 20, 1801, with Matthew Rabun, Henry Graybill, John Veazy, Wm. Lord and Jesse Battle as trustees.[2] Mount Zion was a school which the Bemans—Nathan and Carlisle—made famous throughout the land; and here Wm. J. Northen, afterwards Governor, taught school. At Rockeby, near Sparta, the famous Richard Malcolm Johnson, author of the "Dukesboro Tales," opened a school for boys, which he afterwards transferred to Baltimore, Md. Shoulder Bone Creek, in the western part of Hancock, was the scene on November 3, 1786, of an Indian treaty which promised to end the Oconee war; but under the powerful leadership of the none too scrupulous McGillivray, it was repudiated by the Creeks. Some of the most distinguished men of Georgia have been residents of Sparta, but since these have been given in Volume I, they will not be repeated here. We will only add, in this connection, two names: Hon. George F. Pierce, Jr., a brilliant legislator; and Hon. Wm. H. Burwell, Speaker of the Georgia House of Representatives, for the session just closed.

————

Sunshine: The Home of Bishop Pierce.   Four miles from Sparta stands the cosy and picturesque little cottage in which Bishop Pierce spent the greater part of his life and to which he gave a name

————

[1] Lamar's Digest, p. 22.
[2] Clayton's Compendium, p. 12.

eloquent of the happiness which he there found: Sunshine. The Bishop bought this property from Hardy Culver, an old friend. It was an old plantation, on which originally stood a building with three rooms, somewhat inconveniently situated. The spot which he chose for the site of his dwelling was in an old field, near the road. Whether from the fact that no ray of light was intercepted by a shrub or tree, or from the fact that he loved bright and cheery names, he called the place Sunshine, a name by which it was ever afterwards known; and here he made his abode for over forty years.

Across the way was Rockaby, the home of Richard Malcolm Johnston, the distinguished author of the "Dukesboro Tales;" also an editor and educator of eminent attainments. In a letter to Bishop Atticus G. Haygood, dated February 12, 1885, Col. Johnston, who was then living in Baltimore wrote:

"I was a neighbor to Bishop Pierce for twelve years, my home in Hancock, Rockaby, adjoining Sunshine, which all know to have been the name of his. I had grown already to feel great admiration for one so preeminently gifted, and, for many years, had heard his pulpit eloquence with continual delight. But I did not know until I had become his neighbor that, great as he was in public, he was equally so in private; and a cordial friendship grew between us, notwithstanding our divergence in religious faith. For of all the great men I have ever known he seemed to me the most tolerant toward opinions differing from his own, upon whatever plane of inquiry. I have been in his house and he in mine. We have met at the little creek, the dividing line between our plantations, and fished for minnows together; together we have ridden, in his or my buggy, to and from Sparta. He was ever a sweet consoler to me when suffering from domestic affliction. . . . The sense of humor in him was exquisite and abundant. The twinkling of his beautiful eyes was as catching as fire; . . . He was one eminently sensitive to the sweets of individual friendships. Among those outside of Hancock, my impression is that he was most fond of General Toombs. They had been friends from boyhood. . . . The very last time I saw him, except one, he spoke to me with regret, amounting almost to indignation, of the rashness with which the General was misjudged by persons who did not understand his character, his opinions, his language, and his habits. . . . He was the most beautiful of mankind without, and men of all parties believed that his external beauty was the best expression which physical form and feature could give of the more exquisite beauty within. . . . Of the oratorical excellence of George F. Pierce, of course, the thousands who heard him known. Yet I do believe that his greatest endeavors were expended in the little Sparta Methodist Church. Scores of times I have heard him there, during a period of more than twenty years; there and at the Methodist camp-meeting, a few miles south of the village, in the which time I have listened to outbursts of words which I do not believe were surpassed on the Bema of Athens or in the Forum of Rome.''*

Dixon H. Lewis. This extraordinary man was born in Hancock County, Ga., August 10, 1802. He afterwards removed with his parents to Alabama, became prominent in public life, represented the State in Congress, and, in 1844, was appointed by Gov. Fitzpatrick to fill a seat in the United States Senate, made vacant by the appointment of Hon. Wm. R. King to the Court of France. On the return of Mr. King, in 1846, he desired his old seat back, and entered the field as a candidate. It was a battle of giants. Both men were deservedly popular; but after an exciting contest, one of the most stubborn in the history of Alabama politics, Mr. King, for the first time in his long career, suffered defeat. However, Mr. Lewis did not long enjoy the fruits of his victory. Ill-health overtook him; and while on a visit to New York, soon after the election, he died on October 25, 1846. On receiving the news of his death, the mayor of New York called the municipal boards together and it was resolved to give his remains a public burial. The body lay in state for several hours in the City Hall, whence it was borne to Greenwood Cemetery for final interment. Mr. Lewis was a man of gigantic stature.

Gov. Rabun's Family. Gov. William Rabun, who lived in this county near Powelton, left a family of seven children, including one son, Gen. J. W. Rabun, of Savannah, and six daughters, the eldest of

*George G. Smith, in Life and Times of George F. Pierce, D. D., LL. D.

whom married Rev. J. W. Battle, one of the eight distinguished Battles of Hancock. The other daughters were: Mrs. William Shivers, Mrs. Dr. Bass, Mrs. Lowe, Mrs. Cato, and Mrs. Wooten. Some few years ago the grave of Gov. Rabun was located on a plantation, four miles west of Mayfield. It will probably be marked with an appropriate monument in the near future by his surviving relatives.

HARALSON

General Remarks. On February 5, 1856, an Act was approved creating out of lands formerly embraced in Polk and Carroll Counties a new county, to be called Haralson, in honor of a distinguished soldier and statesman, General Hugh A. Haralson, then lately deceased. The same Act creating the new county provided for its annexation to the Blue Ridge Judicial Circuit, to the Fifth Congressional District, and to the First Brigade of the Eleventh Division of the Georgia militia.* Haralson's representatives in the General Assembly of Georgia, since the organization of the county, have been as follows: K. Merchison, 1857-8; W. W. Sockwell, 1859-60; R. F. Speight, 1861-2; Walter Brock, 1863-4, 1865-6; W. N. Williams, 1868-9-70; William J. Head, 1871-2; R. R. Hutchinson, 1873-4; R. A. Reid, 1875; J. K. Hamber, 1876; A. R. Walton, 1877; Charles Taliaferro, 1878-9; J. M. McBride, 1880-1, 1882-3, 1892-3; S. M. Davenport, 1884-5; R. B. Hutcheson, 1886-7; T. W. M. Tatum, 1888-9; 1890-1; J. J. Pope, 1894-5; Price Edwards, 1896-7; E. S. Griffith, 1898-9; E. B. Hutchinson, 1900-1, 1902-3-4, 1905-6;W. T. Eaves, 1907-8; W. J. Waddell, 1909-10; W. W. Summerlin, 1911-12; and C. L. Suggs, 1913-14. This county has also furnished the following State Senators: Walter Brock, 1868-1872; William J. Head, 1878-9; J. M. McBride, 1884-5; W. F. Golden, 1890-1, 1896-7, 1902-3-4, and E. S. Griffith, 1909-10.

Buchanan. Buchanan, the county-seat of Haralson, was named for President James Buchanan, of Pennsylvania, the last Democratic President of the United States before the Civil War. When the new county was organized, in 1856, the Justices of the Inferior Court were authorized to locate a site for public buildings and,

---

*Acts, 1855-1856, p. 110.

under the instructions prescribed in this Act, the town of Buchanan was founded. Its charter of incorporation was granted on December 22, 1857, at which time the following commissioners were designated to hold office, pending an election, to wit: T. C. Moore, W. N. Williams, Thomas Farmer, John Duke, and Mr. Coston.[1] In 1881, the old charter was superseded by a new one, in which T. H. Riddlepurger, T. J. Lovelace and D. B. Head, as Councilmen.[2] This charter was repealed in 1889 for a still later one, with modifications adapted to growing conditions.

Tallapoosa.   Tallapoosa, the chief town and most important commercial center of Haralson, dates its existence as a village, almost to the county's organization; but its charter of incorporation was not granted until December 20, 1860, when the following commissioners were named, to wit: V. A. Brewster, A. M. Robinson, T. S. Garner, M. G. Harper, and Wm. L. Fell.[3] In 1880 a new charter was granted, in which Charles Taliaferro was named as Mayor, with J. T. Barnwell, W. T. Summerlin, H. M. Martin, and H. A. Kiker, as Councilmen.[4] New charters were subsequently granted in 1888 and 1896. The present public school system was established in 1888. The Tallapoosa Street Railway Company was chartered in 1891, with Messrs. C. B. Hitchcock, R. I. Spencer, D. C. Scoville, and James W. Hyatt as incorporators.[5] Tallapoosa suffered from the collapse of a famous real estate boom in 1893, but for several years past the town has enjoyed a healthy growth.

---

[1] Acts, 1857, p. 178.
[2] Acts, 1880-1881, p. 484.
[3] Acts, 1860, p. 103.
[4] Acts, 1880, p. 411.
[5] Acts, 1890-1891, p. 344.

HARRIS

Hamilton. Hamilton was made the county-seat of Harris County by an Act approved December 20, 1828, at which time it was formally incorporated as a town with the following commissioners: Clark Blanford, Jacob M. Guerry, P. T. Beddell, George H. Bryan, and Norris Lyon.[1] Hamilton Academy was chartered December 22, 1828, with the following trustees: Allen Lawhorn, Wm. C. Osborn, John J. Slatter, George W. Rogers, Daniel Hightower, Thomas Mahone, John J. Harper, H. J. Harwell, and Samuel A. Billings.[2] The town was named for George W. Hamilton, a high tariff Democrat of South Carolina. The county, organized from lands formerly included in Troup and Muscogee, was named for Hon. Charles Harris, an eminent lawyer of Savannah. Some of the distinguished former residents of Hamilton are mentioned in the former volume of this work.

HART

Hartwell. In 1853, Hart County was organized out of lands formerly included in three adjacent counties: Elbert, Franklin, and Madison. Hartwell. the county-seat, was incorporated by an Act approved February 26, 1856, with the following commissioners: James T. Jones, John G. Justice, F. B. Hodges, J. N. Reeder, John B. Benson.[3] Subsequently a new charter was granted in 1885. Hartwell is today a thriving town with strong banks, prosperous mercantile establishments, and a body of citizens unsurpassed.

---

[1] Acts, 1828, p. 149.
[2] Acts, 1828, p. 15.
[3] Acts, 1855-1856, p. 382.

Nancy Hart.	Volume I, Pages 671-673.
The Hart Family.	Volume I, Pages 673-674.
Who Struck Billy Patterson?	Volume I, Pages 674-675.

HEARD

Franklin.   Franklin was made the county-seat of Heard when the county was first organized, in 1830. It was incorporated as a town on December 26, 1831, with the following named commissioners: Chas. R. Pearson, Wm. Adkins, Robert M. Richards, Thomas Erwin, and John C. Webb.[1] The Franklin Academy was chartered at the same time, with Messrs. Nathaniel Lipscomb, Wm. B. W. Dent, George W. Tarrentine, Thos. C. Pinkard, and Thos. Anberg, as trustees.

HENRY

McDonough.   In 1822, Henry County was organized out of Creek Indian lands. The county-seat of the new county was called McDonough, after the gallant hero of Lake Champlain, in the War of 1812, Capt. James McDonough; and was incorporated by an Act approved December 17, 1823, with Messrs. Tandy W. Key, Wm. L. Crayton, James Kimbrough, Andrew M. Brown, and Wm. Hardin, as commissioners.[2] Ten years later an academy was chartered. On December 12, 1854, the McDonough Collegiate Institute was founded, with the

[1] Acts, 1831, p. 83.
[2] Acts, 1823, p. 189.

following board of trustees: Humphrey Tomlinson, Leonard, and Thomas Anberg, as trustees.

Hampton. Originally there was a settlement at this place known as Bear Creek; but on August 23, 1872, an Act was approved granting the residents of this community a town charter and changing the name of the place to Hampton, presumably in honor of the great Confederate cavalry officer, General Wade Hampton, of South Carolina. The corporate limits were fixed at one mile in every direction from the depot of the Macon and Western Railroad. Messrs. W. H. Peebles, S. H. Griffin, R. A. Henderson, Levi Turnipseed and J. M. Williams were designated to act as commissioners pending an election of town officials.[1]

HOUSTON

Perry. Perry, the county-seat of Houston, was named for the hero of Lake Erie, in the War of 1812: Captain Oliver H. Perry, and was made the seat of government when Houston County was organized in 1822, out of a part of the Creek lands ceded under the first treaty at Indian Springs. It was incorporated as a town on December 20, 1828, with Messrs. Giles B. Taylor, James M. Kelly, F. W. Jobson, James E. Duncan, and Allen Chastain, as commissioners.[2] The Houston County Academy was incorporated in 1833. But Perry was not satisfied with one school and proceeded to organize a Baptist College for young ladies, which afterwards grew into the Houston Female College, under which name it was re-incorporated on February 18, 1854, with the following board of trustees: Samuel F'elder, president; John Killen, vice-president; Hugh L. Denard, vice-president; Wm. T. Swift, treasurer; Samuel D. Killen, secretary; Benj. F. Tharp, George F. Cooper, Nicholas Marshburn, Laban Segrist, James E. Barrett, Wm. Summerford, George W. Singleton, and John T. Cooper.[3] Perry

---

[1] Acts, 1872, p. 209.
[2] Acts, 1828, p. 159.
[3] Acts, 1853-1854, p. 125.

was the home of Hon. James M. Kelly, the first Supreme
Court Reporter of Georgia. His grave is in the front
yard of the old home place where Hon. Thos. S. Felder,
afterwards Attorney General of Georgia, spent his
boyhood days. The list of former distinguished residents of the town includes also: Judge Wm. L. Grice,
Judge A. L. Miller, Judge Warren D. Nottingham, Col.
Buford M. Davis, and others. Houston County was
named for an honored chief-executive and patriot of the
Revolution: Governor John Houstoun.

Fort Valley. Fort Valley, one of the famed centers of
the peach-growing industry in Georgia, occupies a site of historic memories, associated with Indian warfare in pioneer days. The town was chartered
by an Act approved March 3, 1856, with Messrs. C. D.
Anderson, Wm. H. Hollingshead, Wm. J. Greene, A. D.
Kendrick, and D. N. Austin, as commissioners.[1] But
the old Fort Valley Academy was chartered twenty years
earlier, on December 24, 1836, at which time the following trustees were named: James Everett, John P. Allen,
Hardy Hunter, Henry Kaigler, and John Humphries.
In 1852, the Fort Valley Female Seminary was granted
a charter, with the following board of trustees: George
W. Persons, John J. Hampton, Wm. A. Matthews, Adol-
phus D. Kendrick, Miles L. Green, Wm. J. Anderson, D.
N. Austin, Judson Kendrick, Wm. H. Hollingshead, Matthew Dawsey, Benj. Barnes, Robt. M. Patterson, and
James M. Miller.[2] At the beginning of the war, plans
for a college were on foot; but the outbreak of hostilities
prevented a consummation of this project. Since Fort
Valley began to ship her wonderful peaches to Northern
and Eastern markets, she has found fame and fortune;
and with fine railway facilities the future of the town is
bright with promise. Fort Valley's public school sys-

---

[1] Acts, 1855-1856, p. 377.
[2] Acts, 1852-1853, p. 326.

tem was established in 1886, is one of the best in the
State, and is under the supervision of a most accomplished educator, Prof. Ralph Newton.

Some additional facts in regard to Fort Valley have
been supplied by a well-informed resident of the town;
as follows:

Very little is now known of the early history of Fort Valley. Matthew
Dorsey and James A. Everett donated land to be used only for church
and school purposes, and on this site has been recently erected the handsome high school building, at a cost of $40,000.00. In 1849 there were three
stores, one academy, one church and 250 inhabitants. There was a gradual
increase in the size and business of the place until 1851, when the Southwestern Railroad was completed to this point. This was followed by a
very rapid growth; homes, stores, churches and hotels were built. Fort
Valley suffered, in common with other towns, from the Civil War. The
best business men were called to the field of battle, and commercial and
industrial pursuits were checked, but after the war is prosperity exceeded
the most sanguine expectations of its citizens. On the night of October
31, 1867, nearly all of the principal business houses were consumed by a
most disastrous fire, but these were soon replaced by handsome brick
buildings.

On Church Street we find the old home of the Hon. Joe Hill Hall but
little changed. Fort Valley stands today in the midst of the best farming
section of Middle Georgia, and is the peach center of the world, famous
as the home of the Elberta and Hiley Belle peach. The land around is
level and especially adapted to peach culture. The enormous increase in
yields each year makes it impossible to estimate what the land is really
worth. Fort Valley is located at the divergence of five railroads. The
place is elevated 170 feet above College Hill, in Macon, Ga., and is the
highest point across the country from the Atlantic to the Gulf. The system
of water-works is furnished by artesian wells, and school advantages are
unsurpassed, and it is an ideal town in an ideal location, with an ideal
citizenship.*

IRWIN

**Gov. Irwin's
Family Record.** Governor Jared Irwin, for whom this county was
named, will always be revered for his uncompromising
opposition to the Yazoo Fraud. It was while he occupied the executive chair at Louisville that the records of this colossal iniquity

---

*Authority: Mrs. S. T. Nell, Fort Valley, Ga.

were by his order committed to the flames. Governor Irwin came of a long line of distinguished Scotch ancestors. His father, Hugh Lawson Irwin, of Mecklinburg, N. C., married Martha Alexander, and five children were the fruit of this union, to wit: Jared, John Lawson, William, Alexander and Margaret. With his three brothers, all of whom were soldiers in the war for independence, Jared Irwin built a fort near Union Hill, his home, to protect this section of Georgia from the Indians. It was called Fort Irwin. The Governor's grandfather, Thomas Irwin, married Margaret Lawson, daughter of Hugh Lawson, Gent., of North Carolina. This aristocratic old pioneer always affixed to his name the mark of his gentle birth. He married Mary Moore, daughter of Charles Moore, Sr., of South Carolina, and sister of Gen. Thomas Moore, of Revolutionary fame. Thomas, the Governor's grandfather, came originally from Scotland, settling first in Pennsylvania. Governor Jared Irwin married his cousin, Isabella Erwin, whose father changed the spelling of his name on account of family differences in matters of religion. Governor Irwin's daughter, Elizabeth, married Simon Whitaker, from which union sprang a son, Hon. Jared I. Whitaker, one of Atlanta's early mayors and quite a noted editor. His younger daughter, Jane, remained unmarried. It was she who succeeded in obtaining from Congress a large sum of money to cover certain expenditures made by her father in equipping troops during the Revolution. She established the fact, in her papers to Congress, that Jared Irwin entered the war as Captain, was promoted first to Major and afterwards to Colonel, and was present with his command in the sieges of Augusta and Savannah, and at the battles of Camden, Briar Creek and Black Swamp, in each of which he distinguished himself for gallant behavior. John Irwin, his son, was a captain in the War of 1812, but died a bachelor. Another son, Thomas, and a nephew, Jared, Jr., were members of the first class to graduate from Franklin College, in 1804, on which occasion both were speakers. Governor Irwin was always prominent in both military and civil affairs, and he was three times elected Governor of the State. His brother, John Lawson Irwin, was a general in the War of 1812, and was buried with military honors, at his home in Washington County, in 1822. The first monument ever erected by the State of Georgia was erected to the memory of Governor Jared Irwin, in the town of Sandersville.*

Irwinville.   Irwinville, the county-seat of Irwin County, like the county itself, was named for Governor Jared Irwin, whose signature was affixed to the famous Act of 1796, rescinding the Yazoo Fraud. It was made the county-seat in 1831, prior to which time the

*Authority: Mrs. James S. Wood, of Savannah.

BURNING THE YAZOO ACT

Gov. Jared Irwin signed the Rescinding Yazoo Act Feb. 13th 1796
and the Yazoo Fraud Papers were burned before the Capitol
Feb 15th 1796 Gov Irwin. stands just behind the Messenger who holds the Papers

Reproduced from an original drawing presented to the Savannah Historical Society
by Mr. Lawton B. Evans

seat of government was for a brief period at Ironville. Irwin was organized in 1818, out of treaty lands acquired from the Creeks. On the outskirts of the town of Irwinville, President Davis was arrested at the close of the Civil War, while en route to his home in Mississippi.*

Ocilla. Ocilla, one of the most progressive towns in the Southern belt, is also one of the youngest. It was granted a charter of incorporation on November 24, 1897, with the following named officials to manage its local affairs: John C. Luke, as mayor, M. J. Paulk, as recorder, and D. H. Paulk, W. M. Harris, and G. L. Stone, as aldermen.[1] In the following year the corporate limits were extended. At the same time Ocilla was created, an independent school district with the following trustees, to wit: J. L. Paulk, L. R. Tucker, A. L. Hayes, J. B. Davis, and J. R. Goethe.[2] The town officials from 1898 to 1901 were: J. A. J. Henderson, mayor; M. J. Paulk, town attorney; C. H. Martin, recorder; and J. C. Luke, D. H. Paulk, G. L. Stone, L. R. Tucker, and C. H. Martin, aldermen. Few towns in Georgia have enjoyed such a phenomenal growth during the past decade as Ocilla. It is located in the center of a rich agricultural belt; is possessed of a wideawake body of citizens whose ambition is to make Ocilla a metropolis; is enabled by its strong banks to finance a constantly increasing volume of business; and is a town fully abreast of the times in its up-to-date public utilities.

JACKSON

Historic Jefferson. This famous old town, the seat of Jackson County, celebrated the one hundredth anniversary of its incorporation in the year

---

*See Vol. I, of this work, Chapter 2.
[1] Acts, 1897, p. 283.
[2] Acts, 1898, p. 241.

1912. Jefferson is not a large town. It boasts a population of only about 1,600 souls; and many wonder why she has not progressed—why Atlanta, Macon, Columbus, and other communities have grown so much faster than the old settlement at Jefferson. But those who wonder look only at material things. Jefferson has not developed very great commercial success; but she has given to the world men who are credited with greater things than building factories and railroads.

Wm. D. Martin: His Splendid Philanthropy. One of the noblest institutions of learning in America is old Martin Institute, located in the town of Jefferson. It was first known as the Jackson County Academy when established in 1818, at which time it was but a one-room log cabin with puncheon seats. But when William D. Martin—than whom Jefferson never boasted a better citizen—donated 150 shares of Georgia Railroad stock to the school in 1859, the name was changed to Martin Institute, in honor of this generous benefactor.

William Duncan Martin was born on Stone Horse Creek, in Hanover County, Va., on January 8, 1771, and died at Jefferson, Ga., on May 21, 1852. He came to Jefferson when well past the meridian of life, and his sole possessions at this time were a horse, a bridle and saddle, and $100 in money. It was rather late for laying the foundations of a fortune. But he applied himself to business, and as the result of prudent economy, supplemented by wise investment, he left an estate valued by his executors at $80,000. Wm. D. Martin was perhaps the first person in America to endow a public school from his private fortune. If this statement is correct, then Martin Institute is the oldest endowed educational institution in the United States; and too much honor cannot be accorded this noble philanthropist for setting a pace which has since been followed by so many wealthy citizens in generous gifts to education.

Martin Institute has shown herself worthy of this unique distinction by giving to the world a host of bright names. Justice Joseph R. Lamar, of the Supreme Court of the United States, who just a few days ago was appointed by President Woodrow Wilson to act as one of the mediators to settle the trouble between our country and Mexico, was taught here. Dr. Henry Stiles Bradley, one of the most powerful preachers in America, was also enrolled as a student. The list likewise includes: Ex-Congressman Wm. M. Howard, who was appointed on the Tariff Board by President Taft; Rev. David J. Scott, D. D., of Texas; Rev. Joseph J. Bennett, D. D., of Georgia; Hon. John N. Holder, of Jefferson, twice Speaker of the Georgia House of Representatives without opposition, and now a candidate for Congress; besides men of prominence in every pursuit and occupation. The shaft erected to the memory of Wm. D. Martin stands in the Methodist church-yard, almost under the eaves of the institution which he endowed; and, as directed in his will, it bears the following quaint epitaph:

> "Remember, man, as you pass by,
> As you are now so once was I;
> As I am now, so you shall be,
> Prepare for death and follow me."

Dr. Crawford W. Long: The Discoverer of Anaesthesia. The typical figure by which Georgia is best represented before the world is not that of a great orator. Millions have never heard or read the matchless orations of Grady, the South's silver-tongued Cicero. It is not that of our beloved poet, Sidney Lanier, though he is loved wherever he is known. It is not that of our great statesman, Alexander H. Stephens, for colossal though his services were they benefitted his own country alone. High above these, rises the figure of an unpretentious country doctor who made the town of Jefferson his home and whose right to the highest niche in Georgia's Temple of Fame there will be none to dispute: Dr. Crawford W. Long. The gift of Sulphuric Ether Anaesthesia made by Dr. Long to medical science not only revolutionized the practice of medicine, but made surgery a profession within itself.

On March 30, 1842, in the little town of Jefferson, Ga., Dr. Crawford W. Long, in an experimental operation, discovered that anaesthesia not only helped to make an operation successful, but rendered it painless. The discovery was not published or paraded before the people; perhaps Dr. Long himself did not realize its untold value; perhaps he did not care to exploit his achievement. But today there is not a physician of any recognized prominence in any part of the civilized world who is not familiar with the name of Crawford W. Long. The little office in which he performed his experiments has been torn away. Until two years ago, a gnarled and knotted old mulberry tree, on the north corner of the public square, marked the exact spot where his first operation was performed, an epoch-making event; but this, too, has now disappeared. Its sacrifice was demanded by a commercial age. Tell it not in Gath, but the tree was given by the town authorities to an old negro for fire-wood. Fate intervened, however; and it was bought from the old negro by Mr. W. H. Smith, of Jefferson, who had a part of it made into gavels, pen staffs, and other articles of use, for souvenirs. On a marble slab, in the brick wall of a building adjacent to Dr. Long's little office, the date of his wonderful discovery has been inscribed. This slab was erected by Prof. S. P. Orr, of Athens, an intimate friend of the Long family. There is also a magnificent monument to his memory on the town square. Dr. Woods Hutchison, of New York, and Hon. Pleasant A. Stovall, of Savannah, made the principal addresses, when the monument was unveiled by the Georgia Medical Society, on April 21, 1910. There is also a handsome brass medallion, on the walls of his alma mater, the University of Pennsylvania, a genuine work of art, moulded by an old college mate.*

Harmony Grove. Long before the days of railroads, there was a famous "star route" through this section, over which the stage.coach made daily trips from the classic city of Athens to the little town of Clarkesville, nestling at the foot of the Blue Ridge mountains. This coach stopped at what was then known as the village of Harmony Grove, where it daily left a pouch of mail for the small group of inhabitants. At this time, there were only four families living in Harmony Grove: the Hardmans, the Shankles, the Hoods, and the Bowdons.

Mr. Seaborn M. Shankle was the pioneer merchant. He owned and operated the first store in what was afterwards the town of Commerce. Subsequent to a marriage of Mr. Shankle's sister to Mr. C. W. Hood, the latter became a member of the firm. By mutual consent this partnership was dissolved when Mr. Hood opened a store of his own, while Mr. Shankle for a short while continued to merchandise alone at the old place of business. Later, he formed a partnership with Dr. W. B. J. Hardman. But, after a few years, the firm of Hardman & Shankle was dissolved also, Dr. Hardman withdrawing from active mercantile life to settle with his family upon a large farm then recently purchased by him, about a mile from the present town center; and from this time on he gave his entire time to the practice of medicine. Mr. Shankle left a large family of children. including Rev. Grogan Shankle, pastor of one of the largest Methodist churches in New Orleans; Mr. Lovick P. Shankle, a well-to-do planter of Banks County; Mr. Marvin Shankle, assistant cashier of the Northeastern Banking Company; Mr. Claude Shankle, connected with the Coca-Cola works in Atlanta; Dr. Olin Shankle, of Commerce, a successful practicing physician; Mrs. Amelia Perkins, of Atlanta, and Mrs. W. B. Hardman, Mrs. J. L. Sharp, and Mrs. W. D. Sheppard, all of Commerce. Mr. Shankle died, on August 22, 1885, leaving to his widow, formerly Miss Victoria Parks, a handsome estate, which, by judicious investment, was afterwards largely increased under her management. She also continued the mercantile establishment for a number of years.

Dr. W. B. J. Hardman lived here until his death, some twelve years ago. At the time of his removal from Oglethorpe County to Harmony Grove, he was the only practicing physician in this part of the county, and his circuit embraced an extensive area. He reared a family of ten children, to-wit.: Rev. Henry E. Hardman, Dr. L. G. Hardman and Dr. W. B. Hardman, of Commerce; Mr. Robert L. Hardman, of Atlanta; Mr. T. C.

---

*Authority: Mr. W. H. Smith, of Jefferson, Ga.

Hardman, of Commerce; Mr. John B. Hardman, of Commerce; and Mrs. W. L. Williamson, Mrs. Gordon T. Jones, Mrs. C. J. Hood, deceased, and Miss Sallie Hardman, deceased, all of Commerce. Mr. C. W. Hood left a family, four members of which survive: Mr. C. J. Hood, formerly Mayor of Commerce and at present cashier of the Northeastern Banking Company; Miss Mary Hood, Mr. C. W. Hood, Jr., and Miss Ruth Hood, besides a widow, formerly Miss Alice Owens, of Toccoa.

To three pioneer citizens, Messrs. Hood, Hardman and Shankle, Harmony Grove became indebted in after years for the old Northeastern Railroad, now the Lula and Athens Branch of the Southern. When the proposed line was first advocated, there was quite a rivalry between Harmony Grove and Jefferson, as to which should secure it, since to include both towns was out of the question. At the time set for a final decision, Jefferson turned up with a third more stock subscribed than Harmony Grove. But Messrs. Hood, Shankle and Hardman, representatives from the latter town, agreed personally to endorse every dollar of the stock, provided the road was built by way of Harmony Grove. This action insured success; for the representatives of Jefferson, failing to offer a similar endorsement, the road was lost.

The First School for Girls. To the old town of Harmony Grove belongs the honor of having launched successfully the first school for girls ever established in the State of Georgia. It was known as the "Female Academy of Harmony Grove," and was chartered by an Act of the Legislature, approved in 1824. The following trustees were named in the Act of incorporation: Russell Jones, William Potts, Samuel Barnett, Frederick Stewart, and John Rhea.* On account of the vast number of schools for women which have since leaped into existence, on both sides of the water, this pioneer charter is a document of prime importance in the history of modern education.

Commerce. With the completion of the Northeastern Railroad a new life began to quicken in the old town of Harmony Grove. Visions of greater things were caught, and even at this early date there was launched a movement, the ultimate outcome of which was a new

----

*Dawson's Compilation, p. 24.

name: Commerce. There was something catchy about the name selected. It registered a key-note of progress and made a distinct bid for trade. The caterpillar had merged into the butterfly; and while the former was doomed to creep, at a slow pace upon the ground, it was the glory of the latter to soar among the flowers. Two splendid young men from Franklin County, Messrs. W. T. Harber and G. W. D. Harber, were the first new merchants to settle in Commerce; but the Harbers were soon followed by Messrs W. A. and J. T. Quillian. Thus stimulated, the growth of the town was now steady, fresh recruits coming from most of the adjacent counties. At present, the population of Commerce is 4,000. It is now a recognized competitor of Athens, doing a business of several million dollars per annum. During the past fall season, one firm alone in a single day bought over $25,000 worth of cotton.

Paved streets, electric lights, an excellent water works system, public schools inferior to none in the State, palatial homes, superb business blocks —these are some of the most striking features of present-day Commerce. Three solid banks furnish ample means with which to finance local enterprises. The oldest of these is the Northeastern Banking Company, of which Dr. L. G. Hardman is president, Mr. C. J. Hood, cashier, and Mr. Marvin Shankle, assistant cashier. The First National Bank, organized some twelve years ago, is now a close competitor. Its officers are as follows: Dr. W. B. Hardman, president; Mr. George L. Hubbard, cashier, and Mr. A. H. Shannon, assistant cashier. Besides these, there is a private bank owned by Mr. Enoch B. Anderson, one of the best-known financiers of Commerce. Five churches minister to the town's religious needs. The late Dr. Henry F. Hoyt, one of the foremost Presbyterian divines of the State, was an uncle of Mrs. Woodrow Wilson. Commerce boasts of two weekly newspapers. The older of these is the *News*, owned and edited by Hon. John F. Shannon. The younger is the *Observer*, of which Hon. Paul T. Harber is editor and proprietor. Two better newspapers are not to be found in the ranks of weekly journalism in Georgia. It was due largely to the prestige of these two splendid sheets that the Georgia Weekly Press Association met in Commerce during the summer of 1914.

One of the largest cotton factories in the State is located at Commerce, known as the Harmony Grove Mills. It boasts a capital stock of $450,000, all of which is paid in. Dr. L. G. Hardman is president and Dr. W. B. Hardman, secretary and treasurer, of this mammoth establishment. There are two oil mills in Commerce, viz., the Commerce Branch of the Southern Cotton Oil Company, with Mr. T. C. Robinson, Jr., as manager, and the Farmers' Oil Mill Company, of which Mr. W. H. T. Gillespie is president and Colonel H. O. Williford, lessee. The Hardman Sanitorium, noted all over Georgia, is located at Commerce, with a corps of able physicians in charge, including Dr. L. G. Hardman, Dr. W. B. Hardman, Dr. Olin Shankle and Dr. M. J. Nelms. The town has its own telephone system, with splendid local exchange in most of the surrounding towns and villages.

But, if anything was still needed to put Commerce upon the map it was supplied a few years ago by the famous Glidden tourists, who passed through the town in making their first tour of the State. Here they spent their last night on the road before reaching Atlanta, and such was the royal reception with which the people of Commerce greeted these visitors from the North that by a unanimous vote it was decided to include Commerce on the return trip back to New York. Stopping over for luncheon they were most charmingly served by the fair maids and matrons of Commerce, on the spacious lawn of Dr. Hardman.

Commerce obtained its charter as Harmony Grove in 1883, and its charter as Commerce in 1903. Hon. William A. Quillian, now deceased, was the first mayor of Harmony Grove. The city is governed today by an efficient corps of public officials, consisting of Mr. E. B. Anderson, mayor; Mr. C. W. Goodin, clerk of council and city treasurer, and Messrs. Claude Montgomery, Frank Wright, T. C. Hardman, E. B. Crow, L. L. Davis and W. D. Sheppard, as aldermen; C. C. Bolton, as chief of police, assisted by Elmer Bailey, and Colonels R. L. J. and S. J. Smith, Jr., as city attorneys. There is not an abler Bar in any town of equal population in Georgia, and among the resident lawyers of State-wide note are: Judge W. W. Stark, a member of the present State Senate, and Colonels R. L. J. Smith, S. J. Smith, Jr., W. A. Stevenson, E. C. Starks, G. P. Martin and W. D. Martin. Dr. L. G. Hardman, perhaps the foremost citizen of Commerce, was a strong minority candidate in the recent election for Governor. He was largely instrumental in placing the present State-wide prohibition law upon the statute books.

JASPER

Old Randolph. Jasper County was first organized as Randolph, under an Act approved December 10, 1907, by Gov. Jared Irwin.* But John Randolph, the great Virginian, for whom this county was first named, having become unpopular in Georgia by reason of his views on certain public measures, the name of the county was, on December 10, 1812, changed to Jasper, in honor of the gallant Sergeant Jasper, who fell mortally wounded at the siege of Savannah. The Act in question reads as follows:

"Whereas it was obviously the intention of the Legislature of Georgia, in designating a county by the name of Randolph, to perpetuate the

---

*Clayton's Compendium, p. 357.

name of John Randolph, a member of Congress from Virginia, whose early exertions in the cause of democracy claimed the approbation and applause of every good citizen of these United States. But whereas the conduct of the said John Randolph, in his official capacity as a member of Congress has evinced such a manifest desertion of correct principles and such a decided attachment to the enemies of the United States as to render his name odious to every republican citizen of this State, etc. Be it therefore enacted that from and after the passage of this Act the County of Randolph shall be called and known by the name of the County of Jasper, any law to the contrary notwithstanding."*

But the public mind is often fickle. Sixteen years later, John Randolph was again in high favor with the people of Georgia; and, in 1828, a new county was formed, bordering on the Chattahoochee River, to which was given the name of the peppery old "School-master of Congress."

Monticello. Most of the early settlers of Jasper County, were native Virginians. This was perhaps one among a number of very good reasons why the county was first called Randolph. It also throws an important side-light upon the naming of the county-seat: Monticello, for the old home of Thomas Jefferson. The town was incorporated by an Act providing for its better regulation, on December 15, 1810, when the following commissioners were named: Richard Holmes, Henry Walker, Stokeley Morgan, James Armour, and Francis S. Martin.* The old Monticello Academy was chartered in 1815; but, on December 23, 1830, the Monticello Union Academy, a more pretentious educational plant, was chartered with the following trustees: David A. Reese, Fleming Jordan, Edward Y. Hill, Moses Champion, John W. Burney, Reuben C. Shorter, and Benj. F. Ward. Monticello is a thriving town, progressive and wideawake, but tempered by a fine conservatism and by a splendid loyalty to the old traditions.

*Lamar's Digest, p. 199.
*Clayton's Compendium, p. 609.

Some additional facts in regard to Monticello have been furnished by a distinguished resident of the town.* Says he: In 1808 a commission was appointed by the Legislature to select and purchase a site for the public buildings of the county, the site to contain two acres. This commission found a very peculiarly formed hill, a central prominence, with ridges radiating therefrom on all sides except the north side, on which was a very steep bluff, descending into a ravine, and from the base of the bluff sprang several bold springs of fine water. The commission also purchased about two acres of this ravine, for the use of the county, and for the preservation of these springs for the public use. Ground for the county buildings was laid off in the form of a square, and in the center was built the first court-house, a small log structure. Around this soon began to grow a village, to which was given the name of Monticello, for the home of Mr. Jefferson. With the advent of the Iron Horse Monticello became isolated, trade going to towns along the line of the Georgia Railroad and to Macon until 1887, when a railroad was constructed through Monticello. At once the little village took on new life, and now has a population of 2,500.

The business people of the city of today are the descendants of the early settlers of the county and of the town. Among the men who first engaged in the mercantile business were Jesse Loyall, Jeremiah Pearson, Manly & Kellam, Buchannan & Jordan, William Cooley, John Baldwin, Samuel Fulton, Sr., Samuel Fulton, Jr., and Hurd & Hungerford, which last named were succeeded by N. B. & L. White. This firm continued until the death of Mr. L. White, after which it became N. B. White and N. B. White & Co., continuing as such until a few years ago, when it terminated on the death of Mr. N. B. White.

The lawyers of Monticello in the early days included Alfred Cuthbert and Joshua Hill, both of whom became United States Senators. John R. Dyer was admitted to the bar in Monticello, and practiced here until his death. Of the early physicians were Dr. Moses Champion and Dr. Milton Anthony, the latter of whom afterwards founded the oldest medical college in the State, at Augusta. Of the early settlers of the county was John Maddux, whose descendants are still in the city and county, all good citizens. Among them was Dr. W. D. Maddux, a noted physician in the section, who died eight years ago, after a long and useful life, spent in the upbuilding of the city and county.

Captain Eli Glover,, of the War of 1812, the Mexican War and Inidan wars, was one of the early settlers whose descendants are still here holding prominent places and doing much for the advancement of the city. The Kelly family was a large one, and while at first they lived in the country they later came into town and have been influential factors in the community for generations. Several of them are now engaged in the mercantile business on a large scale. William Penn settled in Monticello

*Judge A. S. Thurman.

soon after it was laid out, and took a prominent part in the development
of the city, as well as in farming. He also owned several large plantations in the County of Jasper.

With hardly an exception the business men of the city are descendants
of the first settlers. As Monticello was for years without railway connections, the people mingled but little with the outer world. For this reason
there has been but little new blood brought into the county; the same
names that we find in the early days are the same of today. These were
a hardy race and shows in the successful lives of the people. But the original
settlers belonged to a vigorous and virile race of men, and from the loins
of these pioneers who laid the foundations of Monticello have come the
men who direct its affairs today. In the most liberal sense, Monticello is a
self-made town.

First White Child Born in Jasper. Nathan Fish, and his wife, Naomi Phillips, were the parents of the first white child born in Jasper. This child, a son, Calvin Fish, was born December 22, 1807, and died August 1, 1861.

Soldiers of Jasper: Supplemental List. Elijah Cornwell, a Revolutionary soldier, is buried in the Cornwell family cemetery, near Alcovy River, about two miles west of Mechanicsville. He served in. the Virginia army, under General Greene. The Cornwells came originally from Cornwall, Eng. Wiley Hood, soldier in the War of 1812, and in the Florida Indian War, is buried at Murder Creek Baptist Church. William Robertson, soldier in the War of 1812, and in the Florida Indian War, is buried in Rocky Creek Cemetery, in the northern part of Jasper. William G. Smith, born in Virginia, in 1787, a private in Captain William Owen's Company, 2nd (Jenkins') Regiment, Georgia Volunteers and Militia, War of 1812, is buried in the family burial ground, near old Murder Creek Baptist church. His father, Guy Smith, one of the early settlers of Oglethorpe County, was a Revolutionary soldier.

John Clark, volunteer soldier in War of 1812, served in Capt. N. T. Martin's Company, South Carolina Militia.

With his family he settled in Jasper County, in 1830, on the Alcovy River, a few miles from old Bethlehem Baptist church. He died in 1870, at the advanced age of ninety years and is buried in the family grave-yard at the family homestead, where he resided for forty years. He was born in North Carolina. His wife was Miss Susan Parks, of Laurens, S. C. They were the parents of eighteen children and many descendants now live in this county and in various States of the Union.

The Confederate   On the court-house square, in Monticel-
Monument.   lo, stands a handsome granite shaft, erected to the memory of the South's heroic dead. The monument was unveiled on April 6, 1910, at which time Gen. Harrison, who commanded the troops from Jasper County during the Civil War, delivered an eloquent address as the chosen orator of the day. Hon. Harvie Jordan acted as Master of Ceremonies; and Rev. W. D. Conwell offered the prayer of invocation. Mrs. H. C. Hill, on behalf of the local U. D. C. Chapter formally presented the monument to the city of Monticello and to the County of Jasper. To this address Major O. G. Roberts responded for the Confederate veterans; Hon. E. H. Jordan, for the county and Mayor Monroe Phillips for the town. Master Leland Jordan feelingly recited a selection entitled ''The Daughter of Dixie, the Preserver of the Faith,'' while Miss Alice Baxter, Georgia State President, U. D. C., made a most delightful talk. Thirteen little granddaughters of the Confederacy, at a given signal, drew the cord which unloosed the veil. To Mrs. Greene F. Johnson, President of the Chapter, was largely due the success of the movement, culminating in this splendid shaft. The purchasing committee was composed of the following members: Mr. J. J. Pope, Mr. M. Benton, Mr. Eugene Benton, Dr. C. L. Ridley, Judge J. H. Blackwell, Mrs. Monroe Phillips, Mrs. B. Leverett, Mrs. T. M. Payne, and Miss Maud

Clark Penn. The monument is a work of art. It stands thirty-two feet high, and is built of finely polished granite from the quarries of Elbert County, Ga. On the east and west sides there are imported statues of Italian marble, each of which is most exquisitely carved. On the south side of the pedestal is inscribed:

> "Crowns of roses fade, crowns of thorns endure. Calvaries and crucifixions take deepest hold of humanity; the triumphs of might are transient; they pass and are forgotten; the sufferings of right are graven deepest on the chronicles of nations."

On the north side is seen a Confederate battle-flag with the inscription:

> "To the Confederate soldiers of Jasper County, the record of whose sublime self-sacrifice and undying devotion to duty in the service of their country is the proud heritage of a loyal posterity."
>
> "In legend and lay our heroes in gray
> Shall forever live over again for us."

JEFF DAVIS

Hazelhurst. On August 18, 1905, an Act was approved creating the county of Jeff Davis, out of lands formerly embraced within Appling and Coffee counties and designating the town of Hazelhurst as the new county-seat. For additional facts in regard to the creation of this county, the reader is referred to Volume I.

Putting Mr. Davis in Irons: The Story Told by His Prison Physician. Dr. John J. Craven, a distinguished surgeon in the Union army, was the prison physician at Fortress Monroe during the first six months which followed the incarceration of Mr. Davis. Though at first strongly tinctured with the prejudice which prevailed at the North in regard to the illustrious prisoner, Dr. Craven, from intimate personal contact with him from day to day, came to regard his patient with unfeigned admiration. On relinquishing his duties at the famous prison, Dr. Craven published a volume entitled: ''The Prison Life of Jefferson Davis;'' and, besides containing what in the main was accepted at the South as a truthful account written by one who was in a position to know the facts, it sounded the first distinct note of friendliness which was raised at the North on behalf of the great Confederate leader. It served to put Mr. Davis in an altogether different light before his enemies, and it doubtless operated in some measure, as a check upon the vindictive spirit of revenge which was clamoring for his death. Throughout the long and bitter ordeal of imprisonment, there was no hour fraught with greater humiliation to Mr. Davis than when a blacksmith was sent to his cell to manacle this proud chieftain of a vanquished, but brave people, nor can there be found in the transactions of the Federal government a blot which so impugns the humanity of a Christian nation. The subsequent failure of the government to bring Mr. Davis to trial, on the ground that he could not legally be convicted of treason, only shows the needlessness of such indignity to one who was already helpless at the mercy of his foes. After narrating the pathetic circumstances incident to the formal induction of Mr. Davis into prison life at Fortress Monroe, Dr. Craven thus tells how he was manacled:

''On the morning of the 23rd of May, a yet bitterer trial was in store for the proud spirit—a trial severer probably than has ever in modern times been inflicted upon any one who has enjoyed such eminence. This morning Jefferson Davis was shackled. . . . Captain Jerome E. Titlow, of the Third Pennsylvania Artillery, entered the prisoner's cell, followed by the blacksmith of the fort and his assistant, carrying in his hands some heavy and harshly rattling shackles. As they entered, Mr. Davis was reclining on his bed, feverish and weary after a sleepless night, the food placed near him on the preceding day still lying untouched on the tin plate at his bedside.

'' 'Well?' said Mr. Davis, as they entered, slightly raising his head.

"'I have an unpleasant duty to perform, sir,' said Captain Titlow, and as he spoke the senior blacksmith took the shackles from his assistant.

"Davis leaped instantly from his recumbent attitude, a flush passing over his face for a moment, and then his countenance growing livid and rigid as death. He gasped for breath, clutching his throat with the thin fingers of his right hand, and then recovering himself slowly, while his wasted figure towered up to its full height—now appearing to swell with indignation and then to shrink with terror, as he glanced from the captain's face to the shackles—he said slowly and with a laboring chest:

"'My God! You cannot have been sent to iron me!'

"'Such are my orders, sir,' replied the officer, signalling the blacksmith to approach, who stepped forward, unlocking the padlock and preparing the fetters to do their office. These fetters were of heavy iron, probably five-eighths of an inch in thickness, and connected together by a chain of like weight. I believe they are now in possession of Major-General Miles, and will form an interesting relic.

"'This is too monstrous,' groaned the prisoner, glaring hurriedly round the room, as if looking for some weapon or other means of self-destruction. 'I demand, Captain, that you let me see the commanding officer. Can he pretend that such shackles are required to secure the safe custody of a weak old man, so guarded, and in such a fort as this?'

"'It could serve no purpose,' replied Captain Titlow; 'his orders are from Washington, as mine are from him.'

"'But he can telegraph,' interposed Mr. Davis, eagerly. 'There must be some mistake. No such outrage as you threaten me with is on record in the history of nations. Beg him to telegraph, and delay until he answers.'

"'My orders are peremptory,' said the officer, 'and admit of no delay. For your own sake, let me advise you to submit with patience. As a soldier, Mr. Davis, you know I must execute orders.'

"'These are not orders for a soldier,' shouted the prisoner, losing all control of himself. 'They are orders for a jailer—for a hangman—which no soldier wearing a sword should accept. I tell you the world will ring with this disgrace. The war is over; the South is conquered; I have no longer any country but America, and it is for the honor of America, as well as for my own honor and life, that I plead against this degradation. Kill me! Kill me!' he cried passionately, throwing his arms wide open and exposing his breast, rather than inflict on me, and on my people through me, this insult, worse than death.'

"'Do your duty, blacksmith,' said the officer, walking toward the embrasure as if not caring to witness the performance. 'It only gives increased pain on all sides to protract this interview.'

"At these words the blacksmith advanced with the shackles and, seeing that the prisoner had one foot upon the chair near his bedside, the right hand resting on the back of it, the brawny mechanic made an attempt to slip one of the shackles over the ankle so raised; but, as if with the vehemence and strength which frenzy can impart, even to the weakest invalid, Mr. Davis suddenly seized his assilant and hurled him half way across the room. On this, Captain Titlow turned, and, seeing that Davis had backed against the wall for further resistance, began to remonstrate, pointing out in brief, clear language, that this course was madness, and that orders must be enforced at any cost.

" 'Why compel me,' he said, 'to add the further indignity of personal violence to the necessity of your being ironed?'

" 'I am a prisoner of war,' fiercely retorted Davis. 'I have been a soldier in the armies of America, and know how to die. Only kill me, and my last breath shall be a blessing upon your head. But while I have life and strength to resist, for myself and for my people, this shall not be done.

"Hereupon Captain Titlow called in a sergeant and a file of soldiers from the next room, and the sergeant advanced to seize the prisoner. Immediately Mr. Davis flew on him, seized his musket and attempted to wrench it from his grasp. Of course, such a scene could have but one issue. There was a short, passionate scuffle. In a moment Davis was flung upon his bed, and before his four powerful assailants moved their hands from him, the blacksmith and his assistant had done their work—one securing the rivet on the right ankle, while the other turned the key in the padlock on the left. This done, Mr. Davis lay for a moment as if in a stupor. Then slowly raising himself and turning around, he dropped his shackled foot to the floor. The harsh clank of the striking chain seems first to have recalled him to the situation, and, dropping his face into his hands, he burst into a passionate flood of sobbing, rocking to and fro and muttering, at brief intervals:

" 'Oh, the shame! the shame!'

　　*　　*　　*　　*　　*　　*　　*　　*　　*

"On the morning of May 24th, I was sent for about half-past 8 A. M., by Major-General Miles; was told that State prisoner Davis complained of being ill, and that I had been assigned as his medical attendant. Calling upon the prisoner—the first time I had ever seen him closely—he presented a very miserable aspect. Stretched upon his pallet and very much emaciated. Mr. Davis appeared a mere fascine of raw and tremulous nerves—his eyes restless and fevered, his head continually shifting from side to side for a cool spot on the pillow, and his case clearly one in which intense cerebral excitement was the first thing needing attention. He was extremely despondent, his pulse full and at ninety, tongue thickly coated, extremities cold, and his head troubled with a long established neuralgic disorder. He complained of his thin camp mattress and pillow stuffed with hair, adding that he was so emaciated his skin chafed easily against the slats; and, as these complaints were well founded, I ordered an additional hospital mattress and a softer pillow, for which he thanked me courteously. . . . On quitting Mr. Davis, I at once wrote to Major Church, Assistant Adjutant-General, advising that the prisoner be allowed to use tobacco, to the want of which, after a lifetime of use, he referred as one of the probable causes of his illness—though not complainingly, nor with any request that it be given. This recommendation was approved in the course of the day; and, on calling in the evening, I brought tobacco with me and Mr. Davis filled his pipe, the sole article which he carried with him from the Clyde, except the clothes which he then wore.

" 'This is noble medicine,' he said, with something as near a smile as was possible for his haggard and shrunken features. 'I hardly expected it and did not ask for it, though the deprivation has been severe. During my confinement here I shall ask for nothing.'

"He was now much calmer, feverish symptoms steadily decreasing, pulse already down to seventy-five, his brain less excitable, and his mind becoming more resigned to his condition. He complained that the foot-falls of the two sentries within his chamber made it difficult for him to collect his the two sentries within his chamber made it di..cult for him to collect his thoughts; but added, cheerfully, that with this—touching his pipe—he hoped to become tranquil. This pipe, by the way, was a large, handsome one, made of meerschaum, with an amber mouthpiece, showing by its color that it had seen active service for some time, as indeed was the case, having been his companion during the stormiest years of his late titular Presidency. It is now in the writer's possession., having been given to him by Mr. Davis and its acceptance insisted upon as the only thing he had left to offer.''

As a medical necessity, Dr. Craven also succeeded in having removed in the course of time, the cruel shackles which bound his prisoner. He knew that Mr. Davis could never regain his normal strength while the humiliation of such indignity rested upon him; and he allowed himself no rest until the brutal order was rescinded. Without going into further details, Dr. Craven's association with the prisoner ended at the expiration of six months, but Mr. Davis remained an inmate of Fortress Monroe for two full years. Every effort was made by politicians in Washington to secure his execution: complicity in the assassination of Mr. Lincoln, cruel treatment of Federal prisoners at the South, and others; but none of these trumped up charges could be substantiated. Finally, it was decided by the Supreme Court of the United States, headed by Chief-Justice Chase, that the charge of treason against Mr. Davis could not be successfully maintained in the American courts. He was thereupon

admitted to bail; and, though anxious for a trial in which
to vindicate himself at the bar of justice, the indictment
against him was quietly dropped: a tacit recognition of
the iron logic on which the South grounded her rights
under the Federal Constitution.

JEFFERSON

Louisville.   Volume I. Pages 146-155.

Galphinton   Fifty miles southwest of Augusta, on
or "Old Town."   the upper banks of the Ogeechee River,
                      there once stood an old trading post,
the origin of which probably antedates the coming of
Oglethorpe to Georgia. At any rate, the traditions of
the locality indicate that at an early period there were
Indian traders from South Carolina in this immediate
neighborhood, and, if not the first Europeans to establish
themselves upon the soil of the future colony, they at
least penetrated further into the interior. George Galphin was one of this adventurous band. He lived at
Silver Bluff, on the east side of the Savannah River,
where he owned an elegant mansion, conducted an extensive trade with the various Indian tribes, and became
a sort of potentate upon whom the dusky natives of the
forest looked with awe and respect. They usually brought
to him for settlement the issues on which they disagreed;
and whatever he advised them to do in the matter was
ordinarily the final word on the subject, for they acqui-
esced in his ruling as though he were an oracle of
wisdom. The trading-post which he established on the
Ogeechee River was called Galphinton. It was also known
as Ogeechee Town; and, after Louisville was settled,
some ten miles to the northwest, it was commonly designated as Old Town to distinguish it from New Town,
a name which the residents of the locality gave to the

future capital of Georgia. In the course of time, there gathered about the old trading-post quite a settlement, due to the extensive barter with the Indians which here took place at certain seasons of the year; but time has spared only the barest remnants of the old fort. The following story is told of how George Galphin acquired the land on which the town of Louisville was afterwards built. Attracted by the red coat which he wore, an old Indian chief, whose wits had been somewhat sharpened by contact with the traders, thus approached him, in the hope of securing the coveted garment. Said he:

"Me had dream last night."

"You did?" said Galphin. "What did you dream about?"

"Me dream you give me dat coat."

"Then you shall have it," said Galphin, who immediately suited the action to the word by transferring to him the coat.

"Quite a while elapsed before the old chief returned to the post, but when he again appeared in the settlement Galphin said:

"Chief, I dreamed about you last night."

"Ugh!" he grunted, "what did you dream?"

"I dreamed that you gave me all the land in the fork of this creek, pointing to one of the tributary streams of the Ogeechee.

"Well," said the old chief, "you take it, but we no more dream."

There is every reason to believe that the old trading-post at Galphinton was in existence when the State was first colonized. The settlement which gradually developed around it may have arisen much later, but the historians are not in accord upon this point. Says Dr. Smith:* "There may have been, and I think it likely there were, sundry settlers who were scattered among the Indians and who had squatted on lands belonging to them; and it is probable that Mr. Galphin had around his settlement at Galphinton, some of his countrymen before Oglethorpe came, but I find no positive proof of it, and Colonel Jones put the emigration of the Scotch-Irish to St. George's Parish as late as 1868. I find that certainly as early as the time of Governor Reynolds, in 1752, there were grants made to men whom I know were

---

*Story of Georgia and the Georgia People, p. 31, Atlanta, 1900.

in Jefferson.'' Be this as it may, George Galphin himself was an early comer into this region and beyond any question Galphinton was the first locality in Georgia established by white men for purposes of commerce. The site of the old trading-post is now owned by heirs of the late H. M. Comer, Sr., of Savannah.

At Galphinton, in 1785, a treaty was made between the State of Georgia and the Creek Indians, whereby the latter agreed to surrender to the State the famous ''Tallassee Strip,'' between the Altamaha and the St. Mary's; but the compact was repudiated by the Creeks under the artful Alexander McGillivray, under whose leadership was fought the long-protracted Oconee War. Hostilities were not concluded until 1796, when a treaty of friendship was negotiated at Coleraine, confirming the treaty of New York, in 1790, under which the ''Tallassee Strip'' was confirmed to the Indians. This much-coveted bone of contention remained in possession of the Creeks until 1814, when, as a penalty for siding with the British, in the War of 1812, they were forced to relinquish it to the whites.

The Conven- It was at Louisville, in 1798, that the cele-
tion of 1798. brated convention which framed the State
Constitution under which Georgia lived for seventy years, met for deliberation. Similar gatherings had been held in 1789 and in 1795, but few amendments were made to the original Constitution of 1777. On both of these former occasions, the law-makers had embedded in the organic law, a provision debarring ministers of the gospel from membership in the General Assembly of Georgia. Another resolution to the same effect was proposed at this time; but the great Baptist divine, Jesse Mercer, was on hand to challenge the propriety of such an action. When the resolution was introduced, he at once proposed to amend by excluding also lawyers and doctors. He succeeded in making the whole affair so ridiculous that the matter was finally dropped; and since 1798 the legislative doors have swung wide open to representatives of the cloth.

The Convention was composed of the following delegates:

BRYAN—Joseph Clay, J. B. Maxwell, John Pray.

BURKE—Benjamin Davis, John Morrison, John Milton.

BULLOCH—James Bird, Andrew E. Wells, Charles McCall.

CAMDEN—James Seagrove, Thomas Stafford.

CHATHAM—James Jackson, James Jones, George Jones.

COLUMBIA—James Simms, W. A. Drane, James McNeal.

EFFINGHAM—John King, John London, Thomas Polhill.

ELBERT—William Barnett, R. Hunt, Benjamin Mosely.

FRANKLIN—A. Franklin, R. Walters, Thomas Gilbert.

GLYNN—John Burnett, John Cowper, Thomas Spalding.

GREENE—George W. Foster, Jonas Fouche, James Nisbit.

HANCOCK—Charles Abercrombie, Thomas Lamar, Matthew Rabun.

JEFFERSON—Peter Carnes, William Fleming, R. D. Gray.

JACKSON—George Wilson, James Pittman, Joseph Humphries.

LIBERTY—James Cochran, James Powell, James Dunwody.

LINCOLN—Henry Ware, G. Woodbridge, Jared Grace.

McINTOSH—John H. McIntosh, James Gignilliat.

MONTGOMERY—Benjamin Harrison, John Watts, John Jones.

OGLETHORPE—John Lumpkin, Thomas Duke, Burwell Pope.

RICHMOND—Robert Watkins, G. Jones.

SCREVEN—Lewis Lanier, J. H. Rutherford, James Oliver.

WASHINGTON—John Watts, George Franklin, Jared Irwin.

WARREN—John Dawson, A. Fort, W. Stith.

WILKES—Matthew Talbot, Benjamin Taliaferro, Jesse Mercer.

JENKINS

Millen. Millen, the county-seat of Jenkins County, was named for Hon. John Millen, of Savannah, a distinguished lawyer, who, after an unopposed election to Congress, died before taking his seat, leaving unfulfilled a career of brilliant promise in the councils of the nation. The origin of the town dates back to the building of the Central Railroad, but it was not incorporated until September 30, 1881, when it was given a municipal form of government. In 1905, when Jenkins County was organized, the site of public buildings was located at Millen, the leading business men of which town were a unit for the bill. On the court-house square in Millen stands a handsome monument to the Confederate dead, erected under the auspices of the local U. D. C. Millen is the center of important railway and commercial activities and possesses an asset unsurpassed by any community in Georgia in its wideawake and progressive body of citizens.

JOHNSON

Wrightsville.   On December 11, 1858, the new county of Johnson was organized out of lands formerly embraced within Washington, Laurens, and Emanuel counties, and named for the distinguished statesman and jurist, Hon. Herschel V. Johnson. The seat of government was called Wrightsville, in honor of Mr. John B. Wright, a leading pioneer resident. The town was incorporated by an Act approved February 23, 1866, at which time the town limits were fixed at three-eighths of a mile in every direction from the county court-house. Messrs. Jeremiah Parker, Morgan A. Outlaw, N. L. Bostick, Charles W. Linder, and Frederick P. Reins were designated to serve as commissioners, pending an election of town officials as prescribed.* In 1884, this Act was repealed, and in lieu thereof a municipal form of government was authorized in a new charter. Wrightsville is one of the terminal points of the Wrightsville and Tennille Railroad. It is an enterprising town, with wide-awake merchants, good schools, attractive homes, solid banks, and up-to-date public utilities.

Herschel V. Johnson: Some Incidents of His Career.   Both intellectually and physically Herschel V. Johnson was one of the giants of his day in Georgia. He defeated the illustrious Charles J. Jenkins for the high office of Governor, a position which he filled with great ability for a period of four years. His devotion to the Union caused him to be nominated, in 1860, for the

------

*Acts, 1865-1866, p. 296.

second place on the national ticket, with Stephen A. Douglas. Though he recognized secession as a right, he opposed it as remedy for existing evils. In the secession convention at Milledgeville he was one of the most collossal figures, and allying himself with the anti-secessionists he made the greatest speech of his life in an effort to keep Georgia within the Union, but without success. The forces of disruption were too strong to be overcome. There is a story told to the effect that after beginning his impassioned plea for conservatism on the floor of the secession convention, he paused at the dinner hour, yielding to a motion for temporary adjournment. During the noon recess, he either took of his own accord or was persuaded by others to take a stimulant, in order to restore his strength after the exhaustion of his great effort of the morning session. But the result proved most unfortunate. It is said that the conclusion of his great argument was lacking in power due to the effects of the stimulant, and that Georgia was lost to the Union largely because the great speech of Governor Johnson lacked at the close of it the splendid amplitude of power with which it began. This great Georgian was far-sighted. The disasters which were fated to follow the impulsive action of the Secession Convention were distinctly foreshadowed upon his great brain, and he exerted himself to the utmost to avert the impending crisis. But the doom of Georgia was sealed. He afterwards represented the State in the Confederate Senate, at Richmond, and for years after the war he wore the ermine of the Superior Court Bench.

Judge Richard H. Clark,* an intimate personal acquaintance, gives us the following pen-picture of Governor Johnson as he appeared in the earlier days. Says he:

"The first political campaign which brought forth the powers of Governor Johnson was in 1840. It was the most exciting one this nation has ever experienced. There is no space to describe it. Suffice it to say that party rancor was at its highest pitch, and the people, including women and children, were wild with excitement. Governor Johnson was then but twenty-eight years old. His form as large and bulky, his face was smooth and beardless, and his entire make-up gave you the appearance of an overgrown boy. Expecting little when he arose, you were soon to enjoy the surprise of listening to one of the most powerful orators in the State or the Union. His bulky form gave yet more force to his sledge-hammer blows. His oratory, though powerful, was without seeming design or knowledge of it on the part of the speaker. His words escaped without the labor of utterance. His style was animated, but the speaker himself hardly seemed to be conscious of it, so intence was his earnestness. He simply discharged his duty to the best of his ability, and left the effect to take care of itself. This campaign gave him a State reputation."

Governor Johnson embraced, to a limited extent, in later life, the religious philosophy of Emanuel Swedenborg, of whose writings he became

---

*Memoirs of Judge Richard H. Clark, pp. 292-293, Atlanta, 1898.

an industrious student. He married Mrs. Anna Polk Walker, a lady of rare personal and intellectual charms. She was a daughter of Judge William Polk, of the Supreme Court of Maryland, a niece of President James K. Polk, of Tennessee, and a cousin of Lieutenant-General Leonidas Polk, the famous Confederate officer who was both soldier and bishop.

JONES

Clinton.   Clinton, the old county-seat of Jones County, was, in ante-bellum days, an aristocratic community, surrounded by the ample estates of wealthy planters. It was also an industrial center. Here was built one of the first iron foundries in the State, a plant which flourished down to 1864, when the hordes of Sherman left it a mass of ruins, never to be revived. Clinton became the county-seat of Jones when the county was first organized in 1807, out of a part of Baldwin; but it was not incorporated until December 2, 1909, when an Act for its better regulation was approved, with the following named commissioners, to wit: Reuben Fitzgerald, Drury Spain, Wm. Butler, Jacob Earnest, and Wm. Allen.[1] It was re-incorporated on December 4, 1816, at which time Messrs. James Jones, Zachariah Pope, James Sapfold, Ebenezer J. Bowers, John Mitchell, Bolar Allen, and John Parrish, were named commissioners.[2] The town was named for Gov. DeWitt Clinton, of New York, and the county for Hon. James Jones, of Savannah, a member of Congress and a distinguished public man of his day. The latter's name heads the above list of town commissioners, a circumstance from which it may be inferred that he owned an estate in this vicinity, and perhaps the naming of the county for him was due in a measure to his landed interests. The Clinton Academy was chartered on December 15, 1821, with Messrs. James Smith, Gustavus Hendrick, Samuel Lowther, Chas. J. McDonald, and Henry J. Lamar, as trustees. Clinton was once

[1] Clayton's Compendium, p. 520.
[2] Lamar's Digest, p. 1026.

a prosperous town, but it failed to recover from the disastrous results of the Civil War. In the preceding volume of this work will be found some additional facts in regard to Clinton, which need not be repeated here; and we also refer the reader to Volume I for a list of distinguished residents.

Gray, the present county-seat of Jones, is a small village located only a few miles above Clinton, on a branch line of the Central of Georgia. The town was named for James Gray, Esq., and was incorporated in 1872.

Blountsville. Blountsville, formerly a village of some pretentions, but now one of the lost towns of Georgia, was located in this county, at a point where some of the best families of the State were established. It was named for the noted Blount family of Georgia, to which the late Hon. James H. Blount, of Macon, for twenty years a member of Congress, belonged; and of which the gifted Mrs. W. D. Lamar, President of the State U. D. C., is also a member. The old Blountsville Academy was chartered in 1834, with Messrs. Allen Drury, Wm. E. Etheridge, John W. Stokes, Francis Tufts, and John W. Gordon, as trustees.*

Thomas B. Slade: Pioneer Educator. Ten years before Wesleyan Female College, at Macon, performed its historic act of conferring upon a woman her first college diploma, there was a distinguished pioneer educator successfully conducting a school for girls in the town of Clinton. This blazer of trails in an educational wilderness was Thomas B. Slade. Here, on the frontier belt of Georgia, while the prints of the Indian's moccasins was still fresh in the soil, this far-sighted scholar who, with the ken of a prophet, could read the signs of the future, here opened an academy in the year 1828 and started a movement for woman's intellectual emancipation. Professor Slade was born in North

---

*Acts, 1834, p. 6.

Carolina in 1800. For a while, he practiced law with his father, General Jeremiah Slade, in the Tar Heel State. But he was cast in the molds of a great educator, and, relinquishing Blackstone, he wended his way to Georgia, there to become a leader in one of the forward movements of the age. Perhaps the first pledge and token of Fortune's good-will toward him was his marriage to Miss Ann Jacquiline Blount, a lady of kindred intellectual tastes and of fine aristocratic family connections.

In 1836, what was then known as the Georgia Female College, was founded at Macon; and such was Professor Slade's prestige as an educator at Clinton that we find him in this year removing to Macon, to be installed as the first professor of natural sciences in the new institution, with the general oversight of its affairs. He brought with him to Macon his own chemical apparatus for experiments and his own geodus for astronomical studies. Thirty of his pupils followed him from Clinton to form the nucleus of the Georgia Female College; also two of his music teachers, Miss Maria Lord, from Boston, and Miss Martha Massey, the latter a beneficiary pupil. Miss Lord was afterwards well known in Macon as Mrs. Boardman.

Two classes graduated under him before the college was bought by the M. E. Church. He arranged the first curriculum and prepared the first diploma granted by the college, thus marking with his pen a new epoch in the educational history of the world. He removed to Columbus in 1842, where for thirty years as principal and proprietor of a female institute of high grade he continued his great work until advanced years forced him to resign his mantle to younger shoulders. He died in 1882 crowned with the benedictions of a well-spent life. Professor Slade prescribed for himself a high standard of ethics. He was never known to canvas for a pupil nor to reject one because she was unable to pay. It is something in this day and time to realize the distinction due this man who wrote the first diploma ever delivered to a woman and arranged the curriculum for the oldest female college in existence. No fitter epitaph for his tomb could have been written than the words of prophecy fulfilled in Christianity's great forerunner: ''The voice of one crying in the wilderness: Prepare ye the way of the Lord; make his paths straight.''*

The Famous Bunkley Trial.   Some score of years prior to the Civil War there occurred at Clinton one of the most famous court-house trials in the forensic annals of Georgia. Jesse Bunkley, a well-educated youth of profligate habits and a scion of one of the wealthiest families of the county, disappeared from Jones in a very mysterious manner; and, though every effort was made to trace the young man, he could never be found. On the death of his father, the widow Bunkley married a man named Lother, but $20,000 was left to Jessee, provided he should return home, give evidence of improved habits, and establish his

*Authority: Mrs. Edgar A. Ross, of Macon.

identity beyond question. Time brought no solution to the riddle. The belief at last became fixed in the popular mind that he was no longer in life, and accordingly his property was divided among his relatives. Subsequent to this division—perhaps five years thereafter—a man who bore some slight resemblance to Jesse Bunkley appeared upon the scene in Clinton and made a demand for the property, to which he claimed to be entitled.

But the parties in possession demanded, in turn, proof most positive of the claimant's real identity before relinquishing such substantial holdings. On this point, he failed to satisfy them, and not long thereafter the alleged Bunkley was arrested on the charge of cheating and swindling. It was averred in the bill of indictment that the defendant's real name was Barber. On the trial of the case, not less than 130 witnesses were examined, 98 of whom were for the prosecution. Four of the former college mates at Athens of the true Jesse Bunkley were put upon the witness stand. These were Robert Dougherty, Hugh A. Haralson, Henry G. Lamar and Charles J. McDonald—all of them men of distinction. But they could not recognize in Barber the features of an early schoolmate. Even his mother failed to find in his face any familiar lineaments. Barber knew just enough concerning the local environment to suggest that possibly he might have learned the story from the rightful heir. He was utterly at sea in regard to a number of matters concerning which the real Jesse Bunkley could not have been ignorant. He was, therefore, sentenced to prison But there are people who believe to this day that he was the real Jesse Bunkley, whose only offence was that he demanded the restitution of property which was rightfully his own under the laws of Georgia. Judge John G. Polhill presided at the trial; and, in the prosecution of the defendant, Walter T. Colquitt, Robert V. Hardeman and William S. C. Reid—three of the strongest advocates in the State—were associated.

. ———

LAURENS

Dublin. The original county-seat of Laurens was Sumterville, a small hamlet between Rocky and Turkey Creeks, in the north-west part of the county, where the population was chiefly centered. But before any public buildings were erected a large body of land on the opposite side of the river was acquired from Montgomery and Washington, which called for the selection of a new county-site, at some point on the Oconee River, central to the enlarged boundaries. Where the city of Dublin now stands there lived at this time an Irishman who agreed to donate a site for the public buildings, provided he was allowed to name the town for Erin's renowned capital.

This offer was accepted. On December 13, 1810, an Act was approved appointing a board of commissioners to locate the new county-site and to dispose of the holdings at Sumterville. The board was constituted as follows: John C. Underwood, Jethro Spivey, Benjamin Adams, John Thomas, and Wm. H. Matthews.[1] In the year following, Dublin was made the new county-site; and on December 9, 1812, the town was incorporated with Messrs. Neill Munroe, Lewis Kennon, Wm. Tolbert, Eli S. Shorter, and Henry Shepherd as commissioners.[2]

Dublin is located in the center of a rich agricultural belt; and with splendid railway connections it is one of the most important commercial towns of Georgia, with an outlook for the future rivalled by few older communities. Gov. George M. Troup owned two large plantations in Laurens County, which he called Valdosta and Vallombrosa; and, during the last twenty-five years of his life, he was often a familiar figure on the streets of Dublin. Gen. Blackshear, whose famous country-seat "Springfield," was further down the river, made frequent visits to the county-seat. Here also lived at one time a noted jurist, Judge Eli S. Shorter, who afterwards removed to Columbus. Georgia's present Commissioner of Commerce and Labor, Hon. Henry M. Stanley, was a former resident of Dublin; from which town hails also a member of our present Court of Appeals, Judge Peyton L. Wade. Gen. Eli Warren, Hon. Lott Warren, Rev. Kit Warren, Dr. Peter E. Love, Hon. John T. Boifeuillet, and Hon. Warren Grice, may likewise be included among the former residents of Laurens.

Cotton Seed as a Fertilizer. Mr. James Callaway, of Macon, one of the best informed historians and writers in the State, is authority for the statement that Henry C. Fuqua, of Laurens County, Ga., was the

[1] Clayton's Compendium, p. 642.
[2] Lamar's Digest, p. 950.

first person of record to discover the value of cotton
seed as a fertilizer. The discovery was made by accident.

Springfield: The   Major Stephen H. Miller, in his Bench
Home of   and Bar of Georgia, gives the following
Gen. Blackshear.   picture of General David Blackshear's
                        plantation life, at Springfield, on the
Ocmulgee. Says he:*

"Besides his grapery of several acres, General Blackshear owned large
orchards, from which he distilled apple and peach brandies of the purest
kind. Nothing was neglected in the manufacture, from the gathering of
the fruit to the dropping of the rectified spirits from the tube. He usually
gave morning drams to his slaves; and whenever, from exposure to cold
or water, they required a tonic, he ordered them to receive it from his
cellar. It was often the case that, in heavy work—raising houses, building
mill-dams, and adjusting timbers—they were in condition to receive it; but
he never permitted them to have it in such quantity as to produce intoxica-
tion, and he saw nothing to regret from the custom.

"He also cultivated the cane, making more than enough sugar and
syrup for his own use. It was his rule to let his neighbors have whatever
he could spare from his farm. He never profited by scarcity and high prices
in the market. His rates were just fairly remunerative. He never specu-
lated on the necessities of the people. Being a first-rate judge of human
nature, he was not often deceived. To the honest and industrious, he was
ever a friend; to the idle and dissolute he showed no favor. Though obliging in his disposition, he adhered to certain rules which he adopted early
in life:

"1. Never spend any money before you get it.

"2. Never pay other people's debts.

"3. Never pay interest.

"Much is comprehended in these words. They reveal the secret of prosperity, in violence often to the best sympathies. General Blackshear was
governed by principle—not by impulse. Hence his great influence and
success.

"It was customary for the court, including both the judges and the
bar, while journeying on the circuit, to stop with General Blackshear, at
leisure intervals. The dignified Early, the jovial Strong, and other high
functionaries, who enjoined silence in court and held the multitude in awe,
laid aside official consequence, and shot duck and angled for fish with as

much glee as the boys who for the time being furnished them guides and companions. The judges would go to the mill and made upon the sheeting, or creep softly upon the dam, spearing the finny tribe or harpooning a turtle, with perfect relish for the sport. After such achievements, the sideboard was called upon for its quota of refreshment. It was all right then, but a very decided change has since taken place; and sideboards, wine, brandy, and such old-fashioned luxuries have been dispensed with—certainly an improvement on the virtues of our predecessors.''*

Gov. Troup's Will. On file, in the Ordinary's office, at the court house, in Dublin, is the last will and testament of Governor George M. Troup. It is a model of brevity, containing less than two hundred words, but it disposes of what was supposed to be, at the time of his death, one of the largest estates in Georgia. The document reads as follows:

"Georgia, Laurens' County. I wish my executors to keep together, as I leave it, all my property, real and personal, for three years after my decease, endeavoring to improve it as they would their own. 1st. Giving from the proceeds to the heirs, a decent and becoming support, as they had been accustomed to, and 2nd. appropriating any surplus to investment in lands and negroes, Savannah Town property, Savannah Bank Stock, or other subject as they should deem best for the interest of such heirs, the children of Florida Troup late Florida Bryan or Foreman, Oralie Troup and George M. Troup are my only heirs, at the expiration of the three years and on the 1st day of January next thereafter I desire all the said property of which I may die possessed with the increasements both real and personal to be divided as nearly as possible into three equal shares I mean specifically, one share for the children Florida, one share for Oralie and one for G. M. Troup, who are to have and to hold the same to them respectively their heirs and assigns forever with these exceptions, Viz: If Oralie should die without legal lineal heir or heirs then shall her share go to the children of Florida to be equally divided among them or the survivors and if George should die without legal heir or heirs then shall descend to the children of Florida likewise or the survivors and I hereby constitute and appoint G. B. Cummings, James Screven, Thomas M. Foreman, and George M. Troup my executors.

"Signed and sealed this 20th. day of September 1851.

G. M. TROUP   (Seal)

---

*Stephen H. Miller, in Bench and Bar of Georgia, Vol. I.

GOV. TROUP'S OLD HOME:

Remains of the Valdosta Mansion in Laurens County, Showing the
Sandstone Chimney, in the Midst of a Deserted Ruin.

Witness.
WILLIAM WINHAM.
ALEXANDER ADAIR GILTMAN
     his
THOMPSON X SMITH.''
     mark

"The above will was probated and recorded at the June Term of the Court or Ordinary in and for Laurens County in the year 1856. This April 28th, 1911.

W. A. WOOD.
Lauerns County, Georgia.

LEE

Leesburg.   The original county-seat of Lee County was Starksville; but in 1872, the site of public buildings was changed to Leesburg, the present seat of government. The latter place was chosen by the following named commissioners, to wit:, Isaac P. Tison, Henry L. Long, Fred H. West, Wm. T. Saddler, and Virginius G. Hill, who were instructed to choose a site on the line of the South-western Railroad, preferably at or near Wooten Station; otherwise at or near Adam Station. Messrs. Willis A. Jones, Chas. M. Irwin, Wm. C. Gill, and John Paley, were at the same time appointed commissioners to assess damages sustained by the owners of real estate at Starksville, in consequence of such removal.* The site selected was at Wooten Station, the name of which was changed to Leesburg, by legislative Act, in 1874. The town has grown considerably in recent years, sharing in the development which has brought this section of Georgia to the front. Near Leesburg, Gen. Philip Cook owned an extensive plantation, today the property of his grandson, Hon. Philip Cook, Jr., Georgia's present Secretary of State.

---

*Acts, 1872, p. 264.

Chehaw.   Volume I.

————

The particulars in regard to the destruction of Cheraw have been carefully gathered and preserved by White. Says he:[*]

"In March, 1818, Governor Rabun requested General Jackson to station a sufficient military force on the frontier, to protect the most exposed parts against the incursions of the Indians. To this application no answer was given. Governor Rabun, believing it to be his duty to provide for the safety of the frontier inhabitants, ordered Captain Obed Wright, with a sufficient force, to proceed immediately against the Felemma and Hopaunee towns, the inhabitants of which were known to be decidedly hostile, having committed many murders. The orders of Governor Rabun confined Captain Wright specially to this object.

"Captain Wright took up the line of march from Hartford, in Pulaski County, with two companies of mounted men, under Captains Robinson and Rogers, and with an infantry force under Captains Dean and Childs, besides two detachments under Lieutenants Cooper and Jones—in all about two hundred and seventy effective men. When the detachment reached the neighborhood of Fort Early, information came that a celebrated old chief, Hopaunee, whose town had joined the hostile party, had removed; that he was then living in the village upon which the attack was subsequently made; that he was the principal leader of the hostile Indians; and that a great portion of them were under his immediate direction. Captain Wright considered himself authorized to attack it, as one of the Hopaunee towns.

"Accordingly the attack was made on April 23, 1818, and in the course of two hours the whole was in flames. About ten of the inhabitants were killed. General Glascock, of the Georgia Militia, in a letter to General Jackson, dated April 30, 1818, in detailing this transaction says: 'When the detachment arrived at Cheraw an Indian was discovered grazing some cattle. He proposed to go with the interpreter and to bring one of the chiefs with whom the captain could talk. It was not to be. An advance was ordered. The cavalry rushed forward and commenced the massacre. Even after the firing and murder commenced, Major Howard, who furnished you with corn, came out of his house with a white flag, in front of the line. It was not respected. An order was given for a general fire, and nearly four hundred guns were discharged at him before one took effect. He fell and was bayoneted. His son also was killed.'

"Governor Rabun regretted very much this occurrence. Captain Wright was arrested by order of General Jackson, but was released by the civil authorities. Gov. Rabun afterwards had him arrested again. And the

———

[*]Historical Collections of Georgia, Lee County, Savannah, 1854.

President of the United States ordered him to be placed in the custody of the marshal, but he made his escape.''

Palmyra.   Volume I.

Starksville.   In 1826, Lee County was organized out of a part of the Creek Indian lands acquired under the second treaty of Indian Springs—the treaty which cost General McIntosh his life.   But it was not until 1832 that a site was fixed for public buildings.   Starksville was the name given at this time to the new county-seat.   In 1847, due to some dissatisfaction, this Act was repealed.   But Starksville remained the seat of government—though apparently without public buildings, for in 1851 an Act was passed authorizing a court-house and a jail, only to be re-pealed n 1853.   Rented quarters were no doubt occupied.   On December 26, 1851, Starksville was incorporated as a town, with the following named commissioners, to-wit.: George C. Tickner, Willis A. Hawkins, Samuel Lind-sey, Philip M. Monroe, and Edward V. Monroe.*   The Starksville Academy was chartered in 1833.   So far as appears from the records neither a court-house nor a jail was ever built at Starksville.

LIBERTY

**Historic Old Mid-
way: A Shrine
of Patriotism.**   Volume I. Pages 135-138; 726-743.

**One Hundred Years
of Usefulness: The
Midway Centennial.**   Beginning on December 5, 1852, and lasting for three days, there was held at Midway Church, a season of rejoicing, the memory of which still abide in the traditions of the settlement.   It marked the completion of the first one hundred years of existence in the history of the Midway congregation; and, besides drawing a multitude of visitors to the locality, it riveted the attention of the whole nation upon the marvelous record of the little church, whose religious and pa-

---

*Acts, 1851, p. 45.

triotic achievements became everywhere the topic of the
hour. Newspapers devoted columns to it. Ministers of
the gospel preached sermons upon it. Thousands who
possessed no church connection were enthusiastic in
praise of the little district in Georgia; which was the
proud possessor of so much well-deserved renown.

The centennial observance began on the Sabbath. Dr.
I. S. K. Axson, who was then the senior pastor, preached
a sermon appropriate to the occasion. On Monday morning, early, the festivities of the day were inaugurated by
the firing of cannon. Among the invited guests of the
occasion was the Chatham Artillery, of Savannah, whose
iron mortars awoke the echoes of the settlement. Before the sun was well up, the people commenced to gather
from every direction. They came in family carriages,
in farm wagons, and on horseback. The roads leading
to Midway were crowded for miles with travelers; and
by 10 o'clock there was gathered about the Liberty pole
in front of the historic church, a crowd, the like of which
no one had ever seen in the settlement. At a point on
the Sunbury road the procession formed and to the ac-
compaiment of music furnished by the German band from
Savannah, marched to the church. Colonel William Maxwell, though somewhat of a veteran, was the president
of the day; and, bedecked with blue rosettes, made an impressive figure. Assisting him, in the capacity of grand
marshals, were Captain Abiel Winn and Captain Peter
W. Fleming. One of the features of the parade was a
broad banner, on which was inscribed this legend: "Our
Country, Our Whole Country, the Land of the Free and
the Home of the Brave, 1852." It was borne by Mr.
Thomas Q. Cassels, the chairman of the committee on
arrangements, supported by Captain Cyrus Mallard. As
soon as the congregation was assembled within the
church and the prayer of invocation was concluded, an
ode, written for the occasion, by Rev. Samuel J. Cassels,
was sung. Then followed an address by Prof. John B.
Mallard, setting forth incidents and circumstances

connected with the early days of the settlement, the part which it played in the struggle for independence, and its varying vicissitudes of fortune both good and ill. Following the address, there was given a selection by the band, after which the congregation repaired to the spot selected, directly in front of the building for the laying of the corner stone to the proposed monument to the forefathers of the settlement. Here an address was delivered by Rev. John Winn, and a prayer offered by Rev. Charles C. Jones, after which a number of interesting relics and mementoes were placed in the receptacle. Then came a salute from the guns, and the multitude repaired to the tables near-by, where they partook of an elegant out-door banquet upon the lawn, and numerous toasts were proposed. On this occasion, Rev. Samuel J. Cassels, who was an invalid confined to his home in Savannah, sent this toast, which became quite celebrated: "Liberty County—the place of my first and second birth, and yet to be the place of my third."

On the following day, nothwithstanding a downpour of rain, another splendid crowd was present to hear an eloquent address from the special orator of the occasion, Judge William Law, of Savannah, who pronounced an oration the echoes of which have not ceased to vibrate among the sacred timbers.

Religious Work Among the Slaves: The Mission of Dr. Chas. C. Jones. To our good friends at the North it will be a matter of some interest to know that the largest slave-holders in Georgia during the prosperous days of the old regime were the devout Puritans who lived in the Midway settlement. Most of them were rice planters, who cultivated the rich alluvial bottoms, and they were compelled in the nature of things to employ slave labor. As they enlarged the fertile acres which they tilled, they naturally increased the number of slaves which they employed, and, on the eve of hostilities with England, in 1776, it is estimated that one-third of the entire wealth of the Colony of Georgia was concentrated in the Parish of St. John. According to Dr. Stacy, whose observations are based upon the Midway records, the Dorchester colonists brought to Georgia five hundred and thirty-six slaves, and these were divided between seventy-one families. At a period somewhat later, when the community was well established in Georgia, he estimates that it numbered three hundred and fifty whites and fifteen hundred blacks, the average increase of population being in favor of the latter class. With these figures Colonel Jones is in perfect agreement. It was by means of slave labor that the residents of Bermuda Island built Fort Morris. It was also by means of slave labor that the inhabitants of the district usually built the homes in which they lived, but, of course, under intelligent supervision. And the extent to which the Puritan settlers of Midway employed slave labor only tends to prove that the burning issue of American politics during the ante-bellum decade was purely an economic one, the attitude of the individual mind toward which was determined largely by environment.

The rice which was forwarded to Boston to relieve the distress incident to the closing of the harbor to commerce, in 1774, was grown entirely by slave labor on plantations owned by the Dorchester Puritans in the Parish of St. John.

But the care of the slaves was always an object of the utmost solicitude to the residents of the Midway settlement. Between master and servant there was always the closest tie of attachment, and nowhere in Georgia was the feudal relationship characterized by greater tenderness. The religious welfare of the slaves was taken into account from the very start. In the house of worship, which was built by the whites, there were galleries for the accommodation of the colored members, who were never organized into separate religious bodies, but continued to worship with the whites throughout the entire existence of the Midway Church. On Sacramental Sunday both races communed together, the blacks in the galleries above, the whites in the pews below; and in like manner both races were admitted to the ordinance of baptism, beneath the same shelter, and at the hands of the same man of God. However, it was not until the distinguished Dr. Charles C. Jones began his useful labors on the plantations of Liberty County that the work of religious instruction assumed definite and systematic proportions. His field of labor embraced an area of twenty miles square. Besides holding religious services at stated times and places, he compiled catechisms, trained teachers, and in other ways sought to accomplish the religious uplift of the slave. He afterwards wrote a book in which he outlined his methods of work for the benefit of the religious public. Like the noted Dr. John L. Girardeau, of Columbia, S. C., with whom he was afterwards associated, it was his chief delight to preach to the negroes, though a man of marvelous intellect and power; and even after becoming a professor in the Theological Seminary at Columbia he spent his vacations in evangelistic work among the slaves. Altogether, he was the means of converting not less than 1,500 negroes, whose names were duly added to the church rolls.

Laurel View: The Home of Senator Elliott.
Overlooking the Midway River, at Hester's Bluff, stood the old Colonial home of United States Senator John Elliott, one of the most distinguished members of the Midway settlement. His grandfather, who bore the same name, was one of the original settlers, who moved into the district from Dorchester, S. C. His father, by marriage to Rebecca Maxwell, acquired the handsome estate at Hester's Bluff, to which, because of the superb prospect which it commanded, through vistas of the most luxuriant foliage, was given the name, "Laurel View." Senator Elliott married Martha Stewart, a daughter of General Daniel Stewart, an officer of distinction in the Revolution. His wife accompanied him to Washington, D. C., to take her place in the brilliant social circle at the nation's capital. The trip was made overland in a carriage drawn by four horses, and occupied more than a week, but was broken by easy stages and attended by no serious mishap. Senator Elliott wore the toga of the nation's highest legislative forum, from 1819 to 1825. He died at his home in Liberty some two years after relinquishing office, in his fifty-fourth year. His widow afterwards married Major James Stephen Bulloch, a grandson of old Governor Archibald Bulloch; and from this union sprang Martha Bulloch, whose marriage to Theodore Roosevelt, Sr., of New York, made her the mother of the future President of the United States.

Fragrant associations cluster about the site of the old Elliott home at Hester's Bluff. It was one of the stately mansions of the old regime, and though the rigid Puritan code of the Midway settlement outlawed the frivolities typical of cavalier life, it was the abode of generous hospitality and of good cheer. The old home place has long since fallen into ruins; but near the spot on which it once stood there rises today upon the bluff an attractive and up-to-date club-house, the property of an organization, composed of certain members of the Savannah Bar. Judge Paul E. Seabrook, the present lessee of the property, has permitted this organization, as an act of courtesy, to enjoy the privileges of fishing and hunting over the entire estate, and the name Liberty Hall which has been given to the club-house suggests that the traditions of the locality are well preserved.*

———————

Liberty's Oldest Family: The Maxwells.
Before the first emigrant from the Puritan settlement at Dorchester, S. C., located in this beautiful region of live oaks, the Midway district was represented by Audley Maxwell, in the first General Assembly of the Province, in Savannah, in 1751, and to this very day, in the County of Liberty, the descendants of Audley Maxwell are still living

———————

*Consult the author's former work: Reminiscences of Famous Georgians, Vol. I, p. 20. Additional authorities: Judge Paul E. Seabrook, of Savannah; Miss Julia King, of Dunham, etc.

upon the ancestral acres. Mark Carr, who owned the ground on which the town of Sunbury was built, may have been an earlier comer into the district, but his name has long since disappeared from the region. The Maxwell family is of Scotch-Irish extraction. Without a break in the chain of connection its members trace lineal descent to the old homestead on the Nith, in Dumfries, Scotland, the inspirational fountain-source of the famous air:

> "Maxwelton's braes are bonnie
> Where early falls the dew."

"It is said that the family is descended from the earls of Nithdale; but the Georgia Maxwells have always been too democratic to lay any stress upon the claim. Besides, there has been little need for them to go beyond the Revolution for deeds of prowess with which to brighten the family crest. From the south of Scotland, the Maxwells first migrated to the north of Ireland, where they must have lived for some time in the neighborhood of Belfast, and where they continued in steadfast and unbroken allegiance to the kirk. The exact time when the family escutcheon was planted in America is unknown; but there were Maxwells living in South Carolina before the settlement of Georgia. Audley Maxwell came to St. John's Parish in 1748. He did not come from South Carolina, however, but from Pennsylvania; and he seems to have married in Boston, Mass. His wife was Hannah Powell. Locating on a tract of 500 acres at the head of Midway River, he called his home place Limerick, a name which is still to be found on the map, though an old stone well is said to be the sole memorial which today marks the site on which his residence once stood. He was one of the commissioners, of which there were three in number, to lay out the important military road between Sunbury and Darien. Two brothers, James and Thomas, obtained land grants at or near the same time and located— the former at Belfast, the latter at Hester's Bluff, on opposite sides of the Midway River. James was one of the founders of Sunbury. The daughter of Thomas married an Elliott and became the mother of United States Senator John Elliott.

Colonel James Maxwell, a son of Audley Maxwell, was an officer of some prominence in the Revolution. He was also closely associated with Dr. Abiel Holmes, in bettering the conditions of life for the new settlers; and in this connection it may be said that while the Maxwells anticipated the Dorchester colonists by several years in occupying the Midway district they joined them in religious worship and became zealous supporters of the historic old organization. Colonel Audley Maxwell, his son, was another man of mark. He located on Colonel's Island, where he cultivated an extensive plantation, and the old home place, Maxwell Point, on the south end of the island, is still the property of his descendants. Rebecca Maxwell, a sister, married the famous John Cooper, and lived at Cannon's Point, on St. Simon's Island, where they kept open house and entertained English and Scotch lords. The Maxwells have always been handsome in feature, erect and patrician in carriage, and have splendidly exemplified the old school of Southern manners. They have also represented the culture of the Georgia coast. The family of Mr. J. A. M. King, of Colonel's Island, is descended from the first Audley Maxwell and from the noted Roswell King, who founded the town of Roswell.*

John Quarterman: One of the very earliest settlers in
A Patriarch the Midway district was John Quar-
in Israel. terman. Concerning this devout pio-
neer, who was a man eminent for piety, there are only meagre entries in the church records; but he holds an exalted place in the traditions of the settlement. He is today revered as the progenitor of a distinguished multitude of descendants. Embraced among his offspring are eight eminent educators, including the LeContes, seven foreign missionaries, and twenty-three ministers of the gospel. Robert Quarterman, his grandson, was the first native born pastor of the Midway flock and he served the congregation for a period of twenty-four years.

Dr. McWhir: His On the importance of an education, the
Academy Once a early Puritans of Georgia laid great
Noted Institution. stress. It was not long after the Revolution that the foundations of the famous Sunbury Academy were laid, in 1788; and, under the management of Dr. William McWhir, a Scotch-Irishman of rare attainments, it became an institution of high rank and of wide favor. The following brief sketch is condensed from an account by Colonel Charles C. Jones, Jr.,* a scion of the Midway settlement. Says he:

"The most famous institution of learning in southern Georgia, for many years, was the Sunbury Academy. It was established by an Act of the Legislature, passed February 1, 1788, in which Abiel Holmes, James Dun-

---

*Authorities: Colonial Records of Georgia; old residents of Liberty; an article by Miss Julia King, of Dunham, Ga.
*Dead Towns of Georgia, pp. 212-215, Savannah, 1878.

wody, John Elliott, Gideon Dowse, and Peter Winn were named commissioners'. With the sum of 1,000 pounds stirling realized from the sale of
confiscated property, these well-known citizens, after giving bond, proceeded to provide an adequate building in which to house the school; and
in due time the institution was opened. The teacher, whose name was for
the longest period most notably associated with the management of the
Academy and who did more than all others to establish a standard of scholarship and discipline was the Rev. Dr. William McWhir. He was a thor-
ough Greek and Latin scholar, a strict observer of prescribed regulations,
and a firm believer in the virtue of the birch. To the studious and ambitious he always proved himself a generous instructor, full of suggestion and
encouragement. The evening of his days was spent chiefly in the homes
of his old scholars, by whom he was always cordially greeted, and the welcome in turn was peculiarly relished by him when accompanied by a generous
supply of buttermilk and by a good glass of wine. The latter might be
omitted; but a failure to provide the former was a breach of hospitality
which impaired the comfort of his sojourn. The building—a large two story
and a half wooden structure, located in King's Square—was razed to the
ground about the year 1842.''

Two very interesting old heir-looms, formerly the
property of Dr. McWhir, are now in the possession of his
step-greatgrandson, Hon. William Harden, of Savannah,
viz., a gold-headed walking cane and a silver drinking
cup, the latter of which was presented to Dr. McWhir
by his devoted friend, Rev. Murdock Murphy. The silver
cup is shaped like a tumbler, and near the top is engraved the date, 1815. At equal distances apart, there
are three inscriptions engraved upon the sides: ''Charity
in Thought,'' ''Liberality in Word,'' ''Generosity in
Action.'' On the bottom is inscribed: ''Peace and Plenty.'' The gold-headed cane is made of Irish black-thorn,
and is very substantial. On the top is engraved ''W. Mc-
W.'' Not far below the knob is a hole cut through the
stick, on either side of which there is a silver guard,
somewhat like the guards to key-holes. Dr. McWhir
reached the ripe old age of ninety-two years. He sleeps
beside his wife in the deserted little graveyard at Sunbury, where there is much to suggest the pathetic picture which Oliver Goldsmith has drawn of the Village
Schoolmaster. On the marble slab which marks the grave

of this pioneer teacher of Georgia may be deciphered
this inscription, now blurred and indistinct:

> "Sacred to the memory of Rev. WILLIAM McWHIR,
> D. D., who was born in the County of Down, Ireland,
> September 9, 1759, and died in Liberty County, Geor-
> gia, January 31, 1851. In 1783 he came to the United
> States and settled at Alexandria, Va., whence he re-
> moved to Georgia about the year 1793. His long and
> eventful life was devoted to the cause of Christianity
> and Education, and his labors to promote these objects
> were eminently successful."

Midway: The Stewart-Screven Monument. In the center of the historic old church-
yard at Midway, ready to be unveiled
in the fall of this year, stands a magnificent obelisk of marble, erected by the
United States government, at a cost of $10,000, to two
distinguished Revolutionary patriots, both residents of
Midway: Gen. James Screven, and Gen. Daniel Stewart.
President Woodrow Wilson, who married a daughter of
Midway, and ex-president Roosevelt, a descendant of
Gen. Stewart, have both promised to be present at the
unveiling, and to take part in the ceremonies. The shaft
is fifty feet in height and thirty feet square at the base,
with the following inscriptions splendidly cast, in relief, on beautiful copper plates, and set into the pure
white marble:

> (North Face.)
> 1750   1778
> Sacred to the Memory of BRIGADIER-GENERAL
> JAMES SCREVEN, who Fell, Covered with Wounds,
> at Sunbury, Near this Spot, on the 22nd Day of Novem-
> ber, 1778. He Died on the 24th Day of November, 1778,
> from the Effects of his Wounds.*

*Gen. Screven fell mortally wounded about a mile and a half south of
Midway Church. This point is fully ten miles distant from Sunbury. Consequently, it is difficult to understand this variation on the monument. We
are indebted to Hon. H. B. Folsom, of Montgomery, Ga., for a description
of this obelisk, together with the inscriptions.

> (Continued)
> (East Face.)
> Reared by the Congress of the United States as a
> Nation's Tribute to BRIGADIER-GENERALS JAMES
> SCREVEN and DANIEL STEWART.
> (South Face.)
> 1759.   1829.
> Sacred to the Memory of BRIGADIER-GENERAL
> DANIEL STEWART, a Gallant Soldier in the Revolu-
> tion and an Officer Brevetted for Bravery in the Indian
> Wars.
> (West Face.)
> (The west face is fittingly adorned by a copper re-
> lief representation of Midway Church, as perfect as skill
> and enduring copper can make it. No inscription what-
> ever.)

Seven of Georgia's Counties Named for Liberty's Sons. Perhaps the most eloquent attestation of the part played by the Midway settlement in the drama of the Revolution is to be found in the fact that seven counties of Georgia bear names which can be traced to this fountain-head of patriotism.

1. Liberty. This name was conferred by the Constitution of 1777, upon the newly created county which was formed from the old Parish of St. John. It was bestowed in recognition of the fact that the earliest stand for independence was here taken by the patriots of the Midway settlement, whose flag at Fort Morris was the last to be lowered when Georgia was overrun by the British, and whose contributions to the official lists of the Revolution were manifold and distinguished.

2. Screven, formed December 14, 1793, was named for General James Screven, a resident of Sunbury, who fell mortally wounded, within a mile and a half of Midway church, on November 22, 1778, and who lies buried in Midway graveyard.

3. Hall, created December 15, 1818, and named after Lyman Hall, a resident of the Midway district, who was

the first delegate sent from Georgia to the Continental Congress and who was afterwards a Signer of the Declaration of Independence and a Governor of Georgia.

4. Gwinnett, established December 15, 1818, was called after Button Gwinnett, whose home was on St. Catherine's Island, but business affairs connected him with Sunbury, who was also a Signer of the Declaration of Independence, and a Governor of Georgia.

5. Baker, constituted, December 12, 1825, was named for Colonel John Baker, of the Revolution, one of the early pioneer settlers of St. John's Parish.

6. Stewart, organized December 30, 1830, was named for General Daniel Stewart, an eminent soldier both of the Revolution and of the Indian wars. He was a native of the district, a member of Midway church, and an ancestor of ex-President Theodore Roosevelt. He sleeps in Midway burial-ground.

7. Bacon, created by Legislative Act, during the session of 1914, in honor of the late United States Senator Augustus O. Bacon, whose parents repose in the little cemetery adjacent to Midway Church.

LINCOLN

Lincolnton. Zachariah Lamar, of Wilkes, was authorized by an Act approved February 8, 1786, to lay out a town at the mouth of the Broad River, on the south side, to be called Lincoln. It does not appear from the records what was ever done in pursuance of this Act; but, in 1796, a part of Wilkes County was organized into Lincoln, with Lincolnton as the new county-seat. Both the town and the county were named for Gen. Benj. Lincoln, of the Revolution, at one time in command of military operations in Georgia. Lincolnton was incorporated by an Act approved December 19, 1817, with the following town commissioners, to wit: Peter Lamar,

Rem Remsen, and Lewis Stovall.* The Lincolnton Female Academy was chartered in 1836, and was an excellent school for the times. Near Lincolnton lived the noted wit, Judge John M. Dooly, and the distinguished pioneer legislator, Thomas W. Murray. Just six miles above the town is Tory Pond, where, according to tradition, six Tories were hanged. Without railway facilities, the growth of Lincolnton has been retarded; but whenever the iron horse arrives a new era will begin for this fine old ante-bellum town, once the home of such noted Georgia families as the Lamars, the Currys, the Dallases, the Crawfords, the Remsens, the Simmonses, the Flemings, and the Lockharts. Here was born the distinguished Dr. J. L. M. Curry, statesman, diplomat, and educator, whose statue has recently been placed in the nation's Hall of Fame by Alabama, his adopted State for many years.

Skeletons of the Six Tories Found. To discover, after a lapse of a century and a half, the well-preserved skeletons of six men who were buried without coffins, during the Revolution, only six feet below the earth, in a climate which possesses little of the art preservative, is to say the least, a modern miracle. In the absence of scientific verification, the following story, which appeared in the Atlanta Constitution of December 22, 1912, is subject to the usual newspaper discount, but it nevertheless constitutes an item of some interest in this connection. The article reads:

"Skeletons of the six Tories captured at her dinner table and afterwards hanged to trees near her home by Nancy Hart more than a century and a half ago were unearthed last week by a squad of hands at work grading the Elberton and Eastern Railroad. They were buried about three feet under the ground, in what is known as the Heard field, near the mouth of Wahatchie Creek, some half a mile from where it empties into Broad River. The bones are all there, in a splendid state of preservation, but

*Lamar's Digest, p. 1044.

have become disjointed. The skulls, in fact, all the bones of the heads and under jaws, are especially well preserved, and the teeth are perfect. The place where the skeltons were unearthed, together with the fact that they were so close together, near the surface, with no sign or trace of anything like a coffin anywhere around, makes the evidence convincing that these are the bones of the Tories captured by the Revolutionary heroine. The house in which Nancy Hart lived was located on Wahatchie Creek near a spring some half to three-fourths of a mile from where the skeletons were found. The place is now owned by the local chapter of the Daughters of the American Revolution. This place is about thirteen miles from Elberton.''

State Senators. Lincoln during the early pioneer days was represented in the General Assembly of Georgia by the following State Senators: Thomas W. Murray, Robert Walton, Rem Remsen, John M. Dooly, John Fleming, William Harper, Micajah Hanley, John Fraser, Peter Lamar, Benning B. Moore and N. G. Barksdale. Some of the early Representatives were: John M. Dooly, Philip Zimmerman, James Espey, Elijah Clarke, Jr., Samuel Fleming, Wheeler Gresham, Gibson Clarke, Peter Lamar, Thomas Lamar, John Fleming, Thomas W. Murray, John Lamkin, William Jones, William Curry, Nicholas G. Barksdale and John McDowell. William Curry was the father of Dr. Jabez Lamar Monroe Curry, diplomat, statesman, educator and divine, whose statue has been placed in the nation's Hall of Fame by the State of Alabama.*

LOWNDES.

Old County Sites. In 1826 Lowndes County was organized out of a part of Irwin and named for Hon. William Lowndes, a distinguished statesman of South Carolina. Franklinville was the original county-seat of Lowndes; but in 1833 the site of public buildings was changed to Lowndesville.[1] Still later, it was changed to Troupville, a town located in an angle between the Willacoochee and the Little Rivers. On December 14, 1837, Troupville was incorporated with the following-named commissioners, to-wit.: Jonathan Knight, Sr., Jared Johnson, K. Jameson, Francis McCall, and William

[1] Acts, 1828, p. 151; Acts, 1833, p. 317.

Smith.[2]   Finally, when the Atlantic and Gulf Railway was built, an Act was approved November 21, 1859, appointing Messrs. James Harrell, Dennis Worthington, John R. Stapler and William H. Goldwire as commissioners to chose a new county-site on the above-mentioned line, and out of this Act grew the present city of Valdosta, named for one of Governor Troup's plantations.

Valdosta.   Volume I.

LUMPKIN

Dahlonega: Early Gold-Mining in Georgia. According to the testimony of not a few residents in this neighborhood, some of whom have passed the patriarchal limit of four-score years, gold was found in Lumpkin County prior to the date given for its discovery in White County, on Duke's Creek, in 1828. Mr. Reese Crisson, one of the best-known of the practical miners who came to Dahlonega in the early day, was heard to say on more than one occasion that when he came to Dahlonega, in the above-named year, it was some time after the discovery of gold in this neighborhood. Mr. Joseph Edwards, a man of solid worth, still living at a ripe old age near Dahlonega, corroborates this statement. He also was one of the early miners; and, on the authority of Mr. Edwards, gold had been discovered in Lumpkin for some time when he came to Dahlonega in 1828. At any rate, the discovery of gold brought an influx of white population into Cherokee Georgia, some mere adventurers, some possessed of the restless spirit of discontent, ever on the lookout for something strange and new, but most of them men of high character, anxious to develop the rich treasures hidden in the hills of this beautiful section of Georgia. The Indians were still here and must have known of the gold deposits, though perhaps ignorant of their value; hence the name "Taloneka," signifying "yellow metal."

In 1836 the United States Mint was established at Dahlonega. Skilled workmen were brought from Philadelphia to put the mint into operation; and among the number who came at this time was the Rev. David Hastings, a Presbyterian minister, whose cultured family imparted a tone of refinement to the rough mining camp and formed the beginning of Dahlonega's social and intellectual life. His grand-daughter, Miss Lida Fields, was a noted eduactor, whose popular history of the United States is still a standard text-book in the public schools. Governor Allen D. Candler, one of Georgia's most distinguished sons, was born near the old mint. Dr. Benjamin Smith, with his good wife, came from Vermont and

---

[2] Acts, 1837, p. 265.

settled near Leather's Ford. He built a school-house across the highway from his residence, furnished it with maps, black-boards, globes and so forth, and here his own children, together with others in the neighborhood, were taught by Mrs. Smith until the cares of her growing family deprived the community of her splendid services, after which a lady from Athens, Ga., was employed to take up her work.

Here lived the Gartrells, the ,Singletons, the Mangums, the Kennons, and, last but not least, Colonel R. H. Moore. Who does not delight to dwell upon his memory—the handsome, courtly gentleman of the old South, the brave and chivalrous commander of the gallant Sixty-fifth Georgia Regiment? The father of Henry W. Grady, the South's great orator-journalist, came here to marry Miss Anne Eliza Gartrell. His uncle then lived in the house now occupied by Mr. R. C. Meaders. Dr. James Thomas, later president of Emory College, was once a resident of Lumpkin. He came seeking health from mountain air and pure water. Miss Adeline Thomas, afterwards Mrs. Spriggs, was a noted school teacher in her day. Nineteen miles west of Dahloneg, in the upper part of Dawson County, bordering on Lumpkin, are the falls of the Amicalola, renowned for beauty. The peaceful quiet of this lovely region is broken only by the murmur of the water as it leaps from rock to rock, forming a beautiful cascade, 792 feet in height, which fully justifies the meaning of its Indian name, "Soothing Water."

Dr. Matthew Stephenson, one of the best-known men of science in antebellum days, especially in the field of geological research, came to Dahlonega with his gifted wife, a lady educated in the schools of Nashville, under the celebrated Dr. Hume. Three families of the Quillians were formerly residents of this town. Dr. Benjamin Hamilton, an eloquent pulpit orator, with his interesting family, once resided here. Dr. H. M. VanDyke, a noted physician from New York, joined hand and fortune with the little village. The Burnside brothers, James and William, whose father was challenged to fight a fatal duel because he would not give the authorship of a certain communication in his paper, came from Augusta with their widowed mother, who was anxious to spend the remainder of her days away from the scenes of political strife, which had been the cause of her great sorrow. They made good citizens of the place, and now rest in peace in Mt. Hope Cemetery.

At Auraria sleep the remains of a noted woman of this section, Mrs. Agnes Paschal. Gifted in many ways, her strong point was her knowledge of the healing art. Her services in this capacity were in demand far and wide, and she was wonderfully successful in her practice. This elect woman lived to be ninety-four years of age, and of her it can truly be said that she lived not for herself, but for others. She was the mother of Judge G. W. Paschal so distinguished in the legal profession. He removed to Arkansas and became one of the judges of the Supreme Court of that State. Later he went to Washington, D. C., where he was instrumental in founding the Law Department of Georgetown University, and became the first professor of jurisprudence in that institution. Here, too, by the side of her husband rests Mrs. James Wood, so long a resident, known far and wife for her hospitality and practical business qualities, and truly remarkable woman. One mile this side is a heap of stones in a cornfield that marks the place where stood General Winfield Scott's headquarters when he was sent to remove the Cherokees to the West. It was called the ''Station,'' and stood there until recent years.

On the banks of the Etowah, near the home of Mr. John Hutcheson, is ''Guy Rivers' Cave,'' made famous by William Gilmore Sims in his novel of that name. The interpreter for the noted Indian Chief, Gunauluskee, was connected with a family in Dahlonega, and through them comes this story of how it was arranged that he should not be carried to the West. He could speak English, but in a business transaction, a white man had been guilty of an unprincipled act, and thereafter Gunauluskee would never speak a word of English, hence the necessity for an interpreter. He was on the staff of General Andrew Jackson, and had rendered signal service to that intrepid warrior at the battle of Horseshoe Bend, and when the chief gave notice that he would not be taken from his home, a man was found who was willing to undertake the long journey on horseback to Washington, D. C., to interview General Jackson as to what must be done with the brave old man, and he replied in language more forcible than elegant: ''Let Guanuluskee stay in any d—d place he wants to.''

Space cannot be allowed to tell of all who combined to make Dahlonega and its vicinity a center of learning and culture in those early days. The political horizon soon became clouded, and the storm in all its fury broke at length over the country, and there was a general scattering abroad of the families who had lent a charm to this immediate section. The young men hastened to take up arms in defence of the South, and nowhere in all the armies that were marshalled could be found braver, truer soldiers than those from Lumpkin. After the long hard struggle, then came the trying days. Volume I tells of the establishment of the N. G. A. C. College, and Colonel Price's connection with it, but it would be incomplete without mention of others who have made their impress on their great Commonwealth. Wier Boyd, the ''Grand Old Roman from Lumpkin,'' as he was styled, was a prominent figure in the conventions of 1865 and 1877. His record as an able and wise statesman is a part of the history of the two branches of the Legislature of Georgia. Marion G. Boyd, the elder son, led the fight in the Senate of Georgia in 1878 against the abuses of the convict system, and won for himself national fame as an orator. His last appearance in public was at the convention which nominated Governor A. D. Candler in 1898. He was chosen to make the nominating speech, and those who heard him say that it was a marvellous effort from this wonderfully gifted man. J. W. Boyd, the younger son, who is now a citizen of Fairmount, Ga., a lawyer and an accomplished mathematician, as a member of the Senate, was prominently connected with the ''Good Roads'' legislation in the sessions of the Georgia Legislature in 1907 and 1908.

The companion of his father, as well as of a scholarly uncle, B. F. Sitton, both of whom took great interest in whatever would improve the roads of the country, it was to have been expected that he would have been an enthusiastic worker in the cause. Indeed, the whole family lived in the belief that this immediate section would one day become the garden spot of Georgia. Pure and incorruptible, unselfish and patriotic, Lumpkin lost one of her best citizens in his removal from her. A. G. Wimpy, another citizen, around whose name clusters precious memories, was for forty years superintendent of the Methodist Sunday School. Goodman Hughes was a benediction to this section. B. R. Meaders still lives to bless the community. In his long life he has never sworn an oath or touched one drop of whiskey. William J. Worley, whose long useful life has recently closed, was one of four brothers who were born and reared in Dahlonega, and who went nobly forward in defence of their country in time of its peril. ''Service'' was the keynote of his character, and he gave it without stint to every good cause for the advancement of his native town.

Hon. W. H. McAfee, now in Atlanta, a man of sterling worth, was a citizen of this place the greater part of his life. Doctors Hills, Moody, Howard and Chapman were men noted in their profession. Judge Amzi Rudolph, late of Gainesville, was for years an honored citizen of Lumpkin. Mrs. Josephine Whelchel, one of the few remaining residents who was intimately acquainted with nearly all those who have been mentioned in connection with Dahlonega's early history, is still an ornament to the place, with her rare knowledge of so much that is beautiful in nature and art. She is a niece of Harrison Riley and often presided at the table of his splendidly appointed hotel when there were distinguished guests to be ententaind. Among the frequent visitors to this part of the country were United States Senators, judges and other high dignitaries of both State and Nation, and the Riley hotel was their stopping place. Later it was known as the Besser House, and many amusing anecdotes are related by the citizens of this dear old German proprietor. This same building is now known as ''Hall's Villa,'' having been purchased by F. W. Hall, and is a part of his estate, but is no longer used as a hotel, having been superseded by the ''Mountain Club House,'' so favorably known to the travelling public.

This is written to prove that now, as always, the good is far in advance of the bad, and while it must be admitted that there were open bar-rooms and too much drinking, fighting and gambling in the early history of the place, such was likewise true of other sections of Georgia; nor was it altogether fair to have given this place a name which attached to it so long in the minds of those unacquainted with the facts.

One thing more, and this article closes. Dahlonega furnished three colonels for the Southern Army from '61 to '65. They were Colonel William Martin, First Georgia Regulars; Colonel Wier Boyd, Fifty-second Regiment, Georgia Volunteers; Colonel R. H. Moore, Sixty-fifth Regiment, Georgia Volunteers. The young men who have gone from the halls of the N. G. A.

College since its opening have almost, without an exception, reflected honor upon the old school in which they were made strong to fight the battles of life.

McDUFFIE.

Thomson. Thomson, the county-seat of McDuffie, dates its origin as a village from the building of the Georgia Railroad in the early forties. It was named for Mr. J. Edgar Thomson, of Philadelphia, the chief engineer who surveyed the line. Thomson was incorporated as a town on February 15, 1854, with the following-named commissioners, to-wit.: Wiliam P. Steed, Leonard G. Steed, F. F. Reynolds, William M. Pitts, Francis T. Allen, William J. Langston, Adam J. Smith, Joseph H. Stockton, Richard A. Sullivan, Anson W. Stanford, James L. Zachary and Richard P. Thurmond.* The Thomson Male and Female High School was granted a charter of incorporation on the same date, but in a different Act. When the new County of McDuffie was formed in 1870 from Warren and Columbia, the site of public buildings was fixed at Thomson. The growth of the town of late has been rapid. Its best-known citizen is the brilliant historian, editor and party leader, Hon. Thomas E. Watson, but such eminent Georgians as Judge Henry C. Roney, Hon. John T. West and others have likewise been identified with Thomson.

McINTOSH.

Darien. Darien, the county-seat of McIntosh County, is one of the oldest towns of Georgia. It was founded by General Oglethorpe, who here planted a colony of Scotchmen for the defence of the exposed southern frontier. In 1793, when McIntosh County was formed out of Liberty, the site of public buildings was fixed at

---

*Acts, 1853-1854, p. 223.

Darien. The town was incorporated by an Act approved December 2, 1805, providing for its better regulation, and Messrs. William A. Dunham, Virgil H. Vivian, John K. Holzendorf, George Street and Scott Gray were named at this time as commissioners. In 1818 the town was incorporated as a city, with a municipal form of government. Elsewheer will be found a more extended sketch of Darien.

The McIntoshes: A Clan Noted in Georgia Annals. Since the days of Oglethorpe, the distinguished family of this name has been conspicuous in the public life of Georgia. It has produced fighters, some of whom have achieved high eminence, both on land and on sea. It has produced statesmen, one of whom, Governor George M. Troup, held nearly every important office in the gift of the people and defied successfully the power of the United States government in the celebrated clash over State Rights. The family is of Scotch origin. It was planted in Georgia by John Mohr McIntosh,* a Highlánder, whose name was a power in Scotland, but whose support of the Pretender cost him the forfeiture of his estate. The invitation of Oglethorpe, who was seeking for colonists of hardy timber to settle the frontier outposts of Georgia, seems to have reached him at his home near Inverness about the time of his disastrous reverses, and the well-known Jacobite leanings of Oglethorpe only served to re-enforce an appeal which was not unattractive in itself. He resolved to seize this opportunity to recoup his fortunes in the new world. As the head of the Borlam branch of the powerful McIntosh clan, he induced a number of his followers to accompany him to Georgia. The emigrants settled on the site of the present town of Darien. In the frequent wars with the Spaniards, the brave little Scotch colony was almost completely obliterated, and in the assault upon St. Augustine, John Mohr McIntosh was himself made a prisoner; and, being transported to Spain he was immured for months within dungeon walls. He was at first the civil commandant in charge of the settlement, but was later instructed to enroll one hundred Highlanders to serve under him as light infantrymen in General Oglethorpe's regiment. Thus he came to participate in most of the hard fighting. Broken in health by his long imprisonment in Spain, he returned home only to die soon after his arrival in Georgia.

General Lachlan McIntosh, his son, was, like himself, a native of Borlam, in Scotland, and a man of strong martial instincts. He became perhaps the foremost military officer which the State gave to the struggle

---

*White's Statistics of Georgia, pp. 416-421; Stacy's History of the Midway Congregational Church, pp. 280-281; Men of Mark in Georgia, pp. 244-256, etc.

for independence. Due to an unfortunate quarrel with Button Gwinnett, which led to fatal results on the field of honor, the latter falling a victim in the encounter, General McIntosh relinquished the command of the Georgia troops and accepted an appointment under Washington. Though not the aggressor in this unfortunate affair, there was naturally a division of public sentment, Gwinnett having been a Signer of the Declaration of Independence, for which service he was held in grateful esteem, notwithstanding certain grave faults. In his new field of operations, General McIntosh won rapid advancement and received the encomiums of Washington. He returned to take active part in the siege of Savannah, but the theatre of his activities was principally in Virginia, under the great commander-in-chief.

It was his nephew, Colonel John McIntosh, whose gallant defence of Fort Morris, at Sunbury, Ga., received the recognition of the State Legislature, in the gift of a sword, on which was engraved his famous message of defiance to the British officer: "Come and take it!" He participated in numerous engagements, and, at the battle of Brier Creek, where he was made a prisoner, his life was narrowly saved by the timely intervention of Sir Aeneas McIntosh, a kinsman, in the opposite ranks. Colonel John S. McIntosh, his son, was another heroic representative of this martial race. He won his spurs in the War of 1812; and, when hostilities with Mexico began in 1845, he was one of the first to enlist. He bore himself with conspicuous gallantry in several of the fiercest engagements, but in the battle of Molina del Rey he was mortally wounded at the head of his columns. He died in the City of Mexico, where his remains were buried; but subsequently, by vote of the State Legislature, his ashes were exhumed, brought back to Georgia, and laid to rest in the Colonial Cemetery at Savannah. They repose in the vault of his illustrious granduncle, General Lachlan McIntosh.

But the list is not yet exhausted. Commodore James McKay McIntosh, a cousin of the above-named officer, arose to eminence in the United States Navy and died on the eve of the Civil War, at Pensacola, Fla., where he was in command of the navy yard. His sister, Maria J. McIntosh, became distinguished as a novelist. Another sister, Mrs. Ann Ward, became the mother of the accomplished diplomat and lawyer, Hon. John E. Ward, who was the first United States Minister to China. Major Lachlan McIntosh, the father of this brilliant group, was also a man of note in the line of military attainments. Captain John McIntosh Kell, who achieved an immortality of fame, in association with Admiral Semmes, on the decks of the Alabama, was a grand-nephew of Colonel John McIntosh, of Sunbury fame, whose name he bore.

General William McIntosh, the brave chief of the Cowetas, whose friendship for Georgia cost him the sacrifice of his gallant life, in consequence of the treaty at Indian Springs, ceding the remainder of the Creek lands in Georgia to the whites, was likewise a member of this same McIntosh family, and a kinsman, if not a descendant, of John Mohr McIntosh.

of Darien. His father was Captain John McIntosh, and his uncle, Captain Roderick McIntosh, an eccentric character of the Revolution, who espoused the British side of the struggle, but possessed none of the typical vindictiveness of the Tories. Catharine McIntosh, his aunt, married an English army officer by the name of Troup, from which union came the distinguished statesman, Governor George M. Troup, who was one of the foremost public men of his time: an apostle of State Rights and an enemy without compromise to Federal encroachments. It will thus be seen that the McIntosh family has been notably identified with the fortunes of Georgia, from the earliest colonial days down to the present era. Nor has the State failed to give substantial recognition to the claims of this distinguished household; for not only does one of the oldest counties of Georgia bear the proud name of McIntosh; but the counties of Troup and Coweta may likewise be counted among its enduring memorials.

Joseph Woodruff: Patriot and Pioneer. Beginning with the late Colonial period and coming on down through the period of the Revolution, there are few names more frequently found in the early records of this State than the name of a staunch old patriot who spent his last days on Broro Neck, in the County of McIntosh: Colonel Joseph Woodruff. This distinguished officer of the Continental Army was born in London, Eng. On a visit to Bermuda Island, he met and married Mary Forrester; and, after a temporary sojourn in Charleston, S. C., he came to Georgia, in 1788, settling eventually in what was then the Parish of St. John—the Georgia cradle of independence. When Liberty County was organized out of this parish, in 1777, he became one of its stalwart representatives; and later when McIntosh County was formed out of a part of Liberty, in 1793, we find him in that part of the county which was then erected into McIntosh. He was a large land owner, with plantations on various parts of the coast, but was not afraid to jeopardize his holdings in the cause of freedom. At the outbreak of the Revolution, while in command of a galley, he was captured by the British and thrown into prison; but no sooner was he released through the intervention of Tory friends than he hastened to join the Continental Army, in which he served until the surrender of Cornwallis at Yorktown.

Just before the siege of Savannah, Colonel Woodruff was dangerously wounded in the thigh, at Ogeechee Bridge, in 1778. He afterwards served as Deputy Quartermaster-General and sat both in the House of Assembly and in the Executive Council. One of his sons, Joseph Woodruff, Jr., a major in the United States Army, bore a conspicuous part in the war of 1812. His only daughter, Mary, married the gallant Captain Ferdinand O'Neill (O'Neal), a Frenchman who came to America to fight the British. Joining Lee's Legion of Cavalry, young O'Neill accompanied this dashing commander to Georgia and subsequent to the Revolution acquired a plantation on Broro Neck, became one of the founders of the Georgia Cincinnati, served in the Legislature of the State, and took an active leadership in public affairs. Two of his comrades in arms 'settled near him on Broro Neck, Captain Armstrong and Captain Rudolph, the latter of whom died in Captain O'Neill's home, on June 28, 1800. Colonel Woodruff was at one time Collector of the Port at Savannah, probably the last public office which this distinguished patriot ever filled in Georgia. His death occurred in 1799, and he probably lies buried on his plantation at Broro Neck. The burial ground of the O'Neill's has recently been located in the upper part of McIntosh.

MACON.

General Remarks.* The county of Macon was laid out in 1830 from Houston and Marion, and the first court was held at the house of Walter L. Campbell, Judge King presiding. This was on a plantation owned in 1854 by one A. Wiley, and was formerly known as "Barnett's Reserve." Barnett was an Indian, and his Reserve included many hundreds of acres extending from Montezuma toward Marshallville and covering the high table land on the east side of the Flint River. Lanier was made the county-seat in 1838. Oglethorpe in 1854. When the seat of government was changed, there were 679 buildings in the county; total number of free persons, 4,191; total slaves, 2,961.

Flint River, running north to south through the county, was crossed entirely by ferry-boats until 1888, when a bridge was built above Oglethorpe by the town of Montezuma, for the purpose of drawing trade. This bridge is a quarter of a mile long and a fine piece of constructive work. There have been five ferries. The upper ferry, known as "Bryan's," has been discarded. The second, or "Hollingshed's Ferry," is still in use. The third, or "Lanier Ferry," was discarded after the war. The ferry between Montezuma and Oglethorpe was discarded when the county built an iron bridge in 1902. The lower ferry connected Traveler's Rest with Oglethorpe, but when Travelers' Rest was deserted the ferry was abandond. Two railroads now traverse Macon. The Central of Georgia reached Oglethorpe in the summer of 1852, at a cost of $13,342 per mile. The Atlanta, Birmingham and Atlantic was built through Macon in 1903.

There are two "Deserted Villages" in the county—Travelers' Rest and Lanier. There is also one resort, Miona Springs. These are two miles from the site of old Lanier. For years the mineral waters of this locality have been widely known. The tradition in regard to the springs

*For the full and comprehensive treatment of Macon County in this sec tion, we are indebted to Archibald Bulloch Chapter, D. A. R., of which Mrs. J. E. Hays, of Montezuma, is Regent.

is that an Indian girl by the name of Miona was killed by her white lover near the springs, and buried in the surrounding woods. As far back as the days of the Red Men, the Magical power of these waters was recognized. In the eighteen-nineties, Mr. William Minor, of Montezuma, built a hotel here, with outlying cottages, and for several years it enjoyed quite a vogue as a summer resort. The cottages are still occupied in summer, and the place is a great picnic ground.

During the war between the States, Macon County was not lacking in patriotism. The Davis Rifles, with Captain John McMillan, were the first to respond to the call, going from the vicinity of Marshallville. Captain S. M. Prather, from Oglethorpe, carried a company, including Phil Cook, Joel Griffin, Colonel Willis and others. Major J. D. Frederick went as captain of a company from old Lanier. Captain McMullan, of Oglethorpe, mustered in a company of boys, and Major W. H. Robinson organized a company of old men, verifying the truth of what has often been said that the war toward the last "robbed both the cradle and the grave." When peace came Union soldiers were encamped at White Water Creek.

Travelers Rest: A Forgotten Town. In the early twenties two travelers were making their way South, and at sun-down they sought a place where they might find shelter and rest for the night. They found such a place under a friendly clump of trees on a little mound near the road-side. After a refreshing sleep they awoke, and looking around at the beauties of nature, they exclaimed, "This is truly a place of rest," so the spot was called "Travelers Rest." At that time only one house was standing nearby, but Travelers Rest soon became a thriving village. A dozen or more houses were built by John Shines, Daniel Harrison, William Yarbrough and others. Two churches, one hotel, or tavern as it was then called, a Masonic lodge, work shop, grist mill and a very good school were soon erected.

In those days the only means of transportation was horseback and stage-coach, but the little village prospered, and several large stores were built, the people going through the country to Savannah and Augusta for goods, but in 1850 the Central of Georgia Railroad was extended to the new town of Montezuma, Ga., and the little village of Travelers Rest began to fall into decay. The stores were moved to Montezuma, and today only the huge sign post where the sundial stood and the quiet cemeteries with their sleeping dead marks the spot where old Travelers Rest once flourished. The site of the old town is two miles south of Montezuma.

Old Lanier: A Forgotten County Site. Lanier, located 80 miles from Milledgeville, 22 miles from Perry, 25 miles from Americus, and near the center of the county, was made the county-site in 1838. During the years from thirty-eight to fifty-two, Lanier was a thriving town of several thousand population. There were two hotels and two livery stables. Forsyth Ansley owned a brick store, Si Hill a grocery, L. L. Snow a grocery, Enoch Wilson a tailor shop. Among other names connected with its earliest history were Dr. Dennis, Mrs. Mahon, Mrs. Hays, the Corbetts, Dr. Dawson, John M. Giles and a little later W. H. Robinson, Aaron Lowe, the Greers (who afterwards moved to Oglethorpe), Major J. D. Frederick, the Laws, the Underwoods, the Lockwoods and Dr. McKellar. Mrs. W. H. Felton lived a short distance away. The Gileses moved to Perry, the Mahons to Waynessboro or Swainesboro, the Robinsons to Montezuma, the Fredericks and the Feltons to Marshallville. When the court-house was removed to the railroad at Oglethorpe in fifty-two, Lanier saw the beginning of her downfall. Families dispersed houses were torn away, and now on the site of the village, Crepe Myrtle trees mark the location of old walls, once happy homesteads. The ancient grave-yard only remains to tell its tale of the once thrifty past.

> "No more the farmer's news, the barber's tale,
> No more the woodman's ballad shall prevail;
> No more the smith his dusky brow shall clear,
> Relax his ponderous strength and learn to hear;
> The host himself no longer shall be found,
> Careful to see the mounting bliss go round;
> Nor the coy maid, half willing to be prest,
> Shall kiss the cup to pass it to the rest.
> But now the sound of population fail,
> No cheerful murmurs fluctuate in the gale;
> No busy steps the grass-grown footway tread,
> But all the bloomy flush of life is dead.''

Oglethorpe. As far back as 1840, there was a settlement on the site of the present town of Oglethorpe, named for Georgia's illustrious founder. In 1850 the local population numbered 268 whites and 186 blacks. It was a regular stopping place for the stage coach. Mr. E. G. Cabaniss owned 600 acres of land in the immediate neighborhood and when the work of construction along the line of the Central of Georgia began to approach the settlement, Mr. Cabaniss laid out town lots and advertised an auction sale, from the proceds of which he realized a handsome profit. Thus were laid the foundations of the town of Oglethorpe. During the summer of 1852, the Central Railway's southwestern branch was completed to this point, and instantly the town began to bristle with renewed life. Thousands of wagons began to haul cotton into Oglethorpe, some of them coming from as far south as Dothan, Ala., and these wagons always returned loaded with merchandise. There were eighty business houses on Baker Street alone, besides eight hotels, and the population of Oglethorpe before the war has been variously estimated at from 12,000 to 20,000 inhabitants.

Lanier began to decline in prestige with the advent of the iron horse. It lacked railway facilities, and in 1854 the county-site was changed to Oglethorpe. The first court-house was built where the high school now stands, but was burned in 1857. Thirteen years later the jail also was destroyed by fire. The first newspaper was the *Southwest Georgian*, issued by Simri Rose, in 1851. During the same year the first Masonic Lodge was organized. Mr. Posy Stanfield, now of Americus, was one of the charter members.

Among the first settlers were Dr. T. B. Oliver, P. L. J. May, Dr. Black, Major Black, Dr. Head, Henry Johnson, Joel B. Griffin, Colonel A. S Cutts, Major Hansel, General Phil Cook, John M. Greer, Warren Lee, W. J. Collins, Dan Kleckley, Major Miller, Sam Hall, Dr. William Ellis, George Williams, Egbert Alen, Aaron Lowe, Elbert Lewis and Dr. Prottuo. John and Allen Greer came from Lanier in sixty-three.

After a few years of marked prosperity the railroad was extended, but about this time an epidemic of smallpox raged. Numbers of citizens died of the disease. All houses in which there were cases were burned. Houses were moved to Marshallville, Dawson, Americus, Montezuma, Lanier and other places. Oglethorpe never recovered from the smallpox epidemic, but soon adjusted herself to changed conditions. In 1893 there was a long and hard fight for the possession of the court-house, Montezuma trying to move it. After a successful fight the third court-house was built in Oglethorpe. Artesian wells were bored in July, 1884. Among the most prominent citizens who aided in the upbuilding of Oglethorpe were Colonel W. H. Willis, Captain Sneed, Mr. Charles Keen and Colonel William Fish, father of Chief Justice Fish. The prominent doctors of the fifties were Doctors Cotton, Hall, Ainger, Herring, Colzey, Oliver, Head and Woods. Three of the best dwellings in Oglethorpe were built in fifty-one by Dr. Head, Dr. Black and Major Black.

Gen. Philip Cook: An Ante-Bellum Resident. General Philip Cook, soldier, legislator and Secretary of State, was for several years prior to the Civil War a resident of Macon. He lived for a while at Lanier, but later removed to Oglethorpe, where the outbreak of hostilities in 1861 found him engaged in the practice of law. From Oglethorpe he went to the front as a sergeant in the Macon Volunteers. The close of the war found him wearing the stars of a brigadier-general, though he was not a West Pointer. General Cook's father was the famous commandant at Fort Hawkins, during the War of 1812, Major Philip Cook, noted in pioneer days as an Indian fighter. His grandfather, Captain John Cook, was an officer in Colonel William Washington's Legion of Cavalry; while his mother was a daughter of Major John Wooten, who was killed at Fort Wilkinson. He was also lineally descended from the Pearsons, an aristocratic Virginia family distinguished in the Revolution. General Cook's first acquaintance with military life was during the Seminole War, when he volunteered at the age of eighteen. Locating in Americus in 1869 he formed a law partnership with Hon. Charles F. Crisp, afterwards Speaker of the national House of Representatives. While still a resident of Macon in 1865 General Cook was elected to Congress, but he did not take his seat at this time, because of political disabilities. He rendered the State an important service in the Constitutional Convention of 1865 and later represented his district in Congress for three consecutive terms. He also served in both branches of the State Legislature. Governor McDaniel, in 1883, appointed him one of the five commissioners to supervise the erection of the present State Capitol in Atlanta; and this magnificent structure—built within the original appropriation—is a superb monument to the official integrity of this board. In 1890 General Cook was tendered the office of Secretary of

State, a position to which he was twice re-elected. At his death, he was
succeeded in office by his son, Hon. Philip Cook, Jr., who for more than
sixteen years has worthily worn the mantle of his distinguished father.
General Cook received his collegiate education at Oglethorpe University
and began the practice of law at Forsyth, Ga., as a partner of the late
Zach Harman. For a number of years after the war, he conducted extensive farming operations in Lee County, where his plantation became an
arena for advanced scientific experiments. Gifted with a masterful intellect, General Cook was a born leader of men—courageous, upright, patriotic, inflexibly true to his convictions. At the same time, he was governed
throughout his whole life by the law of gentleness, and to know him was
to love him. The Montezuma Chapter, U. D. C., bears the name of this
gallant Confederate soldier and peerless gentleman of the old school.

Marshallville. At what is still known as the cross-roads,
on the site of the present town of Mar-
shallville, Isaac Johnson, in the early part of the last
century, built a house partly of brick. On the opposite
side of the street he erected a blacksmith shop; and from
this modest beginning arose the town. There was also
a blacksmith shop run by a man named Briggs. Soon
a hard-shell church was built, in which three denominations worshipped—the hard-shell Baptists, the Missionary Baptists and the Methodists. This church occupied
the site where Henry Taylor's house now stands, and was
used until the fifties. In 1825 Needham Massee brought
his family from North Carolina to Fort Hawkins, and,
two years later, coming to this county, he bought the
place on the edge of Marshallville, still owned by his
grandsons. In 1832 Daniel Frederick came from Orange-
burg, S. C., and settled on a farm just across the county
line in Houston; but after a short while he removed to
Marshallville, where he bought a farm, which is still
owned by the Fredericks.

During the early thirties a number of families came from the same
section of South Carolina and settled near the border line between Houston and Macon. In the course of time, these families became strong factors in the development of Marshallville. They included the Fudges, who

settled on a place now owned by John Pharr; Conrad Murph, who bought the plantation now owned by Nash Murph, his son; Nathan Bryant, who settled near the Flint River on land still owned by his sons; Dr. D. F. Wade, who lived on a place owned by the late D. B. Frederick; Dr. Hollinshed, with his brother Jim, who lived not far from the river; Frank Baldwin, who settled close to Winchester; William Haslam, who lived in Houston County and moved to Marshallville after the war; George Slappy, who bought the Mulberry place from Mr. Lowman, now owned by his son Jake; Mr. Wells, who lived where Taylor Williams now lives; Mr. Hiley, who settled between here and Fort Valley; Dr. Crocker, who settled on the river; Mr. Harman Staplers, and Lewis Rumph, who settled in Houston County, where his home is still owned by his son Lewis.

Billy Felton settled at Winchester; his son Ham (W. H.) lived at Lanier until after the war, then came to Marshallville; another son, Monroe, settled in Marshallville in 1859.

Major James Belvin and Dr. McGehee settled first in Houston County, but came to Marshallville after the war; George Plant came some time in the thirties. During the early forties Murdock and John McCaskill came from South Carolina, living close to the place where, in the early seventies, they built the beautiful brick colonial home now owned by Lewis Rumph; D. B. Frederick came from South Carolina in fifty-three, and bought a farm from Dr. Wade; Dave Gammage came from Jones County early in the forties and settled here. Others coming in the forties were the Nixons, Joseph Day, who bought out the Edgeworts family, into which Dr. J. W. Roberts, of Atlanta, afterwards married. Seaborn Bryan came in the forties; John C. Sperry came from Twiggs County in the forties and bought out Isaac Johnson; Rev. Joe Edwards, from Prince George County, Va., came in the forties; Dr. Wm. Hafer came from Pennsylvania in the fifties; Billy Martin came from Ireland in the fifties; Shadrock Ware came from Twiggs County in 1855, bought an estate from Dick Orr, which is still owned by his sons; Dr. Cook, brother of General Phil Cook, came from Winnsboro, N. C., at the close of the war; L. O. Niles, a teacher and merchant, came from Massachusetts; Major James D. Frederick moved here from Lanier, and for forty years was chairman of the Board of Roads and Revenues; Colonel Reese, a lawyer, came in sixty-eight from Jasper County. He is the father of Mrs. S. H. Rumph and of Mrs. Nash Murph. Henry Taylor, merchant and planter, came soon after the war; Mary Slappy—afterwards Mrs. Bell Lee—mother of Mrs. Oscar Williams, a woman of unquestioned veracity and memory, who died within the last month at the age of 86, gave the following account of how the county's name originated: A group of young people were together discussing a name for the new nameless town, when some one suggested that it be named for Rev. John Marshall, a preacher who lived close to town, and who was greatly beloved; thereupon the name of Marshallville was adopted. Rev.

John Marshall was son-in-law of Dr. D. F. Wade and father-in-law of Marcus Sperry.

———

Soon after Daniel Frederick moved into Marshallville he laid off the long main street, gave two acres for a Methodist Church, and began selling off lots for building purposes. He erected the homestead in 1845, which is still in possession of his family. In the early fifties, about fifty-five, a Methodist Church was built on this lot, and D. B. Frederick for the Methodists, with William Rice for Baptists, organized the first union Sunday school. D. B. Frederick continued as superintendent of this Sunday School until his death, in 1911—an unusual record. Miss Kate Edwards, sister of Joe Edwards, was one of the teachers in this first Sunday School. Major J. D. Frederick, son of Daniel Frederick, gave the land for a school, which place is still the site of the school building. Walter Frederick and Mrs. Joe Edwards taught in this school for thirty years giving perfect satisfaction. The first store was built by John C. Sperry and the first warehouse was run by Hatcher & Baldwin. The railroad came through in fifty-two, but it was not until after the war that the town was incorporated, and Dave Gammage was the first Mayor.

In the early sixties Dr. G. L. D. Rice gave four acres of land for a Baptist Church, on which a substantial edifice was subsequently built.

———

In the seventies Sam Rumph, at Willow Lake, began to experiment with peaches. Some questioned the wisdom of the venture, but a new era had come for Marshallville. His son, Sam Henry Rumph, a practical planter, continued his experiments, and after years of waiting developed his long-desired and perfect-shipping peach, which he named for his wife, "Elberta." It was some time before the people could grasp the idea of an-

other product besides cotton. Now this is the greatest
peach section in the world, and the Elberta is still the
standard.

There are several homes in and around Marshallville
worthy of especial note. About one mile from and overlooking Flint River is the old Crocker home, built by
Dr. Crocker in 1840. His daughter Mary, who was born
on this place the night the stars fell, married Ham Felton
in this house at the age of fifteen. The house is in perfect preservation, and Dr. Crocker's granddaughter, Mrs.
Walter Walker, occupies the place.

Three buildings were moved from Oglethorpe when
the smallpox began to frighten people away. One was
a hotel moved by Tom Slappy and later bought by Needham Massee. It is about one mile from town, and is still
owned by the Massee family. Mr. Nixon moved a house
in which Mr. Shadrick Ware lived, but the house was
burned in the last few years. The third house moved
from Oglethorpe was the William Haslam house, in which
John Lee lives now. Mr. George Slappy built his Colonial home in sixty-eight, and his family still occupies it.
Mr. W. H. Felton built his home soon after the war, and
his family still own it. One of the oldest homesteads is
the Lewis Rumph house, about six miles from town,
built in the fifties and still owned by Lewis Rumph the
second. Marshallville installed water-works and electric
lights in 1914. One distinction of Marshallville is that
most of the plantations around the town have been handed
down from father to son for a period ranging from fifty
to seventy-five years.

Montezuma.   As late as 1850 the site now occupied by the
city of Montezuma—one of the most beau-
tiful of Georgia towns and a wide-awake center of trade
and commerce—was a low swamp in the midst of a dense
thicket of woods, whose solitudes were broken only by
the clutter of wild game and by an occasional shot from

some hunter's rifle. Wild ducks and turkeys, antlered deer, opossums, coons, and squirrels were found in large numbers. It was a favorite locality for the sportsman— this typical bit of Arcadia; and such, indeed, were its surroundings that even a poet's imagination would have been taxed to evolve a town from this particular spot where—it must be confessed—the hooting of the owl sometimes rendered the night hideous. But a town began to arise on this very spot. Luckily for Montezuma, she possessed the fighting spirit. Mars became her patron deity among the gods. There was also something about her name suggestive of war. In a grapple with Travelers Rest for railway honors Montezuma won. Population began steadily to increase. Almost in a day a new metropolis was born. Some of the more enterprising merchants from Travelers Rest came to Montezuma. In fact, the first business house in the new town was erected by Messrs. Holton and Orliff, who came from Travelers Rest, and it stood where the establishment of Hicks and Black is now located. After plucking the laurels from Travelers Rest, it was necessary to start a prolonged and bitter struggle for existence with Oglethorpe, but Montezuma began to lay her plans for securing the wagon trade on the opposite side of the Flint River, access to which was made easy by a splendid bridge across the stream at Travelers Rest.

Shadrick R. Felton, father of Mr. A. C. Felton, was the founder of Montezuma. He owned all the land upon which the town now stands, and as an inducement for people to locate here the town was laid off into lots, and placed upon the market at a very low price. To facilitate the sale of lots, Mr. Felton gave John T. Brown half interest in all town lots to sell them. Mr. Brown was first railroad agent. The depot was situated where the stand-pipe in front of the Minor Hotel is now. The first hotel was built by S. R. Felton and C. H. Young, and was run by Mrs. Ritley; the second hotel was built by Dr. Manly. The first warehouse was erected by S. R. Felton and John T. Brown; the second by J. O. Jelks and C. H. Young, and managed by Captain W. T. Westbrook. The first dwelling was built by Messrs. Holton & Orliff. The second business house was put up by W. S. Truluck, and the third by D. L. Harrison; the first livery stable by C. H. Young, the first drug store by Dr. S. D. Everett. In 1871 Montezuma elected its first Mayor and Council, with Dr. A. D. Smith as Mayor, and at his death Judge A. J. Hamilton was made Mayor in 1872. He and his wife lived here to celebrate their sixtieth wedding anniversary. In 1860 there were a number of fine families living in Montezuma, among them Mrs. Ann Roach, Dr. Everett, Mrs. Bottome, L. A. Brantley, Norris Brothers and William McLendon. One of Mr. McLendon's daughters married J. E. DeVaughn and another married J. W. McKenzie. The McKenzie family has been very prominent in the upbuilding of Montezuma and Macon County. J. W., T. R. and W. L. McKenzie came here from Drayton in Dooly County as very young men and have since then been prominent merchants, planters and factors in the upbuilding of Macon. In 1871 Jno. F. Lewis established a mercantile and banking business, and put his son, E. B. Lewis, then seventeen years old, in charge of it. Subsequently E. B. Lewis ably represented this district in Congress for twelve years, and has always contributed liberally of his time and means to any and every enterprise intended for the promotion of the town. The Lewis Banking Company, organized in 1871, is still the largest bank in this section. Mr. Lewis organized the First National Bank in 1903, an institution of which he is president.

Mr. J. E. DeVaughn, prominent planter and merchant, moved to Montezuma in 1868 from Jonesboro. Dr. I. X. Cheves and family moved here from Crawford County, and his sons, Rev. A. J. Cheves and O. C. Cheves, were prominent in religious and educational movements. Mr.

Ham Felder was one of the first preachers. The Carnegie Library was built in 1906. Montezuma was considered an unhealthy locality until the first artesian well was bored, in 1883. Subsequently, fifteen wells have been bored, and the town has enjoyed unusual health-giving facilities. The deepest well is 500 feet; the shallowest 45 feet; the largest flow 100 gallons per minute, the smallest 6. The A., B. & A. Railroad came into Montezuma in 1903. Montezuma and Oglethorpe were connected by a ferry-boat until 1902, when an iron bridge was built. Montezuma's business was enhanced by the building of a bridge by the town connecting with the upper part of the county in 1888.

Among the old homes in this neighborhood is the Harrison home, moved from Spaulding. Until a few years ago, on the site of the Library, stood an old hotel, the Roach House, which was moved from Oglethorpe. There are four old plantation homes within a radius of five miles: the Adams place, the Hooks homestead, the Barron home and the Dykes home. Electric lights and waterworks were installed in 1902. The first fire engine was bought in 1885. It is one of the oldest and best in the State. The Montezuma Manufacturing Company and Oil Mill was established in 1901, the knitting mill in 1903 and the fertilizer plant in 1910. The first steamer, "The Montezuma," was run between Montezuma and Warwick, in 1885, the steamer "Ada" in 1886.

The old *Montezuma Record,* now *The Georgian,* was established in 1883. It is one of the pioneer weeklies of this section. In 1911 the Daughters of the Confederacy erected a handsome monument to the heroic men in gray who went from Macon County into the Civil War.

Spaulding. In the year 1868 Dr. W. C. Wilkes, pastor of the Baptist Church at Travelers Rest, conceived the idea of establishing a seminary, and chose as its location a spot close to the home of his friend, Mr. Isaac Cheves, some two miles distant. At once, in order to educate their children, and for the sake of the religious and educational atmosphere, many families moved there and built homes. It was named Spaulding, for Dr. A. T. Spaulding, a Baptist minister. Among the residents were Sam Turner, Tom Sutton, Judge J. H. McClung, John Henry McKenzie, Lee Veal, Mr. Spencer, who built the home afterwards bought by the Maxwells, Shadrick Felton, Warren Davis who built the home later sold to Mr. Veal, J. M. DuPree, Mr. Battle, who built the home now owned by Morgan Chastain and Mr. Truluck, who had the only store. The seminary prospered for six or eight years, but gradually the families moved away, and the seminary lost its prestige. Mrs. Lee Veal taught the first music class. Many Montezuma citizens received early training in the Spaulding Seminary, which was about two miles from Montezuma.

MADISON

Danielsville. Danielsville, the county-seat of Madison County, was named for General Allen Daniel, a soldier of the Revolution and an officer of some note in the State militia. When the new County of Madison was organized in 1811, General Daniel, who owned large interests in the neighborhood, donated the site for public buildings and helped to organize the first court. The town was incorporated by an Act approved November 27, 1817, with Messrs. James Long, Willis Towns and Joseph Vincent as commissioners.* The Madison County Academy was chartered in 1811, when the county was first organized. Near Danielsville stands a famous landmark of Presbyterianism in upper Georgia, known as New Hope Church, considerably more than a hundred years old. Dr. Crawford W. Long, the discoverer of sulphuric ether anaesthesia, was born in Danielsville, a fact in itself sufficient to give the town a deservedly high rank among the historic shrines of the world. Dr. Long's wonderful achievement marked a new epoch in the annals of medicine and made humanity his debtor until the end of time.

*Lamar's Digest, p. 1040.

MARION[1]

Tazewell: A   Eight miles northeast of Buena
Former County-Seat.   Vista, is the charming little town of
                      Tazewell, once the county-seat of
Marion. It is situated on both sides of a small stream
called Buck Creek. For several years after the county
was organized, in 1827, the public buildings were at
Horry; but, on December 27, 1838, an Act was approved
making Tazewell the seat of government, with the following town commissioners: Arthur W. Battle, David
N. Burkhalter, Randell W. Mesten, Zachariah Wallace
and Seaborn L. Collins.[2] Just one year preceding, on
Christmas day, 1837, the old Tazewell Academy was
chartered, with the following board of trustees: Burton
W. Dowd, James Powers, Joseph J. Battle, Robert S.
Burch and C. B. Strange.[3] The handsome school-house
at Tazewell occupies the original plot of ground donated
for this purpose by the State. Visitors are always interested in the old parade ground, where the militia drills
took place before the war, and where many an incident
occurred, such as Judge Longstreet describes in ''Georgia Scenes.'' The first clerk of the court at Tazewell
was Burton W. Dowd. Tony Carroll, an early bailiff,
was one of the famous Carroll triplets, all of whom lived
to be very old men. John Burkhalter, Benjamin Halley,
Jordan Wilcher and Solomon Wall were also prominent
among the early pioneers.

Captain John E. Sheppard, a former resident of
Tazewell, but now of Buena Vista, achieved a record for
gallantry during the Civil War which few, if any, surpassed. Like his Highland ancestors, he was a grim
fighter, though withal a most genial gentleman. On ac-

---

[1] Much of the information contained in this chapter has been furnished
by the following residents of Marion: Mr. Benjamin Powell, Mrs. Sallie
Mitchell Green, Mrs. W. B. Short, and Mrs. Annie M. Munro.

[2] Acts, 1838, p. 127.

[3] Acts, 1837, p. 12.

count of a bullet wound in the head, his life hung in the balance for months, but as soon as he could shoulder his musket he was back again at the front. Not long thereafter, in a fierce battle, his ranking officers were all either killed or wounded, making it necessary for him to assume command of his regiment. On this occasion, it is amusingly told of him that he was not exactly on a war footing, since in lieu of shoes his feet were wrapped in pieces of an old croker sack. Hon. J. E. Sheppard, of Americus, a distinguished lawyer and legislator, is Captain Sheppard's son. One of the oldest residents of Tazewell is William Stewart. His gifted son-in-law, Hon. E. H. McMichael, has frequently represented Marion in the General Assembly of Georgia and was Speaker pro tem. of the last House. There are many attractive homes in Tazewell—a conservative and cultured old town, famed for the hospitality of its citizens.

Horry: A Dead Town. The original county-seat of Marion was Horry, a town located some three miles to the northeast of Tazewell, in what is now the County of Schley. The exact size of the town is today unidentified by any existing landmarks. But it was the seat of government from the time when the county was organized, in 1827, until Tazewell was made the county-seat, in 1838.

Pea Ridge. Before 1830, the site occupied by the present town of Buena Vista was a primaeval forest. When a settlement at last bloomed amid the solitudes it was called Pea Ridge. The nucleus for this settlement is said to have been a cake stand, at which an occasional traveler now and then stopped to appease his hunger; and near this stand, Mr. H. K. Lamb, the pioneer merchant of Pea Ridge, afterwards built a store. This was followed by three grog-shops, each of which flourished like a green bay-tree, after the manner of the wicked, until a great revival broke out at a camp-meeting conducted by Blakely Smith. As a result the taverns were closed.

Proofs of a former occupancy of this region by the Indians still abound in numerous flints, arrow heads and fragments of pottery; and likewise in the names bestowed upon running waters. Many citizens of the county recall a number of Indians who remained in Marion until death removed them; and, among these was a famous conjurer and medicine man called "Old Chofe," who held despotic sway over the negroes, due to his supposed extraordinary powers.

Over on Kinchafoonee Creek, the Butts family was established when the county was first organized. Later on, other staunch pioneer settlers began to drift into this region, bringing with them the following fine old Marion County names: Powell, Wallace, Mitchell, Green, Wells, Blanton, James, Burkhalter, McMichael, Miller, Munro, Stevens, Webb, McCall, McCorkle, Drane, Matthews, Brown, Melton, Lowe, Herndon, Mathis, Gill, Rogers, Sheppard, Dunham, Crawford, Harvey and Merrell. Prof. James Monegan, an Irishman, was the first teacher at Pea Ridge. He is still vividly recalled by a former pupil, Mr. Benjamin Powell, who resides within a stone's throw of where he lived when a boy. Prof. Tom Peter Ashmore, of Greer's Almanac fame, was also an early educator. Hardy Mitchell came from North Carolina in 1840; and, during the first year, lived in what is now the court-yard of Buena Vista.

David N. Burkhalter. But the most dominant figure among the early settlers of Pea Ridge was David N. Burkhalter, who removed to Pea Ridge from Tazewell in 1845. Mr. Burkhalter was a Methodist preacher, a large property owner, and a man of wide influence in public affairs. He was one of the first citizens of the county to represent Marion in the State Legislature. It was long before any railroad penetrated this section, and he usually made the trip to Milledgeville behind two mules. While a resident of Tazewell, he built a church for the Methodists; but, on changing his residence to Pea Ridge, he moved the church, too.

John Burkhalter. John Burkhalter, the latter's father, was a Revolutionary soldier, whose grave on a plantation, some few miles out from Buena Vista is soon to be marked by Lanahassee Chapter of the D. A. R. Mr. Burkhalter was one of the earliest pioneer settlers of the county of Marion, and a man from whose loins have sprung a host of descendants, including the present distinguished chief magistrate of Texas: Governor O. B. Colquitt.

Buena Vista. But Pea Ridge was not a name with which to woo the fickle goddess; and, in 1847, it was changed to Buena Vista, following the famous victory achieved by General Zachary Taylor over the Mexicans. Two years later the county-seat was wrested from Tazewell; and, on January 26, 1850, an Act was approved making permanent the site of public buildings at Buena Vista.* Mr. David N. Burkhalter, to whose vigorous initiative the removal of the county-seat was due, donated the land on which the court-house, the Methodist Church and other buildings were located. New vistas of opportunity were now opened. Soon a railway line was built, while stores, schools, churches and homes began to multiply. Today, in the most progressive sense of the word, Buena Vista is a modern town, equipped with an electric-light plant, with a water-works system, and with other public utilities. It is on the automobile highway between Columbus and Americus, and commands a wide territory rich in agricultural products. The Hoke Smith Institute, named for Georgia's senior Senator, is the pride of this entire section, having twice in succession won the silver trophy for this district. Two giften women of Buena Vista enjoy wide note as educators: Miss Ida Munro and Miss Nettie Powell.

Fort Perry. Near Buena Vista, at Fort Perry, can still be seen the breast-works thrown up by the United States infantry, when they occupied this place as a stronghold during the Creek Indian wars. Just a short distance beyond, at Poplar Springs, quite a band of United States cavalry encamped after fording the Chattahoochee River. Both sites will probably be marked in time with appropriate memorials.

Some of the Noted   Governor O. B. Colquitt, of Texas,
Sons of Marion.   the present chief magistrate of the
                      "Lone Star State," spent several
years of his early boyhood in Buena Vista, a town

---

*Acts, 1849-1850, p. 102.

founded by his grandfather, David N. Burkhalter. Judge
Mark H. Blandford, an Associate Justice of the Supreme
Court of Georgia, opened an offiice at one time in Buena
Vista for the practice of law. Hon. J. E. Sheppard, of
Americus, and Hon. B. S. Miller, of Columbus, two of
Georgia's most brilliant lawmakers, were reared in
Buena Vista. Former State School Commissioner W. B.
Merritt was a native of Marion. Hon. William S. West,
of Valdosta, who, on the death of United States Senator
A. O. Bacon, in 1914, was given an ad interim appoint-
ment to fill this vacancy, was born on a plantation in
Marion. Judge William B. Butt was a native of Buena
Vista, where he practiced law until just a short while be-
fore his election to the Bench of the Chattahoochee Circuit. Marion County furnished three companies of infantry to the Southern army, Colonel Edgar M. Butt,
Captain Taylor and Captain Blandford commanding; in
addition to which a large number of volunteers went to
Griffin and joined a cavalry company, led, during many
fierce battles, by the gallant Captain T. M. Merritt. Some
of the ablest lawyers in the State have practiced at the
Buena Vista Bar. It is still ably represented by a group
of strong men, among whom are Hon. William D. Crawford, Hon. William B. Short, Hon. George P. Munro,
Judge John Butt, Colonel Noah Butt and Colonel T. B.
Rainey.

MERIWETHER

Greenville. In 1827, Meriwether County was formed out
of a part of Troup, and named for General
Meriwether, a distinguished officer of the State militia,
prominent in treaty negotiations with the Indians. The
county-seat, fixed in the year following, was named for
General Nathaniel Greene, of the Revolution. Greenville's charter of incorporation was granted December
20, 1828, with the following residents of the town named
as commissioners: Abner Durham, Joseph Cone, Levi

Adams, Matthew Leverett and Abraham Ragan.[1] The
Meriwether County Academy was chartered on December 22, 1828, with the following trustees, to-wit.: Alfred
Wellborn, John L. Jones, Abraham Ragan, and James
A. Perdue.[2] In 1836 the Greenville Female Academy
was chartered with trustees named as follows: Walton
B. Harris, Joseph W. Harris, Joseph W. Amhoy, Robert
A. Jones, Gibson F. Hill and Wiley P. Burks.[3] Some of
the most distinguished men of Georgia have been former
residents of Greenville, among them Judge Hiram Warner, one of Georgia's ablest jurists; Judge Obadiah
Warren, his younger brother; Hon. Henry R. Harris,
a former member of Congress, Hon. Joseph M. Terrell,
a former Governor and United States Senator; Hon.
William T. Revill, a noted educator, and Judge Hiram
Warner Hill, a member of the present Supreme Court of
Georgia. Governor John M. Slaton was born in Greenville, but removed with his parents to Atlanta, where he
grew to manhood and entered the practice of law.

Memories of   Before the Civic Club of Greenville, dur-
the Early Days. ing the month of January, 1914, Mrs.
             Mary Jane Hill, then in her eighty-
fourth year, read a most delightful paper on the town of
Greenville as she knew it when a girl. Mrs. Hill is the
only child of the late Judge Hiram Warner, and notwithstanding her age, is still in splendid health, with a mind
vigorous in its grasp of things, both past and present.
From this charming paper, a few paragraphs are culled.
Says Mrs. Hill:

"Greenville is an old town whose history dates back to the first settlement of the county. General Hugh Ector owned the land upon which the
town of Greenville was built. I was four years old when my parents came
to make their home here in 1834. We spent the first year in a rented
house on the lot where Mrs. Jno. L. Strozier now lives. This place was
owned by Major Alex. Hall, the grandfather of Mr. A. C. Faver, Mrs. J. R.

[1] Acts, 1828, p. 149.
[2] Acts, 1828, p. 15.
[3] Acts, 1836, p. 8.

Render, Mr. James Hall and other grandchildren now living in the county. Our next-door neighbor was Dr. William Tinsley, a leading physician of the town, and the grandfather of Mrs. R. D. Render, of LaGrange.

"Among the historic houses of Greenville is the one now owned by Mr. Arthur Pinkston. This house was built by a Mr. Hobbs and is one of the oldest in the town. It was for many years owned by Mr. Nathan Truitt, whose wife was sister of Judge James Render. A beautiful daughter, whose name was Elizabeth, was their only child. I attended her wedding when she became the wife of Stephen Willis, of Greene County. Three children came to bless this union, two sons, who are now living in LaGrange, and one daughter, who married Jack Thompson and also lives in LaGrange. After the death of Mr. Willis, his widow married again, Mr. Rachels. She lived to a good old age, and passed away about one year ago. Opposite the Truitt home was that of Mr. Robert Adonis Jones. His family was of the best. His wife, a Miss Macon, descended from that distinguished family for which the city of Macon was named. Mr. Jones died in Greenville and his grave in the cemetery is marked by a slab.

"The building now occupied by the Civic Club and library was the residence of Mr. Isaac C. Bell. Mr. Bell was a tailor with shop in the north side of the square. Mrs. Bell was a woman of beautiful Christian character, whose religious life so influenced her husband as to cause a reformation in him after she passed away. They now sleep side by side in the little cemetery. The next house was the law office of Colonel W. D. Alexander, who came to Greenville from Virginia, and from tradition he rode horseback the whole distance. The lot on the north, where the attractive home of Mrs. W. T. Revill now is, was purchased, according to "old times," by Mr. Levy M. Adams from the Inferior Court, and he erected the first building there. Mr. Adams was clerk of the Superior Court. He was also County Treasurer, lawyer and merchant. His home was noted for its hospitality and he is well remembered by many of the early settlers. The Gresham home, a little to the northwest, which has so long been in possession of the family, was originally owned by Abram Ragan.

"Where the Presbyterian Church now stands, to the west of our home, lived two dear old ladies, the grandmother and great-aunt of Mrs. J. L. Strozier, Mrs. Martha Robertson and Mrs. Judith Mitchell. The friendship formed between these ladies and my mother lasted through her lifetime. Across the street, where now is the Methodist parsonage, lived the family of W. B. Ector.

"Two other houses were in the course of construction on this street, now known as Griffin Street. One of these was bought and has long been occupied by the family of the late Mr. Myron Ellis. The other to the east was built by Mr. Elerby. He lived only a short time in this house which he himself built. He died and now occupies an unmarked grave in the cemetery. My memory does not recall whether there was a house in the corner of this street, now occupied by the Methodist Church. Later, I remember there was a grocery there, made memorable by a bear and dog fight having occurred in the rear of it, and a drunken man sitting on the porch singing a song beginning:—

> "On the wings of love I fly
> From the grocerie to groce-ry."

"This bear fight was an event in the town, but it ended disastrously. So many were attracted to the scene that numbers of them climbed on the roof of the shed attached to the store in order to get a better view, but alas! too many sought this point of vantage, and the roof gave way, hurting several badly. One interested spectator, seated on a barrel under the shed when the roof collapsed, was crushed into the barrel."

Judge Warner's Narrow Escape. Judge Warner was a man of unique character. He was veritably a Roman cast in the molds of the great Cato. One of Georgia's purest sons, he was also one of her bravest—a man to whom the instinct of moral fear was unknown. For the sake of principle he was ready to suffer the stake or the gibbet; but he was never inclined to turbulance. On the contrary, he was slow to anger, even-tempered and calm. The judicial poise of his great mind was seldom disturbed. The following incident of Wilson's raid, in 1865, is narrated by Governor Northen. It will serve to illustrate the character of the old jurist. Says Governor Northen:

"In 1865, just after Johnston's surrender—but before it was generally known—Wilson's Federal raiders were abroad in Middle Georgia, bent on plunder. Vandalism is too weak a work to describe the petty meanness which marked the paths made by bands of Federal soldiers through certain portions of the South; and General Wilson was such an offender in this respect that succeeding generations have used his name to describe rapine and slaughter. Some of Wilson's raiders, visiting Meriwether County, headed for Judge Warner's home. As they approached all the whites on the place fled except Judge Warner and his daughter, Mrs. Hill. The latter, with an infant two weeks old, could not be moved. Her father remained with her. During the morning some cavalry detachments passing by stole what they could carry off. About noon another party arrived and stopping, fed their horses, stole the silverware and robbed the smokehouse. Judge Warner stood by in silence. But suddenly the leader, putting a pistol to his head, ordered him to accompany them. Between the house and the negro quarters was a small woodland. To this grove his captors conducted Warner, and there the leader of the band, wearing the uniform of a Federal captain, took out his watch and said: "I'll give you just three minutes to tell where your gold is hidden." Warner protested that he had no gold. They replied that they had been told that he did have it and that he must give it up. He again denied it. They searched him and found five thousand dollars in Confederate money and fifteen thousand dollars in Central Railroad bills, which they appropriated. At the end of three minutes the captain gave a signal. One of the men took from his horse a long leather strap with a noose at one end. The other extemporized a gallows by bending down the end of a stout sapling. With an oath the officer made him select a larger and stouter tree. Judge Warner remained silent. One end of the strap was adjusted around his neck and the other fastened securely to the tree. The sapling was gradually released until the line became taut, when it was turned loose and the Judge's body dangled in the air. On reviving, he found himself upon the ground, but with the noose still around his neck. The soldiers still surrounded him. Once more he was ordered to give up his gold under penalty of death. He replied as before. Again he was strung up and the sapling released. This was about two o'clock in the day. When he recovered consciousness the sun was nearly down. He lay at the foot of the sapling. The noose had been removed from his neck. The dry leaves of the preceding autumn had been fired, and these were burning within a foot or two of his head. He always thought that the heat of the flames brought him back to consciousness and to life. The soldiers had left him for dead and had set fire to the woods. He was barely able to make his way back to the house, where he lay ill for many days."

Woodbury. Woodbury is a rapidly growing town, with splendid railway connections. It was chartered by an Act approved August 23, 1872, with the following-named commissioners, to-wit.: John R. Jones, David Muse, Henry Worthy, John E. Buchanan and William Wheeler, but the charter was subsequently amended so as to provide for a municipal form of government.* The present public school system was established in 1900, at which time the Woodbury School District was incorporated with the following board of trustees: Dr. J. M. Hooten, B. T. Baker, Dr. H. W. Clements, W. J. Smith and Dr. J. D. Sutton.*

MILLER

Colquitt. In 1856, Miller County was formed from Baker and Early Counties, and named for Hon. Andrew J. Miller, of Augusta, a distinguished legislator, whose then recent death suggested the propriety of some memorial. At the same time, the county-seat was named for Judge Walter T. Colquitt, jurist and statesman, of whose brilliant services the State was during this year bereaved. The town was incorporated on December 19, 1860, with Messrs. Isaac Bush, J. S. Vann, D. F. Gunn, Thomas S. Floyd and F. M. Hopkins, as commissioners.[1] Situated on the Georgia, Florida and Alabama Railway, Colquitt occupies the center of a rich territory, which has just commenced to develop, and the future of the town is bright with splendid possibilities.

Recollections of Andrew J. Miller. He was several times elected President of the Senate, in which position he evinced the highest administrative ability; and when, from political majorities in the Senate, adverse to him for the time being, he was passed over in the choice of presiding officer, his accurate knowledge of parliamentary law always caused him to be appealed to, in open Senate, when difficulties arose, on points of order. During his service of twenty years, he was the coolest, safest, and most practical mind in the Senate.

Frank H. Miller, Esq., in a letter to Major Stephen H. Miller, thus writes of his father. "He was plain and unaffected in manner of speech, suiting the word to the thought and expressing it as plainly as possible. He rarely, if ever used a metaphor. His memory was his most wonderful gift. He never forgot. He could remember the minutest details years after the event occurred. He was small of statue and a man of pleasant address, had blue eyes, which wore the appearance of gray as he grew older, his mouth and nose were large, and his lofty forehead expanded and grew broader the longer he lived. He had an amiable expression of countenance, though there ever appeared around his mouth those small lines which indicated decision of character.''*

MILTON

Alpharetta. In 1857 Milton was organized out of Cobb and Cherokee, and named for Hon. John Milton, who saved the records of the State during the Revolution. Alpharetta was made the county-seat. The town was incorporated December 11, 1858, with the following-named commissioners, to-wit.: Oliver P. Skelton, P. F. Rainwater, J. J. Stewart, Thomas J. Harris and

---

[1] Acts, 1860, p. 86.
*Stephen H. Miller, in Bench and Bar of Georgia, Vol. 2.

Oliver P. Childers.* Though without railway connections, Alpharetta is a thriving town.

MITCHELL

Camilla. When a new county was made from Baker, in 1857, it was given the name of Mitchell, in honor of Governor David B. Mitchell, a distinguished former chief executive, while the county-seat was named for the old Governor's daughter, Miss Camilla Mitchell. The town was first incorporated in 1858. It possesses a splendid public-school system, established in 1889, a number of up-to-date public utilities, and is commercially a prosperous town, with a most encouraging outlook.

Pelham. One of the most enterprising towns of South Georgia is located in this county: Pelham. The town was named for Major John Pelham, an Alabama youth, whose gallantry on the field of battle immortalized him before he was twenty-one. His heroic death has been the inspiration of poems almost without number. General Lee once wrote of him: "It is glorious to see such valor in one so young," and to Stonewall Jackson at Fredericksburg he remarked: "General Jackson, you ought to have a Pelham on each flank." The town was incorporated on September 14, 1881, with Hon. J. L. Hand as Mayor, and with Messrs. Cornelius Lightfoot, G. F. Green, J. C. Rhodes and J. L. Glozier Councilmen. The corporate limits were fixed at one-half a mile in every direction from the Georgia, Florida and Western depot. To meet the demands of growth the town charter was Amended in 1887 and the corporate limits extended.

MONROE

Historic Forsyth. On the highest ridge between Atlanta and Macon, in almost the exact center of the State, stands the old historic town of Forsyth, named for the illustrious diplomat and statesman, John

---

*Acts, 1858, p. 148.

Forsyth. As United States Minister to Spain, Mr. Forsyth negotiated the purchase of Florida from Ferdinand VII. He was also Governor of Georgia from 1827 to 1829, and afterwards a United States Senator. The town of Forsyth came into existence in 1822 when the new County of Monroe was created out of lands then recently acquired from the Creek Indians, at which time it became the new county-seat. On December 10, 1823, it was incorporated as a town, with the following pioneer residents named as commissioners: James S. Phillips, Henry H. Lumpkin, John E. Bailey, Anderson Baldwin and Samuel Drewry.* The town was originally laid off into lots of two and one-half acres each, affording ample room for garden plots and spacious green lawns. In 1855 the town limits were extended one-half mile. The following names of pioneer settlers frequently appear in the early records: Sharp, Roddy, Cabaniss, Thomas, Lumpkin, Sanford, Dunn, Martin, Johnson, Winship, Harman, Purifoy, Bean, Stephens, Litman, O'Neal, Banks, Coleman, Phelps, Turner and Wilkes.

Cyrus Sharp built the first brick store in Forsyth. This pioneer citizen lived to be well past ninety years of age, and embodied in a clear memory most of the chronicles of the town. The first court was held at the residence of Henry H. Lumpkin, a brother of the great chief justice of Georgia. In the year following, a courthouse built of logs rose on the town square. But a stately temple of justice has long since replaced the original structure. On the court-house square stands a handsome bronze memorial to the Confederate dead.

In matters of politics, the early residents of Forsyth were either Whigs or Democrats. Judge E. G. Cabaniss was the leading Whig; Dr. E. L. Roddy the most prominent Democrat. Both belonged to the Masonic order. Judge Cabaniss was worshipful master of the local lodge and Dr. Roddy was the high priest. The representative lawyers were: R. P. Trippe, Zach. E. Harman and Cap-

---

*Acts, 1823, p. 197.

tain James S. Pinckard. The first town paper was *The Bee,* founded by Joe Coran. It afterwards merged into *The Educational Journal,* and later into *The Monroe Advertiser.* At one time it was owned by James P. Harrison, who employed as a printer's devil the afterwards renowned Joel Chandler Harris. Mr. Harris boarded at the home of Mr. Harrison. The paper is now owned by Captain O. H. B. Bloodworth, Jr. Besides Dr. Roddy, the leading ante-bellum physicians were Drs. Stephens, Bean and Purifoy. The pioneer inns at which travelers stopped were the Lumpkin Hotel and the Thomas Hotel. There were three religious denominations: Baptists, Methodists and Presbyterians. But the immersionists outnumbered the others, making Forsyth a distinctly Baptist stronghold.

———

Forsyth was early recognized as an educational center. First the Male Academy was organized. Its charter dates back to February 20, 1854, at which time the following trustees were named: Zach. E. Harman, John H. Thomas, Addison Bean, Benjamin Watkins, Elbridge G. Cabaniss, Dickie W. Collier, William Sims, Sidney M. Smith and Joseph R. Banks.[1] This school afterwards grew into the Hilliard Institute, named for the noted orator and diplomat, Henry W. Hilliard, and finally into what is known today as the Banks-Stephens Institute, a flourishing co-educational high school. The Female Academy, taught by Frances Sturgis, developed into the Monroe Female College, said to be the second oldest in the world. It is now Bessie Tift College, named for Mrs. H. H. Tift, of Tifton, Ga., formerly Bessie Willingham, and is one of the best-known institutions of the South.[2]

On December 23, 1833, the old Monroe Railroad, which ran from Macon to Forsyth, was chartered by an Act of the Legislature, with a capital stock of $200,000, half

[1] Acts, 1855-1856, p. 142.
[2] See Vol. I, pp. 791-793, of this work for a sketch of Bessie Tift.

of which was subscribed in the town of Forsyth.   It
was completed early in the fall, and by means of this
steel highway the ambitious little county-seat of Monroe
became the first interior town of Georgia to connect
with a stream open to navigation.   There was much destruction of property in the town of Forsyth during the
last days of the Civil War, but the old soldiers of the
town, returning home, gave themselves with a will to
the work of rehabilitation.   Some of the new names
which became prominent at this time were Lawton, Willingham, Rhodes and others.   The first military company
of Forsyth was organized under Major Black and went
to the Creek Indian War of 1836 as the Monroe Mus-
keteers.   This company afterwards disbanded, but in
1859 was reorganized as the Quitman Guards, under
Captain James Pinckard.   It was named for Governor
Quitman, of Mississippi, a distinguished soldier of the
Mexican War and a strong advocate of State rights.   The
company is now commanded by Captain O. H. B. Bloodworth, Jr.   Forsyth has grown slowly, but steadily.   It
has always stood for conservatism, and for the safe business methods of the old school.   It has shaped much of
Georgia's history, and has been the home of some of
her most noted men.

Distinguished   From the earliest days, Forsyth was noted
Residents.   as a seat of culture, in consequence of
                 which scores of the best families in the
State were attracted to the town.   Included among the
Georgians of note who have resided here may be men-
tioned: Judge Robert P. Trippe, a former member of
Congress, afterwards a Judge of the Supreme Court of
Georgia; Judge Elbridge G. Cabaniss, a noted jurist;
his son, Judge Thomas B. Cabaniss, a former member of
Congress, and now a judge of the Superior Court; Judge
Cincinnatus Peeples, who afterwards went to Atlanta,
one of the strongest judges and one of the best lawyers

in the State; Judge Alexander M. Speer, an occupant of the Supreme Court Bench; General L. L. Griffin, the first president of the Monroe Railroad, for whom the town of Griffin was named; Colonel A. D. Hammond, Colonel R. L. Berner, Hon. W. H. Head, a distinguished financier and legislator, also a veteran of two wars; Dr. H. H. Tucker and Dr. Shaler G. Hillyer, two renowned Baptist theologians and educators; General Gilbert J. Wright, a noted Confederate brigadier; General Philip Cook, soldier, Congressman and Secretary of State, who once practiced law in Forsyth; Hon. Zach. E. Harman; Hon. O. H. B. Bloodworth, Sr., Hon. B. S. Willingham, widely known as the author of the famous Willingham Prohibition bill, besides a host of others whose names are familiar at almost every Georgia fireside.

Many important political meetings have been held in the grove surrounding the historic home of Judge T. B. Cabaniss, and among the eloquent Georgians who here once thrilled the multitudes in joint debate were Robert Toombs and Alexander H. Stephens. But there are other historic homes in Forsyth. The fine old residence of Dr. J. O. Elrod is associated with memories of four distinguished former occupants: Dr. H. H. Tucker, Judge R. P. Trippe, Judge Alexander M. Speer and Colonel A. D. Hammond. Another historic home was the one built by Captain James S. Pinckard, now the residence of Mrs. Richard P. Brooks, former regent of the Piedmont Continental Chapter, D. A. R., of Atlanta, and founder of the James Monroe Chapter, D. A. R., of Forsyth. This home was headquarters for doctors and officers during the Civil War.

Revolutionary Soldiers. Over the grave of William Ogletree, a Revolutionary soldier buried near Coggans, the Piedmont Continental Chapter, D. A. R., of Atlanta, has unveiled during the present year a handsome marker. Impressive exercises were held in connection with the unveiling, at which time a large number of the old hero's lineal descendants gathered with the Daughters of the Revolution to honor the memory of a revered ancestor. The James Monroe Chapter, of Forsyth, was also present by special invitation. Mr. John Mott made a brief speech, introducing Mrs. Richard P. Brooks, regent of the Piedmont Continental Chapter, who made a fine address. She was followed by the orator of the occasion, Professor J. P. Mott, of Brunswick. Mrs. J. O. Ponder, of Forsyth, regent of the James Monroe Chapter, made a short address on behalf of her chapter, after which the exercises were concluded with a few eloquent remarks by Mr. C. O. Goodwyne, of Forsyth. Four great-great-granddaughters of the old soldier unveiled the marker: Misses Ora Evans, Christine Goodwyne, Nellie Goodwyne and Louise Sutton, all of Monroe.

———

Brittain Rogers, a soldier of the Revolution, is buried in the lower part of Monroe, near Rogers Methodist Church. He was under the command of Colonel Elijah Clarke. He drew a bounty of 287½ acres of land, located in what was then Washington County, now Hancock, on Shoulderbone Creek, as appears of record in the Secretary of State's office, at the Capitol. Mr. Rogers afterwards removed from Hancock and became one of the first settlers of Monroe, where he died. On the monument erected over his grave is the following inscription:

> Sacred to the memory of BRITAIN ROGERS. Born Oct. 11, 1761. Soldier of the Revolution. Member of the Methodist Episcopal Church, 32 years. Died April 22, 1835, in expectation of rest in heaven.

———

Historic Colloden. One of the most noted little towns in the State is situated some sixteen miles from Forsyth, in the extreme southern part of the county—Colloden. It was named for a wealthy Scotch gentleman by the name of William Colloden, an early settler. On account of the healthfulness of the climate, it began at an early date to attract some of the best people of the State, who established and maintained excellent schools here, and who acquired a degree of culture which was not to be surpassed, even in old settled communities like Savannah. The Colloden Female Seminary was a pioneer school founded here by the Methodists; and, under Dr. John Darby, it became quite a celebrated institution. Here the distinguished United States Senator, jurist, and writer of books, Judge Thomas M. Norwood, spent his boyhood days. Here the gifted Alexander Speer, formerly Secretary of State of South Carolina, noted as an orator, both in the pulpit and on the hustings, brought his children to be educated. These became famous men in Georgia: Judge Alexander M. Speer, an occupant of the Supreme Bench, and Dr. Eustace W. Speer, an eloquent Methodist divine and a ripe scholar. The latter was the father of the brilliant Federal jurist, Judge Emory Speer, of Macon. Governor James M. Smith was educated in the Colloden High School. Colonel N. J. Hammond, a former member of Congress and a lawyer with few equals at the bar of Georgia, spent the youhtful period of his life in the town of Colloden; and here two consecrated brothers, Dr. W. F. Cook and Dr. J. O. A. Cook, both of them ministers of note in the Methodist Church, were equipped for useful careers. It will be difficult to find a community of equal size in the United States which can parallel this list. For a number of years after the war, the little town languished; but with the building of a railway line through this part of the county, it has commenced to exhibit distinct signs of revival.

MORGAN

Madison. On December 7, 1807, the County of Morgan was created out of a part of Baldwin, and named for General Daniel Morgan, of the Revolution. Madison was made the county-seat of Morgan by an Act approved December 12, 1809, and was at the same time incorporated as a town, with the following-named commissioners, to-wit.: James Matthews, William Mitchell, James Mitchell, Abner Tanner and John B. Whiteley.[1] There were no better people in Georgia than the pioneer settlers who first came to Morgan, and to judge from the number of charters granted by the Legislature for academies in various parts of the county, there was no failure

[1] Clayton's Compendium, p. 555.

to appreciate the value of learning. Due to unsettled conditions, the growth of Madison was at first slow; but when the Georgia Railway was completed to this place in the eighteen-forties a new era of development began. As editor of a local newspaper, Colonel William T. Thompson wrote his renowned letters under the pseudonym of Major Jones. These gave him a national reputation as a humorist. At a later period, he established the *Savanah Morning News,* which he edited for nearly forty years.

In 1850, two schools of wide note were founded. The first of these was chartered as the Madison Collegiate Institute, with the following board of trustees: Elijah E. Jones, John B. Walker, Zachariah Fears, Thomas J. Burney, Edmund Walker, Charles M. Irvin, William S. Stokes, James F. Swanson, J. W. Fears, Benjamin Harris, Benjamin M. Peeples, Nathan Massey, R. P. Zimmerman, Nathaniel G. Foster and William W. B. Crawford.[2] The other school was chartered as the Madison Female College, with trustees named as follows: Adam G. Saffold, Wilde Kolb, John Robson, William V. Barnley, Lucius L. Wittich, Gay Smith, Alfred Shaw, Thomas P. Baldwin, Hugh J. Ogilby, Thaddeus B. Reese, Dawson B. Lane, Samuel Pennington, William J. Parks, Caleb W. Key, M. H. Hebbard, Isaac Boring, John W. Glenn and J. G. Pearce.[3] Madison has been the home of some of Georgia's most distinguished sons, including United States Senator Joshua Hill, Colonel David E. Butler, Judge Alexander M. Speer, Judge Augustus Reese, the Saffolds, Adam and Reuben; Nathaniel G. Foster, Dr. J. C. C. Blackburn and a host of others. Some of the stately homes of the old regime are still standing in Madison; but while the past is reverenced for its ideals, the progressive enterprise of the town is typical of the new South.

---

[2] Acts, 1849-1850, p. 112.
[3] Acts, 1849-1850, p. 108.

Launcelot John- On a Morgan County plantation origi-
tone's Great nated an economic process which today
Invention. underlies one of the greatest industrial
activities of the world—the manufacture
of cotton-seed oil. As the result of this marvelous invention an industry of vast proportions has been created
and what was formerly considered a waste product has
been the means of putting millions of dollars into the
pockets of the Southern farmer. The first successful
effort ever made to extract oil from cotton seed was made
by Launcelot Johnstone, Esq., within a quarter of a mile
from the court-house in Madison. Mr. Johnstone was
an extensive ante-bellum planter, whose scientific experiments in practical agriculture placed him at least half
a century in advance of his times. The records of the
Patent Office in Washington, D. C., will show that between 1830 and 1832 Mr. Johnston was granted an exclusive patent for a cotton-seed huller, the first device
of its kind ever constructed; and, in operating his patent
he made large quantities of cotton-seed oil, some of which
he used with white lead for house painting. Shingles
which he saturated in cotton-seed oil remained on his
house for more than sixty years. Mr. Johnstone is
buried just in the rear of the old homestead, where, in
a modest way, he began to lay the foundations of what
has since developed into one of the most colossal industries of our age. His crude experiments marked an
epoch in the history of manufacture by wresting from
nature a secret worth untold millions; and though he has
long slept the deep sleep from which no pean of earthly
praise can ever wake him, it is not too late to accord him
the distinction to which he is rightfully entitled as the
real father of the cotton-seed oil industry of the United
States.

Madison's His- White's Statistics of Georgia, published in 1845, con-
toric Homes. tains this statement: "Madison, Georgia, is the wealthiest and most aristocratic village on the stage-coach
route between Charleston and New Orleans." One still finds here much

of this ancient prestige. The old-fashioned homes contain their handsome mahogany, silver, cut-glass, libraries of rare old volumes, paintings, and many of their old jewels and laces. A few of these splendid places have passed into the hands of strangers, but most of them are still owned and loved and lived in by the descendants of their original builders, some occupied by the fourth and a few by even the fifth generation.

Well, indeed, might the Author White have been impressed as he journeyed in the old stage-coach, past the plantation home of Judge Joseph Lumpkin, now owned by Miss Emma High, with its mantels ten feet wide and eight-feet high framing, even on summer days great blazing logs of wood eight feet long (fires were counted healthful every day in the year), swiftly drawing near with crack of whip and blowing horn to the little tavern (now owned by Mr. J. A. Hilsman) on the edge of the town. They doubtless here tarried, where an abundant dinner with much liquid refreshment awaited the travelers. Then with four fresh prancing horses in the harness and more cracking of whip and blowing of horn majestically they swept down what as then the ''Old Indian Trail'' (now West Avenue) past the June Smith House (now occupied by Mr. J. A. Hilsman), the Killian Cottage (former home of Mrs. Grant, who with her husband gave Grant Park to Atlanta, now the home of Mr. W. H. Butts), the Ike Walton place (now closed), the beautiful John B. Walker estate (Mr. P. W. Bearden), the old Butler homestead (Misses Daisy and Bessie Butler), the Peter Walton, Sr., house (Mrs. Godfrey-Walton-Trammell), the Hill house (Mrs. Bowles Hill Obear), the Stokes-McHenry place (Mr. J. G. McHenry), the Kolb house (Hon. John T. Newton), the Jones place (Mr. S. A. Turnell), ''the old house built by the Northern man, who had on his walls tapestry covered with scenes from Lalla Rhook and South American forests'' (Mr. M. L. Richter), the dozen one-story stores, the old court-house with it gray monument on the left, erected in honor of Benjamin Braswell, who left his fortune to educate and clothe indigent orphans of the county.

With many a flourish up to the little wooden post-office building, they were soon off again on the same ''Old Indian Trail'' (now North Main Street), past other splendid residences, the Douglass home (Mr. J. W. and Miss Gertrude Douglas), the Cohen house (Mrs. Rebecca Cohen Pou), the Campbell place (Mr. Mason Williams), the Martin Home (Judge H. W. Baldwin), the Billiups residence (Mrs. Cone-Daniels-Billups), the Saffold mansion (Mr. D. P. Few) with its many splendid columns and large grounds; having caught glimpses on cross streets and parallel ones of other stately well kept places, the old Georgia Female College, whose charter dated only a few weeks later than Wesleyan's; its president's home, Rev. George Y. Browne (Mr. Q. L. Williford), the Wade-Langston home (Mr. H. H. Fitzpatrick), the old Porter place (Mrs. Louise Turnbull), the Judge Stewart Floyd house (Judge Frederick Floyd Foster), the A. G. Foster house (recently burned), the Judge Augustus Reese house (Mrs. Elizabeth Speers), the A. G. Johnson (Mrs. Sallie Johnson Penn), the famous "Mrs. Cook's house" (Mrs. J. B. Childs), a Northern woman, whose only son was the first Confederate soldier from Morgan County killed in batttle and whose mother taught in the little school-house in her back-yard every child in the town from 1845 until 1888, leaving a part of her little fortune for a town clock, and whose memorial is a beautiful fountain on the city square; then the solid old Academy, where Hon. Alex. Stephens began his career as a school teacher, as well as many other buildings noted for their beauty and fame. Leaving the town behind, and approaching the cottage of one who afterwards became the famous guide of General Lee, "Red-Headed Hume" of Virginia (his childhood home), and rolling away amid fertile plantations, the picture left in the mind might well be described in the words of the author of "White's Statistics": "The wealthiest and most aristocratic village on the stage-coach route."*

MONTGOMERY

This charmingly written sketch is from the pen of Hon. H. B. Folsom, owner and editor of the "Montgomery Monitor," published at Mount Vernon, Ga., one of the best-known weekly newspapers in the State. Over 200 miles were traversed by Mr. Folsom in gathering his materials for the above sketch. With an up-to-date photographic outfit, he also took the splendid views which accompany this article, and to say that he has made a most important contribution to the State's historical literature is to assert what every one who reads this luminous account of Gov. Troup's last days must admit. Mr. Folsom prepared this sketch while engaged in an arduous but successful fight before the Legislature to prevent a further partition of Montgomery County's territory by a land-grabbing mania to form new counties in Georgia.—L. L. K.

Gov. Troup's Last Days. Studied words of praise or deep-chiseled marble cannot recall the acts of yesterday. Neither can the future replace the losses of the past; and to touch chords that have ceased to vibrate is but to wait before a fountain whose waters have wasted away. It is not the purpose of this brief sketch to deal with the public life and achievements of one so illustrious in Georgia history, but in limited measure recall the latter-day surroundings of Governor George Michael Troup. His useful life has been and will continue to be a theme for the mature historian: his brilliant career is fixed in history—"A Roman in feature, and a Roman in soul."

*Authority: Miss Bessie Butler, Madison, Ga.

**New Facts
Brought to Light.** Definite record of his closing days has seldom, if ever, been given to public print; errors concerning his resting place are plentiful, though apparently innocent. First-hand information for this sketch comes largely from aged citizens of Montgomery County, who, in their youth, knew the statesman and saw his lifeless body laid away. Permanent evidence of his burial place is had in the native sand-stone wall surrounding his grave in the northwestern part of Montgomery County, where he has rested for more than half a century. Old age and infirmity having overtaken this distinguished figure, he sought the quietude and comfort of numerous homes, visiting them in methodical rotation.

**Valdosta: His
Favorite Mansion.** The Valdosta plantation, in Laurens County, was distinctly the bower of his retirement—his retreat after the cares of State, and the home of his friends. From this abode came some of his strongest documents, dating to within a few days of his death. The Valdosta mansion, for such it was in ante-bellum days, was a large six-room log structure, triple-pen style, divided with halls and nearly surrounded with broad verandas and fitted with chimneys of clay. To this was annexed in 1852 a large room, used as a reception chamber. This was substantially built of 6 x 10-inch dressed timbers, laid edgewise and intricately dovetailed and spiked with hand-forged nails, something of the workmanship being shown by one of the accompanying cuts. The interior was plastered, making it a most durable structure. It was by far the most palatial of the Troup homes, but is now in ruins. The sand-stone chimney, with its liberal fireplace, has to some extent stood the ravages of time. Carved in the upper portion of this chimney, outside, may be seen the Governor's name and the date of construction. This home graced a beautiful eminence, from which, even now,

may be seen the splendid little city of Dublin, seven miles to the north.

The Vallombrosa and Turkey Creek plantations, in Laurens County, formed a part of the Troup holdings, but our research being limited and the intent of this sketch not demanding it, reference to them cannot be accurately made. The other plantations, extending southward on the Oconee River, were the Horseshoe place, in Montgomery (now Wheeler) County; Rosemont, east of the river, in Montgomery County; the Mitchell place, west of the river (originally settled by Hartwell Mitchell, 1814), in Montgomery (now Wheeler) County, opposite Mount Vernon and south of Greenwood. Each homestead has its special interest, for, under his regular plan of visiting, an open and well-ordered home awaited its landlord's coming. Each estate was supervised by an overseer, and each slave had a task assigned for the day. Perfect system regulated all labors.

Dies on the Mitchell Plantation. Shortly before the Governor's death a message from the overseer on the Mitchell place, William Bridges, announced an unruly disposition on the part of a certain negro slave. With his faithful coachman, the aged Governor was soon at the lower plantation, thirty-five miles from Valdosta. It is needless to say that proper chastisement broke the unruly spirit; however, cruel treatment of slaves was unknown on the Troup plantations. On reaching the Mitchell place, fatigued by the hurried trip, the Governor became ill, and five days brought the end. He was removed from his residence, nearby, long since decayed, and tenderly cared for at the home of Overseer Bridges, where he died April 26, 1856. Smart Roberson, a colored slave, was mounted on a spirited young horse and dispatched to Glynn County to bear the sad tidings to Colonel Thomas M. Forman, his son-in-law (husband of the eldest daughter, Florida, who died two years before). Before reaching his destination, the steed was overtaxed by his rider's haste and fell by the wayside. Faithful Smart, undaunted, pressed on on foot and delivered his message. Madison Moore, the coachman, with a vacant seat, returned post-haste to Valdosta for the younger daughter, Oralie, and other members of the family.

———

How the Old Governor was Buried. With few members of the family present, preparations were made for the burial. A coffin was made from wide boards taken from the porch of a new home of Peter Morrison. The plank having been laid but unnailed, were easily removed by willing hands. This enclosure was constructed at the workshop of John Morrison, two miles from the Troup residence. His handiwork was aided by his son, Daniel, together with the assistance of Duncan Buchanan. The nails were wrought by Peter Morrison, the blacksmith. The Colonel was a regular patron of this little shop. On the lid of the box brass tacks formed this humble tribute: "An Honest Heart." The venerable statesman was enshrouded in a winding sheet (the custom of the day) prepared by Mrs. Elizabeth Morrison, whose skill, like that of Dorcas of old, should be told as a memorial. She was the wife of the old woodworker. Material for the shroud was taken from a bolt of white linen, a portion of which also lent comfort to the rude coffin.

———

Gov. Troup's Tomb. The statesman was laid to rest at Rosemont, beside the body of his brother, Robert Lachlan Troup, to whose memory a shaft had been erected by the Governor and his son, G. M., Jr. (the latter having died two years after his father). The marble shaft, about ten feet tall, was finished in

TOMB OF GOV. GEORGE M. TROUP:

On the Rosemont Plantation In Montgomery Co., Ga.

Augusta, and stands in the center of the enclosure. On
the front face will be seen the inscription:

> Erected by G. M. Troup, the Brother, and G.
> M. Troup, Jun., the Nephew, as atribute of
> affection to the memory of R. L. Troup, who
> died September 23, 1848, aged 64 years. An
> honest man with a good mind and a good heart.

After the Governor's burial there was recessed into
the front of the base a marble slab, 2 x 3 feet, and seen
through the open door of the enclosure, bearing this
inscription:

> GEORGE MICHAEL TROUP.
> Born Septr. 8th 1780.
> Died April 26th 1856.
> No epitaph can tell his worth.
> The History of Georgia must perpetuate
> His virtues and commemorate
> his Patriotism.
> There he teaches us
> the argument being exhausted,
> to Stand by our Arms.''

The enclosure, a most creditable affair, about 17 x 25
feet, is made of sand-stone, quarried from Berryhill Bluff,
on the Oconee River, near by, and fragments left by
workmen may now be seen strewn in the rear of the tomb.
the splendid iron door, oft-times ajar, whose lock
has long since been removed, was cast by D. & W. Rose,
of Savannah. Governor Troup rests (according to the
best information) on the right of the shaft, the single
box coffin being used to avoid excavation too near the
pedestal. There, among the wildwood, may be seen a
rose bush, still blooming, the tribute of a faithful slave
woman, long since in her lowly grave, among those of
her kind. Near the tomb, which is now surrounded by
a friendly little clump or trees (reduced in size, contrary
to wishes of its owner), stood the Rosemont homestead,
owned at the time of his death by R. L. Troup; but in

his will, dated only two days before death overtook him, Rosemont, with all personal property, was consigned to his brother, the Governor, and nephew, G. M. Troup, Jr. As exceptions, a 15-year-old colored girl was given to a friend, and the sum of 3,000 in cash assigned to Robert T., son of Dr. James McGillivray Troup, the youngest of the six Troup brothers, then residing in Glynn County. One of our illustrations shows half a section of the Rosemont dwelling, a double-pen log affair, many years ago cut from its mate and removed to a distant part of the field, but still well preserved. A deserted and lonely old barn now stands vigil over the site of this once happy retreat. Broad fields of cotton and corn have displaced the luxuriant forests of bygone days, the sound of the hunter's horn and the bay of the hounds is hushed forever, for during his earlier manhood the field and stream were resorted to by Governor Troup and his brothers.

Of the Horseshoe place nothing remains of former days, and it, too, is forgotten by the tiller of the precious soil as he sows and reaps on historic ground. Allowing a reference to the Turkey Creek plantation, and to further show the indomitable will power of the beloved statesman, it may be said that, just prior to his last journey to the Mitchell place, he wrote his overseer on the Turkey Creek farm, concerning a dispute with a neighbor of that community: "If I have not right on my side, I will surrender, but not compromise." Doubtless his last message.

———

Gov. Troup's Life as a Planter. But back to old Valdosta! There remains on this massive plantation a number of the Troup slaves and their descendants, and their accounts of former (possibly happier) days would fill a volume. Here, as on his journeys, the celebrated executive was surrounded by a full retinue of servants, who responded to his every beck

Grove of Trees Surrounding Gov. Troup's Tomb on the Rosemont
Plantation, near Soperton, Ga.

Old Barn on the Rosemont Plantation, Appurtement to
the Former Homestead

TWO INTERESTING VIEWS OF ROSEMONT.

and call. Some of these were: George Baker, body servant; Timothy Baker, footman; Madison Moore, coachman; Richard Baker, horseman; George Hester, car-
penter and all-around man. He, it is said, built the Valdosta annex referred to, being at the time, also a licensed
pilot on the Governor's river steamer. A special pair
of carriage horses, three single buggy horses and three
saddle horses were kept groomed for the master's use.
Space will forbid a further reference to the home life.
Betsy Hester, of continued memory, was the house servant, and, with many others, lived to a ripe old age. The
servants are buried in a plat set aside for the slaves, and
many of their graves are well marked. George Baker
was well educated, and was allowed to assist the Colonel
with his reading and writing. The Governor retired at
four in the afternoon, invariably, and arose at seven in
the morning—ready for all contingencies.

Sad, and as voices from the past, come the stories
told by these trembling lips, and dimmed eyes that seem
to review the days filled with happiness to them. Now
and then a tear is shed in memory of the past. Time, in
its eternal passage, has dealt gently with some of them,
now ready for the grave—willing to follow their master
to the ground made sacred to them by his habitation and
kindness to them. These human landmarks, modest in
form and bowed with age, are still beautiful reminders
of the past and preservers of memories which die not,
though the years come and go. But the departed master! Sadly lingering thought: He sleeps in a tomb his
loving hands built for another, and their dust is mingled together 'neath the shades of Rosemont, where the
soft-moving waters of the Oconee murmur an eternal
requiem of peace.

————

Mount Vernon. One of the oldest counties in the State,
Montgomery, was organized in 1793
from Washington and Wilkinson Counties, and named
for Major-General Richard Montgomery, who fell at the

siege of Quebec in 1775. Due to unsettled conditions along the border, growing chiefly out of the Oconee War, it was fully twenty years before a permanent site for public buildings was finally made. At last, on November 30, 1813, an Act was approved by Governor Early, making the county-seat permanent at a place to be given the name of Washington's home on the Potomac River. The Mount Vernon Academy was chartered in 1810, and later, on December 11, 1841, the Montgomery County Academy was granted a charter with the following board of trustees, to-wit.: John McRae, Sr., Wiley Adams, John Paterson, William Joice, Anthony Phillips, Joseph Ryals, Andrew Williamson, William Clark and James Chaney.* Brewton-Parker Institute, located between Mount Vernon and Ailey, on the Seaboard Air Line, is one of the flourishing high schools of the State, founded by Rev. J. C. Brewton, D. D. Rather a seat of culture than a center of trade, the capital of Montgomery County has entered upon a new era of growth since the completion of the Seaboard Air Line, and the prospects of the town, from a commercial point of view, are bright with promise. There is not a richer agricultural belt in Georgia than the one which immediately surrounds Mount Vernon. This section of Georgia was largely settled by Scotch-Irish immigrants from the State of North Carolina, and there are scores of families living in the county whose representatives still bear the names of Highland clans.

Much of the original territory of Montgomery has been taken to form other counties in Georgia.

Richard Montgomery We are indebted to the pen of Dr. William B. Burroughs, of Brunswick, for the following sketch of Major-General Montgomery, for whom this county was named. Says he:

"Richard Montgomery was born in the north of Ireland 1737. At the age of 22 we find him with Wolfe at the storming of Quebec; he

---

*Acts, 1841, p. 4.

was in the campaign against the Spanish West Indies, and shortly after quit his regiment and returned home. In 1772 he returned to America, bought an estate on the Hudson, and married a daughter of Robert R. Livingston. When the Revolution broke out he joined the Colonists and was made second in command in 1775 under General Schuyler. In the expedition against Canada General Schuyler being sick, he took command and was was commissioned Major-General before he reached Quebec. He had every difficulty to contend with—mutinous troops, scarcity of provisions and ammunition, want of clothing, deserters, etc. The eloquence of a Chatham and a Burke lauded his merit in the British Parliament. The Colonial Congress passed resolutions of grateful remembrance, profound respect, high veneration, and voted to erect a monument in front of St. Paul's Church, in New York City. The monument is still standing, and bears the following inscription:

> 'This
> monument is erected by order of Congress
> 25 of January 1776
> to transmit to Posterity a grateful remembrance of the patriotic Conduct, enterprise and perseverance of Major-General RICHARD MONTGOMERY, who after a series of success, amid the most discouraging difficulties Fell in the attack on Quebec, 31 December 1775, age 37 years.'

"In 1818 his widow made a request to the Governor of Canada, Sir John Sherbroke, to allow his remains to be disinterred and brought to New York. The request was granted and the State of New York caused the remains of this distinguished hero to be brought from Quebec and placed in St. Paul's Church in New York."

MURRAY

Spring Place. Spring Place, the historic old country-seat of Murray, is redolent with time-honored memories. Early in the last century a mission was planted here among the Cohutta Mountains by the pious Moravians. It flourished for years, but with the removal of the Cherokee Indians to the West it was discontinued. In 1832, when Murray County was organized out of a part of the Cherokee lands and named for Hon. Thomas

W. Murray, of Lincoln, Spring Place was made the county-seat, a distinction which it retained until 1912, when the county-seat was removed to Chattsworth. As yet no public buildings have been erected in the latter town, and the question of a permanent site is involved in some dispute. Spring Place was the home of a noted Indian chief, Vann, whose residence is still standing, one of the few landmarks of a vanished race. John Howard Payne, the famous author of "Home, Sweet Home," was here detained as a prisoner in 1836, on the eve of the Cherokee removal. Spring Place was chartered as a town in 1834, with the following commissioners: William N. Bishop, John J. Humphries, John S. Bell, Seaborn Lenter and Burton McGee.*

Fort Mountain. Six miles and a half to the northeast of Spring Place looms a peak of the Cohutta Mountains, near the summit of which can still be seen the ruins of an old fort, the origin of which is shrouded in a thick veil of traditions. This ancient landmark of a region famed for its great natural beauty is known as Fort Mountain, so called from the remnants of this old fort, some of the legends connected with which reach back over a stretch of four centuries to the romantic days of De Soto. But no one who thoughtfully examines what is left of the old fort can accept readily the account which credits its erection to the Spaniards. There were originally not less than twelve walls in this defensive stronghold. Its erection required time; and, according to the Spanish narratives, less than two weeks were spent in this region, after which the gold seekers proceeded to what is now the city of Rome. Two stopping-places of De Soto have been identified as towns included within the original limits of Murray County, viz., Gauxule and Conasauga; but since in both of these towns he was accorded friendly receptions there existed no occasion for hostile maneuvers, such as the building of a fort would lead us to infer. The rules of historical criticism forbid an assumption that the ruins on Fort Mountain date back to DeSoto, but a former occupancy of this region by Europeans is strongly intimated, if not unmistakably proven, by these remains. We are indebted to Professor S. W. McCallie, State Geologist, for a table of measurements, showing how each of the twelve walls of the old fort ran. This table is given below, as follows:

----

*Acts, 1834, p. 248.

SE.   40 feet to pit; 160 to gate at spring.
 N.   60   "
 E.   70   "
 N.   20   "
S. 80° E.   60   "   (2 towers)
NE. 100   "
S. 80° E.   70   "
 E.   20   "
 N. 120   "
NE.   90   "
N. 10° E.   30   "
NE.   80   "

Says Prof. McCallie: "The old fort is located just a short distance from the highest point of the mountain. Some 250 yards from the main gateway to the fort is a spring. The walls are nowhere more than two feet high, but have a base of more than twelve feet. The masonry about the gateway is somewhat massive. All the stones in the wall can be removed by two men, except for a few boulders in a section over which the wall passes. There are many loose fragments on top of the mountain, from which the fort was no doubt constructed."

But, while DeSoto may not have built the stronghold on Fort Mountain, the antiquarians are for the most part agreed that he visited what is now Murray County, during his famous quest for gold in 1540. In support of this tradition, we quote from an original source "The Travels of a Portuguese Gentleman," translated by Richard Haklupt:

Says this account: "As the Governor (DeSoto) came to a town called Conasauga there met him on the way twenty Indians, every one loaded with baskets of mulberries and butter and honey in calabashes. . . . From the time the Governor departed from Conasauga he journeyed through a desert to Chiaha (where the town of Rome now stands). This town was on an island between two arms of a river and was seated high upon one of them. The river divideth itself into those two branches. DeSoto rested there thirty days, and the Indians told him of a rich country toward the North where there was to be found copper and another metal of the same color, save that it was finer and a far more perfect color, which they called talla-nuca, or yellow earth." It is a well-established fact that from the earliest times copper was dug from the hills of Murray County by the Cherokee Indians. The hinges on the doors of the old Mission at Spring Place are of beaten copper, and are said to have been made by the red men. Colonel Charles C. Jones, Jr., our foremost historical scholar, identifies Gauxule, the town mentioned in the Spanish narratives, as Coosawattee Old Town, in which is now Murray County; and Conasauga he identifies as a town on what was afterwards the site of New Echota, at the confluence of the Conasauga and Coosawattee Rivers, in what is now Gordon County, Ga. En route from Nacoochee Valley to

Gauxule only five days were spent by the Spaniards; between ?? ? ?? Gauxule and Conasauga they consumed only two days; and between Conasauga and Rome they occupied only twelve days; so it hardly seems probable that the stronghold on Fort Mountain was built by DeSoto, though it may have been constructed by Eureopeans, and possibly by Spaniards at a later period.

Indian House: The Home of Chief Vann.   Outlined against the blue Cohutta Mountains, at Spring Place, is a famous old red brick mansion, known as the "Indian House." It was built by Chief Vann and today stands strong and unwrecked by time. The brick used in construction was hauled from Savannah, while the quaintly constructed stairway, which has no visible support, and high hand-carved mantels were brought from beyond the seas.

Dark and fearsome tales are told of its early days, blood-stains still to be seen on attic walls, and mysterious hints of secret places containing hidden treasure, known only to the Indian, and never divulged to the white man. Vann was one of the two chiefs who befriended the Moravian missionaries who, in 1901, established the Moravian mission at Spring Place, the first mission to the Cherokee Indians. This mission was built near the large spring from which Spring Place had its name, and was an unpretentious log house.

In 1865 the structure was demolished, and no trace now remains, but a few rocks mark the spot where Rev. Abraham Steiner and G. Byhan labored so faithfully. Later many other missionaries were employed to teach the people the arts of civilized life. Mr. Steiner is authority for the statement that Chief Vann built the first wagon in the Cherokee Nation, for which he was severely censured by the Council, and forbidden the use of such a vehicle. The objection was, "If you have wagons, there must be wagon roads; and if wagon roads, the whites will be among us."

Just where Chief Ridge lived has been the subject of much discussion. He was born about 1771 at Hiawassee, his father a full-blooded Cherokee and his mother a Cherokee half-breed. By the Indians he was called Kah-ming-da-ha-geh ("man who walks on the mountain top"). He became at the age of twenty-one a member of the Cherokee Council, and when he rode to the Cherokee Council Ground on an old white horse, poorly clothed and with few ornaments, he was ridiculed, and some of the chiefs proposed to exclude him from their council. He soon won their confidence and became one of the chiefs of their nation. His son, John Ridge, attended the missionary school at Spring Place, and later an Eastern school. Tradition asserts that either Major Ridge or his son John Ridge built the old Indian House south of Spring Place which at the Indian exile passed into the possession of Farrish Carter, and is still owned by the

Carter family, members of which, down to the fourth generation, gather
yearly at the quaint old house, which still claims its narrow stairway, tiny
windows and hand-carved mantels.*

Traditions of   It is not known with certainty when the first settle-
the Cherokees   ment of whites was made within the limits of what
                    is now Murray County, but there is a tradition to the
effect that white traders from this section participated in the battle of
King's Mountain, during the Revolution, none of whom ever returned to
their cabin homes. Toward the latter part of the eighteenth century a
number of white families from the Carolinas and from lower Georgia
settled at what was then called Vann's Station, on the site of the present
town of Spring Place. The Cherokees had at this time become fairly
civilized. They occupied fixed places of abode, some of them owning negro
slaves, with whom they cultivated extensive tracts of land in the fertile
valleys. The most conspicuous among the leaders of the nation at this
time were half-breeds like Ridge, Vann, Hicks, Boudinot, and Ross.

Chief Vann's father was a full-blooded white. His name was James
Vann; and, to escape the consequences of a homicide committed by him
in South Carolina, it is said that he fled to the Indians for protection.
The exact time of his appearance upon the scene is unknown. He married
an Indian girl, acquired a large tract of land on Mill Creek, and owned
a number of slaves. His property at his death was inherited by his sons,
of whom there were several. In an old court record (1834) may be found
an injunction against one William M. Bishop, forbidding him to trespass
on twenty-three specified lots of land belonging to Joseph Vann. Dr.
George Mellen, in an article on the old Federal road, refers to the owner
of the famous Vann House as David Vann; but Rev. W. J. Cotter, a distinguished octogenarian, who spent his boyhood in Murray County, speaks
of him as Chief Joseph Vann, adding that he knew this noted old Indian
chief well. Mr. Cotter's exact words may be found in an article published
in the *Wesleyan Christian Advocate* during the year 1910. He describes
the chief as over six feet in height. He says that he was possessed of very
large means; that he employed skilled workman in building his house,
and that when completed and furnished it was one of the handsomest homes
in the State. We have no record as to when this house was built, but in
Ramsey's Annals it is stated that the Moravian missionaries were given
land by Chief Vann near his own house on which to erect their mission
house in 1801. Although the mission house was not finished until 1817,
the first missionaries, Rev. George Byhon and Rev. Abraham Steiner, were

---

*Miss Willie S. White, of Dalton, contributes this sketch. The author-
ities consulted by her are as follows: White's Statistics, Rev. A. R. T.
Hambright and Mr. F. T. Hardwick.

here long before this date. The old mission house was torn down by Mr. Lem Jones about 1865.

————

Chief Ross lived where the city of Rome now stands, and dated his letters "Head of the Coosa," but he later moved into Tennessee to Ross's Landing, now Chattanooga. He was a man of splendid talents, had a well-selected library, and had much to do with the litigation between the Cherokees and the State of Georgia, appearing for them in various courts, and finally carrying his contention, which was that the State of Georgia had no jurisdiction over the Cherokee country, to the Supreme Court of the United States, and there gained it before the nation's highest tribunal. In this case he exhibited so much statesmanship that Henry A. Wise, of Virginia, on the floor of the House of Representatives, declared in answer to a speech of Forsyth, of Georgia, one of the most eloquent men of his time, that Ross was in nothing inferior to Forsyth.

Chief Ridge was a full-blood Cherokee, a man of much intelligence, but of little education. His home was at the Carter Place. He was friendly to the State of Georgia, and by every means within his power sought to persuade the Indians to accept the government's proposition for a removal to the West.

Spring Place was incorporated in 1834, and was made the county-seat of Murray. It was first called Poinset, but the people disliked the name and called it Spring Place. The records show that on September 19, 1834, Abner E. Holliday and Matthew Jones deeded forty acres, lot No. 245, to the county, "for the purpose of placing a county-site upon." The first court, presided over by Judge John W. Hooper, was held in the old mission house. There is a record of the names of the first grand jury. The first true bill was against George Took for murder. It is said that Judge O. H. Kenan was the first judge who succeeded in enforcing respect for the law.

As early as 1833 a stage route was operated between Spring Place and Athens, Tenn. Horses were changed every eighteen miles. There were post-offices along the route, one of which was located at what is now Eton. The Federal road was the great highway of the time. The first representative as William N. Bishop.

About this time a Moravian mission was established at New Echota, which was then the capitol of the Cherokee nation, situated four miles north of the present site of the town of Calhoun, Ga. The first Moravian missionary to New Echota was the Rev. Samuel Worcester. Through his influence a Cherokee youth, who attended his school, was sent North to a Moravian mission school, at Cornwall, Conn. While there he came under the notice of the distinguished Congressman, Elias Boudinot, whose portrait now hangs in the hall of Independence in Philadelphia.

Congressman Boudinot was so pleased with the Indian youth that he adopted him and gave him his name. It was through this relationship

SEQUOYA:

Inventor of the Cherokee Alphabet.

that the young chief became acquainted with the lovely young girl, Harriet Gould, who later became his wife. Her father, Captain Benjamin Gould, was an officer in the United States army. The young chief and his wife went to New Echota to live among the Cherokees. She soon became the idol of the tribe, and during the twelve years which she spent in New Echota she labored faithfully for the uplift of her adopted people. She taught the young Indians to read and write in their native tongue by means of the syllabary, which the Cherokee Indian, Sequoyah, had just invented. Her husband, a leader in all the affairs of the tribe, was editor of the *Cherokee Phoenix*, a paper which was printed in the Cherokee language at New Echota, and was published from 1828 until 1834, when it was suppressed by the Georgia authorities.

With these splendid influences at work the Cherokees were rapidly moving toward a high type of civilization. But dark days were ahead; for the treaty of New Echota was soon to be signed. Under the terms of this treaty, though obnoxious to ninety per cent. of them, the entire nation was forced to move West and leave forever the land of their fathers. But Chief Boudinot's wife was not to live through the heart-rending scenes of the removal. After a short illness she passed away, and her grave is the only one distinctly marked among the many hundreds of New Echota. Her name is carved on a tombstone erected by Chief Boudinot before the removal of the Indians, and is made of marble brought from Connecticut, her native State.

To show how the Cherokees were progressing at this time the files of an old paper contains the following: "At a meeting of the National Council of the Cherokees, the following resolution was adopted: 'Resolved by the National Committee and Council that an agent shall be appointed to solicit donations in money from individuals, or societies, in the United States for the purpose of establishing a National Academy or College for the Cherokees.'" The resolutions were signed by John Ross, president of the National Committee; by Major Ridge (his mark), Speaker of the National Council; Pathkiller (his mark), Principal Chief of the Cherokee Nation; by Charles R. Hicks, virtual Head Chief and Treasurer; Alexander McCoy and Elias Boudinot, respectively, clerks of the two branches of the Legislative Department of the Government.

It was finally the assumption of national sovereignty and plenary powers which incited the Georgians to take measures which ultimately resulted in deportation. The removal by force of fourteen thousand people from their homes caused great commotion throughout the whole world. The papers of the day were full of it, a great many taking the part of the Indians. It is said that General John E. Wool, an officer under General Scott, commanding the regulars, and General Richard G. Dunlap, commanding the Tennessee Volunteers, had their sympathies so enlisted on the side

of those doomed to exile that they recoiled before the task which confronted them. Even some of the civil officers looked upon the movement
as brutal and outrageous, and so' expressed themselves. Consequently we
cannot wonder that a man of poetic temperament, like John Howard
Payne, should have been moved to compassion for these poor savages;
so much so, indeed, that while on a visit to Georgia he openly expressed
his sentiments in regard to them. Hearing this, and fearing the effect
on the Indians, Captain A. B. Bishop, who commanded the soldiers stationed at Spring Place, sent an armed guard to Chief Ross's home,
where the poet was stopping, to arrest the poet and to bring him to
Spring Place for imprisonment. One of the guards was John Oates, a
man well-known to the people of this section. Payne was arrested at
the home of John Ross, in Bradley County, Tenn., only a few miles from
the State line. On the positive testimony of John Oates, it was not in
the jail at Spring Place that Payne was imprisoned, but in the Vann
House. Said he to one who heard the statement from his own lips. ''I
knew him well. He was at the old brick house—never in jail for a single
moment.'' The guard stationed there was known as the Georgia Guard.
commanded by Captain A. B. Bishop. He was released without an hour's
delay when the fact was ascertained that he was innocent.*

MUSCOGEE

Columbus.   Volume I, Pages 816-822.

Girard: Where the   On Sunday afternoon, April 16,
Last Fighting of the   1865, the last engagement of the
War, East of the Mis- Civil War, east of the Mississippi
sissippi, Occurred.   River, was fought at Girard, on the
slopes of the Chattahoochee, opposite
the city of Columbus. It was incident to the celebrated
cavalry raid into Georgia of General James H. Wilson.
West Point was captured on the same day, but at an
earlier hour. We quote the following brief account of

---

*Much of the material for this article was furnished by Mrs. Warren
Davis, of Dalton, Ga. The authorities consulted by her were as follows:
Rev. W. J. Cotter, Mr. Jesse Jackson, Dr. George Mellen, White's Historical
Collections, etc.

the engagement at Columbus from Professor Joseph T. Derry's Military History of Georgia.*

"At Columbus, on the same day, April 16—a week after General Lee's surrender—Howell Cobb made a gallant attempt to defend the bridges over the Chattahoochee, fighting on the Alabama side, but was overwhelmed by the Federal forces, who took possession of the city, capturing 1,200 prisoners and 52 field guns. Colonel C. A. L. Lamar, of General Cobb's staff, was among the killed. The ram Jackson, which had just been built for the defence of the Chattahoochee, was an armament of six seven-inch guns, was destroyed, as were also the navy yard, foundries, arsenal, armory, sword and pistol factory, shop, paper mill, cotton factories, 15 locomotives, 200 cars and a large amount of cotton."

Upwards of twenty companies were organized and equipped in Columbus for Georgia's defence during the Civil War, and some of the officers who went from Columbus achieved high distinction, among them General Paul J. Semmes, General Henry L. Benning, the Iversons, father and son; Colonel John A. Jones, Colonel James N. Ramsey, Major Raphael J. Moses, and several others. General Semmes and Colonel Jones were both killed in the battle of Gettysburg, while Major Moses, as Confederate Commissary for the State of Georgia, executed the last order of the Confederacy, in a transaction relating to the disposition of $10,000 in silver bullion.

The Killing of Ashburn: An Episode of Reconstruction.
There occurred at Columbus during the period of reconstruction an episode which plunged the whole nation into a fever of excitement, and which evinced a fixed purpose on the part of the people of the South to maintain the integrity of an Anglo-Saxon civilization. It was the killing, by unknown parties, of G. W. Ashburn, an offensive partisan, who represented the most extreme type of radicalism. He was a member of the Constitutional Convention of 1865, in which body he made himself peculiarly odious to the white people of Georgia. The feeling of revulsion naturally reached a climax in Columbus, where he lived

with the negro element of the population—an object of great loathsomeness to the Caucasian race. The following account of the trial is condensed from various sources:

The killing of Ashburn occurred on the night of March 31, 1868. He is said to have been a native of North Carolina, from which State he came to Georgia some thirty years prior to his death. There is very little known concerning him prior to the era of military usurpation, which, in addition to unloosing upon Georgia a swarm of vultures from other sections, developed the baser instincts of men who were already residents of the State and who identified themselves for vicious purposes with these ignoble birds of prey. There were undoubtedly some good and true men who, from conviction, advocated a policy of non-resistance; but they were few in number. Ashburn's mysterious taking off, therefore, at a time when passion was inflamed, when civil courts were suppressed, when Georgia's sovereign Statehood was outraged in the most flagrant manner, and when there was no redress for the whites except through the instrumentality of the Ku-Klux, was a matter little calculated to produce surprise, though it created a tremendous sensation. The military authorities took the matter in hand and caused arrest on suspicion of the following parties: William R. Bedell, Columbus C. Bedell, James W. Barber, Alva C. Roper, William D. Chipley, Robert A. Ennis, William L. Cash, Elisha J. Kirkscey, Thomas N. Grimes, Wade H. Stephens, R. Hudson, W. A. Duke, J. S. Wiggins, and R. A. Wood. Besides these, there were several negroes implicated. It seems that even the blacks entertained toward Ashburn a feeling of mingled fear and disgust.

For the purpose of trying these alleged offenders, a military court was organized at McPherson Barracks, in Atlanta. The counsel for the prisoners included Alexander H. Stephens, Martin J. Crawford, James M. Smith, Lucius J. Gartrell, Henry L. Benning, James N. Ramsey and Raphael J. Moses. On the side of the prosecution, General Dunn, the judge advocate, was assisted by ex-Governor Joseph E. Brown and Major William M. Smythe. While in prison the defendants were subjected to great indignities. They were eventually admitted to bail, however, in the sum of 32,500 each, and not less than four hundred citizens of Columbus, representing both races, signed the required bonds.

It was on June 29, 1868, that the court was duly constituted, but, at the request of Mr. Stephens, a postponement was granted until the day following. The trial then began with the filing by Mr. Stephens of an answer in plea to the specific charges, in which, on behalf of the several prisoners, he entered a plea of not guilty to the crimes set forth. At the same time, the rightful jurisdiction of the court was was traversed. With slow progress the case proceeded until the twentieth day, when orders were received from General Meade suspending the investigation until further notice from headquarters. On July 25, 1868, the prisoners were taken to Columbus, under guard. It was at this stage of the proceedings that they were finally admitted to bail; and, for reasons best known perhaps to the military authorities, the trial of the alleged murderers was never resumed.

Governor Brown's part in the prosecution of the Columbus prisoners charged with the murder of Ashburn only served to increase the obloquy in which he was held at this time by Georgians, due to his course in supporting the election of General Grant and in upholding the policy of Reconstruction. The following explanation of his course in the Columbus affair has been given by Colonel Isaac W. Avery, his accredited biographer. Says he:

"Weighing the evidence in the matter fairly and dispassionately, it may be shown that Governor Brown, in taking part in this prosecution, was governed by proper motives and rendered a service, both to the State and to the prisoners. He alleges that General Meade employed him, on the condition which he insisted upon making, that he—Governor Brown—should control the case, and that, upon the restoration of civil law, the case should be surrendered by the military authorities. His employment prevented the retention of very extreme men. The corroboration of Governor Brown, in this statement, has been very striking. It has been argued against its credibility that during General Meade's life, when the latter could either have verified or denied it, no explanation was made by Governor Brown of his conduct in the matter. Major A. Leyden, of Atlanta, who talked with General Meade several times about the affair, says that he was assured by General Meade that his fears for the prisoners would not be realized. Mr. John C. Whitner, of Atlanta, states that Detective Whiteley, who worked up the evidence for the prosecution, told him that the understanding when Brown was employed was that the military trial was to be remanded to the State authorities, on the reorganization of the civil government. General William Phillips, of Marietta, testifies that Governor Brown consulted with him at the time on the subject and explained to him his attitude of mind. Major Campbell Wallace, in an interview at the time with General Meade, confirms Governor Brown's statement. Many years ago Governor Brown gave his version of the affair to Hon. Alexander H. Stephens and Dr. J. S. Lawton."

**Recollections
of General Mir-
abeau B. Lamar.**
There are few persons who remember General Mirabeau Lamar. It was nearly eighty years ago that he left Columbus to achieve renown in the war for Texan independence; and barring only an occasional visit home he remained an exile throughout life from the land of his birth. But Judge Alexander W. Terrell, of Texas,* an eminent jurist and diplomat, who is still living at the ripe old age of eighty-four years, enjoyed the personal acquaintanec of this extraordinary man who, next to Sam Houston, was the most illustrious of Texans. Says he:

"The career of Mirabeau B. Lamar—patriot, soldier, statesman, poet—was one of the most remarkable in history. He was descended from a French Huguenot, who, after the destruction of La Rochelle, in 1628, found refuge in America. Lamar was born in Georgia, in 1798, and there he grew to manhood. He acquired only a common school education, for he preferred hunting, fencing, and horseback exercise to the confinement of the class-room. But he delighted in reading the ancient classics and the standard English authors, and thus acquired so correct a knowledge of the structure of his own language that few excelled him as a forceful and eloquent speaker."

"I first saw General Lamar in 1853, when his long, jet black hair was tinged with gray. He was of dark complexion and about five feet ten inches tall, with broad shoulders, deep chest and symmetrical limbs. From

---

*Sketch of Mirabeau B. Lamar, Vol. VII, Library of Southern Literature. Atlanta, 1909.

under his high forehead blue eyes looked out in calm repose; while his clean-cut, handsome features bespoke an iron resolution.

"When twenty-eight years old he married Miss Tabitha Jourdan, to whom he was tenderly devoted, for he had loved and courted her for years, and her death, while yet in the bloom of youth and beauty, so overwhelmed him with grief that he left Georgia—a homeless wanderer. In 1835 Lamar was next heard from on the frontier of Texas where, like Sam Houston, he appealed to the settlers with impassioned eloquence to revolt against the tyranny of Mexico. There was a strange parallel in the lives of these two great men. Each of them, when crushed by domestic affliction, fled from home and friends. Each emerged from self-imposed exile to advocate on a foreign soil the cause of civil freedom; each became commander of a revolutionary army, and then president of a new republic; each remained unmarried during all the fierce years of the Texan Revolution, and each found at last in married life his supreme happiness with wife and children."

"On March 6, 1836, the Alamo at San Antonia was stormed by an invading army under Santa Anna, the president of Mexico, all its defenders were massacred; while a few days afterward one hundred and seventy-five volunteers were butchered in cold blood at Goliad by his orders, and after having surrendered. Two weeks afterward Lamar appeared again on the coast of Texas, at the abandoned town of Velasco, and started on foot to join the Texan army. Colonel Fannin, who was butchered at Goliad, had been the bosom friend of Lamar, and the latter was eager to revenge his murdered friend. On April 20, 1836, Houston's army, after a forced march of two days and a night, with no other food than parched corn, confronted on the smooth prairie of San Jacinto the army of Santa Anna, which outnumbered them two to one. That afternoon Walter P. Lane, while skirmishing, was attacked by three Mexican lacers, who wounded him as his horse fell. Lamar rushed to his rescue, and killing one of the enemy, put the others to flight, though wounded himself. The Texan infantry saw the heroic act, and shouted in admiration. He had won his spurs, and Houston at once put him in command of the cavalry, with the approval of all its officers. The next afternoon, at 4 o'clock, the Texan infantry advanced toward the Mexican line to the tune of an old love-song; but when finally within forty paces of the Mexicans the band struck up "Yankee Dooodle." With clubbed rifles and knives they rushed upon the foe, hewing them down in the fierce onset. Lamar, though wounded, led the Texan cavalry on the right wing like an avenging fury. He remained in the pursuit until sunset, and with his cavalry captured Santa Anna. The battle was over in eighteen minutes, and the Mexicans slain or made prisoners outnumbered the Texans two to one. The latter lost only three men killed and twenty-seven wounded.

"Never before nor since in the annals of war was such a victory won by volunteers in an open field over such a superior force of disciplined troops, and never was a victory more far-reaching; for it secured independence, resulting in the annexation of Texas to the Union, which provoked the war of 1846 with Mexico. Under the treaty of Guadalupe Hidalgo our flag was carried across the continent, while the area of the Union was doubled. Within ten days Lamar was made Secretary of War; in four weeks the Cabinet appointed him commander-in-chief of the army; in four months he was elected Vice-President of the Republic, and in three years President without opposition. No private soldier ever rose so rapidly from the ranks to supreme authority through so many important offices, militay and civil. His style as a writer was not unlike his nephew's, L. Q. C. Lamar, the United States Senator.''

"During Lamar's term as President the frontier was extended and protected, Mexican invasions were repelled, Texan independence was recognized, treaties were made with great European powers, immense tracts of land were surveyed and dedicated to higher education, and a free school system was established—the second on the Continent. France sent her minister to the Republic of Texas, and his residence, built with the gold of Louis Philippe, may still be seen in Austin. Time and official station had not yet soothed Lamar's domestic grief, and it was not until after seventeen years of loneliness that he met and married, in 1851, Miss Henrietta Maffitt, the beautiful and accomplished daughter of John Newland Maffitt, the great Methodist revivalist and orator of the South. When afterwards, in 1857, he was United States Minister to the Argentine Republic, a beautiful Indian girl inspired his heart to compose "The Daughter of Mendoza," his best-known poem. After the end of his term as President, he kept severely aloof from partisan strife, and found his chief pleasure in the endearments of home, where he died, at Richmond, Texas, December 19, 1859. No suspicion ever tarnished his reputation.''

————

General Lamar* is buried at Richmond, Texas, his old home. The grave is covered by a horizontal slab of rough granite, about six feet and a half long by four in width. It was quarried from the hillsides of his adopted State. At the end of this slab, there rises a splendid shaft of Italian marble, twelve feet high, which rests

———

*Tombs and Monuments of Noted Texans, by Mrs. M. Looscan in Wooten's Comprehensive History of Texas, Vol. I, p. 702, Dallas, 1898.

upon a pedestal four feet square. On the west side of the shaft, in bold relief, is chiselled a shield bearing the name, LAMAR, encircled by a beautiful wreath. Just a little below the point of the shield, on either side, project the muzzles of two cannon from among the leaves and flowers. On the east side of the shaft is the simple inscription:

> EX-PRESIDENT OF TEXAS
> DIED
> Dec. 19, 1859.
> Aged 61 years, 4 mos. & 2 days.

NEWTON

Early Times in Newton.* In 1822 Newton County was well-nigh an unbroken forest. There were no cleared lands except Indian maize and bean patches. There were no public roads; simply Indian trails. As soon as the lands were surveyed settlers began to occupy them at once. They cleared and cultivated fields of corn, wheat and other cereals. The men had patches of tobacco; the women had patches of indigo. No cotton was raised, except enough to make necessary clothing. The cotton was seeded by hand, for there were no gins; before carding it was first washed and then carded by hand, spun on spinning wheels, and finally woven on looms into cloth. The cotton, or spun thread, or woven cloth, was dyed blue by means of indigo, yellow with copperas, or whatever color was desired, with other coloring materials. The cloth thus made, white or colored, was then cut and sewed by hand into such garments as would hide human forms. Foreign fashion had not then invented Balkan blouses or hobble skirts.

At this early date, the forests were made up of oaks of different kinds, hickories, symmetrical pines and other growths. Among them were interspersed chestnut trees, from two to three or more feet in diameter, loaded with burrs containing sweet, palatable nuts. In September

*To Mrs. Wm. C. Clark, of Covington, we are indebted for most of the materials contained in this chapter. She was greatly assisted in the work of gathering data by Rev. A. C. Mixon, to whom grateful acknowledgments are likewise made.

or October the burrs generously opened, and after a rain or a brisk wind, nuts could be gathered by the bushel. Many of these the children treasured up for winter enjoyment. On what remained, the frisky squirrels feasted and the grunting swine fattened. Chinkapins were scattered all along up and down the little streams. Their little burrs, too, opened and disclosed little round fruit, large as a bullet and black as the eyes of a pretty girl. These were good to eat, and, besides, furnished materials for such innocent games as "Hull Gull," "Even or Odd" and "Jack in the Bush, Cut Him Down." Children have no such pleasure nowadays. Chestnut trees and chinkapin bushes are now as scarce as hen teeth in Newton. Another feature of former times in Newton was the abundance of various kinds of birds. Pigeons came in immense flocks in fall and winter, to gather up the acorns. Millions of blackbirds, in gangs half a mile long, came in winter and spring to pick up the uncovered grain in the farmers' fields. Of other birds, some have disappeared, others are scarce, none are abundant.

Covington: Its Indian Legend. Covington, the county-seat of Newton, is situated on the Georgia Railroad, 41 miles from Atlanta and 130 miles from Augusta. There is a creek which bounds the north and south of the town bearing the name of Dried Indian; and the legend which tells us of the naming of this stream comes from the long ago. When the earliest settlers came into this section, the red men dwelt upon the banks of this stream. Many were the attempts, often unsuccessful, made by the brave pioneers to rout these warlike inhabitants. At last they were all put to death and to flight save one old chieftain, who, single-handed and alone, still breathed the defiant spirit of his race. But one day, while asleep, he, too, was overtaken and captured. To prevent his escape, the old Indian was bound hand and foot with white oak lithes. He was then tied to a tree and pierced with many arrows. Death ensued, but still the settlers were unappeased, and, after cutting his body with deep gashes, they took him to a rocky steep on the banks of the stream, and there left him to dry in the sun. The creek was named Dried Indian from this incident.

The first church in Covington was a Methodist Church, and was built on the banks of this creek. When the town began to grow, the old church building was sold to the negroes, who have since transformed it into an up-to-date church, with handsome leaded windows and electric lights. Just west of this old church, in a very large grove, stood the old manual training school established in Covington some time in the early thirties by Dr. Olin. It was the property of the Methodists of Georgia. But the school was not a success, and through the efforts of Dr. Ignatius Few, the first president of Emory, this school was sold and some of the buildings were removed to Oxford as a beginning for the school known later as Emory College. Colonel W. W. Clark bought the site and the main building of the Manual School, converting it into an elegant Colonial home, which stands today as the home of Colonel Clark's daughter.

Covington was incorporated as a town in 1822 and as a city in 1854. The earliest settler on the site of the present town was Mr. Carey Wood, a pioneer citizen, who in after years became its most conspicuous landmark. From a list of the board of trustees of the old Southern Female College, at Covington, may be obtained the names of some of the prominent residents of the town in 1851, when the college was chartered, to-wit.: Joseph A. Anderson, William L. Conyers, John P. Carr, John B. Hendrick, Joseph H. Murrell, Robert O. Usher, Thomas F. Jones, William P. Anderson, Columbus L. Pace, John Harris and John J. Floyd. The present public school system of Covington was established in 1887. Some of the early representatives of Newton County in the General Assembly of Georgia, most of whom resided in or near Covington, were: Luke Robinson, Josiah Perry, Martin Kolb, McCormick Neal, John Bass, Richard L. Simms, A. F. Luckie, John Harris, Parmedus Reynolds, John Loyall, Richard Loyall, Felix Hardman, Isaac P. Henderson and Alfred Livingston.

*Acts, 1851-1852, p. 313.

Covington's Ante-Bellum Homes.[*] If one is fond of contrast let him ride from Atlanta to Covington and back again the same afternoon. Atlanta, our young and marvelous city of magic; our farewell to the past, our card to the future. Covington, of the ancient regime; far, far older; a fine old lady, sitting serenely in her old brocade, with a smile of contentment, viewing unmoved the passings years. Some clever analyst once said that the architecture of a section is the only perfect and accurate history of its past; it cannot lie. The splendid old homes of Covington, which have been so perfectly preserved, tell the story of the refined and advanced civilization that once obtained there, making it one of the most aristocratic social and political centers of Georgia. Oxford College is only two miles away, and the proximity of this seat of learning naturally gave Covington an atmosphere of culture. Crossing the square and passing out Floyd Street you come to the home of Carey Wood, who, in company with three other adventurous pioneers, was the first settler of Covington, then backwoods, or a mere crossroads on the public highway leading to Augusta. This house, so perfectly preserved with its dignified white columns, and fine air of conservative dignity, so simple yet so suitable, was, as originally built, the first frame house erected in Covington. The first four rooms of this pioneer house, two above and two below, are still a part of this old dwelling as it now stands. They were added to from time to time until long before the war the domicile achieved its present form, since when it has remained unaltered.

Carey Wood and his descendants were a large part of old Covington. His two daughters, Laura and Pauline, married two brothers, Colonel Robert Henderson, who was made a general on the battlefield as he was dying, and Colonel Jack Henderson, both of the Confederate army. Another of his daughters, Mary Jane, married Ozborn T. Rogers and resided in a splendid old Georgia mansion. General Robert Henderson lived subsequently in the old Cary Wood homestead, which is now the residence of Mr. and Mrs. T. S. Swann. Two of General Henderson's daughters reared in this old house, Mrs. Lod Hill, of Atlanta, and Mrs. E. Y. Hill, of Washington, Wilkes County, are prominent women well known throughout the State. Robert R. Wood, of Atlanta, is a grandson of Carey Wood. Mrs. Louise Green, the well-known artist of Atlanta, is his granddaughter, and his daughter, Mrs. Ozborn T. Rogers, of the famous old Rogers house, now lives in Decatur. Carey Wood married a Miss Billups, of South Carolina, and coming to her husband's home in Georgia, she brought the nurse of her childhood with her as a body servant. At the time of this old negro's death, fifty of her descendants, none of whom had ever been sold, were owned by Carey Wood, and maintained either in his or his children's home, in addition to which he had many other slaves.

Further out Floyd Street, adjoining the old Wood place, is the former home of Judge John Floyd, one of the foremost citizens of Covington. This

---

[*]Article written by Mrs. Thad Horton, of Atlanta.

THE CRADLE OF EMORY COLLEGE:

Home of the Late Col. W. W. Clark, Covington, Ga., Including Part of the Old Normal School Established by Dr. Olin.

beautiful old house has its colonnade at the very edge of the sidewalk, and a view looking towards the square with the fluted columns of this old home on one side and the green odur hanging trees on the other is so picturesque that it deserves to be perpetuated. Just across from the Floyd house is the old Usher residence, now the home of Jack Henderson, a son of Robert Henderson. Jack Henderson married Miss Usher, whose father built this beautiful old residence.

The best built and the most archtectural of the many old homes of Covington is the old Rogers mansion, now the residence of Mrs. Joseph Wright, formerly the well-known Miss Corrie Carr. This splendid old brick house, which would be a credit to any city, was built by Colonel Thomas Jones, the father of Colonel Thomas Floyd Jones, of South Georgia. Originally the tract comprised fifty-five acres. A spacious lawn surrounded the house, there being no neighbors on either side, as there are now. The picturesque old English-looking residence stood on a noble eminence with its well designed loggia, overlooking the town. A high open brick wall surrounded the house garden, which was laid out in formal flower beds. These beds were surrounded by a boxwood hedge, planted by Mrs. Rogers herself, now a venerable lady of 82, who tells me that some forty years ago this hedge had grown to be waist high. The old walls and boxwood hedges have all been moved away; neighbors have established themselves to the right and left, but the fine old house still overlooks the city from its splendid eminence. The brick used in its building are said to have cost $10,000. for all the interior walls are of solid masonry. But shortly after the war, the old house with its sur ounding acres were sold for the meager sum of $3,800.

The most picturesque home in Covington is decidedly the old Neal homestead. It was sold many years ago to David Spence, whose daughter, Mrs. Sheppard, inherited the place, and whose family now resides there. This most typical and picturesque old home, with its outside chimneys and noble Grecian portico, was built by McCormick Neal, the brother of the late T. B. Neal, of Atlanta, the brother, also, of the late Mrs. Pittman, the late Mr. Keely and of Mrs. E. H. Thornton. The beautiful old cedar trees and boxwood hedges were planted by Mrs. Neal herself many years ago. She has many descendants and relatives in Atlanta, among them Mrs. Emma Neal Douglas, whose recent work among the convicts of the Federal prison has endeared her to all benevolent people.

On ringing the doorbell to ask permission to take a photograph of the old place, I was invited to enter, which gave me an opportunity to study the plan of the house and see the woodwork, which is always a most interesting feature of old ante-bellum houses. The woodwork is of white and gold, the mantel in the quaint old drawing room one of the most charming colonial designs I have ever seen, and worthy of reproduction in the finest latter-day mansions.

Most of the old homes in Covington are in a state of splendid preservation and in perfect repair. Indeed the spirit of repair pervades the town;

the old Bob Wood place was being done over inside and out, and the old
Rogers or Wight home was in the hands of interior decorators. But every
now and then I came upon some beautiful old welling gray with time, and
these were by far the most interesting and romantic of all. One of
these was on the corner just above the old Neal residence. A mass of
crimson crepe myrtle flaunted itself against a background of antique
white clapboards. The gardens to the front and to the side and the
rear were mellow with age, and seemed to have been undisturbed for
years by a single footfall. Moss and lichens and pretty tender weeds
grew everywhere. It was, I ascertained, the home of Mrs. Virginia Usher
Camp, the widow of Septimus Camp, who died a few months after his
marriage, leaving his bride this beautiful old home, where she has continued
to reside entirely alone for the last fifty years. No wonder the garden
seemed undisturbed, with only her light footfall passing through there.
Mrs. Camp showed us through her home, and gave us as souvenir the
published scores of some songs of her own composition. Later we had
water from her picturesque and moss-grown old well. Although Mrs. Camp
has owned this place for fifty years, it has an even more ancient history,
having been for a generation earlier than its purchase by Septimus Camp
the home of the well-known Batts family, of Georgia. The daughter of
the house, Miss Adelaide Batts, married E. W. Marsh, then one of the
merchant princes of Atlanta. Her children, McAllen (Batts) Marsh and
Mrs. Green Adair, still reside here.

It is hard to say which was the most charming, the ride to Covington
or the ride home again. Perhaps the latter—we had so many things to
think of. As we sped along, the dusk began to thicken. In an incred-
ibly short time we were speeding through the cool moist air of Druid
Hills; next we were home. But though we were back again, the glamour
was still upon us—the glamour of the old South.

**Henry Ivy: Revolu-
tionary Soldier.** Henry Ivy, or Ivey, perhaps a South
Carolinian by birth, was a soldier
in Washington's army at Valley
Forge, but he moved into Newton with his family, including two sons, soon after the county was opened
to settlement. He died before the day of pensions,
carrying to his grave the marks of his warfare, especially during the bleak winter at Valley Forge. His
death occurred in 1839 or 1840, at the age of four-score
years. With his wife, who preceded him to the grave,

he is buried at Red Oak Cemetery, eleven miles south of Covington. Like many of his patriotic comardes, he went to his last resting-place, "unknown, unhonored and unsung," but in the sky above him waves the starry emblem for which he fought, symbolizing the greatest power on earth.

Pioneer Temperance Movement. During the early days of Newton County it was quite the fashion to partake of fiery intoxicants. Every household had its decanter of spirituous liquors. If a neighbor came in, even before breakfast, he was invited to take a social drink, and he seldom refused. Between the years 1824 and 1826 the first move in the direction of temperance was inaugurated by the adoption of what is still remembered by some of the older generation as the Washington pledge. Temperance organizations were formed throughout the country, in the constitutions of which this pledge was embodied; and the effect upon the local population was marked. At the old Red Oak Methodist Church, Dr. Alexander Means, of venerated memory, delivered a lecture on temperance, the impression produced by which upon the popular mind was most profound. As a result there was formed a small temperance society, the members of which abandoned the use of alcoholic stimulants, except for medicinal purposes; removed their decanters from the bureaus and sideboards and taught their children "to touch not, taste not, handle not the unclean thing."

The Indian Fishery. In the southern part of Newton County, near the junction of South and Yellow Rivers, there is a famous shoal called "The Indian Fishery." It acquired this name from the fact that large numbers of Indians camped here at one time to trade and to fish. The savages gathered for this purpose in the early spring, because at this season a great many salt-water fish called shad came up to the shoal. These were very fine fish, weighing from two to four pounds each. But shad no longer abound in the stream at this point.

Pioneer Industries of Newton. Captain John Webb, in association with a Mr. White, built the first cotton mill in the County of Newton. It was erected on the Alcova River, about ten miles south of Covington. Some time later this co-partnership was dissolved, after which Mr. White built a cotton mill a short distance down the same stream. At both places flour mills, with quite a large capacity, were also erected. During the Civil War, White's mill was burned by the Federals. Webb's mill was destroyed by fire at a much later period.

Porterdale.   Three miles southwest of Covington, at Porterdale, are located the largest cordage mills in the world. In 1868 Colonel E. Steadman bought 1,012 acres on and around the site now occupied by this great establishment. He included in his purchase a section of Yellow River, at a point on which, then known as Cedar Shoals, he established a township called Steadman. Here he afterwards erected a mill known as the Cedar Shoals Factory, where cotton and woollen fabrics were both manufactured. This plant was operated by Mr. Steadman for years, after which he sold the property to the late O. S. Porter, Esq., who converted the same into a mill for the manufacture of twine; and later formed a combination with the Bibb Manufacturing Company, out of which grew the famous Porterdale Mills. The town of Steadman has given place to Porterdale, Ga., a town of 1,500 inhabitants, and the terminus of a branch line of the Central Railroad.

Mr. G. C. Adam's Fine Work.   In 1893, Mr. G. C. Adams, County School Commissioner of Newton, introduced in the rural districts of this county an innovation which has since met with almost universal adoption, viz., the free transportation of school children to the rural schools of the district. His modest experiments marked the beginning of the present transportation system now in operation throughout the United States. Nor has the progress of this reform movement been restricted to this side of the Atlantic Ocean. It has spread even to England, where the periodicals have published full accounts of the system, with detailed maps of Newton County, including the various routes. In 1894 Mr. Adams also organized the Boys' Corn Club in the South. His object was to encourage the boys to remain on the farms, by developing a wholesome spirit of rivalry among them. This movement was at once adopted by all the Southern States, and today the number of workers enlisted in this crusade for the betterment of farm life in the South reaches far up into the hundreds of thousands.

Newton's Window at the State Capitol.   At the State Capitol, in Atlanta, there is a leaded window put there by the citizens of Newton County in 1895, the year of the Cotton States and International Exposition. Instead of having the regulation display, the citizens placed this window in the Georgia building and afterwards, through the co-operation of Hon. L. F. Livingston and Captain John Milledge, it was placed in the library of the State Capitol, where it depicts the marvelous resources of Newton. The central panel, portraying the county's water powers, was the gift of the Bibb Manufacturing Company, of Porterdale, Ga.

Rev. A. C. Mixon: Newton's oldest Resident. Much of the information contained in this work relative to Newton County has been furnished by a gentleman, now in his ninety-fourth year, who has been a resident of the county since his earliest infancy: Rev. A. C. Mixon. The home of this revered patriarch is at Mixon, twelve miles south of Covington. His father bought a tract of land in this section of the county when there were no roads in this part of Georgia—nothing but Indian trails; and here, on what was then the frontier belt of the wilderness, exposed to the danger of savage attacks, Mr. Mixon was born in 1821. President Jefferson and Emperor Napoleon were still alive—the former an old man at his country home in Virginia, the latter a prisoner on the Isle of St. Helena. Mr. Mixon is the oldest living graduate of Emory College, and the oldest resident of Newton County; but his eye is still bright, his step elastic, and his memory of past events as clear as a crystal morning. He is a splendid talker, a man of varied and wide information, and a most genial gentleman. Because he has kept his heart pure, he finds the evening of his life serene; and may his golden twilight linger long.

Col. Alfred Livingston: His Escape From the Indians. Colonel Alfred Livingston was one of the most noted men of Newton. He reached a phenomenal age, somewhere up in the nineties, and reared a son who represented his district in Congress for twenty consecutive years. There were many incidents of a most dramatic character in the long pilgrimage of Colonel Livingston, but nothing to surpass his wonderful escape from the Indians, when a lad. As told by one conversant with the facts, the story runs as follows: On the border of Taliaferro County, touching Greene, there lived in the pioneer days of our country a little family consisting of three members, father, mother and son, who were fighting hard to exist, with the odds heavily against them. Many were the hardships and dangers to which they were exposed on the perilous belt of the frontier. Indian tribes were all around them, and they were most hostile to these struggling settlers.

One day the father was called away from home on business which required his absence for several days, and his final word of warning was:

"Be careful of the Indians, and be ready for an attack at any moment."
The first day passed without incident, and as the shadows lengthened mother
and son began to make ready for the night. The rude home was provided
with cumbersome doors and shutters, but these were made fast. Strange
to say, the only weapon in the cabin with which to repel a hostile visit
was an axe, but this was made sharp in case of need. With every precaution
taken, they prepared to retire. But no sleep awaited them, for the watchful Indians had seen the husband and father leave his little home early
that morning, and they knew that now was the hour for attack, hoping to
count two scalps in their belt before midnight. As mother and son sat
around the little hearthstone, suddenly a wierd scream pierced the stillness
of the outer world, and both knew that in a few moments the house would
be surrounded by the fierce men of the forest.

Impelled by a sudden impulse the mother seized the axe and stationed
herself at the window, while the lad, armed with a cudgel, stood guard
at the door. The Indians, with a war-whoop, began to surround the little
cabin. The first point of attack was the door, but this was securely fastened,
and foiled here, they next addressed themselves to the rudely shuttered
window. At a single stroke the frail protection fell to the floor, and a
warlike Indian thrust his head through the opening. The mother aimed
well with her axe, and the head of the savage intruder was severed from
his body. The other Indians were greatly enraged. When the limp body
fell to the ground outside a second Indian thrust his head in, and quickly
he, too, fell to the ground in a lump beside his comrades.

Three times with unerring stroke did this brave woman fight for her
offspring, and when the third body fell to the ground outside the survivors
decided to attack the house by a descent through the chimney. One of the
redskins clambered on the roof and swung himself down into the little
room. But the mother was alert, and with one well-aimed blow the fourth
victim was sent to a bloody death. Only one other redskin remained. When
his companion failed to return, he became terrified and fled. All night
the inmates of the cabin watched and waited, expecting a return of the
enemy at any moment. But the night dragged slowly away without further
incident, and dawn's first rays of light found the watchers ready to perform
the gruesome task of burying the dead. The mother decided to make a
large fire from the accumulated brush around the house, hoping thereby to
deceive the Indians, but when the savages approached near enough to
perceive the ruse they became infuriated, and rushing upon the helpless
woman scalped her.

Though in mortal pain, she possessed sufficient presence of mind to
show no signs of life, until the Indians finally left her for dead. At last
when she could hear no sounds from the redskins she arose and started
back to the cabin, her only thought being her boy. She had not dragged
herself far before she saw her husband returning, but ere he reached her
she fell to the ground in a fainting condition. The distracted husband bore

her tenderly into the house, where she breathed her last in a very short while. The lad, who had gone in search of his father, returned just in time to see his mother's eyes close in death. This son was Alfred Livingston. Removing to Newton County years afterwards he bought property in the western part of the county, calling the place at which he settled Bethany, in honor of the historic old church in Taliaferro County, to which his family belonged before he came to Newton.

Oxford. Oxford, the seat of Emory College, came into existence with the great school of Methodism which was here located in the mid-thirties, bringing to this little college town some of Georgia's best families. It was incorporated as a town on December 23, 1839, with the following-named commissioners, to-wit.: Richard L. Sims, Ignatius A. Few, Samuel J. Bryan, Acchelaus H. Mitchell, Harmon Lamar and James H. Bryan.[1] The Oxford Female Academy was incorporated on December 19, 1840, with the following board of trustees: James O. Andrew, William Capers, Augustus B. Longstreet, Samuel J. Bryan, Richard L. Sims, William H. Mell and George Lane.[2]

Some of the most distinguished men of the State have been residents of Oxford. The list includes: Bishop George F. Pierce, one of the greatest orators of the American pulpit; Judge Augustus B. Longstreet, author of "Georgia Scenes;" Justice L. Q. C. Lamar, a son-in-law of Judge Longstreet, afterwards a member of Congress, a United States Senator, a Cabinet officer under President Cleveland, and an occupant of the United States Supreme Court Bench; Bishop Atticus G. Haygood, theologian, educator, author and administrator; Bishop James O. Andrew, first Bishop of the M. E. Church, South; Dr. Ignatius A. Few, a noted pioneer educator and divine; Dr. Alexander Means, an eminent

[1] Acts, 1839, p. 80.
[2] Acts, p. 7.

scholar, poet and man of science; Dr. Isaac S. Hopkins, afterwards president of the Georgia School of Technology; Bishop Warren A. Candler, one of the founders of the great Methodist University which bears his family name, and to the chancellorship of which he was called; Hon. Robert U. Hardeman, former State Treasurer of Georgia, and a host of others.

Justice L. Q. C. Lamar. Perhaps the most illustrious graduate of Emory College was the renowned jurist and statesman: L. Q. C. Lamar. Entering the freshman class in 1841, he received his diploma in 1845. Some few years later he married Virginia Longstreet, the beautiful daughter of the president, and when Judge Longstreet removed to Mississippi to become the head of the new university, he soon followed, to spend the remainder of his life in his adopted State. He became a member of Congress, an envoy to Europe, on behalf of the Confederate government, during the Civil War, a Senator of the United States, a member of the Cabinet of President Cleveland, under the latter's first administration, and finally an Associate Justice of the Supreme Court of the United States. But he never ceased to love Georgia. Throughout his whole life, he remained loyal to Emory, and nothing delighted him more than to recount the recollections of his long sojourn of four years at Oxford. In the commencement address which he delivered in the summer of 1870, before the alumni of the college, he paid the following beautiful tribute to the old town. Said he:

"No spot on earth has so helped to form and make me what I am as this town of Oxford. It was here, in the church which stands a little further up the street that I became fully impressed with the value and peril of my soul, and was led to pour out my contrite confessions. It was in yonder building, which now seems so deserted, that I became conscious of power. It was here, in the Phi Gamma Society, that I received my training as a debater. I see before me now many who wrestled with me in the arena of argument. There sits a man who was one of the first—he was, indeed, actually the second—to suggest that I had powers within me to stir men's hearts and to convince the reason. Wesley Hughes was the first. I know not where he is, but I send to him my greetings wherever he may be. There sits the venerable man who, when I delivered by graduating address, in approval of its sentiments, placed his hand upon my head and gave me his blessing. There is another old man who sat at the very fountain head of my mind, and with loving hand directed the channel in which it was required to flow and who, when I arrived at manhood, gave me my betrothed bride, who has ever since held the choicest place in my affections and made my life one constant song of joy.''

Zora Fair: A Heroine of the Civil War. Still fragrant in the memory of the town of Oxford is the daring exploit of a beautiful South Carolina girl, who refugeed to this remote Georgia village during the Civil War. Her name was Zora Fair. She was living with an uncle, Mr. Abram Crews, in the famous old city of Charleston, when the latter was detailed by the Confederate government to run the blockade to Europe. Before embarking upon this perilous enterprise, he sought to find a safe retreat for his family, and, having friends in the little village of Oxford, he brought them hither, and with the other members of his household came Zora Fair. She was a frail slip of a girl, but she came of courageous stock, with wonderful powers of endurance, as events were to prove, and with a spirit as brave as ever animated the maid of Orleans. The story is too long to be told in this connection, but those who wish to read an account of this brave girl's heroism can find it in ''Grandmother Stories,''* a charming little book written by Mrs. Howard Meriwether Lovett, of Augusta. It is enough for present purposes to say here that, disguising herself as a mulatto negress, she crossed the Yellow River, on a partially destroyed mill dam, and made her way on foot to Atlanta, where, passing the enemy's lines, she gained access to General Sherman's headquarters, possessed herself of certain secrets pertaining to the Federal plan of campaign; and, narrowly escaping death under fire of a sentinel's gun, she returned with blistered feet to Oxford, from which place she sought to communicate by letter with General Joseph E. Johnston, then at Lincolnton, N. C. But, unfortunately, the brave girl's message fell into the hands of the Federals. Troops were sent to Oxford to effect her capture, but she remained in hiding until danger was well past. If the letter had reached General Johnston there might have been a different story for the historians to tell. This daring exploit originated in the fertile brain of the young girl herself. She undertook its bold and hazardous evecution without help; and though it failed of success, it proclaimed her a brave and fearless girl, possessed of the spirit of the true heroine; and her name deserves to be embalmed for all time to come in the grateful affections of her beloved Southland.

OCONEE

Historic old Watkinsville. Watkinsville, the county-seat of Oconee, is one of the most historic towns of Georgia, reaching back over the dusty stretch of more than a hundred years to the heroic age of the

*Grandmother Stories, by Howard Meriwether Lovett, pp. 163-171.

pioneers. In 1801, by an Act of the Legislature, Clarke
County was formed out of a part of Jackson, on what was
then our western border, and named for the valiant Revolutionary leader, General Elijah Clarke; while the
county-seat of the new county was called Watkinsville,
in compliment to Hon. Robert Watkins, of Augusta, one
of the State's ablest lawyers. Thomas Booth was probably the earliest settler on the site of the future town,
but Dr. Harden soon followed him and built a handsome
home on what is still known as Harden's Hill, later the
property of Hon. B. E. Thrasher.

Bishop Haygood's One of the first lawyers to open an
Old Home. office at Watkinsville was Green B.
Haygood, Esq., whose son, Atticus G.
Haygood, a native of this town, was destined to become
a prince of preachers and one of the tall landmarks of
Southern Methodism. Bishop Haygood filled many arduous roles. As a minister of the Gospel he possessed
few equals. As an educator he stood at the very fore-
front. As a profound theologian he moulded the minds
of men. As a writer he wielded not only a trenchant,
but a fearless pen; and as a bishop of the church he
proved himself to be a man of God divinely called to a
great work. On account of some of his advanced views,
especially on the race problem, he did not escape criticism, but he lived to witness a radical change of sentiment on this line, and to inaugurate a new era in the
South. His sister, Laura, a noted educator, who devoted
the last years of her useful life to missionary work in
China, was likewise a native of Watkinsville.

Rev. John Calvin Johnson, a name which no one in
Watkinsville can mention except with honor, was for
years a commanding figure among the pioneers, a man
of great influence with the people and of great favor with
God. Walter Johnson, his son, was for years tax-col-
lector of the county, while his grandson, John Calvin, Jr.,

afterwards held the office of Ordinary. Oconee's earliest probate judge was Asa M. Jackson, a man greatly beloved, whose tenure of service covered a period of forty-seven years, one of the longest in the history of the State. His successors in office have been: James R. Lyle, B. E. Thrasher, H. A. Thomas, John Calvin Johnson, Jr., and A. H. Morton. The first court-house was a frame building, reared in 1806. It was afterwards replaced by a large structure of brick, covered with blue stucco and shaded by immense oaks. This fine old building was erected by John Birch, grandfather of the late Chancellor Walter B. Hill, of the University of Georgia.

Recollections of Judge Overby. Judge Basil H. Overby, one of the first advocates of temperance in Georgia, though not a resident of Watkinsville, was affiliated to some extent with the people of the town by ties of marriage. His first wife was a daughter of John and Sarah (Barton) Thrasher, and by reason of this fact he was always close to the people of Watkinsville and often a visitor here. There was not a finer character during his day in Georgia than Judge Overby: eloquent, magnetic, fearless, public-spirited. His daughter-in-law, Mrs. Earle Overby, perhaps the best loved woman in Watkinsville, still treasures among her keepsakes a little pamphlet which bears this title: "Basil Overby Union, Daughters of Temperance, No. 11." It is dated 1853; and, in view of the marvelous world-wide growth to which the great W. C. T. U. movement has attained, it is a matter of the most intense interest to scan the pages of this little pamphlet, in which the modest beginnings of a great modern reform are reflected in print. Mrs. Overby is a brilliantly cultured woman, a great lover of books; and such is the esteem in which she is held by every one in Watkinsville that a splendid library has been established, bearing her name; and this library is one of the glories of the little town.

Judge Overby's second wife was the youngest daughter of General Hugh A. Haralson, and a sister to Mrs. Logan E. Bleckley and Mrs. John B. Gordon. Though he died early in life, Judge Overby has left the impress of his genius upon the State. Nor does the man who espouses a weak cause, when a tremendous moral issue is at stake, deserve any less to be admired than the man who presides over a great tribunal of justice or leads an army to battle. His children by the first wife were: Barton, Nick, Earle, Mrs. James Middlebrooks, Mrs W. W. Price and Mrs. Robert Winship. There was only one child by his second marriage, a daughter Lizzie, who married Captain Charles W. Williams. The latter was given a General's commission at the outbreak of the Spanish-American war, but died of yellow fever in the Philippines. Basil O. Lenoir, a son of Mrs. James Middlebrooks by her first marriage, is today one of the most useful men in the government service, entrusted frequently with delicate and difficult commissions.

Pioneer Families of the Town. To mention by name only some of the other pioneer families of Watkinsville, the list includes: the Greshams, the Lees, the Applings, the Elders, the Thomases, the Ligons, the Billupses, the Paines, the Taneys, the Harrises, the Durhams and many others. In 1871, by an Act of the Legislature, Athens was made the county-seat of Clarke, a removal credited to Judge Emory Speer, even then a power in politics, though a young man in his twenties. Great dissatisfaction was aroused, especially in the territory around Watkinsville; and such was the pressure brought to bear upon the Legislature that, on February 25, 1875, a new county called Oconee was created out of Clarke, with Watkinsville for its county-seat. Since 1819 only two men have suffered the death penalty in Oconee, a record which attests the law-abiding character of its citizens. But there is little cause for astonishment. The ethical standard was set years ago when Micajah Bone, Esq., was presented to the Grand Jury for swearing and for taking his Maker's name in vain.

Graves of Revolutionary Soldiers. In the county cemeteries near Watkinsville the graves of four Revolutionary soldiers have been located. These are Josiah Elder,* David Thurman, Colquitt Freeman and John Freeman. Applications for markers have already been made by Mrs. Robert Smith, at Watkinsville.

OGLETHORPE

Historic Old Lexington. Much of Georgia's history, in ante-bellum days, was made by a group of statesmen whose homes are yet standing amid the historic shades of the little town of Lexington. Gilmer, Upson, Lumpkin, Cobb, Crawford—these are names which have made the annals of Georgia resplendent.

*Not David Elder, as stated in Vol. I.

But here they are found in the minute-books of church sessions, and in the records of town meetings, while the great men who modestly wore them were known chiefly as neighbors, whose crowning traits, in village eyes, were those of the country gentleman of the old school. On December 19, 1793, Oglethorpe was formed from a part of Wilkes, and under the provisions of this same Act Lexington was made the county-seat. The town was incorporated by an Act providing for its better regulation, on November 24, 1806, at which time the following town commissioners were named, to-wit.: Matthew Gage, George Phillips, John Gresham, Thomas W. Cobb and George Paschal.* The famous Meson Academy, at Lexington, is almost as old as the town itself. It was founded as the Academy of Oglethorpe County, but on November 27, 1807, it became Meson Academy, in honor of a wealthy townsman, Francis Meson, who bequeathed to the school a large estate, real and personal. At the same time the following board of trustees was chosen to govern the school under its new name: John Lumpkin, William Harris Crawford, Benjamin Baldwin, George Phillips, James Luckie, Obediah Jones and Thomas W. Cobb. The Presbyterian Church at Lexington is the oldest church in the Synod of Georgia. In the cemetery adjacent to this historic landmark sleep Governor George R. Gilmer and Hon. Stephen Upson, for each of whom a county has been named. Here lies also the founder of the church, Rev. John Newton, a prince of pioneer evangelists, and here rests Carlisle McKinley, a noted Georgia poet and a kinsman of the martyred President.

Recollections of General Oglethorpe. "It is an interesting fact in the history of this celebrated man that he lived to see the infant colony become a great and free State. Among the very earliest to call on John Adams, the first Ambassador of the United States to the Court of St. James, was Oglethorpe. He who had planted

---

*Clayton's Compendium, p. 307.

Georgia and nursed the royal colony in its feebleness, joined hands with him who had come to the British Court the representative of its national independence. Well might Edmund Burke tell him that he was the most extraordinary person of whom he had ever read; for he had founded the province of Georgia; had absolutely called it into existence, and had lived to see it severed from the empire which created it and become an independent State.

"The evening of his life was mild and pleasant. His bodily and mental vigor remained to the last; and, in the society of one of the most delightful literary circles of England, composed of Johnson, Goldsmith, Wharton, Burke, Burton, Mrs. Garrick, Mrs. More, and others, he passed in London, or at Cranham Hall, the quiet and peaceful hours of social life. Hannah More, whose praise is itself renown, thus graphically describes him in a letter to her sister: 'I have got a new admirer, and we flirt together prodigiously. It is the famous General Oglethorpe, perhaps the most remarkable man of his time. He is the foster brother of the Pretender, and much above ninety years old. The finest figure you ever saw. He frequently realizes my ideas of Nestor. His literature is great; his knowledge of the world extensive; and his faculties as bright as ever. He is one of the three persons mentioned by Pope still living: Lord Mansfield and Lord Marchmont are the other two. He was an intimate friend of Southern, the tragic poet, and all the wits of the time. He is perhaps the oldest man among the gentry now living; and he could have entertained me by repeating passages from Sir Eldered. He is quite a preux chevalier—heroic, romantic and full of the old gallantry.' ''*

The Lumpkin Family Record.   Among the earliest settlers of Oglethorpe were the Lumpkins. They came from Virginia, and, according to land-grants, there were quite a number of them, and they appear to have taken an active part in the Revolution. John Lumpkin was the father of the two distinguished Georgians: Governor Wilson Lumpkin and Chief Justice Joseph Henry Lumpkin.

Wilson Lumpkin was twice married. His first wife was Elizabeth Walker, who bore him seven children:

1.   Lucy, who married Middleton Pope; of which union was born Sarah, who married David C. Barrow, the father of Hon. Pope Barrow, former United States Senator from Georgia, and of Dr. David C. Barrow, Chancellor of the University of Georgia.

2.   Ann, who married Augustus Alden.

3.   Pleiades Orion, who married Margaret Wilkinson.

---

*Wm. Bacon Stevens, M. D., D. D., in History of Georgia, Vol. I, pp. 207-8, New York, 1847.

4. Wilson.

5. William.

6. Elizabeth, who married O. B. Whatley.

7. Samuel H.

Governor Lumpkin's second wife was Annis Hopkins, who bore him two children:

1. John C.

2. Martha, who married Thomas M. Compton. It was in honor of the Governor's youngest daughter that the Southern terminus of the Western and Atlantic Railroad was christened Marthasville. In 1847 the name of the village was changed to Atlanta.

Joseph Henry Lumpkin married Callender Grieve. She bore him five children:

1. Marion McHenry, who married General Thomas R. R. Cobb, of which union were born several daughters, one of whom married Augustus L. Hull, another Captain Henry Jackson, and the youngest Hon. Hoke Smith, Secretary of the Interior, Governor and United States Senator.

2. Joseph Troup, who married Margaret King.

3. Callie, who married Porter King, from which union came Hon. Porter King, former Mayor of Atlanta.

4. William Wilberforce, who married Louisa King, from which union came Colonel Edwin K., a prominent lawyer of Athens, and Hon. Joseph Henry, Associate Justice of the Supreme Court of Georgia.

5. Lucy, who married William Gerdine.

6. Edward P.

7. James M.

8. Charles M.

9. Miller G.

10. Robert C.

11. Frank, who married Kate Wilcox.

Hon. Samuel Lumpkin, late Associate Justice of the Supreme Court, was a nephew of Wilson and Joseph Henry Lumpkin. The late distinguished John H. Lumpkin, of Rome, jurist and Congressman, was also a kinsman.

Oglethorpe's Famous Quarries. Some of the finest granite in the State is quarried today on land which formerly belonged to the estate of Governor George R. Gilmer, near Lexington, but which is now owned by Judge Hamilton McWhorter, of Athens. The magnificent Georgia State monument in Chickamauga National Park was built of stone from these quarries; and there is not a memorial in the park more universally admired. Nor is this due so much to the artistic design of the monument as it is to the superior quality of the stone out of which this splendid shaft is fashioned.

· PAULDING

Van Wert. In 1832, Paulding County was organized out of a part of the Cherokee lands and named for the celebrated John Paulding, one of the captors of Major Andre. Under the provisions of this same Act, Van Wert was made the county-seat. This town, named for a companion of John Paulding, who aided the latter in making his famous capture, was incorporated by an Act approved December 27, 1838. It became an important center for the slate-mining industry in Georgia, and was made in 1866 a terminal point of the Cartersville and Van Wert Railroad, but with the rise of Rockmart, only half a mile distant, Van Wert began to decline, and is today only a suburb of the latter town.

Dallas. On December 20, 1851, an Act was approved taking from Paulding and Floyd Counties a large body of land, out of which to form the new County of Polk. In readjusting the border lines, Van Wert was left on the edge of the new county, making it necessary to choose a new county-site for Paulding. Accordingly, the Inferior Court judges were authorized to select a new site for public buildings, and out of this legislative enactment grew the present town of Dallas, named for Hon. George M. Dallas, of Pennsylvania, who was afterwards made Vice-President of the United States. The town was incorporated on February 8, 1854, with the following commissioners, to-wit.: John S. Poole, Garrett H. Spinks, James H. Ballinger, Hezekiah Harrison, and James S. Hackett. The Male and Female Academy was chartered in 1860.

PICKENS

Jasper. In 1853, Pickens County was organized from Cherokee and Gilmer, and, under the provisions of the same Act, Jasper was made the county-seat, named for Sergeant Jasper, while the county itself memorialized General Andrew Pickens, both Revolutionary patriots of South Carolina. Perhaps a large element of the county's population at this time was from the Palmetto State. The town was incorporated December 22, 1857, with the following-named commissioners, to-wit.: A. K.

Blackwell, John A. Lyon, Adin Keeter, L. W. Hall and George W. Harman.[1]

PIERCE

Blackshear. Blackshear, the county-seat of Pierce County, was incorporated as a town on December 16, 1859, and was named for General David Blackshear, of Georgia, a noted Indian fighter. The county itself, formed out of Appling and Ware, was named for President Franklin Pierce. On December 7, 1860, the old Blackshear Academy was chartered, with the following board of trustees: J. A. Harper, E. D. Hendry, D. R. Milton, C. S. Youmans, John W. Stephens, John T. Wilson, Benjamin Blitch, William Goettee, John M. Jenkins and James B. Strickland.[2] The present public-school system of Blackshear was established in 1893. Hon. W. G. Brantley, a former member of Congress, and Hon. J. Randall Walker, a newly elected member, are both natives of Pierce. This was also the home of Hon. John C. Nicholls.

PIKE

Zebulon. In 1822, Pike County was organized out of Monroe. Under the provisions of an Act, approved in the year following, the county-seat was located at a little village called Newnan, commissioners for which were named as follows: Samuel Mitchell, William Mitchell, William Myrick, Nicholas Johnson and Hugh F. Rose.[3] But Zebulon became the county-seat within a short while thereafter, and was incorporated as a town in 1825. Both the county and the county-seat were named for the famous explorer, General Zebulon M. Pike. With the establishment of the town, a school was started for boys, and on December 25, 1837, a charter was granted for the Zebulon Female Academy, the trustees of which

[1] Acts, 1857, p. 180.
[2] Acts, 1859, p. 134.
[3] Acts, 1823, p. 186.

were named as follows: Robert Walker, John Hall, Richard S. Walker, Jeptha V. George, Thomas B. Daniel and William Harris.* In 1852, a charter was granted for the Zebulon Branch Railroad, to connect either with Barnesville or with some convenient point on the Macon and Western Railroad.

Barnesville. Prior to the year 1820 Gideon Barnes, with his family, left his native State of Virginia and came to Georgia, bringing with him five or six head of stock and five slaves. Charles Wallace Graddick, his great-grandson, has in his possession the original deed to a lot of land, for which Gideon Barnes traded an Indian pony in full payment thereof. On this lot, near the western stage route, where the roads from Zebulon to Forsyth, Jackson to Thomaston, intersected he built a log cabin for a home, and one for a store, and the settlement was known as Barnes' Inn. One of the slaves could cook like ''de fo'ks in Virginny,'' and the fame of the inn went abroad in the land. The primitive house stood for many years and was enlarged from time to time. A shed to the front made a long veranda that boasted benches and a shelf the length of the house, on which were stationed, like sanitary sentinels, tin wash-pans, buckets and towels, proving that clean hands and a pure heart were prenatal with the plucky·little city that makes no false claims in her plea for civic justice. Here youths and maidens loitered on the Sabbath day, and John Alden and Priscilla lived again.

Willis Jay Milner, was the next settler recorded. In 1823 he made a trip to Jasper County, and brought his bride on horseback to his cabin in the woods. He built and sold seven houses in as many years in the vicinity of Barnes' Inn, and thus came into existence Barnesville, one of the proudest little cities in Georgia. Among those who laid the foundation were Jack Jenkins, Zack Fryer and Josiah Holmes. Later came Charlie Turner, Alvis Stafford, Dan Hightower and the Elder boys, Jack and Hub. The Elder boys were successful young merchants, and during the famine in Ireland they shipped a cargo of corn to the sufferers across the water. Soon church spires pointed heavenward, and two remarkable schools attracted families worth while. Dr. Holly and Dr. Blackburn were the first physicians. They were followed by Dr. Wright, Dr. McDowell and Dr. Perdue, who were pillars of faith in time of need. Dr. Lavender and Dr. Fogg were the dentists who did perfect work, with no promise of the painless impossible. After recovering from the shock of war the ambitious village set stakes for a full-fledged city, and is steadily pulling to them. The Murphys, Blalock, Frank Reeves, Robert Mitchell and many other families of sterling worth added merchants, farmers, manufacturers and

---

*Acts, 1837, p. 15.

professional men to the high-toned citizenship. Charles E. Lambdin founded
Gordon Institute and every March an appreciative people delight to honor
his memory with exercises of Founders' Day. And the buggy factories
have had much to do with the making of the town. Jackson G. Smith's two
sons and C. O. Summers were born to the genius of the business, and
within a few years the Franklin Company has made a marvelous record.
The only misfortune Barnesville feels, and to which she yields, is her
political geography, which nothing can remedy but the wisdom of granting
the new County of Lamar.

Authority: Mrs. J. W. Reeves, Barnesville, Ga.

POLK

Cedartown. Under an Act approved February 8, 1854,
the site of public buildings for the new
County of Polk was made permanent at a place called
Cedar Town. At the same time a charter of incorporation was granted, in which the following commissioners
were named, to-wit.: Augustus N. Verdery, Benjamin F.
Bigelow, Brooks M. Willingham, Jesse M. Wood and
Hezekiah Witcher.[1] But Cedartown was already an important village when Polk County was organized. On
December 19, 1834, the Cedar Town Academy was char-
tered, with Messrs. John Kerley, Jacob Scott, Larry
Witcher, John Witcher, Sr., and Ephraim Mabry as trus-
tees. As a community of cultured people, Cedartown
began to attract attention long before the Civil War;
and, on March 5, 1856, a somewhat ambitious local enter-
prise bore fruit in a charter for the Woodland Female
Academy. The trustees of this institution were: Edwin
Dyer, Edward D. Chisholm, Springer Gibson, Thomas
H. Sparks, William Newton, David S. Anderson, A. N.
Verdery, William A. Mercer, Abner Darden, Carter W.
Sparks, Joel H. Ferrell, Wilson O. B. Whatley, Alfred
F. King, Edward H. Richardson, William Peek, Lazarus
W. Battle and William E. West.[2] This list is important
at the present time, chiefly for the list of pioneer names

[1] Acts, 18k53-1854, p. 224.
[2] Acts, 1855-1856, p. 288.

which it still preserves. Cedartown has enjoyed a rapid growth of late years. It is the home of Hon. W. J. Harris, Director of the Federal Census; of Hon. G. R. Hutchins, a distinguished lawyer and legislator; and of other noted Georgians. In Volume I of this work will be found an extended list of former residents, to which number may be added Hon. Frederick L. Blackmon, a brilliant Alabama Congressman.

Rockmart.   One of the best-known towns of Georgia before the war was the old town of Van Wert, the original county-site of Paulding; but when the new county of Polk was created in 1851, out of a part of Paulding's territory, Van Wert was included in the section allotted to Polk. This necessitated a change in the seat of government from Van Wert to Dallas, the present county capital. Cedartown was made the county-seat for the new County of Polk, while Van Wert, stripped of her civic honors, was left near the eastern edge of the new county, with her proud spirit broken by her adverse fortunes. Van Wert began to decline; but with the development of the slate industry in this neighborhood, subsequent to the war, arose the modern town of Rockmart, less than a mile distant. On August 26, 1872, Rockmart was granted a charter of incorporation with Hon. C. T. Parker as Mayor, and with Messrs. W. Ferguson, Thomas Moon, T. G. Ingraham, W. H. Hines, and S. K. Hogue as Councilmen.[1] The name "Rockmart" indicates the chief industry of the town. This name was coined from the two component words "Rock" and "Mart." The quarries at this place are world-renowned. Today Van Wert is only a suburb of Rockmart.

PULASKI

Hartford.   The original county-seat of Pulaski County was Hartford, a town which long ago ceased to exist. Its charter bears date of December 10, 1811, at which time it was chartered with the following named commissioners, to-wit.: Thomas A. Hill, Solomon A. Hopkins, Elijah Wallace, William Lyon, and Henry Simmons.[2] The town was named for Nancy Hart, of Elbert, one of the most famous heroines of the Revolution. Only the barest fragments of this old town still survive. Pulaski County was formed in 1808 out of Laurens. One of the earliest settlers at Hartford was Dr. Joseph Reid.

---

[1] Acts, 1872, p. 244.
[2] Lamar's Digest, p. 936.

Hawkinsville. In 1837, the county-seat of Pulaski was removed to Hawkinsville, a prosperous town on the opposite side of the Ocmulgee River, after which the fortunes of Hartford began to decline. Hawkinsville was incorporated as a town on December 2, 1830, with the following residents of the town named as commissioners:: Robert N. Taylor, John Rawls, John McCall, Jacob Watson and David B. Halsted.* The Hawkinsville Academy was chartered in 1831, with most of the above-named residents as trustees. Surrounded by a rich agricultural section and connected with the outside world by railway and steamboat facilities, Hawkinsville is one of the most prosperous towns of the middle belt.

How the Name Originated. It is the general belief that the town of Hawkinsville was named for the distinguished Revolutionary soldier and friend of Washington, afterwards a United States Senator from North Carolina, and for sixteen years resident agent among the Creek Indians of Georgia: Colonel Benjamin Hawkins. But the late Judge J. H. Martin, of Hawkinsville, at one time State Commander of the United Confederate Veterans, held to an altogether different view. In a published letter on this subject, Judge Martin says:

"The general and popular opinion is that the town of Hawkinsville was named for General Hawkins, or old Fort Hawkins, but this is not true. Pulaski County was organized in 1808, and the town of Hawkinsville incorporated in 1830. The court-house was moved from Hartford to Hawkinsville in 1836. At the time the town was surveyed and laid off Mr. John Bozeman, father of Judge C. M. Bozeman, deceased, and grandfather of our present esteemed townsman, Colonel F. H. Bozeman, was running a hotel built of logs on the lot now known as the brick kiln lot and lying immediately south of and adjoining the road leading on to the public bridge across Ocmulgee River. A Jew, whose name was Levy, kept a little store on the north side of the road, the river being then crossed on a flat boat. Out in the country and near by lived a countryman named Hawkins, who bought a peck of salt from Levy, and as the measure was

*Acts, 1830, p. 314.

'short Hawkins went on to Levy, Hawkins declaring Levy had swindled him and Levy declaring the salt had settled down. When Hawkins attacked Levy, Levy went through the back window and ran across the road to the hotel and begged Mrs. John Bozeman to protect him against the assault of Hawkins. The town was named for this man Hawkins. The name first selected was Tarversville, for the Hon. Hartwell Tarver, of Twiggs County, but as there was a Tarversville in Twiggs County this name was dropped and Hawkinsville substituted.

"Judge C. M. Bozeman, then a boy, was present and with the party surveying and laying off the town. My information was obtained from Judge Bozeman. Col. F. H. Bozeman says that he has often heard his father narrate the facts. Judge P. T. McGriff and Judge Bozeman were intimate friends and doubtless he has heard Judge Bozeman speak of the matter. In order to perpetuate as far as I can the statements of Judge Bozeman, one the most reliable men the county ever had, this article is written.''

PUTNAM

Historic Old Eatonton. Eatonton, the county-seat of Putnam, was named for General William Eaton, an American soldier of fortune, whose brilliant exploits in Tripoli were the talk of the State when the bill creating Putnam County was introduced in the Legislature of Georgia. In the year 1805, General Eaton, at the head of a small force, numbering perhaps five hundred men, marched across the Lybian desert to effect the successful capture of Derne, the second largest city of Tripoli. The expedition was planned in the interest of the rightful Pasha. General Eaton held the town against three repeated assaults of the Arabs, but was finally obliged to relinquish it, on account of a treaty of peace concluded with the usurper by the United States Consul-General at Algiers, acting in agreement with Commodore Rogers, who commanded the American fleet.

Situated on a high ridge in the center of the county, Eatonton is 22 miles distant from Milledgeville, 22 from Greensboro, and 22 from Madison, and is on a branch line of the Central of Georgia running from Milledgeville to Covington. The town was laid off soon after the county was organized. On December 12, 1809, for the better regulation of local affairs, an Act was approved conferring plenary powers upon the following commissioners: Barnes Holloway, Lewis Kennon, John C. Mason, Henry Brown and William Wilkins.[1]

Two years later, on December 15, 1809, the famous Union Academy was chartered with the following board of trustees: Brice Gaither, Robert Iverson, Simeon Holt, Edward Lane and Barnes Holloway.[2] This was the school where the afterwards celebrated William H. Seward, of New York, taught the youth of Putnam County during his brief sojourn in Georgia, when quite a young man. It was located near the famous Turner plantation, some nine miles from Eatonton, and was burned to the ground soon after the war. On December 4, 1816, the old Eatonton Academy was chartered by the Legislature, at which time the following citizens were named as trustees: Christopher B. Strong, Thomas Hoxey, Coleman Pendleton, William Williams, John J. Smith, John C. Mason, Irby Hudson, William Wilkins and William E. Adams.[3]

Eatonton has been the home of some of the best people of Georgia, not a few of whom have been men of distinction. The hospitality of the town is famed throughout the South; and few communities have surpassed it in the graces of social life or in the charms of intellectual culture. The stately old homes of Eatonton, built on the classic models of ancient Greece and embowered in the luxuriant shade of forest oaks, are reminiscent of the best days of the old South. Here lived the Reids, the Wingfields, the Nisbets, the Terrells, the Lawsons, the Meriwethers, the DeJarnettes, the Lamars, the Holts, the Abercrombies, the Hudsons, the Branhams, the Adamses, the Dennises, the Hurts, the Cozarts, the

[1] Clayton's Compendium, p. 555.
[2] Clayton's Compendium, p. 581.
[3] Lamar's Digest, p. 10.

Trippes, the Shorters, the Turners, the Jenkinses, the Edmonsons, the Maddoxes, the Flournoys, the Hardemans, and scores of other aristocratic old families, whose names have long occupied a large place in the heraldry of Georgia.   The old colonial home of Colonel Sidney Reid is now owned by Mr. T. G. Greene, a wealthy citizen, who maintains it in a style worthy of its splendid historic traditions.   The Edmondson country-seat, once surrounded by its thousands of acres, is a few miles out from Eatonton, where a member of the family still owns a large tract of the original land.   Mr. John T. Dennis owns the old William Dennis home, which is just below the Edmondson place.

Eatonton was one of the early Georgia towns to organize a U. D. C. Chapter, with Mrs. Josesph S. Turner as president, and recently this chapter—the Dixie—has erected a handsome Confederate monument on the town square.   During the past year a D. A. R. chapter has been organized, with Mrs. Francis Hearn as regent and Miss Martha V. Edmondson as vice-regent.   It has been given the name of Samuel Reid, a distinguished former resident of Eatonton and a grandfather of Mrs. John M. Slaton, the wife of Georgia's present Governor. Perhaps the longest tenure of service on record in the office of Postmaster belongs to Mr. Sidney Prudden, a life-long resident of Eatonton, who held this office for fifty years.

The Old Cemetery.   In the Academy grove is the old cemetery of Eatonton, a sacred area of ground, in which some of the oldest inhabitants of the town sleep.   Most of the monuments are yellow with age, and from not a few of them, due to the destructive forces of time, the inscriptions have disappeared.   Here lies Irby Hudson, for years Speaker of the Georgia House of Representatives, and one of the earliest champions of co-operative effort in behalf of internal improvements.

Within this same enclosure sleep the Branhams, the Shorters, the Meriwethers, the Cozarts, the Coopers, the Trippes, and scores of others, whose names appear on the oldest records of the town.

Union Church. Until recent years, there stood in this same grove, sacred to the earliest memories of Eatonton, an ancient structure known as old Union Church. It was built in 1819, and, when first erected, was said to have been the finest in the State outside of Augusta and Savannah. The church belonged jointly to four denominations: Methodists, Baptists, Presbyterians and Disciples of Christ, each of whom, on successive Sabbaths, used it for divine worship. Whenever there was a fifth Sabbath in the month, it was used by the Masons. The church was abandoned by the Methodists in 1857, by the other denominations in 1897 and was finally torn down and removed. But it still lives in literature; for the silver tones of the old bell, which for so many years called the little hamlet to worship, has furnished the inspiration for an exquisite poem entitled: "The Old Church Bell," written by Colonel William H. Sparks. The opening stanza of the poem reads as follows:

> "Ring on, ring on, sweet Sabbath bell,
>   Thy mellow tones I love to hear.
> I was a boy when first they fell
>   In melody upon mine ear.
> In those dear days, long past and gone,
>   When sporting here in boyish glee
> The magic of thy Sabbath tone
>   Awoke emotions deep in me."

Colonel W. H. Sparks, the author of this poem, was a native of Putnam County; and, after a lapse of many years, the above lines were written on a return visit to his boyhood's friend, Mr. Edmond Reid. It was at Eatonton, in 1833, during a church convention, that a schism occurred in the Baptist ranks, and from this old church the celebrated Jesse Mercer, with other devout spirits, organized the Missionary Baptists.*

**Pioneer Settlers
of Putnam.**   Volume I.

To this list may be added: Thomas Edmondson, William Dennis, Joel Hurt, Wilson Bird, Andrew Jeter, Alexander Harrison, B. W. Clark, Rowell Ingram, Washington Rose, David Bledsoe, Nick Tompkins, Henry Branham, Allen Lawrence, Nathaniel Walker, Caleb Spivey, Isaiah Boswald and Alexander Reid.

Rising Star Lodge. One of the oldest Masonic lodges in Georgia is the Rising Star Lodge, at Eatonton, the origin of which dates back to the earliest days of the town. It commenced work under a dispensation bearing date of January 8, 1818, which was the third anniversary of Andrew Jackson's celebrated victory over the British at New Orleans. The charter was obtained on October 12, 1818, from Alexander McHunter, Grand Master, and Paul M. Thomason, Grand Secretary of the Grand Lodge of Georgia Masons, and the following named residents of Eatonton were the charter members:

George M. Walcott, Worshipful Master; Augustus Haywood, Senior Warden; Lloyd Harris, Junior Warden; Henry Granham, Secretary; Emmet Shackelford, Treasurer; Irby Hudson, Senior Deacon; William Evans, Junior Deacon; Isaac Holland, Tyler; John H. Broadnax and West Goodrich.

In 1827, the number of this lodge was changed from 33 to 4, which rank it still holds, making it one of the oldest in the State. The old Masonic Hall at Eatonton was erected in 1820. It has withstood the storms of almost a century of time, showing that the best of materials

---

*Miss Martha V. Edmondson, of Meda, Ga.

were used in its construction. The building is today owned by Mr. Champion, and is used as a storeroom.

Distinguished Res-   Volume I.
idents of Putnam.

Boyhood Haunts of Joel Chandler Harris, the South's **"Uncle Remus."** most noted man of letters, was born in 1849 in the town of Eatonton. His father, a farmer, died while the child was still an infant. The mother was very poor, and the boy was probably the least noticed youngster of the neighborhood. Some of his childhood playments still live in the old town of Eatonton. One of them, Charles A. Leonard, knew him when he was quite young. Says Mr. Leonard:

"Our playground was divided between Big Gully and Mr. McDade's livery stable. In the latter were fine horses, while the Gully was a good place in which to pay hide-and-seek. At the stable we sometimes had the privilege of riding the horses to the blacksmith's shop, and when the drovers came we were allowed to exercise them. Midway between Big Gully and McDade's lived an old free negro named Aunt Betsy Cuthbert, whose abilities in making potato biscuit, ginger cakes, and chicken pies could hardly be equalled.

"We entered the school taught by Miss Kate Davidson, where there was little play, except at recess; and it seemed then that school held from sup-up to sun-down. After a while we entered the male academy. It was not long before we made the acquaintance of one of the larger boys, Hut Adams, and when out of school we were boon companions, playing marbles, jumping holes and enjoying similar amusements. Whatever Hut did was right, even to foraging on Mr. Edmund Reid's watermelon patch. We organized what was known as the Gully Minstrels. Hut was manager, I was treasurer, and Joe was the clown, with a fiddle, which he couldn't play. But he would make a noise, which would bring down the house. The price of admission as ten pins.

"Hut, about this time, became the possessor of a shot-gun, in which Joe and I were as happy as he, and nearly every Saturday we would be off for the fields or woods, Joe's part and mine being to carry the game. Sometimes we would get a chance to shoot just once when the hunt was over. Besides his love for hunting, there was nothing which gave Joe more delight than to play pranks; and, since he was clever enough to get the best of us each time, he enjoyed it to the full limit."

But life was a very serious matter in those days. It was just at the beginning of the war, and few were the years which could be devoted to school. The next step in his life is best told in his own words. They are taken from an interview which he gave to one of the Atlanta newspapers a few years before he died. Says he:

"It so happened that I was in the post office at Eatonton, reading the Milledgeville papers, when the first number of *The Countryman* was deposited on the counter where the newspapers were kept. In reading it through, I came upon an advertisement wheih announced that the editor wanted a boy to learn the printer's trade. This was my opportunity, and I seized it with both hands. I wrote to the editor, whom I knew well, and the next time he came to town he sought me out, asked if I had written the letter with my own hand, and, in three words, the bargain was concluded.

"The paper on which I started out in life," said Mr. Harris, in after years, "was unlike any other one; it stands solitary and alone among newspapers. It was published nine miles from any post office, on the plantation of Mr. Joseph A. Turner. Over the roof of the printing office the squirrels scampered about and the blue jays brought acorns there to crack them. What some people call loneliness was to me a great blessing. I used to sit in the dusk and see the shadows of life's great problems flitting about me, and I then had time to think about them. So far as I learned it, the printer's trade was a liberal education; and Mr. Turner owned a large private library, full of the best books. It was specially rich in the various departments of English literature, and it would have been the most wonderful thing in the world if, with nothing to do but set a column or so of type each day, I had failed to take advantage of the library, with its perfect mine of treasures.

"Mr. Turner was a man of varied accomplishments. He was a lawyer, a scholar and a planter. He owned a large plantation, and he managed it successfully; he acquired a good law practice; and he was one of the most public-spirited men in middle Georgia. He was pronounced in his views on the questions of the day, an independent thinker, a good writer, and, best of all, so far as I was concerned, he took an abiding interest in my welfare, gave me good advice, directed my reading, and accorded me the full benefit of his wisdom and experience at every turn.

"For the rest, I managed to get along like any boy would. I was fond of setting type, and when my task was over I would hunt or fish or read. Then at night I used to go to the negro cabins and hear songs and stories. It was a great time for me."

It was in Mr. Turner's library that the future creator of Uncle Remus acquired the literary taste which was to add so much richness to his art in later years; among books like Shakespeare, Moore, Byron, Burns, Goldsmith, Grimm's Fairy Tales, the Letters of Junius, and scores of others. The raw material with which he was to build his stories in later years he found amongst the slaves. The character of Uncle Remus itself was composite. The original was, in most respects, an old negro named George Terrell, owned by Mr. Turner before the war. Until a few years ago, the little cabin in which George Terrell lived was still standing; it has since been torn down. His descendants are yet to be found in Eatonton, and one of his contemporaries, a type of his kind, so bent and crippled it is hard to tell whether he is man or beast, still hobbles about the town.

In the ancient days, Uncle George owned an old-fashioned Dutch oven, on which he made every Saturday the most wonderful ginger cakes. These and persimmon beer, which he brewed himself, he would sell to the children of planters for miles around. It was his custom to cook his own supper on this old oven; and at twilight, by the light of his kitchen fire, he used to tell his quaint stories to the Turner children, and at the same time to Joel Chandler Harris. Men now, who were boys then, still relate the joy they felt at listening to the story of the "Wonderful Tar Baby," as they sat in front of the old cabin, munching ginger cakes, while Uncle George was cooking supper on his Dutch oven.

Another prototype of the original Uncle Remus was Uncle Bob Capers, a negro owned by the well-known Capers' family, and hired by them as teamster to the cotton factory at Eatonton. Joel Harris, before he went to Turn-wold to set type for *The Countryman*, lived with his mother near the home of this old darkey, from whose lips came many of the tales which delighted the children of the neighborhood.

Although but a mere youth, Mr. Harris very early burst into print. He wrote many anonymous articles for *The Countryman*, but the first compositions to which he signed his name were brief paragraphs; and the first poem which appeared from him was in the issue of September 27, 1864, entitled: "Nelly White." He was then little more than fifteen years old.

But the Turner plantation was in the direct path of Sherman's "March to the Sea." General Slocum's staff enjoyed the hospitality of the place for several days, and when they marched on there was not much left. The youth now felt that it was time for him also to move on. The year 1868 found him in Savannah, on the editorial staff of the *Morning News*. His employer was William T. Thompson, the famous humorist; and his office boy, Frank L. Stanton, afterwards the famous poet, with whom he was long associated on the staff of the *Constitution*. He married Miss Essie La Rose, a lady of Canadian birth; and in 1876 the family refugeed to Atlanta to escape an epidemic; and here he became immortal.*

*Condensed from "Memories of Joel Chandler Harris," a work edited by Ivy L. Lee.

The Old Lamar Homestead. About eight or ten miles south of Eatonton is the old Lamar homestead. It was established in 1810 by John Lamar, a thrifty planter, and years afterwards became the property of Mr. Mark Johnson. The house still stands [1895] in good condition: a fine, old-fashion, two-story, frame building, constructed after the strong and enduring models of the period. Little River winds near by, and cultivated fields offer a wide prospect. Here, at the home of his grandfather, on September 17, 1825, was born the future statesman and jurist, Lucius Quintus Cincinnatus Lamar. To his latest days he retained a longing for the old place, and delighted to indulge in reminiscences of the old life when a child. There extended along the entire front of the mansion a wide gallery; and the whitewashed walls of the airy rooms were hung with pictures. One of these, symbolizing a nightmare, was the work of "Uncle Mirabeau." It portrayed a beautiful woman asleep upon a sofa, and, thrust through the window above her, a great shadowy horse's head. An immense front yard was filled with grand oaks and poplars. To the east lay rolling lands. In the rear, a widespread plain shelved gently down to the river, which gave to the owner of the farm the sobriquet of "Little River John."

The house was a relay; and down the far-reaching red lane which stretched away like a long orange ribbon, the stage coach daily passed with rattle and halloo and call of bugle, emptying its bevies of bustling and hungry, but genial, travelers for the midday meal.[1]

With the old couple lived a bachelor brother, Zachariah[2]—a self-taught man—who, like many others, in old plantation times, gave himself up to the ideal world of literatuer and history, without any further purpose than the enjoyment of its fairyland; and over all his surroundings was cast the glamour of the realm of letters, in which he lived. When he led in family prayer, he did not think it inapt to thank God for heroic examples of Roman or English or American history, for the march of science, or for exemption from the crimes and miseries of the less favored lands into which his geographical studies had led him last. So when son after son was born to the head of the house this bookish enthusiast claimed the privilege of naming his infant nephews after his favorite of the moment, and the amiable and doubtless amused parents consented. Thus Lucius Quintus Cincinnatus, Mirabeau Bonaparte, Jefferson Jackson, Thomas Ran-

[1] Edward Mayes in Lucius Q. C. Lamar: His Life, Times and Speeches.
[2] This was none other than Colonel Zachariah Lamar, of Milledgeville, the father of Mrs. General Howell Cobb, of Athens. Colonel Lamar married somewhat late in life. He was a man of rare culture and of ample means, and spent his younger days in the Lamar home at Eatonton.

dolph and Lavoisier Legrand [a grandchild] indicated how his interest shifted from history to politics, and from politics to chemistry.*

At this old homstead, buried in a quiet garden by the side of his daughter, Evalina, lies John Lamar—father of the second President of the Republic of Texas and grandfather of the great jurist, cabinet officer and legislator, whose mature years were identified with the State of Mississippi. He must have been a man of rare mold to have been the progenitor of such an offspring. The grave is well kept, and is marked by a slab of plain marble, with the following inscription, written by Mirabeau:

"In memory of JOHN LAMAR, who died August 3, 1833, aged sixty-four years. He was a man of unblemished honor, of pure and exalted benevolence, whose conduct through life was regulated by the strictest principles of probity, truth and justice; thus leaving behind him, as the best legacy to his children, a noble example of consistent virtue. In his domestic relations he was greatly blessed, receiving from every member of a large family unremitting demonstrations of respect, love, and obedience."

Genealogy of the Lamars. There is a tradition amongst the Lamars of Georgia that the family was planted in Maryland by four brothers, who fled from France in the celebrated exodus consequent upon the revocation of the edict of Nantes, in 1686, but the records show that emigrants of the same name were living in Maryland much earlier; and the probabilities are that the first Lamars came to America to escape the oppression of Protestants under the administration of Cardinal Richelieu.

John Lamar was the earliest member of the family to plant the escutcheon in Georgia, settling on Beach Island, in the Savannah River. His grandson, John Lamar, lived first in Warren County, but in 1810 moved into Putnam and established the famous Lamar homestead, some eight or ten miles to the south of Eatonton.

---

*William Preston Johnston, in the Farmer's World of February 5, 1879.

He married his cousin, Rebecca Lamar, and became the head of one of the most noted of Georgia households.

Two of his sons achieved eminent distinction. The elder L. Q. C. Lamar, Sr., succeeded to the Superior Court Bench before he was thirty-five years of age, and was almost immediately styled "the great Judge Lamar." He also revised Clayton's "Georgia Justice," a rare book, and compiled the Georgia Reports from 1810 to 1820. Yet he died before reaching the full maturity of his powers. The younger, Mirabeau B. Lamar, became the second president of the Republic of Texas. He began life as an editor and was successively a poet, a soldier, a statesman and a diplomat. He published a volume of poetry entitled: Verse Memorials.

There were two other sons, Thomas Randolph and Jefferson Jackson, besides five daughters, one of whom, Loretta Lamar, married Colonel Absalom H. Chappell, member of Congress, jurist and author of "Georgia Miscellanies." To them were born J. Harris Chappell, the first president of the Georgia Normal and Industrial College, at Milledgeville; Thomas J. Chappell, who served in both House and Senate of the State Legislature; and Lucius H. Chappell, ex-Mayor of Columbus, besides other children, including a daughter, Mrs. Toomer.

L. Q. C. Lamar, Sr., married Sarah, daughter of Dr. Thompson Bird, an eminent physician of Milledgeville, and granddaughter of Colonel Micajah Williamson, a comrade-in-arms of General Elijah Clarke.

Eight children were born of this union, five of whom reached adult years.

L. Q. C. Lamar, Jr., the eldest, married Virginia, daughter of Judge A. B. Longstreet, president of Emory College and author of "Georgia Scenes." He located in Oxford, Miss., for the practice of law, became a member of Congress, a commissioner of the Confederate government to Europe, a Senator of the United States, a member of President Cleveland's first Cabinet, with the portfolio of Secretary of the Department of Interior, and, last but not least, an Associate Justice of the Supreme Court of the United States—one of the most eminent Americans of his day and generation.

The other children of L. Q. C. Lamar, Sr., were Dr. Thompson B. Lamar, who commanded the Fifth Florida regiment during the Civil War, and surrendered his heroic life, in battle, near Petersburg, Va., in 1864; Jefferson M. Lamar, another Confederate martyr, killed at Crampton's Gap in Maryland; Susan, who married a Mr. Wiggins, and Mary Ann, who first married James C. Longstreet, Esq., and afterwards John B. Ross, of Macon.

William Bailey Lamar, an eminent lawyer and jurist, who represented Florida in Congress for several terms, is a son of Dr. Thompson B. Lamar. Judge Lamar now resides in Washington, D. C. Lucius M. Lamar, who served in both branches of the State Legislature, achieved distinction on the field of battle, and died while United States marshal for the Southern District of Georgia, was a son of Jefferson M. Lamar.

———

But the honors of the family are not yet exhausted. The achievements of individual members in other branches are not less distinguished.

Henry G. Lamar was an eminent jurist and statesman, who represented Georgia for several terms in Congress. He was also a popular candidate for Governor before the convention which nominated Joseph E. Brown, in 1857. His daughter Victoria became the first wife of Judge Osborne A. Lochrane, Chief Justice of the Supreme Court of Georgia. Another daughter married Hon. Augustus O. Bacon, afterwards United States Senator.

Dr. James S. Lamar was an eminent scholar and divine, who wrote "The Organon of Scripture, or the Inductive Method of Biblical Interpretation." He married Mary Rucker, of Elbert County, Ga., and of this union was born Hon. Joseph Rucker Lamar, who served for several years on the Supreme Bench of Georgia, and who, though a Democrat in politics, was in 1910 appointed by President Taft to the Supreme Bench of the United States, a tribute of the highest character to his professional attainments. In 1914 he was appointed by President Wilson as representative from this country to meet with representatives from Argentina, Brazil and Chili in a conference, the object of which was to accomplish by mediation a pacification of Mexico.

Colonel Zachariah Lamar, of Milledgeville, was a distinguished man of affairs. His son, John Basil Lamar, wrote "The Blacksmith of the Mountain Pass," among a number of other stories. He was killed at the battle of Crampton's Gap, in Maryland, while serving on the staff of his brother-in-law, General Howell Cobb, of Athens. Mary Ann, daughter of Colonel Zachariah Lamar, married General Howell Cobb, and from this union sprang Major Lamar Cobb, for years secretary of the board of trustees of the University of Georgia; Judge Howell Cobb, long judge of the City Court of Athens; Judge John A. Cobb, of Americus, Ordinary of Sumter County; Judge Andrew J. Cobb, formerly an occupant of the Supreme Bench of Georgia; Mrs. Alex. S. Erwin, and Mrs. Tinsley W. Rucker.

Basil Lamar was a soldier of the Revolution and a planter. Two of his sons, Peter and Ezekiel, became distinguished. For years, Colonel Peter Lamar was a dominant figure in politics. He lived in Lincoln County and married Sarah Cobb Benning, a granddaughter of Colonel Thomas Cobb, of Columbia. His son, Lafayette Lamar, was a prominent lawyer, who organized a company at the outbreak of the war, and died at Warrenton, Va., in 1861.

Prudence, one of the daughters of Basil Lamar, married a Winn, and became the grandmother of two distin-

guished Georgians: Richard F. Lyon, who served on
the Supreme Bench of the State, and Jabez Lamar
Monroe Curry, diplomat, statesman, author and divine.
Dr. Curry was United States Minister to Spain and trus-
tee for the Peabody and Slater funds. The State of
Alabama has placed his statue in the nation's Hall of
Fame, in Washington, D. C.

Gazaway B. Lamar, an early Congressman from
Georgia; Colonel C. A. L. Lamar, one of the joint
owners of the slave ship "Wanderer," who lost his life
near the close of the war at Columbus; Rebecca Lamar,
the famous heroine of the Pulaski, a vessel lost at sea,
off the coast of Hatteras, in 1836; Colonel Albert R.
Lamar, who was the secretary of the Secession Convention and editor for years of the *Macon Telegraph*—a man
of brilliant gifts; Joseph B. Lamar, who removed to
California, and after representing Mendocino County in
the Legislature was elevated to the Superior Court
Bench; Rev. Andrew J. Lamar, of Nashville, Tenn., a
great-grandson of Governor James Jackson; Hon. Warren Grice, the State's present attorney-general. These
and scores of others who have risen to equally high distinction belong to the Lamars of Georgia.

QUITMAN

Georgetown. Georgetown was made the county-seat of
Quitman when the county itself was first
organized from Randolph and Stewart, in 1858, and
named for Governor John A. Quitman, of Mississippi.
But the town itself was not incorporated until December 9, 1859, when the following commissioners were entrusted with its local affairs: D. Morris, E. C. Ellington,
L. C. A. Warren, N. T. Christian and John E. Riordan.*
Georgetown was named for its well-known predecessor in
the District of Columbia.

*Acts, 1859, p. 156.

RABUN

Clayton. Rabun County was organized in 1819 out of Cherokee lands, then recently acquired by treaty; but it was not until December 13, 1823, that a county-seat was chosen. Clayton was at this time made the permanent site of public buildings and given a charter of incorporation with the following board of commissioners: Benjamin Odell, Edly Powell, John Dillard, Edward Coffee and Solomon Beck.[1] The town was named for Judge Augustin S. Clayton, of Athens, and the county for Governor William Rabun. On December 25, 1821, the Rabun County Academy was chartered, with the following trustees: Chesley McKenzie, Andrew Miller and James Dillard.[2] Two of Georgia's most distinguished sons were former residents of Rabun: Chief Justice Logan E. Bleckley and Dr. H. V. M. Miller, a former United States Senator.

————

"The Demosthenes of the Mountains." Though a native of the State of South Carolina, it was among the mountain ranges of Rabun that the boyhood days of this distinguished physician and orator were spent. On the political hustings, it is doubtful if either Toombs or Stephens surpassed Dr. Miller. Before he was thirty years of age, his rare powers of eloquence caused him to be dubbed "the Demosthenes of the Mountains," and without relinquishing his interest in the great profession of medicine he arose by sheer force of genius to a seat in the United States Senate. As a man of broad culture, familiar with both the ancient and the modern classics, his superior has not appeared in the public life of Georgia It is to be regretted that he has left behind so little in the way of literary memorials. On account of the issues of Reconstruction, he was debarred from the upper house of Congress until the closing days of the session for which he was elected; and there was consequently no opportunity for the great orator to distinguish himself in this high forum. Perhaps the only fragment of his eloquence in print is the impromptu effort which he delivered in his old age over the bier of Alexander H. Stephens.

---

[1] Acts, 1823, p. 197.
[2] Acts, 1821, p. 125.

Hooper Alexander, Esq., a kinsman, has recently prepared for publication
an excellent sketch of Dr. Miller, in which he records this estimate of him.
Says he: "Dr. Miller was the wisest man I ever knew. His judgment of
men was keen, his foresight of events marvelous. His education was self-
acquired, his learning prodigious, his memory astounding. In medicine he
was pre-eminently successful, but believed little in drugs. I have heard him
say that it was doubtful if medicine had not done as much harm as good.
When the merit of some remedy was argued, about which he was skeptical,
and cases were cited of cures wrought, he would say: 'The Hottentots have.
proven by experiment that a loud noise will remove an eclipse of the sun.'
In opinion he was broadly tolerant, possessed of the most implicit faith in
God. In church membership he was a Methodist, and adhered closely to
his church organization, though he always claimed that the present form
of church government by bishops was unscriptural and opposed to Wesley's
teaching. It was also a favorite theme with him to tease his brethren of
the Methodist pulpit by quoting an entry from Wesley's Journal about
having baptized somebody in Savannah 'by immersion, according to the
Word of God and the practice of early Christians.' It was another of his
favorite themes to insist that the Presbyterian Shorter Catechism was the
only proper religious system on which to bring up the young. From all
which things I am led to conclude that he believed the Word of God a
bigger and broader thing than any church. In personal character Dr. Miller
was superb. There was no vestige of anything mean or little in his
nature. He was completely and essentially a gentleman. And the one
thing in this world which he hated was a lie." The Miller Rifles, a company organized in Rome at the outbreak of the Civil War, was named for
Dr. Miller. It was incorporated in the famous Eighth Georgia Regiment, of
which the gallant Bartow was in command. The Doctor himself went to
the front as the surgeon of this regiment. He was in charge of the field
hospital when Bartow fell at Manassas; and the handsome oil painting of
this brave officer, on the walls of the Carnegie Library in Atlanta, was
the gift of Dr. Miller.

RANDOLPH

Cuthbert. In 1828, Randolph County was formed out of
Lee and named for the celebrated John Ran-
Randolph, of Virginia. Some twenty years before this
time, Mr. Randolph had been honored in a like manner,
but in protest against some of his unpopular views the
name of the first County of Randolph was changed to
Jasper. But the great Virginian was now again riding
the crest of the wave. Lumpkin was the original county-

site of Randolph, a town named for Governor Wilson
Lumpkin; but when Stewart County was created in 1831
Lumpkin became the county-seat of the new county, while
Cuthbert was made the county-seat of Randolph. The
town was named for one of the Cuthberts, presumably
Hon. John A. Cuthbert. Its charter of incorporation was
granted in 1834. As an educational center, Cuthbert has
long enjoyed a wide repute. On December 25, 1837, the
old Randolph Academy was incorporated with the following board of trustees: David Holman, Oliver H.
Griffith, Alexander Hendry, Thomas Jenkins and William
Taylor.[1] Andrew Female College, one of the best-known
educational plants in Georgia, was chartered on January
15, 1854, with the following board of trustees: Andrew
L. O'Brien, Henry L. Taylor, Sidney C. DuBose, Otis
P. Bell and William H. Brooks.[2] Cuthbert is today a
wide-awake commercial town, with good banks, prosperous business establishments, fine schools and up-to-date
public utilities.

The Cuthberts.   Volume I, Pages 877-878.

**Andrew Fe-
male College.**   Volume I, Pages 878-879.

Shellman. On the site of the present town of Shellman there formerly
stood a little village called Notchway. To this village in
the year 1837 William F. West brought his wife and child, the latter an
infant of only six months. This child, now Mrs. Eliza Ellis, is today
Shellman's oldest resident. The first dwelling was a small cabin built by
Wash Stanton just west of where the Central of Georgia depot now stands,
and when this little structure was enlarged to meet the needs of a depot
in 1858, the settlement, in honor of its first station agent, John Ward, took
a new name, and became Ward's Station The line was then known as
the Southwest Georgia Railroad. In 1870 the town's population was only
seven souls. Today it is estimated at 1,200. In 1871 the first public building was erected, with a school-room on the lower floor and a Masonic hall

---

[1] Acts, 1837, p. 4.
[2] Acts, 1853-1854, p. 116.

on the upper. But in 1888 Colonel R. F. Crittenden and Captain H. A. Crittenden bought the negro church on the east side of town for school purposes, and when these quarters were outgrown the town raised $800 for remodeling the structure, which served until 1898, when the present property was acquired. Mr. W. F. Shellman, of Savannah, gave $100 of the above sum, and in honor of this gentleman the school became Shellman Institute, and the town itself Shellman. The Methodist Episcopal Church was organized in Masonic Hall in 1876, with Rev. John West as pastor. In 1880 this denomination built its first house of worship, a structure remodeled in 1890. There was a strong Baptist community centered at Rehobeth, just north of the town, as early as 1845, but the first church of this faith was not built at Shellman until 1886, and finally in 1904 the old structure was superceded by the present handsome edifice of brick. Some time in the early seventies Mr. J. B. Payne began what has been successively a saw mill, a grist mill and an oil mill. The present structure was built in 1901 by Mr. W. J. Oliver. As business increased the demand for banking facilities increased likewise, and in response to these demands came the Shellman Banking Company in 1890 and the First National Bank in 1900. Shellman's business activities have been mainly dependent upon its surrounding agricultural lands. In consequence of this fact, three guano mixing plants are supported. The first white child born in Shellman was Virginia Phelps, whose parents, Thomas Jay and Annie Phelps, were the first couple to be married in the town. The first public school teacher was Rev. R. A. J. Powell. The first member of the General Assembly from Shellman was Colonel R. F. Crittenden, 1871-1872 and 1882-1883. His successors in office from this town have been: I. A. Martin, 1894-1895, and J. N. Watts, 1911-1912. Shellman's first State Senator was Captain H. A. Crittenden, 1907-1908, followed by J. N. Watts, 1913-1914.*

RICHMOND

Fort Augusta: 1736.   Volume I, pp. 113-117.

Treaties Made Several important treaties with the Geor-
at Augusta. gia Indians were made at Augusta. The
first of these was negotiated by the royal
Governor, Sir James Wright, on June 1, 1773. In satisfaction of certain debts due the traders, a large tract
of land was ceded at this time by the Indians, including

---

*The data for this sketch was supplied by Mrs. Eilza Ellis and Capt. H. A. Crittenden, and compiled by Mrs. John Gordon Black, historian, assisted by Mrs. J. N. Watts, regent, Noble Wimberly Jones Chapter, D. A. R.

both the Creeks and the Cherokees, whose dominion adjoined in this part of the State. Out of the lands acquired under this treaty was subsequently formed the large County of Wilkes, originally a sort of frontier kingdom, which became the parent of a numerous offspring. On the part of the Crown, two commissioners signed the compact: Sir James Wright, baronet, captain-general and commander-in-chief of the Province of Georgia; and Hon. John Stewart, Esq., his Majesty's sole agent for and superintendent of Indian affairs in the southern district of North America. On the part of the redskins, it was witnessed by chiefs, head-men and warriors of both tribes.

During the struggle for independence both the Creeks and the Cherokees sided with the British. In consequence, there was a forfeiture of land to the State at the close of hostilities. On May 31, 1783, a treaty was made at Augusta with the Cherokee Indians, whereby a tract of land was acquired in the upper part of the State, out of which the County of Franklin was afterwards formed. Governor Lyman Hall, General John Twiggs, Colonel Elijah Clarke, Colonel Benjamin Few, Hon. Edward Telfair and General Samuel Elbert, witnessed the compact, as commissioners appointed by the Legislature of Georgia. There was no further trouble with the Cherokees for a number of years. On November 1, 1783, a treaty was made at Augusta with the Creek Indians, whereby a tract of land was acquired in the lower part of the State, out of which the county of Washington was subsequently erected. The commissioners, on the part of the State, were: General John Twiggs, Colonel Elijah Clarke, Hon. Edward Telfair, Hon. Andrew Burns and Hon. William Glascock. But the Creeks, under the bold leadership of the noted Alexander McGillivray, repudiated the agreement; and out of this bone of contention grew the Oconee War. The settlers in the new County of Washington were constantly harrassed by hostile incursions and depredations. Subsequent treaties were made at Galphinton, at Hopewell, and at Shoulder Bone, but to little purpose. McGillivray was an artful dodger. At last the newly organized Government of the United States took the matter in hand. Under the personal eye of Washington, the treaty of New York was negotiated in 1790 by Secretary Knox, of the Department of War. But still further difficulties ensued, and it was not until 1796 that a final treaty of friendship and good-will was concluded at Coleraine, ratifying the treaty of New York and bringing the Oconee War to an end.

Historic Old St. Paul's. Volume I, pp. 117-122.

Meadow Garden. Volume I, pp. 122-125.

Sand Bar Ferry: Four miles southeast of Augusta lies
A Famous one of the most famous duelling
Duelling Ground. grounds in America: Sand Bar Ferry.
It occupies both banks of the Savannah River at a point which in past years, before the old ferry gave place to the present modern steel bridge, was well adapted by reason of its peculiar environment to the purposes of a field of honor. Here, in the days gone by, personal combats without number have been fought under the Code Duello, Georgians resorting to the Carolina side and Carolinians betaking themselves to the Georgia side, each to adjust their differences according to the only mode of arbitrament which then prevailed among gentlemen. Happily this method of redress has long since passed. For more than a generation not a drop of blood has been spilled on the old duelling ground, and its hostile meetings are today recalled only by the gray-beards whose memories reach back to the old regime, when the duelling pistol dominated the public life of the South. But we are fortunate in finding for our

readers an article which describes this noted resort of the duellist as it appeared forty years ago. It was written by Colonel James T. Bacon, editor of the *Edgefield Chronicle,* who often visited the spot; and, without reproducing the article in full, its salient paragraphs are as follows:

"There is not a spot of greater interest in any part of our country than the secluded glade known in the history of the South, of South Carolina and Georgia, especially, as Sand Bar Ferry. A commonplace name enough, but attached to a glade or fairy ring set apart for the conventional duelling ground when the Code Duello was the first resort of gentlemen in settling personal difficulties.

"In some respects it would seem that this spot were fashioned for some such purpose, so quiet, so perfectly secluded, so easy of access and at the same time so out of the way that a most bloody duel could be fought to a finish before authority from any point could arrive to interfere.

"This historic duelling arena lies three miles southeast of the city of Augusta, over what was once a wheel-scarred and rugged road, heavy in places with fine sand, and again marshy where it dipped into a bit of low land or struggled through a tongue of undrained swamp. The road lies along pleasant farm lands, and plume-like elms meet in leafy arches overhead. Now it runs deep into the heart of the dim swamp, now close along the margin of the rushing, muddy, turbulent Savannah, bordered by thousands of the trailing water willow.

"This duelling ground lies on either side of the river. With the belligerents of the Carolina side, who wished to settle differences with leaden arguments, the fairy ring beneath the hoary moss-draped trees on the Georgia side was chosen as the scene of action. With those already in trouble on the latter side, the clean, firm sands of the wide river bank were preferred. On the Georgia side the famous spot might well be mistaken for the artificial work of man, fashioned with a view to the purpose which it served. The ground is as level as a dancing floor; a soft carpet of moss covers it, through which the vivid fruit of the partridge vine or ground ivy glows like the crimson stain of blood. All around tall cedars, feathery elms and towering gums, interspersed with a few black-boled pines, draped with long streamers of the funeral gray moss, shade the traveler from the too-ardent rays of the semi-tropical sun.

"On the left the river runs, broadening out into wide shallows, the sand bars shoaling out from either bank, until at low water, or during the summer months, persons standing on the further end of the bar could clasp hands across the bed of the then placid river. On the right a thick hedge of flowering juniper shuts off the view of a most prosaic object, a railroad trestle poised high, and spanning the river from bank to bank.

On the Carolina side white chalk cliffs loom up, cut by a road that winds up and up until lost to sight over the high brow of the white bare hills.''

———

''It is a singularly quiet place, this famous Southern duelling ground; the natural face of which seems never to change. No sound breaks the stillness, but the occasional flutter of the winged inhabitant of the bushes, the lap of the water over the sand bars, or the grinding wheels of an occasional vehicle that has just been ferried over.

''Many of the lagoons have never been explored, and just how many there are cannot, seemingly, be ascertained. Dense canebrakes, absolutely as impregnable as a stone wall, shutting out daylight in their vicinity, cut off communication except where the tilled lands skirt them, or where a narrow and tortuous passage leads into the Savannah. It is a curious phenomenon that, however high the river rises, or however low it sinks, the waters in the lagoon remain the same—weird, ghostly, mysterious, a freak of nature in her most sombre mood—spots of eternal mourning, may-hap for bygone transgressions—blots upon the fair face of nature beneath the ardent Southern sun.

———

''But let us climb up to the top of the high white cliffs of Beech Island, on the South Carolina side, whence spreads out the level duelling ground. The September moon is rising, and the silence is intense; almost palpable or tangible, as it were. The reddening gum leaves flutter in the lazy breeze—flurrying lightly over the moss with a sound that might be made by the ghostly footsteps of the things unseen. Even the bird voices seem far away and hushed; the moonlight filters through the whispering pines that complain in far-off hushed undertones; and standing there one feels as though civilization and the fret of life and the strife of man had been left many miles behind, and that the land in which it is always afternoon—if not black night—were well at hand.

''Beech Island is a fair and blessed land, but there hangs a dark and bloody fringe along some of her borders.''

———

Poets' Monument: On April 28, 1913, a handsome gran-
Mrs. Cole's Gift. ite memorial to four renowned Georgia poets: Sidney Lanier, Father
Ryan, James Ryder Randall and Paul H. Hayne, was
unveiled with impressive ceremonies, in the presence of
a vast throng. The monument was a gift to the city

from Mrs. E. W. Cole, of Nashville, Tenn., formerly a resident of Augusta, and the speech of presentation, an exquisite literary gem, was made by Chancellor James H. Kirkland, of Vanderbilt University. This attractive memorial stands on Greene Street, a thoroughfare noted for its numerous artistic charms. The structure consists of four ornamental pillars, resting upon a massive base and supporting a handsomely carved roof. Enclosed within is a square of granite, on the four sides of which are these inscriptions:

SIDNEY LANIER.
1842-1880.
"The Catholic man who hath mightily won
God out of knowledge and good out of infinite pain
And sight out of blindness and purity out of a stain."

FATHER RYAN.
1842-1886.
"To the higher shrine of love divine
My lowly feet have trod.
I want no fame, no other name
Than this—a priest of God."

JAMES R. RANDALL.
1839-1908.
"Better the fire upon the roll,
Better the blade, the shot, the bowl,
Than crucifixion of the soul,
Maryland, my Maryland."

PAUL HAYNE.
1830-1886.
"Yet would I rather in the outward state
Of song's immortal temple lay me down,
A beggar, basking by that radiant gate,
Than bend beneath the haughtiest empire's crown."

Surrounding the monument there are four marble seats. With the single exception of Lanier, these gifted men of genius were for a number of years associated with the intellectual and social life of Augusta, while two of them—Hayne and Randall—lie buried in the city cemetery in a section known as "Poets' Row." We quote from a local newspaper* the following brief account of the exercises of unveiling:

Long before the hour of 5 o'clock the crowd began to gather around the monument, and soon the 400 seats placed on the green were filled, as was the driveway around, with automobiles.

When Mrs. Cole and the members of her party arrived they were seated near the stand, upon which the Mayor and members of Council were seated and also the clergy of the city, and those who were to take part in the program.

When the hour of 5 struck more than a thousand people were present and the audience was a most representative one, citizens of all ages being present from the eldest citizen to babies in the arms of their nurses.

The first thing on the program was the unveiling of the monument, by little Cornelia White, the daughter of Mr. and Mrs. W. B. White, and Master Whiteford Cole, Jr., son of Mr. and Mrs. Whiteford Cole, of Nashville.

Hon. Linwood Hayne, who presided over the exercises, then introduced the Rev. S. B. Wiggins, pastor of St. John's Methodist Church, who made the opening prayer. A chorus of about seventy school children, trained by Miss Harris, then sang sweetly, "Maryland, My Maryland," with an accompaniment of harp and violin.

Chancellor Kirkland, of Vanderbilt University, was introduced by Mr. Hayne, and he presented the monument, on behalf of Mrs. Cole, to the city of Augusta in a most eloquent speech, which was listened to with the closest attention and received with the heartiest applause. Chancellor Kirkland paid a beautiful and fitting tribute to the four poets, in whose memory the monument is erected, and in glowing terms mentioned their separate claim to fame and their loyalty to the Southland, in whose honor their most inspired songs were sung.

Chancellor Kirkland was followed by the Rev. M. Ashby Jones, who accepted the monument in behalf of the city. Dr. Jones always rises to an occasion as few can, and his beautiful, inspiring and uplifting speech of acceptance and appreciation was expressed with his customary felicity of expression and eloquent earnestness.

Dr. Jones spoke beautifully of the inspiration this monument would be to the young men and women of the city; of its perpetual appeal to them to demand the best and to seek the highest ideals. He closed by saying: "I accept, in behalf of all Augusta, this beautiful expression of your love for this city, and thank you that you have helped and honored us, for this day and for the days that are to come."

*The Augusta Chronicle, issue of Tuesday, April 29, 1913.

Following Dr. Jones, Mr. William H. Hayne delivered an original ode, written in honor of the occasion, that was a gem of poetic thought and charming expression. One of Father Ryan's beautiful poems, put to music by Miss Harris, was then sung by the chorus to a familiar air. The services were concluded with a short prayer and benediction uttered by Father Kane, of St. Patrick's Church.

At the conclusion of the exercises Mrs. Cole was surrounded by countless old friends in the city, many of whom had not had the pleasure of meeting her personally since they were young folks together. The shadows of evening were falling before the crowd finally dispersed.

Barrett Plaza: The Walsh Monument. Directly in front of the Union Station, on Barrett Plaza, facing the city of Augusta, whose busiest section lies between the plaza and the river stands a handsome statue in bronze of one of the most beloved of Augustans: United States Senator Patrick Walsh. Coming to Augusta from his boyhood home in Ireland, he became in the course of time editor and owner of the *Augusta Chronicle,* one of the most powerful individual factors in the development of his adopted town and one of the most commanding figures in the political life of Georgia. Before reaching the end of his days—a period all too short—he wore by executive appointment the toga of the American Senate, succeeding in this high forum the lamented Alfred H. Colquitt. With impressive ceremonies, on June 20, 1913, occurred the formal exercises of unveiling. Two distinguished Georgia editors, Hon. Clark Howell, of Atlanta, and Hon. Pleasant A. Stovall, of Savannah, both warm and intimate personal friends of the deceased, delivered the principal addresses. We quote the following account of the exercises from a newspaper report:*

There were probably 3,000 people gathered on Barrett Plaza at 6:15 o'clock when the heroic bronze statue of the late Senator Patrick Walsh, mounted on a mammoth marble pedestal, was presented to the city and accepted by Mayor L. C. Hayne from the Walsh Memorial Association.

---

*From the Augusta correspondent of the Atlanta Constitution, in issue of June 21, 1913.

The address of the occasion by Hon. Clark Howell, of Atlanta, and Hon. Pleasant A. Stovall, of Savannah, both of whom knew Mr. Walsh intimately, were sympathetic and held the rapt attention of the big crowd.

Grandnieces of Mr. Walsh, Misses Catherine Smith and Marie Walsh, pulled the cords which loosened the veil from the statue. A commodious stand was erected on the north side of the monument, on which were seated the members of Mr. Walsh's family, the speakers of the day, Mayor L. C. Hayne, of Augusta; members of the city council and other city officials and a number of Mr. Walsh's closest personal friends, who were extended special invitations to occupy seats upon the stand.

Secret orders of which Mr. Walsh was a member attended the exercises in a body. These orders were the Ancient Order of Hibernians, the Knights of Columbus and the Elks. The cadet body of the Academy of the Sacred Heart also attended the ceremonies en masse.

Following the introductory music, the invocation by Rev. P. H. Mc-Mahon, of Washington, Ga.. a close friend of the late Senator, and the unveiling, the bronze figure was presented to this city by John J. Cohen, president of the Walsh Memorial Association, existence of which dates from the day of Mr. Walsh's funeral in March, 1899, Mr. Stovall and Mr. Howell delivered their addresses, following in the order named. The acceptance speech was delivered by Edward B. Hook, who spoke for Mayor Hayne.

The monument is 8 feet in height, placed on a pedestal of practically the same height of white marble, on the adverse side being engraved a laurel wreath. Above and arching over the wreath is engraved a fitting sentiment. On the reverse side are engraved facts relative to Mr. Walsh, the date of his birth, death and others. Cost of the erection is stated to be about $10,000.

This descriptive account of the monument is taken from a local newspaper:*

The statue is placed facing North. The features brought out true to life, the broad brow, the determined jaws, eyes of the same calm, benign and steady gaze of the Senator of life, the hair, side whiskers and goatee appearing just as in the latter years of his life. The figure shows him wearing a long buttoned frock coat, with the right hand thrust into the bosom of his coat and the left hand hanging by his side, holding a scroll typifying the editor and the lawmaker. The weight of the figure is upon the right foot, while the left is placed slightly forward. The general attitude is that of the speaker.

The pedestal is circular and about five feet in height. Carved in relief on the obverse side is an olive wreath, inside of which are the dates "1840" and "1899." "Patrick Walsh" is carved in bold characters in relief directly above the wreath. On the reverse side appears this inscription, the lines being engraved below each other in the respective order: "Editor of

_____

*Augusta Chronicle, issue of June 21, 1913.

The Augusta Chronicle, Mayor of the City of Augusta. Member of the Georgia Legislature. U. S. Senator. A Patriotic Citizen. A Loyal Friend. A Lover of Humanity. Erected by His Fellow Citizens.''

The base of the pedestal is a square block of marble, measuring six feet on the side, placed on a concrete foundation. The foundation has been covered with soil and grass planted, which is now growing luxuriously.

Major Archibald Butt: A Hero of the Titanic. On board the ill-fated Titanic, which struck an iceberg in mid-ocean, on the evening of April 15, 1912, was a gallant son of Augusta—Major Archibald Butt. At the time of his death Major Butt was one of the best-known men in American public life, having served as chief of the President's military staff, under two national administrations, and for eight years no one ever attended the brilliant social functions at the White House without being impressed by the erect and graceful figure of the handsome officer. The disaster in which he lost his life was the greatest marine tragedy of modern times—an ocean holocaust, in which over 1,500 souls perished. The Titanic was the greatest vessel afloat. She was making her maiden voyage from Liverpool to New York; and some of the most eminent men of the world were on board. The unwritten law of the sea—"women and children first"—was rigidly enforced; but the innate chivalry of Archibald Butt made it a needless one, so far as it concerned himself. He was not among the number saved. Only the meagerest details of the colossal tragedy reached Washington after days of anxious waiting; and when hope for the brave officer's rescue was finally abandoned, Mr. Taft's comment, made with moisture in his eyes, was this: "He died like a soldier and a gentleman." The President afterwards came to Augusta for the express purpose of paying a heart-felt memorial tribute to his beloved chief of staff.

Archibald Willingham Butt came of an old Augusta family, and on the banks of the Savannah River at this place he was born on September 26, 1866. Here he grew

up, attending the local schools; but, losing his father
when quite a lad, it was mainly by his mother's hand
that the youth was reared. The latter was a Miss Boggs.
It was the ardent wish of the boy's mother to see her
son in the pulpit, and with the hope of making a minister
of Archibald she sent him to Sewanee. But the lad's
ambition was to enter the army—the life which fasci-
nated him most was the soldier's. As a sort of compromise, on leaving college, he drifted into journalism, but
without relinquishing his dream. In the course of time,
he became the Washington correspondent of the *Atlanta
Journal,* and by a most singular coincidence one of his
associates on the paper at this time was the brilliant
Jacques Futrelle, who was destined to share his watery
grave in the mid-Atlantic.

Major Butt's nearest surviving relatives are his two
brothers, Edward H. Butt, of Liverpool, and Lewis Ford
Butt, of Augusta. John D. Butt, a third brother, met
death in a railway accident a number of years ago.
About the same time he also lost an only sister. When
on a visit to Atlanta, some few months before the tragic
disaster, Major Butt incidentally remarked: "My ambition is to die in such a manner as to reflect credit upon
the name I bear." He may not have recalled this wish
amid the waters of the Wild Atlantic, on the night when
his brave soul went out; but his ambition was fully realized. The citizens of Augusta have planned a memorial
bridge in his honor to span the Augusta Canal and to
keep his name in green remembrance amid the scenes of
his youth. At Sewanee, Tenn., a memorial tablet has
already been unveiled in the halls of his alma mater,
and a handsome monument has also been erected by his
comrades of the army in Arlington National Cemetery,
Washington, D. C.

Archibald Butt: On April 15, 1914, the handsome me-
Memorial Bridge. morial bridge erected by the citizens
of Augusta in honor of Major Archi-
bald Butt was dedicated in the presence of a vast throng

of people, numbering perhaps 5,000. It spans the Augusta Canal at the intersection of Fifteenth and Greene Streets, near the site of Major Butt's old home. Ex-President of the United States Hon. William H. Taft delivered the principal address of the occasion, in addition to which the Masonic rites constituted a most impressive feature of the exercises. From a detailed report of this impressive ceremonial the following account is taken:*

Simple but impressive exercises attended the dedication here today of the Butt memorial bridge, erected as a tribute to the memory of the late Major Archibald Willingham Butt, aide to former Presidents Taft and Roosevelt, who perished in the Titanic diaster on April 14, 1912.

Former President Taft, a delegation of Masons from the Temple Noyes Lodge, of Washington, of which Major Butt was a member; local Masons and members of the Butt Memorial Association, participated in the services, which were held on the handsome new bridge spanning the canal at Fifteenth and Greene Streets.

Arrangements had been completed for the dedication to be held yesterday afternoon, but on account of rain it was necessary to postpone the ceremonies until today.

The formal dedication of the bridge was preceded by the laying of a cornerstone with ritualistic ceremonies by the Masons'.

Former President Taft, the first speaker, spoke feelingly of his former aide as a "Southerner through and through."

"I like to think of him," said Mr. Taft, "as the best type of the new South, with its full flavor of the chivalrous and patriotic sentiment of the old South, strengthened by the trials of war and its consequences, mellowed by success in its struggles against obstacles after the war, and turned into the deepest loyalty to the flag by the Spanish-American war, and a sense of a full share in the power and responsibility of the government of the country.

"He was a Southerner through and through. He had the tradition of the South deep-seated in his nature. But he had the self-control that enabled him with entire self-respect to pass unnoticed expressions of prejudice or criticism toward what he held dear, made thoughtlessly, or upon the assumption that he was not a Southern man."

The bridge proper is constructed of concrete. At each of the two approaches are two massive lions, carved from limestone, one bearing a bronze shield engraved with the coat of arms of the United State, another with the Georgia coat of arms of the Butt family and the fourth the Temple-Noyes Lodge coat of arms. Four tall columns surmounted by bronze eagles

*Augusta correspondent of the Atlanta Constitution, in issue of April 15, 1914.

rise from the four corners of the central arch of the structure. In the center is a bronze bas-relief of Major Butt. A bronze tablet bears the following insciption, which was written by former President Taft:

"In honor of Archibald Willingham Butt.
"Born in Augusta, Ga., September 26, 1865.
"Graduated University of the South, 1888.
"Major in United States Army, trusted aide-de-camp to two Presidents.
"Major Butt went to his death on the steamer Titanic after the rescue of the women and children from that ill-fated vessel, April 14, 1912.
"In memory of his noble and lovable qualities as a man.
"His courage and high sense of duty as a soldier.
"His loyalty and efficiency as a public servant.
"His fellow citizens of Augusta dedicate this bridge."

A beautiful and unexpected feature of the day's exercises was the presentation to the citizens of Augusta of another handsome memorial of the late Major Butt, through Mr. LeRoy Herron, worshipful master of the Washington Masonic Lodge, in the form of a life-size copper reproduction of Major Butt.

At 3 o'clock yesterday afternoon, immediately after its delivery, the handsome statue was set up in the lobby of the Bon Air Hotel, where the entire party and many other visitors for the memorial exercises are stopping, and was admired by thousands of people. This morning it was removed to a location near the tablets on the bridge, and was conspicuously a part of today's exercises.

———

Dennis Cahill: An Irish Hero. On the banks of the Augusta Canal, near the Butt Memorial Bridge, there stands a pyramid of rough stones, erected to commemorate an act of heroism, no less grand in its humble way than the one which glorified the last moments of Major Butt, on board the ill-fated Titanic. Inscribed upon this pile of rock is the following epitaph:

Dennis Cahill by a deed of self-sacrifice such as all humanity claims and counts among the jewels hallowed this spot and rendered his name worthy of such lasting memory as these rugged stones and this simple tablet can secure, for here he gave his life in a vain attempt to save from drowning a child having no claim for his sacrifice save humanity and helplessness, July 29, 1910. Born Parish of Castlemagner, County Cork, Ireland, June, 1861.

———

Colonel Samuel Hammond: Revolutionary Patriot.   One of the most illustrious soldiers of Georgia in the first war for independence was Colonel Samuel Hammond, whose conspicuous part in the siege of Augusta has embalmed him in the lasting gratiture of this metropolis and in the love of all Georgians. Colonel Hammond, at the beginning of the last century, represented this State in Congress, after which he became by appointment of President Jefferson the first Territorial Governor of Missouri. His last years were spent at Varello, his country-seat, on the south Carolina side of the Savannah River, near Augusta. To recall the patriotic services of Colonel Hammond there stands on Greene Street a handsome memorial to this distinguished soldier and civilian. It consists of a solid block of rough-hewn granite, surmounted by a bronze bust of Colonel Hammond, in the uniform of a Continental officer. The inscription on the monument reads as follows:

SAMUEL HAMMOND. Born in Richmond County, Va., Sept., 1757. Died at Varello, near Augusta, Sept. 1842.

Captain of Minute Men at Great Kanawha, 1774.
Long Bridge, Norfolk, 1775.
Aid to Gen. Hand at Pittsburg, 1778.
Colonel of Cavalry under Washington, 1779.

With Gen. Greene in every important engagement through Virginia, the Carolinas and Georgia. On the front line at Eutaw, Cowpens and King's Mountain. At the Siege of Charleston, Savannah, and Augusta. Member of Congress from Georgia, 1802. Appointed by President Jefferson in 1805 to the Command of Upper Louisiana. First Territorial Governor of Missouri. Secretary of State in South Carolina, 1831. He gave sixty years of public service to the cause of America. This memorial in his honor placed by the Augusta Chapter, Daughters of the American Revolution, as the filial tribute of his grandson, Hugh Vernon Washington.

On March 28, 1913, in the presence of a large gathering of representative Augustans, the handsome memorial to Colonel Hammond was unveiled with ceremonies befitting the occasion. Rev. M. Ashby Jones, one of the most eloquent men of the State, delivered the principal address. We quote from a local newspaper the following brief account of the exercises:

At the hour of 5 o'clock a crowd of interested spectators gathered and the presentation ceremonies began upon the arrival of Mrs. Ellen Washington Bellamy, of Macon, who is one of the donors of the monument, the other donor being her brother, the late Hugh Vernon Washington, of Macon, a grandson of Colonel Hammond.

Judge William F. Eve presided and introduced the Rev. M. Ashby Jones, who was to present the monument to the city of Augusta in behalf of the donors.

Dr. Jones was never more eloquent than on this occasion.

Hon. Linwood C. Hayne, mayor of Augusta, was next introduced. Said he:

"To that generous-hearted kinswoman of Macon who, by this act, has demonstrated that the present is not an age entirely of utilitarianism, good people everywhere, with one acclaim, will give applause and reverence. From her own purse, she has made this generous donation to the history of the republic, and perpetuated for all time to come the memory of Sam Hammond—warrior, hero and patriot; and for this contribution which not only extols the patriotism of her valiant grandsire, but reflects the highest credit on her patriotic liberality, Augusta makes her most grateful acknowledgement, and pledges herself to guard with the highest loyalty and fidelity this sacred spot dedicated alike to the heroism of Samuel Hammond, the defender of Augusta, and to the loyal affection of the patriotic donor of this most striking testimonial to the heroism of the days of the revolution, when the land was young."

Mrs. Bellamy then spoke a few words of appreciation, explaining that it was the wish of her brother, the late Hugh Vernon Washington, of Macon, that this monument be erected in Augusta, whose history their illustrious ancestor helped to make, and that the monument was his gift, as well as hers. Besides the many friends present, the representatives of the Hammond family, were Mrs. Bellamy, of Macon, and Mrs. McKie, a granddaughter of Colonel Hammond, who now lives in North Augusta, and her son, Mr. McKie.

The Seizure of the Arsenal. Perhaps the most dramatic event in the history of Augusta was the seizure of the United States Arsenal at Summerville, on the eve of the Civil War. It followed almost directly upon the adjournment of the famous Secession Convention, which carried the State of Georgia out of the Union. As told by Proferror Joseph T. Derry, the story of this bold exploit, which was undertaken successfully by the volunteer troops of Augusta, is as follows:

"The arsenal, situated near Augusta, consisting of a group of buildings on the summits of salubrious sand hills, contained a battery of artillery, 20,000 stand of muskets, and a large quantity of munitions, guarded by a company of United States' trooops, under command of Captain Arnold Elzey, of Maryland. The occupation of this arsenal was necessary. The sentiment favoring the seizure was increased by the arrival, on January 10th, of an ordnance detachment, which had been ejected from the arsenal at Charleston. On January 23, Governor Brown, accompanied by his aide-de-camp, Hon. Henry R. Jackson, who had experienced military life as a colonel of a Georgia regiment in Mexico, and Hon. William Phillips, visited Captain Elzey and made a verbal request that he withdraw his command from the State. Upon his refusal to do so, Colonel Alfred Cumming, of the Augusta battalion of militia, was ordered to put his force in readiness for action, to support the Governor's demand. . . . At the same time, some eight hundred volunteers of the city were put under arms, and others came in from the country. The Augusta volunteers engaged in the capture of the arsenal consisted of the following companies: Oglethorpe Infantry, Clinch Rifles, Irish Volunteers, Montgomery Guards, two companies of minute men, one of which became the Walker Light Infantry, Washington Artillery, and Richmond Hussars. The ranks of these companies had been filled by young men eager to serve, and they averaged at this time one hundred men each. They were splendidly equipped and thoroughly drilled. In addition to these there were about two hundred mounted men from Burke County and a company of infantry from Edgefield district, S. C. Brigadier-General Harris was in chief command, aided by Brigadier-General Charles J. Williams, of Columbus, and Lieutenant-Colonel Alfred Cumming was in immediate command of the armed force, consisting of the Augusta Battalion, companies A and B of the minute men, and the militia. No hostile demonstration was to be made until the 24th, and it was then happily obviated by the action of Captain Elzey. In the conference which fixed the terms of the withdrawal, the Governor, was accompanied by Generals Harris and Williams, Colonel W. H. T. Walker and his aides, Colonels Jackson and Phillips, all of whom joined the Governor in assurances of esteem for Captain Elzey, together with a desire that the unhappy difficulties which had arisen might be adjusted without hostilities. Walker, a comrade of Elzey in the Federal service, seized the latter's hand and assured him that he had done all that could be required of a brave man. Elzey, overcome by the situation which presaged the breaking up of the old army and the deadly conflict of former friends, could only reply by throwing his arm around his comrade silently, while tears filled the eyes of those who witnessed the scene. Walker became a Major-General in the Confederat Army, was distinguishd for his reckless daring, and finally gave his life in the great batttle on the hills around Atlanta. Elzey also entered the Confederate service as soon as circumstances permitted, and was one of the most distinguished representatives of Maryland in the Army of Northern Virginia. His cool and intrepid action on the field of First Manassas won for him the rank of brigadier-general and the title of "the Blucher of the day" from the lips of President Davis. Under Jackson he achieved additional renown and was promoted to the rank of major-general, but wounds received before Richmond in 1862 deprived the cause of his further active service in the field. After a salute of thirty-three guns, the Stars and Stripes fluttered down the garrison staff.''

Origin of the Children of the Confederacy: Augusta the Birthplace.

This patriotic society originated at the Third Annual Convention of the Georgia Division of the U. D. C., which met at Augusta, on October 14, 1897. The following story contains an authoritative account of how it arose: "In the afternoon of the 14th, Miss Bunnie Love, of Atlanta, read a strong paper advocating the organizing of children's chapters of Daughters of the Confederacy, but Mrs. McDowell Wolff had before this organized a band of children in Savannah and called them Children of the Confederacy. A committee was appointed by Mrs. Eve, the president, as follows: Miss Bunnie Love, chairman; Mrs. W. F. Eve, Miss Rosa Woodberry, Mrs. R. E. Park, Mrs. B. O. Miller.

"This committee was given authority to draw up the plans for organizing these chapters as branches of the main division.

"The committee was afterwards changed to the following personnel: Mrs. Charles Rice, chairman; Mrs. McDowell Wolff, Mrs. William M. Nixon, Miss Susie Gerdine, Miss Sallie Jones, Miss Bunnie Love.

"The report of this committee was read at the Rome Convention October, 1898, and adopted, after which a letter was read from Mrs. McDowell Wolff, on the importance of teaching the children true history. Mrs. Charles Rice, of Atlanta, offered the following resolution:

"'Whereas, Mrs. E. P. McDowell Wolff originated the Order of Children of the Confederacy in Georgia, be it

"'Resolved, That in recognition of this act of patriotism she be known as the Founder of the order, and her name be thus inscribed upon documents wherein the names of the officers appear.' This resolution was unanimously adopted.''

--- --- ---

Georgia's Oldest Bank. Georgia's oldest bank was chartered by the Legislature, on December 6, 1810, and was styled the "Bank of Augusta." Its capital stock was $300,000, divided into shares of $100 each; and of this sum $50,000 was reserved for the State of Georgia, subject to the approval of the law-making authorities. In the event the State became a stockholder in the bank, it was stipulated that the Governor, Treasurer, and Comptroller-General, should be entitled, at each succeeding election, to name two members of the board of directors. As given in the bank's charter, the original board of directors consisted of the following stockholders: Thomas Cumming, its first president; John Howard, Richard C. Tubman, John McKinne, James Gardner, Hugh Nesbit, David Reid, John Moore, John Campbell, John Willson, Anderson Watkins, John Carmichael, and Ferdinand Phinzy. The charter was signed by Gov. David B. Mitchell, as Governor, and by the presiding officers of the two law-making bodies: Hon. Jared Irwin, President of the Senate, and Hon. Benjamin Whitaker, Speaker of the House of Representatives.*

--- --- ---

Whitney's Cotton Gin. ''Whitney's plan of getting his gins into use was unpopular among the farmers. He would either buy the cotton himself, or charge one-third of it for ginning. He did not at first sell his gins. The farmers generally thought Whitney was trying to keep the use of his gins too much within his own control. Much began to be said about the 'gin monopoly.' All of this was unfortunate for Whitney, because, although others claimed it, the honor of having invented the cotton gin clearly belongs to Eli Whitney. . . . After the gin was invented, Whitney established his machines in various places in Georgia for the purpose of buying and ginning cotton. One of these was near Augusta, about two miles south of the city. The dam is still seen which held the water to furnish the power. Whitney's machines were at first called cotton engines, but this name was soon contracted into cotton gins.''*

ROCKDALE

Conyers. In 1870, Rockdale County was organized from Newton and Henry, with Conyers as the county-seat; but Conyers was at this time a town of some importance, on the line of the Georgia Railroad. Its charter of incorporation was granted on February 16, 1854, with the following-named commissioners, to-wit.: A. C. Hulsey, Daniel Zachery, Stephen Mayfield, A. R. Richardson and James J. Poole.[1] In Volume I of this work will be found an extended sketch of the town of Conyers.

SCHLEY

Ellaville. In December 22, 1857, an Act was approved creating the new County of Schley out of lands formerly including in Sumter and Marion and the judges of the Inferior Court were authorized to choose a site for public buildings. Ellaville, the county-seat, was incorporated as a town on November 23, 1859, at which time the following pioneer residents were named as commissioners: J. Stephens, H. Davis, R. Burton, H. L. French and Mr. Strange.[2] The town was reincorporated in 1883.

SCREVEN

Jacksonboro. Volume I.

Sylvania. In 1793, Screven County was formed out of Burke and Effingham, with the old town of Jacksonboro as the county-seat, and for nearly fifty years there was no change in the seat of government. But

---

[1] Acts, 1853-1854, p. 259.
[2] Acts, 1859, p. 154.

in 1847 a new town rose in the wilderness. On a fifty-acre tract of land purchased from Charles Church and Azeriah Ennis at this time was founded the present town of Sylvania. The commissioners who made this purchase and who located the new county-seat were: John R. Kittles, Willis Young, William Lovett, John Roberts, Moses N. McCall, Solomon Zeigler and John A. Gross.[1] Sylvania was incorporated as a town on February 20, 1854, with the following commissioners: Dominick J. Dillon, Winsley Hobbey, Daniel E. Roberts, William Williams and Charles Church.[2] With solid banks, wide-awake business establishments, good schools and attractive homes, Sylvania is today one of the most progressive towns of Georgia. Hon. George R. Black, a former member of Congress, lived at Sylvania. His father, Hon. Edward J. Black, was also at one time a resident of Screven.

Historic Traditions:
A Tragedy of
the Swamp.   Pages 474-478.

Recollections of   Major Stephen F. Miller has sketched
Edward J. Black.   for us the following portrait of Edward J. Black, a distinguished resident of Screven. Says he:

"Mr. Black was for six years a member of Congress—from 1839 to 1845. He made several speeches, which gave him a high rank in debate and for elegant scholarship. His diction partook of the purity of Wilde, with much of his elevation of sentiment; and it also possessed some of the causticity of Randolph when impaling an adversary. The comparison is not intended to be perfect, but merely to denote qualities more or less developed. Mr. Black was unquestionably a man of genius. His nature was impulsive, his organization acute. He felt a passion for excellence and took proper models in history for his guide. Enjoying wealth and position, he lived to see much of the world. His imagination was too prolific and his taste too severely disciplined to be content with the attainable;

---

[1] Acts, 1847, p. 75.
[2] Acts, 1853-1854, p. 270.

and he looked for something which is not permitted to man—the sublime
in both the intellect and the affections. Like other men of genius, he
possessed a constitutional malady which preyed upon his spirits. He was
often sad, perhaps murmured unwisely, demanding why he was smitten.
But . . . in the dying hour he saw that all was right; the gloom
vanished and the darkness of this world gave way to the light of another.
The author was acquainted with Mr. Black. They spent an evening together, more than twenty years ago [1855] at the mansion of a well-known
citizen [General Blackshear, of Laurens]. He was fully what he claimed
to be, both in the vivacity of his wit and in the art of making others
happy by his conversation. He was then in the zenith of his manhood,
apparently free from disease, and bade fair to survive the humble invalid
who now dictates this greateful offering to his memory.' "[1]

SPALDING

Griffin. Griffin, the county-seat of Spalding, was named
for General L. L. Griffin, the first president of
the old Monroe Railroad, now a part of the Central of
Georgia. It was granted a charter of incorporation in
1843, at which time it was one of the flourishing railway
towns of Pike. Later on, in 1851, when Spalding County
was organized out of Pike and Henry, Griffin became the
county-seat of Spalding. But, to go back a few years, the
old Griffin Male and Female Academy was chartered on
December 4, 1841, with the following named trustees,
to-wit.: Pitt S. Milner, William M. Leak, James L.
Long, James Butler and Wesley Leak.[2] From a list of
trustees named in the charter of Marshall College, an
institution founded in 1853, the names of some of the
prominent citizens of Griffin for the decade just before
the Civil War have been obtained. These trustees are
named as follows: Jesse H. Campbell, Augustus L.
Brodus, Alfred Buckner, J. Q. A. Alford, Parker Eason,
Hendley Varner, Andrew W. Walker, James H. Stark,
all of the Flint River Baptist Association; William R.
Phillips, representing the City Council of Griffin; Ware-
ham W. Woodruff, from the Presbyterian Church; William Freeman, from the Methodist Church; William West-

---

[1] Stephen F. Miller, in Bench and Bar of Georgia, Vol. 1.
[2] Acts, 1841, p. 6.

moreland, from the Christian Church; Charles H. Johnson, from the Odd Fellows, and Jason Burr, from the Methodists.* During this same year, the old Griffin Collegiate Seminary was rechartered as the Griffin Female College and entered upon what promised to be a career of great usefulness; but, like the ambitious enterprise launched by the Baptists, it went down before the oncoming storm of the Civil War. The first monument erected in Georgia to the Confederate dead stands in Griffin, a town whose homes were converted into hospitals for the sick and wounded, whose devoted women became ministering angels at the couches of the suffering, and whose loyalty to a Lost Cause, manifested in a thousand tender ways, has made its very name forever fragrant with the sweetest of Confederate memories. Some of the State's most noted men have lived in Griffin, but since a list of these residents has been given in Volume I of this work, it is needless to repeat them here. Today Griffin is one of the chief manufacturing towns of Georgia, a city whose pulsing arteries of commerce bespeak the vigorous young blood of a new Dixie; but one needs only to enter the stately old homes of Griffin to find that in everything worth while the ideals of a gentler time are still preserved.

Some of Griffin's Attractive Homes. Griffin is a city of beautiful homes. Some of these were built in the spacious days of the old regime, and have come down to the present time rich in the lore of a former generation. Judge Robert T. Daniel's home is one of the fine old landmarks. It was built by his grandfather, General E. P. Daniel, in the early days of Griffin. The old Bailey home, built by Colonel David J. Bailey, a former member of Congress, is today owned by his daughter, Mrs. C. H. Tebeault, of New Orleans. The old Female College, built in the eighteen-fifties, and used as a hospital during the Civil War, one of the oldest structures in Griffin, is now owned and occupied by Mr. Thomas R. Mills. The old Reid house, built by Judge John B. Reid, was subsequently occupied for a number of years by Hon. James C. Freeman, a former member of Congress. Today it is owned and occupied

---

*Acts, 1853-1854, p. 127.

by Mr. Thomas Nall. The Chapman house, built by one of Griffin's wealthy pioneer citizens, is today the home of Captain W. J. Kincaid, perhaps the most important factor in the modern industrial life of Griffin, a man who built the first cotton mills and whose vast energies have been devoted without reserve to the growth of his adopted town. The Stark house, built by Judge William A. Stark, is now owned and occupied by Mr. Robert F. Strickland. The home of Mrs. John B. Mills was formerly owned by Mr. Obadiah Gibson, afterwards by Mrs. Emily Lewis, and now by her granddaughter, the present occupant. The Henry P. Hill home is today occupied by his widow, who here resides with her daughter, Mrs. Fleming G. Bailey. The Ben Milner place is now the property of Mr. Henry Walker, of Monroe. The handsome old Sims house became in after years the home of Mr. Joseph D. Boyd. Mary Villa, built by Colonel L. T. Doyal, is now owned by Dr. M. F. Carson. Other beautiful homes in and around Griffin are owned by the following substantial citizens: Judge J. J. Flint, Mr. Seaton Grantland, Mr. James M. Brawner, Hon. W. E. H. Searcy, Jr., Hon. W. E. H. Searcy, Sr., Judge T. E. Patterson, Mr. Douglas Boyd, Mr. Junius Gresham, Mr. W. H. Powell, Dr. J. C. Owen, Judge Lloyd Cleveland, Mr. B. R. Blakely, Mr. W. H. Newton, Mr. C. E. Newton, Mr. J. P. Nichols, Mrs. Edward C. Smith, Mrs. B. C. Faircloth, Mr. W. B. Matthews, Mr. B. B. Brown, Mr. David Johnson, Mr. Lee Manley and others. Overshadowed by ancestral oaks, not a few of the fine old mansions of Griffin picture to the mind's eye what Mrs. Heamans has portrayed in one of her most exquisite poems as the "stately homes of England."

STEPHENS

Toccoa. On August 18, 1895, an Act was approved creating the new County of Stephens, out of lands formerly embraced within Habersham and Franklin, and bestowing upon said county the name of the Great Commoner, Alexander H. Stephens. Toccoa was designated as the new county-seat. This town sprang into existence during the early seventies, when the old Charlotte Air Line, now the Southern Railway, was completed to this point. In 1875, a charter of incorporation granted to the town by the Superior Court of Habersham was confirmed by the General Assembly of Georgia. At this time the corporate limits were fixed at three-quarters of a mile from the public square in every direction. The town was named for a small stream, which at a distance of some two miles from the town center makes a gigantic leap forming one of the most magnificent cascades in America. It was called by the Indians "Toccoa," a term signifying "the beautiful." The present public school system was established in 1892. With the building of a branch line from Toccoa to Elberton the growth of the town received a decided impetus. Today there is not a more progressive or wide-awake town in the State than Toccoa. Its high altitude gives it an unsurpassed health record, while the rich valley lands in this neighborhood bring an abundant tribute to its markets, making it the center of a constantly growing trade.

STEWART

Lumpkin. Lumpkin was the county-seat of Randolph from 1828 to 1831, when it became the county-seat of Stewart, a county organized out of lands formerly included in Randolph. The town was named for Hon. Wilson Lumpkin, one of Georgia's most distinguished sons. It was settled by a fine class of people, but has never grown to any extent, for the reason that more than any other community of equal size in Georgia it has helped to build other towns and cities. Some of the most successful business men of Atlanta were trained for mercantile life in the country stores of Lumpkin— merchants like the Boyntons and the Rawsons. General Clement A. Evans, Captain William H. Harrison, Judge Marshall J. Clarke and Major Sidney Root were also at one time residents of this same town, whose virile elements of strength have galvanized the whole State. From an old list of stockholders of the famous Lumpkin Independent Academy, the names of quite a number of early pioneers have been obtained, to-wit.: James Clarke, Willard Boynton, James Redingfield, Loverd Bryan, Matthew McCullar, Hollis Boynton, Marmaduke Gresham, Benjamin May, Nathan Clifton, Nicholas E.

Morris, William A. Rawson, Charles S. Gaulden, Joseph
J. Boynton, John G. Singer, John Singer, Jr., John Rich-
ardson, Mary A. West, John Talbot, William H. Hard-
wick, Matthew Wright, Daniel Matheson, M. D. Doney,
E. W. Randle, James M. Mitchell, Francis Douglas,
Joseph Glenn, Charles W. Snow, William Foster, A. H.
Dickerson, Thomas H. Everett, David Harrell, William
Shields, Robert A. Hardwick, Moses Parker, E. A.
Mitchell, William A. Fort, George B. Perry, Bedford S.
Worrell, Edward E. Rawson, Blanton Streetman, Ran-
dolph Pearson, Jacob Ramser, John Crocker, Tomlin-
son Fort, Miles K. Harman, Isham Watkins, Peter Adley,
Artimus Lewis, Daniel A. Garrett, Madison Hill, Eras-
mus T. Beall, Harris Dennard and John M. Simpson.[*]

SUMTER

Americus. When the first immigrants reached this locality some of the aborigines still remained.
Settlers were attracted to this point by the fact that
the spot where the town is now located was the center of
the granary of the Creek Nation. There was a tradition
among the Creeks that this section of the country had
never failed, in all the annals of time, to produce a good
crop of maize. After the Indians left they would, from
time to time, return, loath to leave the spot where they
had been most contented. It was the custom of the red
men, in the cultivation of their special products, to bore
a hole in the ground with a stick about fifteen inches
deep and to place therein a fish as fertilizer, then dropping upon the fish a grain of corn.

Americus is located on the banks of "Au Muckalee"
Creek. This beautiful Indian name was corrupted by
the whites into "Muckalee." The meaning of the word
is "pour upon me," the creek taking its name from a

---

[*]Acts, 1842, pp. 9-10.

spring about ten miles distant from Americus. The town was incorporated in 1832, and one of the first things the citizens did was to erect an academy and make provision for educating the poor. There was an Act providing that no teacher should receive funds out of the poor-school fund "unless examined and found qualified by the justices of the Inferior Court, or a majority of them."

In the following year, 1833, "Sumter County Academy" was incorporated, with the following-named gentlemen as trustees: John J. Britt, Joseph Mims, Robert Savage, James Glass, William S. Horton, Thomas Johnston and Daniel M. Little. The new trustees appointed in 1835 were as follows: William Pegg, Mark M. Brown, John T. McCrary, Jesse Harris and Thomas Gardner.

Elections were held at the house of Sydney Smith, and Horton and Harris, instead of as formerly, at D. W. Mann's. Americus camp-ground was incorporated in 1840, with the following named as trustees: William L. McKee, William P. Hames, John W. Lommy, Quinny Bass, William Pegg and Joseph M. Wyatt. Farmer's Academy was chartered by an Act of 1842, and the appointed trustees were: Frederick J. Greene, Wyatt R. Singleton, William M. Wimbush, Joseph A. S. Turner and Thomas J. Baisden. Names aforesaid are given principally as showing a list of those among the earliest settlers.

In building the Southwestern Railroad, now the Central of Georgia, and the first railroad through this section of country, the prime mover in this undertaking was the Hon. T. M. Furlow, who was a most active spirit. By a liberal contribution he procured a deflection of the proposed road from Lumpkin to this point. Also, in the building of the Americus, Preston and Lumpkin Railroad, which is now a part of the Seaboard Air Line system, Colonel S. H. Hawkins contributed more of means and energy, to this vast enterprise, than any one else. He was president of the company, and gave to Americus what was so greatly needed, a competitive line. Since then the little city, from a population of 3,800, has grown to its present proportions.

In 1910 the United States census gave to Americus a population of 8,200, but the town has steadily grown since then, and now, in 1914, it is estimated at over 10,000 souls. The area of the little city is five miles square. The streets are paved with wood blocks, and there are forty miles of paved sidewalks. The fine water-works are owned by the city. There are two electric light plants, and 20 miles of sanitary sewerage, 4 State banks, and 2 savings banks. An excellent climate—with a supplement of pure artesian water, six public schools, three colleges, including the Third District Agricultural College—these are among the attractions of Americus. Here also is the source of the largest musical conservatory in the State, "the Bell Piano Schools." The town also boasts a fine tourist and commercial hotel and a $30,000 Carnegie Library, and best of railroad facilities, with twenty-four passenger trains daily. Division head-quarters for the Seaboard Air Line Railroad are here located, and Sumter County is the "banner good roads county" of the State. Americus is on the Atlanta-Andersonville highway, located 175 miles southwest of Atlanta, and last, but not least, there are eighteen churches of all denominations.*

Andersonville: The Monument to Major Henry Whirz. Some few miles to the north of Americus, on the line of the Central of Georgia, is Andersonville, a small town made famous during the Civil War by the establishment here of a noted Confederate prison and, later by the execution of Major Wirz, the officer in charge, at the hands of the Federal authorities. Soon after the close of hostilities, a cemetery was opened at Andersonville by the United States government. Most of the Federal soldiers who fell in the various engagements in this section of the State toward the close of the struggle are here buried. The area is well kept and is beautified by a number of attractive monuments.

---

*Information kindly furnished by Mrs. C. A. Fricker, Regent, Council of Safety Chapter, D. A. R., of Americus, Ga.

During the Presidential campaign of 1876, the charges against Major Wirz were revived in the most sensational manner by James G. Blaine, in the national House of Representatives. His purpose was to arouse the spirit of sectional strife in order to compass the defeat of the national Democratic ticket. There was an evident drift at the North toward Democracy; and the shrewd political orator sought, by waving the bloody shirt and by coupling the alleged prison horrors at Andersonville with the name of Democracy, to make the latter odious to the people of the Northern States. He first declared that the author of the gigantic murder and crime at Andersonville was Mr. Davis; and he next proceeded to observe that neither the deeds of the Duke of Alva in the Low Countries, nor the massacre of St. Bartholomew, nor the thumb-screws and engines of torture of the Spanish inquisition, could compare in atrocity with the hideous outrages perpetrated upon Federal soldiers in the Georgia prison. The speech was well calculated to inflame the popular mind. It was virtually an indictment of the Southern people, and was also an artful bid for votes at the North, with which to suppress the Bourbon Democracy at the South.

But the effect of the speech was neutralized in the most unexpected manner by Benjamin H. Hill, of Georgia. The latter had been the spokesman of Mr. Davis in the Confederate Senate. He was well acquainted with the facts in the case, and the reply which he made to Mr. Blaine on this occasion was overwhelming. He not only exonerated Mr. Davis, but he put the responsibility for loss of life at Andersonville upon the United States government, in consequence of the policy which made medicines contraband of war. Such a thing, declared Mr. Hill, not even the Duke of Alva had dared to do. He also pictured the destitution at the South during the last years of the struggle, and the insufficiency of our meagre resources to provide food and clothing for our own soldiers; whereupon he again taxed the Federal government with the blame for having deliberately and wilfully refused to agree to an exchange of prisoners, when such conditions were known to exist. He furthermore quoted official reports to show that there were more Confederate soldiers who died in Northern prisons than there were Federal soldiers who died in Southern prisons. The speech of Mr. Hill gave an altogether different aspect to the bill of indictment. It turned the tables upon the wily statesman from Maine, and when the popular vote was cast in the ensuing election it was found to be decidedly in favor of the Democratic ticket. Not until three States were disfranchised by the returning boards was Mr. Hayes finally seated. Thus were the tactics employed by the great Republican leader to discredit the South distinctly repudiated by the American people at the polls.

James M. Page, formerly a lieutenant in Company A of the Michigan Cavalry, has published a volume entitled "The True Story of Andersonville; or a Defence of Major Henry Wirz." He spent seven months in the prison at Andersonville, and with ample opportunities for observation he fastens the blame for the so-called outrages upon Secretary Stanton, of the United States War Department. On May 12, 1911, there was unveiled at Andersonville, under the auspices of the United Daughters of the Confederacy, a handsome monument to the memory of Major Henry Wirz, the commanding officer of the prison. Hon. Pleasant A. Stovall, of Savannah, was the orator of the occasion. His address was a masterful review of the unvarnished facts of history connected with the execution of this gallant Confederate officer. Major Wirz is buried in Mount Olivet Cemetery, on the outskirts of the nation's capital, in the District of Columbia. His last resting-place, near the main entrance, is marked only by an obscure little headstone, rising scarcely more than an inch above the ground, on which the only inscription chiseled is the pathetic monosyllable: WIRZ.

TALBOT

Talbotton. Talbotton, a town rich in historic associations, was made the county-seat of Talbot by an Act approved December 20, 1828. At the same time a charter of incorporation was obtained, with the following named commissioners, to-wit.: H. R. Ward, George W. B. Towns, John B. Davis and William Goss.[1] The commissioner whose name appears second in this list was none other than Governor George W. Towns, who was baptized with the "B" in his name, but subsequently dropped it as an unnecessary letter. Both the town and the county were named for Hon. Matthew Talbot, one of the early Governors of Georgia. Between 1828 and 1836 not less than ten academies were chartered in the County of Talbot, a showing which well attests the intellectual character of the early pioneers who settled this region. The Female Academy of Talbotton was chartered on December 23, 1830, with the following board of trustees, viz.: James Bell, Elisha Tarver, Henry Mims, Norborn B. Powell, Robert G. Crittenden, Charles Smith and John P. Blackburn.[2] This pioneer school for young ladies developed into the famous LeVert Female College, named for the noted Madame LeVert, one of the most gifted women of her day. She spoke fluently a number of

---

[1] Acts, 1828, p. 149.
[2] Acts, 1830, p. 9.

foreign languages, wrote a book on travel, and for years dominated the intellectual and social life of the State. Madam LeVert was a granddaughter of George Walton, an early Governor of the State, and one of the Signers of the Declaration. While residing with her son, then Governor of West Florida, she named the future capital of the State—Tallahassee. The commissioners of the LeVert Female College were as follows: Thomas B. Turner, Thomas A. Brown, Allen F. Owen, Josiah M. Matthews, Edmond H. Worrill, James P. Leonard and John T. Blount, all of whom were previously trustees of the Talbotton Female Academy. Besides these were added: William B. Marshall, Harrison W. Hagerman, Andrew W. Wynn, William B. Brown, Francis M. Murray, David Kendall, Washington C. Cleveland and Hiram Drane.[1] But the old college suffered to such an extent from the impoverished condition of the State subsequent to the war that its doors were eventually closed. In 1833 the legal titles to the college property were transferred to the town of Talbotton for educational purposes.[2] Collingsworth Institute, founded by Josiah Flournay as a manual-labor school, was chartered on December 29, 1838, and named for a devoted Methodist preacher. The sum of $40,000 was bequeathed to the school by its generous founder. Here two members of the noted Straus family, Nathan and Isidor, afterwards millionaire merchants of New York, were educated. Judge William A. Little, formerly on the Supreme Bench, and Hon. Walter B. Hill, late chancellor of the University, were born at Talbotton. Here also lived the Gormans, the Leonards, the Blounts, the Searcys, the Powells, and scores of other aristocratic old families, whose ample mode of life is attested by the fine old mansions which still survive in different parts of the county as stately memorials of a gentler era.

[1] Acts, 1855-1856, p. 280.
[2] Acts, 1883, p. 646.

The Straus Family. One of the most noted households in America of Jewish origin was identified for nearly a full decade with the little town of Talbotton, in this rich agricultural belt of middle Georgia. Here it was that the business career of the famous Straus family began; and from a modest corner store in what was then a mere country village dates the origin of the great mercantile establishment of R. H. Macy & Co. in the great commercial metropolis of the continent. It is useless at this late day to conjecture the motives which induced Lazarus Straus to exchange his home in distant Bavaria for the little town in Georgia, to which he brought his household goods; but he settled in Talbotton in 1854, Two of his boys—Isidor and Nathan—were old enough to be sent to school. Accordingly he placed them in the care of good Methodist teachers at Collingsworth Institute. Oscar was still an infant. There was nothing of bigotry in the heart of Lazarus Straus. He was broad minded, a man of whom his neighbors thought well; but he was also progressive, energetic, wide-awake, possessed of the typical instinct of his race for trade and barter. Removing to Columbus in 1862, where a somewhat wider arena was found for his business activities, he remained in Columbus until 1865, when the raiders of General Wilson made the town a visit, which left it prostrate in the ashes of war. Lazarus Straus then removed to New York. Here he organized what eventually became one of the largest establishment in the country engaged in the importation of chinaware. In 1887, Isidor and Nathan purchased an interest in the great department store of R. H. Macy & Co., an establishment of which the Straus brothers in time became the sole owners. Both of them began to accumulate millions and to make themselves felt, not only in the business life of the great metropolis, but in its philanthropies, in its politics, in its moral and social reforms. Oscar chose a professional career. Graduating from Columbia College with the highest honors of his class, he began the practice of law. But ill-health thwarted his ambitions. He thereupon entered his father's place of business, where his legal acquirements proved of immense advantage. But he was not prevented by business engagements from taking an active part in politics; and he demonstrated his capacity for public life to such an extent that President Cleveland appointed him Minister to Turkey. Although a Democrat, he was retained at Constantinople by the McKinley administration. Besides winning the approval of the home government, he also gained the friendship of the Sultan, who wished to decorate him, a compliment, however, which his patriotic scruples forced him to decline, since it was not in accord with the spirit of free institutions. When the Department of Commerce and Labor was created, Mr. Roosevelt conferred upon him this important portfolio, and he entered the President's Cabinet, the first member of his race to be accorded this honor since the birth of the Federal Constitution—though Judah P. Benjamin was given a similar distinction under the government of the Confederate States. In 1909, Mr. Straus again received from President Taft the Turkish Ambassadorship.

Few Americans of the present generation have been more signally honored. Isidor Straus, the eldest of the brothers, perished at sea on board the ill-fated Titanic, which encountered an iceberg while making her maiden voyage, and sank in mid-ocean on the morning of April 16, 1912. Mrs. Straus, refusing to leave her husband's side for a seat in one of the life-boats, perished with him in the wreck. The body of Mr. Straus was subsequently recovered, but the ocean's sandy bed is the last resting place of his beloved wife: a true woman of Israel.

TALIAFERRO.

Crawfordville. Crawfordville, the county-seat of Taliaferro, was named for the great William H. Crawford, who, next to Mr. Stephens, was perhaps Georgia's greatest statesman. The town was incorporated by legislative act, on December 27, 1826, with the following-named commissioners, to-wit.: Herman Mercer, Thomas Chastain, Wylie Womack, Sherwood Towns, William Little, John Murphy, and John W. Jordan.* Stephens Institute, located here, is a flourishing high school. Crawfordville is not a large town, but as the old home of Alexander H. Stephens, the Confederate Vice-President, it is one of the political Meccas of America.

Liberty Hall.   Pages 142-153.

The Arrest of   While a prisoner at Fort Warren, in Bos-
Mr. Stephens.   ton Harbor, Mr. Stephens kept a diary, in
                     which he carefully recorded from day to
day the events of his prison life. He also interspersed it with observations on the philosophy of government, with comments upon current topics, and with various other things. The references to Linton Stephens are both numerous and tender. On almost every page there is some allusion to his half brother, a reminiscence or a prayer, in which Linton was the central thought. Chap-

*Acts, 1826, p. 169.

ter after chapter from the Bible was also copied into the
diary to beguile the tedium of imprisonment; and the
manuscript of this journal, in after years, furnished the
basis for the statesman's great literary masterpiece,
"The War Between the States." On the death of Mr.
Stephens the diary became the property of his nephew,
the late John A. Stephens, whose children have recently
given it to the public. The opening chapter of the diary
contains an interesting first-hand account of the author's
arrest. It runs as follows:

Liberty Hall, Thursday, May 11, 1865—This was a most beautiful and
charming day. After refreshing sleep, I arose early. Robert Hull, a
youth, son of Henry Hull, of Athens, Ga., spent the night at my house.
I wrote some letters for the mail, my custom being to attend to such business as soon as breakfast was over; and Robert and I were amusing our-
selves at Casino, when Tim [a negro servant] came running into the
parlor, saying: "Master, more Yankees have come; a whole heap are in
town, galloping about with guns!" Suspecting what it meant, I rose,
told Robert I supposed they had come for me, and entered my bedroom
to make arrangements for leaving, should my apprehension prove true.
Soon, I saw an officer with soldiers under arms approaching the house.
The doors were all open. I met him in the library. He asked if my name
was Stephens. I replied that it was.

"Alexander H. Stephens?" said he.

I told him yes. He then said that he had orders to arrest me. I inquired his name and asked to see his orders. He replied that he was
Captain Saint, of the Fourth Iowa Cavalry, or mounted infantry, attached
to General Nelson's command; he was then under General Upton; he
showed me the order by General Upton, at Atlanta, directing my arrest and
the arrest of Robert Toombs; no charge was specified; he was instructed
to come to Crawfordville, arrest me, proceed to Washington, arrest Mr.
Toombs, and then carry both to General Upton's headquarters.

I told him I had been looking for something of this kind; at least,
for some weeks, had thought it not improbable, and hence had not left
home; that General Upton need not have sent any force for me; that had
he simply notified me that he wished me at headquarters, I should have
gone. I asked how I was to travel.

He said: "On the cars."

I then learned that he had come down on the train, arriving just before
Tim's announcement. I asked if I would be permitted to carry any clothing. He said "Yes." I asked how long I might have for packing. He
said: "A few minutes—as long as necessary." I set to packing. Harry

[the chief man servant] came in, evincing great surprise and regret, to pack for me. The captain then said:

"You may take a servant with you if you wish."

I asked if he knew my destination. He said:

"First, Atlanta; then, Washington City."

I called in Anthony, a black boy from Richmond, who had been waiting on me for several years, and inquired if he wished to go. I told him I would send him from Washington to his mother in Richmond. He was willing, so I bade him be ready as soon as possible.

In the meantime, Mr. Hiddell [secretary to Mr. Stephens] had come in; he was living with me and had gone out after breakfast. None of my brother's family residing at the old homestead happened to be with me; however, Clarence, who was going to school at the Academy, hearing of what had occurred, I suppose, came over with some friends from town. It was about ten A. M. when Captain Saint arrived. In about fifteen minutes—not much over—we started for the depot, Anthony and I, with the captain and squad; friends, servants, and Clarence following, most of them crying. My own heart was full—too full for tears.[1]

———

Beside His Beloved Brother. On September 5, 1914, the mortal ashes of Judge Linton Stephens—after a lapse of forty-two years—were brought from his old home in Sparta and laid to rest beside those of his renowned brother, on the lawn of Liberty Hall. The exercises of reinterment were simple. Judge N. E. Harris, Governor-elect, who read law in the office of Judge Stephens at Sparta, delivered the principal address. If anything could make the sleep of Mr. Stephens sweeter it would be the consciousness that an act of poetic justice has at last been performed.

———

TATTNALL

Reidsville. The original county-seat of Tattnall was on the Ohoopee River, near Drake's Ferry. In 1832, Reidsville became the seat of government, but the town was not incorporated until December 31, 1838, when the following commissioners wer named, to-wit.: Shadrach Hancock, John A. Mattox, John Brazzell, William Rogers and John A. Rogers, Jr.[2] Reidsville is today

———

[1] Recollections of Alexander H. Stephens, containing the Prison Diary of Mr. Stephens, 1865.

[2] Acts, 1838, p. 123.

a flourishing town, with up-to-date public utilities, a fine
group of banks and with a splendid body of citizens.

TAYLOR

Butler. Butler, the county-seat of Taylor County, was
named for General William Orlando Butler, a
distinguished soldier of the Mexican War and a candidate for Vice-President on the ticket with General Lewis
Cass, of Michigan. He was also a poet of some reputation and the author of a celebrated song called "The
Boatman's Horn." The county was named for General
Zachary Taylor. Butler was incorporated as a town on
February 8, 1854, with Messrs. C. Y. Perry, Ezekiel
Royal, Isaac Mulky, James T. May, and P. C. Carr as
commissioners.[1] Though not a large, it is quite a cultured, community, composed of fine old families, which
have long been resident in this section of Georgia.

TELFAIR.

Jacksonville. Jacksonville, the original county-seat of Telfair, was
founded soon after the county was created in 1807, but
was not chartered until 1815, when the following commissioners were
named: Chas. McKinyan, Abel L. Hatton, Wm. Harris, Nathaniel Ashley,
and Noah Palmour.[2] The Jacksonville Academy was chartered on December 10, 1841, with the following trustees: Mark Wilcox, Sargeant S. Freeman, Henry E. Turner, Alex. T. Dopson, Cornelius R. Ashley, Chas. J.
Shelton, Duncan McRae, Peter H. Coffee, and John G. McCall.[3] Gen.
John Coffee, a soldier of note, memorialized by one of the counties of
Georgia, lies buried five miles south of Jacksonville; and presumably in
this same neighborhood sleeps his son-in-law, Gen. Mark Wilcox, for
whom a county has likewise been named. Jacksonville is today only a
small village.

McRae. In 1870 the site of public buildings was changed
to McRae, a town which was four years later
incorporated with the following-named commissioners,
to-wit.: Daniel M. McRae, William McRae, John Mc-

[1] Acts, 1843-1853, p. 232.
[2] Lamar's Digest, p. 1015.
[3] Acts, 1841, p. 5.

Daniel, Sr., J. Dougherty and R. Rivers.* With splendid railway facilities, McRae is rapidly becoming an important commercial center. The surrounding country is rich in agricultural products, and the fame of the little town as a wide-awake community has traveled abroad. McRae possesses a number of strong banks, several handsome business blocks and scores of flourishing establishments. South Georgia College, an institution under Methodist control, imparts to the town an atmosphere of culture and attracts from a distance quite a large number of students.

TERRELL

Dawson. On February 16, 1856, an Act was approved creating the new County of Terrell from parcels of land described as follows: From Lee County, districts three and twelve; from Randolph County, districts four and eleven; and from Kinchefoonee County, now Webster, district seventeen. To the county thus formed was given the name of Terrell, in honor of Dr. William Terrell, of Sparta, Ga., one of the most distinguished physicians and one of the most useful public men of the State. The site for public buildings was located by the county authorities near the center of the new county on lands belonging to Moses H. Baldwin, and from this pioneer resident one hundred acres of ground were purchased, at the rate of $25 per acre, on which to locate the future county-seat. The town was called Dawson, in honor of a distinguished United States Senator, then lately deceased, Hon. William C. Dawson, of Greensboro, Ga.

Regulations for the government of Dawson were adopted by the President and Councilmanic Board, under an Act of the Legislature approved December 22, 1857. The first mayor or president of Dawson was Rev. Jesse M. Davis. The pioneer councilmen were: Moses H. Baldwin, George Bunch, James W. Shropshire, Francis D.

*Acts, 1874, p. 157.

Bailey and Patrick H. Mills. John L. Allison was the
first town marshal, Benjamin F. Brooks, the first treasurer, and Patrick H. Mills, the first clerk of council. As
a preparation for building the town, Daniel Lawhorn
was paid $100 for surveying town lots. At the same time,
Calvin Register received $110 for clearing the public
square and putting the streets in order. The first session of the Inferior Court was held under a large red
oak tree, which stood near the old Farnum stables, at
the extreme west end of Lee Street, in the fall of 1856.
The first term of the Superior Court was held in the
following spring, with Judge David Kiddoo on the Bench
and Hon. D. B. Harrell as solicitor-general. The first
county officers were: Daniel Harden, treasurer; Ludwell
E. Leonard, Ordinary; Myron E. Weston, Clerk of Court;
A. J. Baldwin, Sr., Sheriff, James W. Bone, Tax Collector; Samuel P. Williams, Representative, and John B.
Vanover, Senator.

J oseph D. Reynolds superintended the building of the
original court-house, for which he was paid the sum of
$5,440, covering presumably the entire cost of the struc-
ture. The first County School Commissioners were:
Moses H. Baldwin, B. L. Winbourn and Eli G. Hill. In
1857 a post-office was established in the town, with R. W.
Nelson as the postmaster in charge. The first train to
pass through Dawson came over the line of the Central
of Georgia in the summer of 1858. Captain W. C. Thornton, who died in Virginia during the Civil War was the
first soldier buried in the cemetery at Dawson, but of
those who enlisted from Terrell, Robert Hayes was the
first to lose his life on the field of battle. In 1866, Messrs.
E. and J. E. Christian founded the *Dawson Journal,*
which they continued to own and edit for several years.

The first marriage license on record was issued to
Michael Burk and Sarah Middelton, June 2, 1865, and
the ceremony was performed by Rev. Patrick H. McCook.
Two of the pioneer educators of Dawson were Prof.
Thomas Brantley and Prof. M. A. McNulty, who con-

ducted flourishing schools. Prof. J. W. F. Lowrey was also an early instructor who stamped his impress indelibly upon the town. Rev. John Martin was the first Baptist pastor. The little building in which he preached stood very near the site of the present handsome structure. The first Methodist Church is still standing on South Main Street. Its pastor was a Rev. Mr. Williamson. This house of workship was used until the congregation grew large enough to warrant the building of the commodious edifice near the centre of the town.

Camp Exile.   During the sixties a gun shop was located in Dawson, which continued in operation until the surrender. When the torches of Sherman's army had left Atlanta in ashes and driven her defenceless women and children into an unsheltered exile, the Governor of the State arranged for transportation of some three hundred refugees to Dawson, and these were quartered at what has been known as "Exile Camp." Not by leaps and bounds, but by slow degrees, Dawson has progressed from a village in the wilderness to a city beautiful. Many of the evils which menaced the first years of the town's existence have been uprooted. Her handsome business blocks, her imposing public buildings, her paved streets, and her many beautiful homes, with their well-kept lawns and flower gardens, all attest the fact that Dawson is destined to become one of the most important commercial centers of a region which literally flows with milk and honey.

Some of the Early Settlers.   Examining some of the early documents of the town we find the following records: Charter members of the Methodist church, 1857—Mr. and Mrs. Moses H. Baldwin, Mr. and Mrs. B. H. Brown, Mr. and Mrs. J. B. Perry, Mr. and Mrs. W. P. Vinson and Dr. and Mrs. C. A. Cheatham. Trustees of the Baptist Church—John T. Walker, William C. Thornton, John A. Bishop, Benj. F. Cook and Harrison Ethridge. Pioneer physicians —Dr. Jim, Huff, Dr. J. W. Shropshire, Wr. C. A. Cheatham, Dr. J. T. Lamar, Dr. B. R. Reeves, Dr. Hiram G. Johnston, Dr. S. F. Lasseter, Dr.

Joseph Gilpin. Pioneer lawyers—James R. Bynum, F. D. Bailey, James A. Wilson, Frank Harper, Reuben Fitzgerald, C. B. Wooten, Richard Maltby, Ed Bass. Other men of note—J. B. Perry, Allen Lowrey, J. W. F. Lowrey, M. H. Baldwin, R. S. Cheatham, C. W. Jones, Jared Irwin, S. R. Weston, A. J. Baldwin, Sr., M. S. Glass, J. M. Simmons, Thomas Caldwell, J. E. Loyless, J. C. F. Clark and W. N. Watts.*

Herod Town Memorial Unveiled. Eight miles to the south of Dawson there formerly stood an Indian village known as Herod Town, whose chief, Old Herod, was a staunch friend of the whites and, according to local tradition, joined forces with Andrew Jackson when the latter, at the head of his troops, reached this town in 1818, en route to Florida, to quell the Seminoles. There is still a settlement at this place, which, in honor of the old chieif, has since retained the name of Herod. On November 20, 1913, to commemorate the heroism of these friendly Indians, a handsome boulder of marble was unveiled with impressive ceremonies, on the site of Herod Town, by Dorothy Walton Chapter, D. A. R., Mrs. W. A. McLain, regent, and the occasion was signalized by the presence of many distinguished visitors, including the State regent, Mrs. S. W. Foster. Promptly at 10 o'clock, the members of the chapter, with their invited guests and a large company of town people, swelling the number of spectators to several hundred, repaired in automobiles to Herod Town, where, under the serenest of autumn skies, mellowed by the soft tints of Indian summer, the exercises of unveiling took place, followed by a magnificent repast on the grounds. Mrs. M. C. Edwards, historian of the chapter, has preserved the following account of the exercises:

The Dorothy Walton Chapter of the Daughters of the American Revolution staged near Dawson an event which had engendered profound interest throughout southwest Georgia. It was the unveiling of a magnificent boulder at the site of a former Indian village, Old Herodtown, to commemorate the historical fact that General Andrew Jackson at the head

---

*For the information contained in this sketch of Dawson, we are indebted to Mrs. J. S. Lowrey, State Historian, D. A. R.

of nine hundred Georgia militia, together with friendly Indians, reached this spot in the year 1818, in his march through Georgia to subdue the hostile Indians, and was joined at Herodtown by Chief Herod and his friendly braves. An almost perfect Indian summer day made the occasion an ideal one, and the impressive exercises were witnessed by a large crowd assembled from the adjacent towns and cities to participate in this event.

The programme was initiated by an impressive invocation from Dr. J. A. Ivey, one of the oldest and best-known Baptist divines in the State. This was followed by a most charming address by the Dorothy Walton Chapter regent, Mrs. W. A. McLain, who in chaste language and impressive manner extended a most cordial welcome to all those who participated in the exercises. Mrs. McLain, who does all things well, acquitted herself in her usual successful manner. The audience then rendered "America," led by the school children of the hospitable little village of Herod. Miss Aphia Jackson gave as a reading the stirring defiance of Osceola in a very striking manner. The salute to the flag given by the daughters was itself a striking feature, but perhaps the most beautiful picture of the occasion was when little Hildah Gumm and Lindah Harris removed from the magnificent boulder the flags which draped it. This was followed by the address of the State regent, Mrs. S. W. Foster, and those who know her wonderful capacity, her unlimited fund of information, and her graceful and forceful delivery, alone, could realize the treat received by the audience.

In a brief and appropriate manner Judge M. C. Edwards introduced the speaker of the day, Hon. Lucian L. Knight. Few orators have been produced by the State of Georgia who surpass Mr. Knight on any occasion, but it seemed peculiar, that here, the time, the place, and the man had met, and his address proved to be a gem. It combined within itself the choicest thoughts which he had garnered as a trained reporter and erudite scholar, a profound thinker and a gentle poet expressed in the sublimest flights of the silver-tongued orator. Those who sat under the sway of his eloquence could almost see the village re-peopled with its vanished inhabitants. This was followed by "The Star Spangled Banner," and the exercises were closed by benediction by Rev. E. F. Morgan, pastor of the Dawson Methodist Church.

A large number attended from various places, and among the guests of honor were Hon. Lucian L. Knight and Mrs. S. W. Foster, of Atlanta; Messrs. T. C. Parker, Charles C. Holt and F. E. Land, of Macon; Mesdames George McDonald, R. L. Walker, S. D. Zuber and R. D. Gay, of Cuthbert; Colonel and Mrs. R. F. Crittenden, of Shellman; Mrs. C. A. Fincher and Mrs. Frank Harold, of Americus, the Stone Castle Chapter of the D. A. R. and many others.

Charles W. Harris was in charge of the barbecue, and the delicious meat done to turn flanked by generous platters of Brunswick stew would have alone sufficed, but the table literally groaned under delicacies prepared by the daughters, which did furnish a menu equal to any Georgia product dinner.

The magnificent pile of granite will be a constant reminder to youth who pass there, that this section is not barren of tradition and memories, and its erection by the victor to the conquered has been one of the most delightful events yet to occur in this section.

Mrs. W. A. McLain entertained in honor of the guests at a 6 o'clock dinner at her palatial residence in Dawson. Appointments, decoration and cuisine were perfect, and the occasion was one of the most recherche of the year.

MRS. M. C. EDWARDS, Historian.

Only a paragraph from the speaker's address can be given. Said he: "Madam Regent, it was a tender thought of your chapter to memorialize this village of a vanished race, and nothing could better typify the heroic virtues of the noble savage than this exquisite boulder of stone quarried from his own hills. It is also most appropriate, for the purposes of this unveiling, that you should have chosen a day in this beautiful season of the year, when the foliage of the trees is deepening into russet, emblematic of the dark-hued warriors who once roamed these woods; when the reddening sunsets recall his council fires; when the mellow musk bespeaks his harvest fields of maize; when the plaintive wind, like a wandering minstrel, tells the pathetic story of his conquered tribe, or in a softer key, sings of his wooing in the golden moonlight by the winding waters; when the hazy air is reminiscent of his pipe of peace; and when the oaks and the maples are trembling in the soft vestments of Indian summer. We can think of him now without an unkindly recollection. For, the icy touch of the frost king has softened the steel-like glitter of his eagle eye, and, on this autumn day, we can come to this place of his former abode, with tears for his fate and with laurels for his fame."

Judge James M. Griggs: His Monument. One of the classics of the American Congress was a speech delivered in the national House of Representatives during the Spanish-American war period, by a distinguished former representative of this district: Hon. James M. Griggs. Brilliant as a statesman, just and impartial as a jurist, without reproach as a citizen, and fearless and upright as a man, Judge Griggs was beloved by all classes of the people, to whom unstintedly he gave the resources of his great mind. In the heart of his adopted town, where Stonewall and Lee Streets intersect, there stands a superb memorial to Judge Griggs, reflecting the esteem in which he was held by his fellow citizens. The memorial is admittedly a work of art. Upon a solid granite base rest two beautifully polished columns, surmounted by a cornice, on which is chiselled in large letters the name:

| "GRIGGS" |

At either side, just over the flowered capitals, is a wreath of bronze. Between the pillars, on a solid block of stone, is a handsome bust of the late Congressman. This also is executed in bronze. It is a splendid likeness, and taken in connection with its superb setting, it constitutes an exquisite memorial to one whose fame will ever be tenderly cherished by the people of Dawson. Inscribed upon a plate, on the west side of the monument, is the following epitaph:

| To the memory of JAMES MATTHEWS GRIGGS, who represented with conspicuous ability and fidelity the Second District of Georgia in Congress, from March 4, 1897, to the date of his death, January 5, 1910, this memorial is erected in his home town by the people of the district. He loved and honored the people. They loved and honored him. |

On the east side, in gilt letters, is chiselled this inscription:

| As great as the greatest; as humble as the lowest. |

At the unveiling, which occurred in the summer of 1913, Hon. Henry M. McIntosh, of Albany, Ga., a devoted friend, acted as master of ceremonies. Hon. William M. Howard, of Lexington, a colleague in Congress, to whom Judge Griggs was warmly attached, delivered a masterful address in presenting to the Congressman's home town this beautiful monument which, on behalf of the community, was accepted by Hon. M. J. Yeomans, in a graceful speech, enriched with tender sentiment.

THOMAS

Thomasville. In 1825, Thomas County was formed from Baker and Decatur. Just one year later— December 22, 1826—on lot number thirty-nine, district thirteen, was located the new county-seat called Thomasville. Presumably both the town and the county-seat were named for General Jett Thomas, who built the old State-house at Milledgeville, though local traditions are not entirely in accord with this supposition. As provided in the original Act of December 24, 1825, preliminary elections were held at the house of Charles Kingsley. On December 26, 1831, the town was incorporated with the following-named commissioners, to-wit.: Isaac P. Brooks, Edward Remington, Malcolm Ferguson, James Kerksey and Murdock McAuley.* In 1856 a new charter was granted, providing for a mayor and six aldermen, with an increase of territory.

Under an Act approved December 24, 1825, Duncan Ray, Archibald McMillan, Paul Colson, Hardy Bryan and Malcolm Ferguson were appointed Commissioners of the Thomas County Academy, and the proceeds from the sale of town lots in Thomasville went to this board. A building was soon erected, and Mr. Cresman taught forty (40) pupils at the corner of Madison and Monroe Streets. He was succeeded by Mr. Rolph, who boarded with Colonel Mike Young, and taught until 1837.

---

*Acts, 1831, p. 237.

Next year Mr. Scott, who boarded with Mrs. McLean, taught in the new building, corner of Broad and Monroe Streets. January, 1838, the old building was renovated, and the upstairs converted into a music room, with Mrs. Metzler and Miss Sophia Metzler teaching the girls, Mr. Scott still teaching the boys, in the new building.

In 1835, the prominent residents of Thomasville were Messrs. Ed. Remington, Isaac Brooks, James and William Kerksey and Dr. Gauley. Mr. James Kerksey had the first store, on corner of Broad and Jefferson Streets. Prior to 1840, among the prominent families in Thomas County were the Neelys, Blackshears, Youngs, Jones, Hayes, Rays, Hadleys, Dixons, Parramores, Adams, McMaths, Bryans, Dekles, Chastains, Hancocks, Singletarys, Cones, McCanns, Wards, Hartwells, Mitchells and MacIntyres. Prominent Congressmen who have resided at Thomasville were James L. Seward, Peter E. Love, A. T. MacIntyre and S. A. Roddenbery.. Among the most distinguished jurists and lawyers have been J. R. Alexander, August H. Hansell, William M. Hammond, A. T. MacIntyre, Jr., and Arthur Patten.

Fletcher Institute, a school founded by the Methodists, was chartered on February 9, 1854. Young's Female College was granted a charter on December 17, 1860. The trustees of the latter school were: Thomas Jones, James J. Hays, James L. Seward, Augustin H. Hansell, William J. Young, A. T. MacIntyre and David S. Brandon.* This institution grew out of the philanthropy of Elijah R. Young, who left the sum of $30,000 with which to start a school for the education of girls. From 1875 to 1900, Thomasville was a prominent winter resort, but the Piney Woods Hotel was burned, and the transient tourists lost to the city. However, a few still occupy during the winter excellent homes in the vicinity of Thomasville.

---

*Acts, 1860, p. 176.

Senator-Elect Hardwick. Georgia's new Senator-elect, Hon. Thomas W. Hardwick, was born in Thomasville, Ga., on December 9, 1872; and though he has since spent the greater part of his life elsewhere, Thomasville has always felt a deep maternal pride in his public honors.

———

Roddenberry Park. During the last week in July, 1914, an appropriation of $5,000 was made by Congress for an additional purchase of ground, adjacent to the post-office building in Thomasville, this extension to be known as Roddenbery Park, in honor of the late Hon. S. A. Roddenbery, Congressman from the Second District. It was a departure from long-established custom to pay a tribute of this kind to a deceased member of Congress; but such was the esteem in which the lamented Georgian was held by his associates, irrespective of party affiliations, that no serious opposition was registered. Judge Roddenbery was a tower of strength in the cause of temperance, giving it the advocacy of a most intense moral earnestness. He was at all times and under all circumstances a staunch friend of the common people, whose burdens he carried upon his drooping shoulders to the very last; and even when the sands of life were running low he refused to take a much-needed rest, remaining at his post of duty like the sentinel of Herculaneum. He was a foe without truce or compromise to whatever bore the semblance of graft; a legislator who scorned to reckon with expediency when Conscience said, "It is wrong;" and a man whose worst enemy could not speak of him except in terms of unqualified respect.

———

The Le Conte Pear. It was in the neighborhood of Thomasville that the famous Le Conte pear was first cultivated on a scale which began to attract the attention of fruit growers in other parts of the world.

Colonel L. L. Varnadoe, a native of Liberty County, Ga., purchased a plantation near Thomasville at the close of the Civil War, and on removing to this plantation he brought with him a cutting from one of the pear trees, called a Chinese Sand Pear, on which John Le Conte had been experimenting. Colonel Varnadoe's success was phenomenal, and from this one cutting has come a yield whose value and extent defies the mathematician. Judge John L. Harden, of Savannah, a kinsman of the Le Contes, is quoted by the late Dr. Stacy, of Newnan, on the subject of the Le Conte pear, to the following effect:

"In 1850 my great uncle, John LeConte, purchased from Thomas Hogg, a nurseryman of New York, a small pear tree. He was told by Mr. Hogg that the fruit was of inferior quality, and fit only for preserving; that it would not mature its fruit so far north as New York, but that it might do so in the South; that it was the Chinese Sand Pear. The tree was given to my mother, and when it grew large enough it produced fruit which, to our surprise, was of excellent quality. The original tree in forty-five years old, 1895, and is still productive and vigorous, although sadly neglected. It has borne twenty bushels in one year, after allowing for what may have been stolen."

At the close of the late war, the people of Liberty County were in straightened circumstances, and quite a number of them emigrated to southwestern Georgia. Among them was Colonel Leander L. Varnadoe, a native of the County and a member of the old church. Upon the suggestion of his uncle, Mr. William Jones, that the tree might be propagated from the cutting, and that the fruit might be profitably raised in the section whither he had moved, Colonel Varnadoe secured quite a number of cuttings and took them with him and planted them at his home near Thomasville. He was soon delighted to see that the idea was a happy one, and to find himself the owner of an orchard of vigorous trees, yielding abundantly of luscious fruit for the market. Cuttings were soon in great demand; and from this little beginning the whole Southern country has been covered with Le Conte pear trees. Many have made not only livings, but even fortunes, by investing in them.

To give some idea of the impoverished condition of our people at the close of the war and to show what a happy hit was the idea of promoting the cultivation of this pear from cuttings, I narrate the following incident: On the return of Colonel Varnadoe from the war, it is said that his first bill of fare was so meagre and uninviting that he jocosely remarked to his wife:

"Annie, if you can, you may do so, but I cannot say grace over such a dinner."

Some few years after his removal to Thomasville, he was offered $10,000 cash for his pear farm, which he very wisely refused. The old mother tree, from which the millions now in cultivation throughout the South-land have sprung, was seen by the writer some time ago. It is sixty inches in circumference, and twenty-four feet in height. Until recent years it has shown no symptoms of blight. Such a tree is not only worthy of mention but deserves a conspicuous place in a collection like this.*

———

Two Great Law-yers Vanquished. Stephen F. Miller, in his Bench and Bar of Georgia, narrates the following story of a lawyer who once practiced at the Thomasville bar:

"Some years ago a very romantic story was circulated in the news-papers, in which Mr. [John] Taylor [formerly a lawyer of Thomasville], was the leading hero. The scene was laid in Arkansas. It appears that a rich planter had insulted the wife of his overseer. She made it known to her husband, who took the liberty of caning his employer on sight. The planter some days afterwards shot the overseer, killing him instantly. He was prosecuted, but his money saved him from conviction. In the meantime he had spoken slanderous words concerning the widow, who brought her action for damages. The day of trial arrived. Sargent S. Prentiss and Albert Pike appeared as counsel for the defendant. The case was called in regular order; and such was the array of influence, the great wealth of the defendant, the ability of his lawyers, and the humble condition of the plaintiff, that even the young attorney who brought the action shrank from it and abandoned his client to her fate. The jury sounded the case again; and, no one responding, he appealed to the gal-lantry of the bar. There was walking in the lobby of the court-room a slender, woebegone-looking personage, with a high forehead, pensive features, thin, compressed lips and wandering blue eyes—his visage of sandy complexion. He heard the appeal, and advancing within the bar modestly informed the court that he would represent the plaintiff. All eyes were turned on the stranger. No one knew him.

"This was a perplexing moment. The judge remarked that no gentle-man could be permitted to act as counsel without a commission. The stranger drew from his pocket divers pieces of parchment bearing signa-tures and court seals from Virginia, Georgia, Alabama, Mississippi, Arkan-sas, Texas and possibly from other States, conferring on John Taylor

---

*James Stacy, in History of the Midway Congregational Church.

the privilege of counsellor, attorney at law, and solicitor. His name was then entered on the docket, and, asking a short indulgence, he found some one who kindly gave him the names of the witnesses, and they answered to the call. He opened the case by reading the declaration and proving the words. He said but very little more, and gave way to the defence. Prentiss made one of his fine speeches, expended his wit freely, and also aimed a sneer at the plaintiff's counsel, whom he described as a reckless adventurer, unable to live by his profession in any of the States in which he had been incautiously licensed.

"The learned Pike, with the garlands of poetry on his brow, rose to continue the argument of his friend Prentiss. The character of the plaintiff was denounced. The obscure attorney who had volunteered services came in for a share of his piercing wit and mischievous humor. Here the speaking for the defence closed with a flourish of exultation.

John Taylor stood before the jury. With his clear, piping voice, distinct in every syllable and full of feeling and intellect, he took up the evidence, applied the law, and then made himself known. He ridiculed the false wit and vulgar impudence of the opposing counsel, until even the gallant Prentiss and the manly Pike felt themselves as children in the hands of a giant. Court, jury, spectators, bar—all gazed with wonder. Taylor rose higher and higher in his flights, until the audience was fairly spellbound. He saw his advantage, knew his powers, and felt that the jury would give the full damages claimed in the declaration. He then turned to the spectators, who were much excited, and implored them not to lay violent hands on the defendant—not to ride him on a rail. They must forbear doing what justice prompted on the occasion. Fifty thousand dollars would be some punishment to a creature so sordid. Let him live to endure the scorn of honest men. The jury retired, and soon brought in a verdict for fifty thousand dollars! Taylor was immortal. The author does not vouch for the correctness of this story, but, from his own knowledge of Mr. Taylor and the inspiration under which he often spoke, he is inclined to believe it. This extraordinary man practiced law for several years in southern Georgia. He would have electrified even the Senate of the United States.*

Boston. Boston, an enterprising town of South Georgia, the rapid growth of which in recent years has kept well abreast with the development of this section, was chartered by an Act of the Legislature, approved October 24, 1870, designating Thomas Adams, B. A. Stone, A. B. Carson, J. Long and J. J. Hatchell to serve as commissioners pending an election to be held on the second

*Stephen F. Miller, in Bench and Bar of Georgia, Vol. I.

Monday in June, 1872. The corporate limits were made to embrace one mile square with the depot of the Atlantic and Gulf Railroad as the town center.[1] To meet the demands of growth, an Act was subsequently passed by the Legislature amending the old charter and giving the town a municipal form of government. On October 14, 1891, a charter was granted to the Boston and Albany Railroad, the stockholders of which were: M. R. Mallette, J. W. Taylor, D. R. Blood, A. B. Cone, W. M. Brooks, T. T. Stephens, E. R. Whaley, J. C. Stanaland, J. S. Norton, H. A. Vann, and F. C. Ivey.[2] The present public school system of Boston was established in 1891.

TIFT

Tifton. Tifton, the county-seat of Tift, began to exist in 1857 with the erection of a saw-mill on the site of the present town by Captain H. H. Tift. The subsequent history of this wide-awake young metropolis of the wire grass, which, in 1905, acquired its new honors as a county seat, has already been fully outlined in Volume I, to which the reader is referred.

TOOMBS

Lyons. In 1905 the County of Toombs was formed out of Tattnall, Montgomery and Emanuel Counties, and under this same Act Lyons was made the new county-seat. The town was chartered with a municipal form of government in 1897, but was founded a number of years prior to this time by Mr. H. C. Bagley, who here located a station on the old S. A. M. Railway, along the line of which he was then engaged in developing town sites at strategic points.

[1] Acts, 1870, p. 169.
[2] Acts, 1890-1891, Vol. I, p. 441.

TOWNS

Hiawassee. Hiawassee, the county-seat of Towns, was named for the picturesque river upon whose banks it is most charmingly situated. In 1856, when the County of Towns was formed out of Union and Rabun Counties, in this enchanted land of the mountains, Hiawassee was made the new county-seat. The town was incorporated on October 24, 1870, with the following-named commissioners, to-wit.: William T. Crane, A. M. Maulden, R. A. Brown and Dr. P. W. Rillion.* In 1857, a charter was granted for the Hiawassee Railroad Company to run from some point in the County of Rabun, at or near the town of Clayton, there to connect with the Northeastern Railroad; thence running down the valley of the Little Hightower, through Towns, Union and Fannin counties to the Tennessee line, in the direction of the Ducktown copper mines. But this charter failed to materialize into a steel highway, due to the on-coming of the Civil War.

Recollections of Gov. Towns. Governor Towns was a Chesterfield in his address. Nothing could exceed the suavity of his disposition and the ease of his manner. He was truly a refined man, courteous and unpretending with the plain, and diplomatic with the precise; it was constitutional, therefore pleasant to all. He had a friendly word and a kind recognition for each individual. His manner claimed no superiority over other men, and yet it signified that he was good as any of them He never appeared upon stilts, nor did he forget his self-respect in his most careless moods. At the bar his rank was decidedly high as an advocate. He possessed all the requisites of an orator to control the jury. In its subdued tones his voice was like plaintive music. The intonations were faultless. His language, at such times, was the poetry of emotion; his gestures adapted themselves, without consciousness on his part, to the circumstances of the case. The human heart was an open thing to him. He could play upon it in smiles or in tears, with almost the skill of Patrick Henry; yet he lacked the thunderbolts of that Jove of eloquence, to rival the grandeur of the storm. With these elements of

*Acts, 1870, p. 204.

success, ripened into maturity by practice and established in many a contest, Governor Towns had before him as inviting a prospect as ever allured the imagination. There had been a Forsyth, with his fluent simplicity and his inimitable sneer; a Berrien, with his music of phrase and his classic gestures; a Wilde, polished in diction and lofty in thought; a Colquitt, with his arrows of eloquence, barbed for the rhinocerous or softened for the hare; yet it was the prestige of Governor Towns to differ from them all—perhaps to excel them all—in the spontaneous gushings of the heart, in the electric sympathy which, kindling with the orator's emotion, blazed in every bosom—court, jury, bar, audience, all melted, all subdued, by the occasion. Such was the man and such the prospect, when he retired from the executive chair, in 1851. But a few months revolve; then suddenly the scene is changed; the tongue of the orator is palsied; his frame a hopeless wreck.*

TROUP

La Grange. In 1826, Troup County was organized out of a part of the recently acquired Creek Indian lands and named for Governor George M. Troup, the stalwart chief executive who forced the Federal government to redeem its obligation to the State, with reference to the Indian tribes. LaGrange, the county-seat of Troup, was named for the chateau of General Lafayette in France. The town was granted a charter of incorporation on December 16, 1828, with the following-named commissioners, to-wit.: Richard A. Lane, James Simmons, John Herring, Dowe Perry, and Howell W. Jenkins. But the old Troup County Academy was chartered a year earlier. On December 26, 1827, this pioneer school was incorporated with Messrs. Samuel Reid, Richard A. Lane, Whitfield H. Sledge, Henry Rogers and Charles L. Kennon as trustees.

But the prestige of LaGrange as an educational center grows out of its enterprise in founding two successful seminaries of learning for young ladies. Thomas Stanley, in the early thirties, here established a school for girls, out of which grew the LaGrange Female College, one of the pioneer institutions of Methodism in Georgia. It was chartered on December 17, 1847, as the LaGrange Female Institute, with the following board of trustees,

viz.: Sampson Duggar, Hampton W. Hill, Daniel Mc-
Millan, Orville A. Bull and Thomas B. Greenwood.* On
December 26, 1851, by legislative act, it became the La-
Grange Female College, a name which it still retains.
The Southern Female College was founded in 1845 by
Rev. Milton E. Bacon, a noted Baptist educator. It was
incorporated as the LaGrange Female Collegiate Semi-
nary, afterwards as the Southern and Western Female
College, and finally, on February 17, 1854, as the Southern
Female College, by which name it is still known. La-
Grange is today one of the most progressive towns of the
State, a wide-awake trade center, with up-to-date public
utilities, solid business establishments, sound banks and
many palatial homes. Such noted men as General Hugh
A. Haralson, Hon. Benjamin H. Hill, Hon. Julius A. Al-
ford and others, have been residents of this historic old
Georgia town.

———

James H. Cam- On the site of the present town of La-
eron: Pioneer. Grange, the first house was built by
James H. Cameron, a pioneer settler of
Scotch descent. It was a structure of logs, built after
the fashion which then prevailed on the frontier; but in
later years this primitive dwelling was replaced by a
handsome edifice. James H. Cameron's daughter, Frances, married Gen. Alfred Austell, who afterwards founded in Atlanta, the first national bank ever organized in
the Southern States. The Cameron family was established in Troup by five brothers: David and Thomas
settled in the neighborhood of Franklin, an Indian trading post which afterwards developed into West Point;
while James H., B. H., and William Cameron settled
near the center of the county, in the neighborhood of
what is now the city of LaGrange. These sturdy Scotchmen came into Troup soon after the county was opened
to settlement. They were the sons of James Cameron,
who emigrated from Scotland to North Carolina, in 1770,

———

*Acts, 1847, p. 120.

participated in the war of the Revolution, and some time after the close of hostilities came with his family to Georgia, first locating in Jasper.

Tomb of Gen. Hugh A. Haralson. Underneath a substantial monument in the town cemetery at LaGrange sleeps a distinguished soldier and civilian, after whom Georgia has named one of her counties: General Hugh A. Haralson. Three of his daughters married eminent men. One became the wife of General John B. Gordon, Governor and United States Senator. Another married Chief Justice Logan E. Bleckley, while a third married Hon. Basil H. Overby, a pioneer advocate of temperance and the first Prohibition candidate for Governor of Georgia. The inscriptions on the Haralson monument are as follows:

> On the west side: "Sacred to the memory of GEN. HUGH A. HARALSON, who departed this life Sept. 25, 1854, in the 49th year of his age." On the south side: "Here we have buried our head, husband and father. We must not murmur. What God does is right."

Burnt Village: a Tale of the Indian Wars. Pages 460-464.

West Point. When the lands in this part of Georgia were first acquired by the whites, there was located on the site of the present town of West Point a trading post known as Franklin. It was the center of quite an important traffic with the Indians, who came hither to exchange peltry—sometimes for firearms, but more frequently for fire-water; and since the trading post was conveniently located with reference to both the Creeks and the Cherokees, these tribes were often seen here, long after the treaty of Indian Springs, under which all the lands between the Flint and Chattahoochee were ceded to the whites. In the neighborhood of the old trading post there arose a village, the population of which was augmented by new settlers when Troup County was formed out of a part of the Creek Indian lands. Two of the earliest pioneers, whose quest of fortune brought them to this remote part of the wilderness, were Thomas Winston and O. D. Whitaker. Mr. George H. Winston, the former's son, became a very prominent man in the social and public life of Troup. His acquaintance with West Point began when the village was still known by the name of Franklin, and he learned to speak with ease both the Creek and Cherokee languages, through frequent contact with the Indians who came here to trade. In 1832 the name of the town was changed to West Point. Three years later the corporate limits were extended, and on December 25, 1837, a charter was granted to the West Point Academy, with the following board of trustees, to-wit.: Benjamin P. Robertson, William Reid, Dickerson Burnham, John M. Russell, John C. Webb and Edward B. Terrell. Some of the last fighting of the Civil War occurred at Fort Tyler. But while the town of West Point is rich in heroic memories, it is likewise suffused with the spirit of the new era. Its public-school system is unsurpassed in the State. Commercially the town is prosperous, with a wide-awake body of citizens, whose business activities are financed by sound banking institutions.

———

Fort Tyler: The Last to Surrender. Fort Tyler, overlooking West Point, was the last Confederate fort to yield to the enemy during the Civil War. The date on which this surrender took place was April 16, 1865, and in the desperate fight which occurred at this time General Robert C. Tyler, the commander in charge, was killed while making a gallant defence of the town. The reader is referred to Volume I of this work for a more detailed account of the battle at West Point. The local U. D. C. chapter bears the historic name of Fort

Tyler and, under the auspices of this chapter, a handsome Confederate monument was unveiled on Memorial Day in 1901.*

TURNER

Ashburn. Volume I, Pages 982-984.

To supplement the historical sketch of Ashburn contained in the preceding volume of this work, we take pleasure in publishing the affidavit hereto attached:

We, the undersigned, certify that there was a public road here, where Ashburn now stands, before the town was ever built, and was known as the Troupville Road, and was built by the Government.

Also that there were settlers here during the war, and some of them yet here, and who have done much more in the upbuilding of the county than the newcomers.

Further, that one of the natives, D. H. Davis named the town of Ashburn for W. W. Ashburn, who gave the land for the town.

Chandler & Gorday was the first business firm of Ashburn. The natives are: Henderson, Paulk, Whiddon, Cravey, Hamons, Hobby, House, Story, Hall, Champion, Rainey, Pate, Pitts, Bowman, Kerce, Cone, Clements, Bass, Stephens, Pittman, Weavers, Gordays, Judges, Thomas, Fletchers, Wells, Hawkins, Chandlers, Davis, Brock, Covington, Averys, Mays, Fitzgeralds, Kendricks, Lamberts, Curtoy, Hart, Wilder Smith, Handcock, Lukes, Sumners, Fords, Tisons, Kings, McCalls, Shivers, Marshalls, Filyaws, McLendons, Wheelers, Fountains, Webbs, Suggs, Roso, Townsends, Branches, Springs, Rooks, Mills, Barfields, Williams, Royals, Youngs, Browns, Yawn, Wiggins.

Signed:

W. A. Story,	J. A. Clements,
A. L. Bobby,	D. G. Barfield,
D. F. Avery,	Z. Bass (Atty.),
D. N. Shiver,	W. C. Cone,
J. J. Covington,	S. M. Shivers,
J. L. Bass,	T. T. Fillyaw,
J. R. Stephens,	John D. Hobby,
J. W. Henderson,	G. W. Turner,
J. E. Paulk (D. D. S.),	E. Y. Paulk (Tax Collector T. Co.),

*The statement made in Vol. I to the effect that the above monument was unveiled by the Ladies' Memorial Association is erroneous.

A. E. Bass,
W. H. Wheeler,
H. S. Story,
Ben Cravey,
Joshua Owens,
M. Owens,
E. T. Pate,
James Cravey,
T. A. Kendrick (Confed. Vet.),
J. R. Brock,
Mrs. W. L. Pittman,
W. L. Pittman (Tax Receiver T. Co.),
J. L. Royal,
A. B. Wells,
B. F. Rainey,
J. B. White, Sr. (1849),
Dav. Cravey,
A. P. Hamons,
Joe McHandcock (Ordinary, T. Co.),
S. D. Gladden,
J. H. Story,
W. E. Branch,
J. J. Davis,
J. J. McDowell,
H. M. Cockrell (Confed. Vet.),
B. H. Cockrell (Dept. Clerk, Supr. Court, T. Co.),
D. H. Hamons,
R. D. Law,
S. Bailey (70 years),
W. D. Ross,
A. J. Pitts,
C. T. Royal, Sr.,
W. M. Massey,
L. T. Nipper,
B. E. Smith,
C. C. Story,
E. B. Hamons,
Mrs. A. B. Wells,
Homer Adams,
A. J. Story,
G. R. Luke, M. D.,

O. W. Smith,
D. F. Bowman, Sr.,
J. T. McLendon,
W. J. Luke,
W. A. Nipper,
Mrs. Zary Nipper,
W. L. Luke,
Warren L. Story, Md.
J. R. Rainey,
J. A. King (Sheriff, T. C.),
T. D. Marshburn,
W. K. Wiggins,
J. W. Hobby,
M. M. Pate,
B. J. Wills,
T. A. Judge,
W. T. Smith,
Jas. M. Rainey,
J. M. Pate,
J. C. McLendon,
Allen Owens,
R. N. Wiggins,
G. M. Hawkins,
A. J. Sumner,
G. W. Hobby,
T. M. Roberts,
G. C. Avery,
J. E. Roberts,
B. D. White,
B. S. Pate,
J. M. Courtoy,
John Pate,
M. L. Dowdy,
Mrs. Polly Dowdy,
W. B. Brock,
Mrs. Bettie Brock,
Nas Rainey,
Mrs. Mollie Rainey,
R. W. Lambert,
H. Pitts,
W. J. Musselwhite,
D. W. Spires,
A. H. Pitts,

GEORGIA, TURNER COUNTY:

Personally, comes before me an officer duly authorized to administer oaths, H. M. Harp, who, being duly sworn, says on oath that the foregoing is an exact copy of names attached to the foregoing certificate.

H. M. HARP.

Sworn to and subscribed before me
this January, 1914.

C. W. DEARISO,
Not. Public Turner County, Ga.

TWIGGS

Old Marion.
Volume I.

Jeffersonville. The original county-seat of Twiggs was Marion, a town whose name no longer appears upon the map of Georgia. On February 11, 1850, an Act was approved authorizing a removal of the county-seat to such a place as the Inferior Court might designate on certain lands owned by Henry Solomon. The same Act prescribes that the new county-seat was likewise to be called Marion. But the removal contemplated in this Act was not accomplished until years afterward, when the site of public buildings was fixed at Jeffersonville, a town named for the great Sage of Monticello. This town grew out of an Act approved December 25, 1837, creating the Jeffersonville Land Company, the declared purpose of which was to form a village, and to erect a female college. The stockholders in this enterprise were: John R. Lowery, Jesse Sinclair, George W. Welch, Kelly Glover, Joshua R. Wimberley, Peter G. Thompson, Thomas J. Perryman, Milton Wilder, William Choice, William E. Carswell and Isaiah Atteway.*

UNION

Blairsville. In 1832 Union was organized out of a part of the Cherokee lands, with Blairsville as the county-seat. The town was named for Francis P.

---

*Acts, 1837, p. 144.

Blair, Sr., of Kentucky, and was incorporated by an Act approved December 26, 1835, with the following-named commissioners, to-wit.: Philip D. Maroney, Thomas Kelly, David Hawkins, Ebenezer Fain and Hugh Capehart.[1]   On December 21, 1833, the Blairsville Academy was granted a charter, with Messrs. John Sanders, Richard Holden, John Butt, Jr., Moses Anderson and Thomas Colling as trustees.[2]   Charmingly situated among the Blue Ridge Mountains, Blairsville is an attractive little town needing only railway facilities to stimulate it into a vigorous growth.

————

UPSON

Thomaston.   On December 15, 1824, an Act was approved creating a new county out of lands formerly embraced within the limits of Pike and Crawford, and, in honor of a distinguished ante-bellum lawyer, Hon. Stephen Upson, of Lexington, it was called Upson.   The name given to the seat of government was Thomaston, presumably for General Jett Thomas, a gallant officer of the War of 1812, and a practical engineer, who built the first State Capitol at Milledgeville; but while such is the presumption there is nothing in the records to establish the fact.   The site for public buildings was made permanent at Thomaston on June 11, 1825, at which time a charter of incorporation was granted to the town, with the following-named commissioners, to-wit.: Edward Holloway, Robert W. Collier, James Walker, Sr., James Cooper and Joseph Rogers.[3]

One of the first communites in the State to realize the possibilities of the iron horse as a motive power of commerce, the people of Thomaston began early in the thirties to agitate the building of a line of railway between Thomaston and Barnesville, and on December 23,

---

[1] Acts, 1835, p. 113.
[2] Acts, 1833, p. 7.
[3] Acts, 1825, p. 23.

1839, an Act was approved chartering a company to build this road. The stockholders named in this pioneer charter were: Robert Redding, David Kendall, Thomas F. Bethel, Thomas Flewellen, Thomas Thweatt, Thomas Beall, William Lowe, Milus R. Meadows, Allen M. Walker, Nathaniel F. Walker, William A. Cobb, Edwin C. Turner and John Castlen.[1] Since it was out of the question to secure a trunk line, Thomaston undertook to do the next best thing, viz., to build a spur line to Barnesville, there to connect with the old Monroe Railroad, now a part of the Central of Georgia. Some few years later, on February 9, 1854, a charter was obtained for the Thomaston Railroad Company to construct a line from Thomaston to West Point, with the following stockholders named in the charter: Thomas F. Bethel, Curran Rogers, Thomas W. Reviere, David Kendall, William Lowe, Jesse Sternes, Nathaniel Walker, James M. Smith and William A. Cobb.[2]

Both of these lines were eventually constructed. But the one between Thomaston and Barnesville became embarrassed by debt and in 1860 was sold under judgment by the sheriff of Upson to the following parties, to-wit.: Andrew J. White, Curran Rogers, Woodson and Bowdre, William Lowe, James Trice, B. B. White, James M. Middlebrooks, Jesse Sternes, Thomas S. Sherman, B. B. King, D. R. Beall, Duke Williams, Thomas Cauthron, Simeon Rogers, John C. Drake, Isaac Cheney, James M. Smith, Benjamin Bethel, David Kendall, Sylvanus Gibson, William Spivey, Jonathan Colquitt & Co., John Traylor, William A. Cobb, William Stephens and Daniel Denham.[3] The Thomaston Academy was chartered in 1825, soon after the county was organized.

On December 23, 1857, the town was reincorporated with the following-named commissioners: John C. Drake, John Thompson, William Carraway and Norman Brice.[4]

[1] Acts, 1839, p. 101.
[2] Acts, 1853-1854, p. 428.
[3] Acts, 1860, p. 199.
[4] Acts, 1857, p. 103.

There was not a community in the State more fortunate in its pioneer settlers than Thomaston. Some of them amassed large wealth, built spacious and splendid old homes, and dispensed a hospitality in keeping with the best days of the ancient regime. Thomaston is today quite an important commercial and manufacturing center, with a number of prosperous financial and business establishments. Robert E. Lee Institute is one of the best-equipped high schools in the Southern States, and its principal, Prof. F. F. Rowe, one of the South's foremost educators.

Some of the Early Pioneers. In addition to the pioneers mentioned in the foregoing sketch of Upson, there were others no less prominent whose names deserve mention. On the list of incorporators of the old Upson Camp Ground, for which a charter was granted by the Legislature, in 1837, we find Peter Holloway, James Hightower and Wm. G. Andrews, all of whom were men of means, possessed of large landed estates. Rev. Zachariah Gordon, a Baptist minister, owned a plantation on the Flint River as early as 1833, and here his distinguished son, General John B. Gordon, was born. Jacob and Butler King, cousins of Zachariah Gordon, were also pioneer settlers. Dr. Curran Rogers was an early physician. His father, Simeon Rogers, was one of the first comers into Upson. "Rogers's Factory," a noted landmark of the county for years and one of the pioneer industrial enterprises of Georgia, was burned by the Federals in 1865. It stood within easy walking distance of Thomaston. Colonel Roland Ellis, of Macon, is a grandson of this early settler. Rev. Simeon Shaw, a former missionary to Japan, is also one of his descendants. The gifted Mrs. Loula Kendall Rogers married his son. Still another pioneer family of Upson were the Myricks, a family of wide note in the public life of Georgia. The first Mayor of Thomaston was Dr. John Calvin Drake, a man greatly beloved by the people of Upson. His wife, a woman of marked intellect and character, was spared to him for more than sixty years. She bore him a large family of children, one of whom married General George P. Harrison, of Alabama, a distinguished Confederate officer. Mr. G. A. Weaver, Sr., of Thomaston, also married a daughter of Dr. Drake. Throughout the entire war period, this noted physician, too old to serve in the ranks, practiced without fee in the families of the soldiers, giving them freely of his professional skill. After the war he was sent to the Legislature, but the fiery tempered old gentleman let the radicals seat William Guilford, a negro, before he would take the oath of allegiance prescribed by the military government. Dr.

Drake was born in North Carolina, of Revolutionary ancestors. Judge Travis A. D. Weaver, a native of Greene County, Ga., was also an early settler of Upson. He was a courtly old gentleman, a Mason, a steward in the Methodist Church, and a man of deep religious faith. His father, Benjamin Weaver, was a soldier of the Revolution. Mr. G. A. Weaver, Sr., and Professor W. T. Weaver, sons of Judge Weaver, each became men of mark in Georgia, the former as a captain of industry, the latter as a leader of the hosts of education.

Helped to Make Washington's Casket. Old man John Webb was an interesting figure in Thomaston for many years. He kept the old Webb House, made coffins, and married five or six times. He was born in Maryland and at an early age was apprenticed to a cabinetmaker in Alexandria, Va., named Greene. This gentleman secured a contract to make the coffin which today holds the remains of George Washington. John Webb helped his employer to make this coffin in 1832. Every scrap of the old casket, out of which the body was taken, found a most jealous custodian in Undertaker Greene, who treasured it in his possession with a miser's care; but John Webb was fortunate enough to secure a part of the old coffin, and when he came to Georgia a few years later it was still among his treasured effects.

Upson in the Civil War. More than 1,200 men enlisted in the Confederate Army from Upson. Colonel James M. Smith, afterwards Governor of Georgia, was practicing law in Thomaston when the war began. He left here as Captain of Company D, in the Thirteenth Georgia Regiment. General John B. Gordon, one of the most illustrious of Confederate leaders, to whose command was entrusted half of Lee's army at Appomattox, was born on a plantation in Upson. Colonel P. W. Alexander, afterwards celebrated as a war correspondent, was a young practitioner of law at Thomaston, at the outbreak of hostilities in 1861. Captain J. W. F. Hightower, a gallant cavalry officer, commanded Company E, in the Third Battalion of Georgia Reserves. His sons, R. E. Hightower, president of the Thomaston Cotton Mills, and W. C. Hightower, of the Britt-Hightower Stock Company, are representative and prosperous business men of Thomaston. Dr. E. A. Flewellen was a prominent surgeon in Bragg's army. He died at the Rock, in 1910, at the age of ninety-one years, unmarried. He left a large estate, but was a somewhat erratic old gentleman, who selected his own monument a few months prior to his death. On the list of the slain at Sharpsburg, Md., in 1862, was the name of gallant Ed Dallas, first lieutenant of the Upson

Volunteers, Company D, of the Thirteenth Georgia Regiment. He left a wife and six children. Somewhere, near the waters of the Chesapeake, he fills an unknown grave, but his memory is still cherished and revered in Thomaston, where four of his sons today reside. In the U. D. C. Chapter-room, at the R. E. Lee Institute, there is a blood-stained battle flag presented to the chapter on the 26th of April, 1913, by the Davis family of Thomaston. It tells a splendid story of heroic daring, one of which his descendants to the latest generation may well be proud. James R. Davis, a beardless boy, in the Upson Sentinels, Company A, Forty-sixth Georgia Regiment, saw the color-bearer shot down at Franklin, Tenn. Without waiting for orders, he grasped the broken flagstaff and pressed forward until he was shot through the lungs and from the loss of blood fell exhausted upon the field of battle. He recovered from the effects of his wound, but died later of tuberculosis. At the commencement of the war, W. T. Weaver and G. A. Weaver, were students at Emory College, Oxford, but fired by the martial spirit they joined a lot of college boys and set out for Macon, where they enlisted as private soldiers. Each of these boys gave a good account of himself at the front.*

The Confederate Monument. In the spring of 1908 a handsome monument was unveiled at Thomaston to commemorate the heroism of the Confederate soldiers who went to the front from Upson. Judge J. E. F. Matthews, Ordinary of the county, delivered a masterly address on this occasion, in which he cited many important facts of local history connected with the war between the States. This address, which was afterwards published because of its historic value, contains a full roster of the companies going to the war from Upson. The following passage is quoted from the address of Judge Matthews:

"Fifty-one Confederate soldiers who died in the hospitals in Thomaston, Ga., in 1864, have at the heads of their graves in the Thomaston Ceme-. tery marble slabs with inscriptions showing that they were from a half dozen different Southern States, to-wit.: South Carolina, North Carolina, Alabama, Mississippi, Louisiana, Arkansas, Tennessee and Georgia. Some of the graves are marked 'Unknown.' "

Distinguished Residents of Upson. On the honor roll of Upson's distinguished residents there are many bright names. Foremost upon the list comes General John B. Gordon, the renowned hero of Appomattox, Governor, United States Senator and Commander of the United Confederate Veterans. Congressman George Carey,

---

*Much of this information was furnished by Mrs. Kate Weaver Dallas, of Thomaston, Ga.

during the last years of his life, came from Columbia County to Upson. Rev. Daniel J. Myrick, one of the ablest of Methodist theologians and scholars, was born at the Rock. His work on "Scripture Baptism," is still one of the recognized standards. Bishop Warren A. Candler, of Atlanta, is a cousin, and Judge Shelby Myrick, of Savannah, is a grandson of this noted Dr. Myrick. Rev. W. L. Pickard, D. D., the newly elected president of Mercer University, at Macon, was born in Upson. This was also the birthplace of Rev. B. J. W. Graham, D. D., one of the present editors and owners of the *Christian Index*. The beloved Dr. Thomas R. Kendall, of the Methodist Episcopal Church, South, spent his boyhood days in Upson; and here his talented sister, Mrs. Loula Kendall Rogers, was born. The latter has written many exquisite gems of song. Reared in luxury, her beautiful ante-bellum home was one of the landmarks of the old South. Professor G. F. Oliphant, the well-known superintendent of the Academy for the Blind, at Macon, was reared and educated at Thomaston, where he was a member of the first graduating class to receive diplomas from R. E. Lee Institute. Later he was for a number of years president of this school. Hon. Charles S. Barrett, the official head of the Farmers' Union, began his career as a planter in Upson. Here he also married and taught school. Dr. Lincoln McConnell, the noted Baptist evangelist, one of the most successful lecturers on the American platform, purchased not long ago the old Respass place, a few miles out from Thomaston, and here he spends a part of each year.

WALKER

La Fayette. La Fayette, the county-seat of Walker County, was originally known as Chattooga, and, under this name, it was made the site of public buildings when the county was first organized out of a part of Murray, in 1833. But later the name was changed to La Fayette, in honor of the illustrious French nobleman, who gave his sword to America during the Revolution. Two local academies were granted charters of incorporation, the Chattooga Academy, in 1836, and the La Fayette Female Academy, in 1837, and by glancing over a list of trustees chosen for the latter school we may obtain the names of some of the leading pioneer citizens. The trustees of this school were: William Quillian, James Hoge, A. L. Barry, Spencer Marsh and David L. Seward.* Between a Federal force, under

---

*Acts, 1837, p. 8.

General Gideon J. Pillow, and two detached columns of Confederate troops, a battle was here fought on June 24, 1864, known as the battle of La Fayette. The town has of late enjoyed a substantial growth. Its milling interests are quite large, besides which it supplies an extensive mountain trade, and is a wide-awake commercial center, with a good banking capital, an excellent public-school system, and a fine body of citizens.

Georgia's Monument at Chickamauga. On the historic battle-field of Chickamauga, near the famous La Fayette road, in what is now Chickamauga National Park, stands the superb Georgia monument, a shaft of granite, colossal in proportions, ornamented with bronze figures and entablatures. In the preceding volume of this work a description of the monument is given more in detail. It is perhaps the most exquisite work of art and the most impressive memorial structure on the entire field—an object of universal admiration. But equally admired by every one is the felicitous inscription from the pen of Major Joseph B. Cumming, of Augusta, himself a gallant survivor of the sixties. It reads as follows:

> "To the lasting Memory of all her Sons who fought on this Field—those who fought and lived and those who fought and died, those who gave Much and those who gave All—Georgia erects this monument."

To accomplish the ends of brevity, the Chickamauga Park Commission, as then constituted, used only a part of the inscription composed by Major Cumming, and perhaps it loses nothing in effect for this conciseness. But the inscription as written by Major Cumming is a literary unit, a model of condensed expression. It came to him on a summer evening, with the suddenness of an inspiration; and it then and there received a form which was never afterwards altered or amended. As originally penned, the inscription is a gem worthy of preservation as a whole; and, with the author's permission, it is herewith reproduced in full:

> To the lasting Memory and perpetual Glory
> Of all her Sons, who fought on this Field,
> Those who fought and lived and those who fought and died,
> Those who gave Much and those who gave All
>
> GEORGIA
>
> Erects this Monument.
> Around it sleep Slayer and Slain
> All brave, all sinking to rest
> Convinced of Duty done.
> Glorious Battle! Blessed Peace!
> This Monument stands for both of these—Glory and Peace;
> For this Memorial of her soldiers' valor
> Georgia places on a foundation, laid for it,
> In this day of Reconciliation,
> By those 'gainst whom they fought.
> Glory and Peace encamp about this stately Shaft!
> Glory perennial as Chickamauga's flow,
> Peace everlasting as yon Lookout Mountain.

Rossville: The Historic Home of an Indian Chief. Rossville, a present-day village, near the Tennessee line, was the old home of the famous chief of the Cherokee nation, John Ross. He was the leader of his people at the time of the removal of the tribe, in 1837, and for more than twenty-five years thereafter he continued to be the recognized head of the government in the Far West. Opposed to the treaty of removal, he headed a faction of the Cherokees known as the Ross party, in opposition to the one headed by Ridge; but he was acquitted of complicity in the murder of the treaty-makers. John Ross was an eloquent public speaker and one of the foremost orators of the Cherokee nation. The home in which the old chief lived at Rossville is still standing, though today a weather-beaten and spectral old ruin. It was built by John McDonald, a Scotch trader among the Cherokees, who married an Indian maiden of the full blood. Mollie, a daughter of this union, on flowering into womanhood, became the wife of Daniel Ross, a native of Inverness. There is quite a bit of forest romance connected with this affair. The elder Ross, soon after the Revolution, was dispatched from Baltimore to trade with the Indians; and while passing down the Tennessee River he was captured by the Cherokees, who, for some reason, were not friendly to his enterprise; and it was only through the strenuous intercession of John McDonald, a fellow-countryman, that his life was spared. The other members of the party met death in the wilderness. Daniel Ross became an inmate of the McDonald home, and falling in love with the dark-eyed Mollie he eventually married her. John McDonald gave his son-in-law a good start in business by purchasing a fine stock of merchandise for him, and the foundations of the little building of hewn logs in which he kept store are still to be seen near the gate of the old Ross home. Here, on October 3, 1790, the future chief of the Cherokee nation was born. In after years, he enlarged the house built by his grandfather, adding thereto a council chamber, 23 feet in length. At first there was only one door to the council chamber, but subsequently, by way of precaution, two others were added, one of which opened into his bed-room. There was a post office established at Rossville as early as 1819, to which the mails were brought by stage-coach lines, connecting on the south with Augusta, Ga., and on the north with Nashville, Tenn. Elsewhere will be found a brief account of the removal of the Cherokee Indians, one of the most pathetic chapters in the history of the State. John Ross died in Washington, D. C., August 1, 1866, while on a visit to the national seat of government, at the ripe age of seventy-six years. The site of the present city of Chattanooga was formerly called by the name of Ross's Landing.

WALTON

Cowpens.   Under the Lottery Act of 1818, Walton County was formed out of lands then recently acquired from the Indians and named for Governor George Walton, Signer of the Declaration, and one of Georgia's most illustrious sons. In the same year a strip of land was acquired from Jackson, and three years later there was an exchange of certain parcels with Henry and a portion set off to Newton, while in 1914 a part was taken to form Barrow. The original county-seat of Walton was Cowpens, a village named for the scene of a famous Revolutionary battle in South Carolina. Judge John M. Dooly, the celebrated wit, presided over the first session of the Superior Court in Walton. It was held at Cowpens, in a log house, which, according to an old account, contained cracks "large enough to throw a small shoat through," while the clerk of the court carried his most important papers in the crown of his hat.

But Cowpens is illustrious in its memories. It ceased to be the county-seat after two years, but as a suburb of Monroe it long continued to enjoy aristocratic honors. Colonel John Addison Cobb, two of whose sons, Howell and Tom, became illustrious in the annals of Georgia, was one of the first settlers at Cowpens. Here, too, lived Colonel William H.

Jackson, a son of the fiery old Governor who fought the Yazoo fraud. He married a sister of Colonel John A. Cobb; and of this union came the future Chief Justice of Georgia, Judge James Jackson. Professor Williams Rutherford lived here at one time. He married a daughter of Colonel John A. Cobb; and of this union sprang one of Georgia's brainiest women, the gifted educator and historian, Miss Mildred Rutherford, a native of Cowpens. Here also at one time lived Judge Junius Hillyer and his son, Judge George Hillyer. On what afterwards became the Grant place, in the present environs of Monroe, lived the great Wilson Lumpkin, afterwards United States Senator and Governor; but the pioneer's cabin in which he then resided gave way in after years to the elegant home of Colonel John T. Grant.

Monroe. It was during the era of good feeling, under President Monroe, that the permanent county-seat of Walton began to blossom amid the wilderness. Hence the name Monroe. Its charter of incorporation was granted on November 30, 1821, with the following-named commissioners, to-wit.: Elisha Betts, Vincent Haralson, James West, James Moody and George W. Humphreys.[1] Two of these, Elisha Betts and Vincent Haralson, were also trustees of the Walton County Academy, along with William Johnson, Timothy C. Word and Wilson Whatley.[2] On the site now occupied by Mr. John Arnold's residence stood the Female Seminary of Monroe. Miss Martha Printup was the first teacher. After the war Miss Jennie Johnson was for a time in charge. Miss Johnson subsequently married Judge John P. Edwards, clerk of the court for nearly forty years. The Male Academy stood in the McDaniel grove. Here, for a number of years the afterwards noted Dr. G. A. Nunnally, a prince of educators, taught the youth of Monroe. Later he became the first principal of Johnston Institute, a school endowed by Nehemiah Johnston, a wealthy citizen of the town. Mr. Johnston was a man of Northern birth, who came to Monroe some time before the Civil War and amassed a fine property, but died without heirs, bequeathing a large part of his estate to education.

[1] Acts, 1821, p. 125.
[2] Acts, 1821, p. 3.

On the site of Mr. C. T. Mobley's home, Prof. A. J. Burruss, for a long time, taught a school for boys. Prof. Burruss was a splendidly equipped teacher, whose memory is still green in the hearts of his old pupils. Johnston Institute at a later period was destroyed by fire, to be replaced by the present handsome public school building of Monroe. Only a small part of the original sum bequeathed by Mr. Johnston still remained, but this remnant has been invested in a school near the cotton mills, to which the generous donor's name has been given. Only a short distance out from Monroe stands the Fifth District Agricultural School, a prosperous State institution. In 1882, a line of railway running from Monroe to Social Circle was completed, and later a line to Gainesville, each giving the town a renewed commercial impetus. With up-to-date public utilities, Monroe is fully abreast of the times, boasting two cotton factories, an oil mill, several strong banks, and scores of wide-awake business establishments. Monroe has been the home of many distinguished Georgians, including the Colquitts—Walter T. and Alfred H. It is still the home of Governor Henry D. McDaniel, the town's foremost citizen, and one of the most beloved of Georgians. In the neighborhood of Monroe was fought the famous battle of Jack's Creek, in 1787.*

Isaac Smith, a soldier of the Revolution, sleeps near Monroe, in a grave unmarked.

Social Circle. Located at the junction of the Georgia Railway with the Georgia Midland, Social Circle is a town of wide-awake industrial and commercial activities, owning one of the largest fertilizer plants in

*Two articles on Walton County, one by Judge Ben J. Edwards, and one by Mrs. G. A. Lewis, constitute the sources from which much of this information has been derived.

the State, besides a cotton mill, two banks, and numerous
mercantile establishments. It is said that the town derived its name from an incident in pioneer times, when
a party of convivial spirits were here seated around a
camp fire, freely imbibing the ardent. One of the number,
in a moment of hilarity, made the remark, to which the
others readily gave assent, that here was a ''social
circle,'' and from this circumstance arose the name of
the present town. The Social Circle Academy was
granted a charter on December 22, 1828, with the following board of trustees, to-wit.: Wilson Whatley, Joseph
Peeples, Weldon Jones, James Philips, and Elisha Henderson.[1] But the town itself was not incorporated until
December 22, 1832, when the following commissioners
were named: Wilson Whatley, Samuel Catley, Lewis
Maine, George W. Walker and S. J. T. Whatley.[2]

WARREN

Warrenton.   In 1793, Warren County was organized out
                of Richmond, Columbia and Wilkes Coun-
ties, with Warrenton as the county-seat. Both the town
and the county were named for General Joseph Warren,
who fell mortally wounded in the battle of Bunker Hill.
The town was incorporated on December 10, 1810, with
the following-named commissioners, to-wit.: David Bush,
George Cotton, Chappel Heath, Jeremiah Butt and Hamilton Goss.[3] Six years later, on December 18, 1816, the
old Warrenton Academy was granted a charter of incorporation, with trustees named as follows: Samuel
Lowther, Peyton Baker, Arthur Moncrief, Edward Don-
oho, Rufus Broom, Archelaus Flewellyn, Turner Persons, George W. Hardwick and Dennis. L. Ryan.[4] In
1838 the town limits were fixed at a distance of one mile

[1] Acts, 1828, p. 15.
[2] Acts, 1832, p. 98.
[3] Clayton's Compendium, p. 607.
[4] Lamar's Digest, p. 12.

from the court-house. As a community, Warrenton has always been noted for its conservatism, and while it has not grown as rapidly as some other towns of the State, it has always maintained a high standard of public morals and a reputation for strict integrity in matters of business. It is today a wide-awake town, with up-to-date public utilities, a number of good banks, several handsome mercantile establishments, and many beautiful homes. The present public school system of Warrenton was established in 1893.

Bird's Iron Works. Probably the first iron works established in Georgia were built at Ogeechee Falls, in Warren County, by William Bird, an enterprising pioneer, who prior to his removal to Georgia founded the town of Birdsboro, Pa. Mr. Bird was the grandfather of two noted Southern orators: Hon. William L. Yancey, of Alabama, and Colonel Benjamin C. Yancey, of Georgia. The iron works established at this place in the early part of the last century are described at some length in William Bird's will, recorded in the Ordinary's office at Warrenton. He bequeathed this property to three sons.

WASHINGTON

Sandersville: Early Days Recalled.* When the County of Washington was created, in 1784, the Oconee River formed the western boundary of the State of Georgia. Indian depredations were of almost daily occurrence, and because of conditions on the frontier twelve years elapsed before a county-site was selected. In 1796 a Mr. Sanders donated the land selected for this purpose, which then formed a part of his

---

*Much of this information has been obtained from residents of Sandersville, including Mrs. D. C. Harris, Mrs. S. J. Bayne, and others.

plantation, and in honor of this liberal pioneer the town was called Sandersville. His store at the cross-roads furnished a nucleus for the new county-seat, which was destined to a slow but steady growth.

On November 27, 1812, the town was incorporated with the following-named commissioners: David Martin, Samuel Richmond, Simeon Rogers, John Matthews and Isham H. Saffold.[1] At a very early period the State chartered an academy, the support of which was for years maintained by a lottery authorized for this purpose, and among the original trustees were: Benjamin Skrine, Henry Crowell, Tillman Dixon, Morgan Brown, Frederick Cullens, John Irwin, James Kendrick, Nathaniel G. Rutherford and John Williams.[2] On December 26, 1851, the famous Washington County Female Institute was chartered, with the following board of trustees: William Smith, Green Brantley, Joseph Banks, James R. Smith, Augustus A. Cullens, William Hodges, Nathaniel W. Haines, Isham H. Saffold and James S. Hook.[3] Three of these failed to serve, whereupon Benjamin Tarbutton, E. S. Langdale and Heywood Brookins were added to the list. Some few years later a school for boys, taught by Colonel John W. Rudisill, was merged with the institute, despite the opposition of many who did not believe in co-education. Prof. A. C. Thompson was afterwards, for years, principal.

As a seat of culture, Sandersville looked with distrust upon railroads, and it was not until 1876 that a short line was built connecting Sandersville with the Central of Georgia. Even then there were citizens who refused to patronize the line, preferring to haul their goods by wagon. In 1886 a road was built connecting Sandersville with Augusta. For several years before the war there was a stage line running to Sparta; also one leading to Dublin, on which a semi-weekly service

[1] Acts, 1851-1852, p. 332.
[2] Georgia Laws, 1819, p. 50.
[3] Lamar's Digest, p. 948.

was maintained. Besides, Sandersville was on the mail route between Savannah and Milledgeville, and when the stage reached the suburbs the carrier always blew a bugle to announce his arrival. The first postmaster of the town was Major Heywood Brookins.

Sandersville is today a progressive and wide-awake community, with up-to-date public utilities. Its schools are among the best in the State of Georgia. But the special pride of Sandersville is the Rawlings Sanitarium, an institute whose fame has traveled abroad. The present staff is composed of Dr. William Rawlings, Dr. O. L. Rogers, Dr. T. B. King and Mr. O. L. Herndon, with a corps of twenty-five efficient nurses. The town is built on a ridge occupying the highest point between Savannah and Macon; and is surrounded by an agricultural section second to none in Georgia. Says a well-known gentleman:* "The town is not of mushroom growth, but everything has been planned and operated upon sound business principles, and as a result we have no failing merchants and broken banks, but all kinds of business moving along as systematically and as gently as the deep current of a mighty river. From the ashes have sprung magnificent dwellings, and the sweet aroma of prosperity like a pavilion overshadows our town."

The Fire of 1855. On March 24, 1855, occurred what is locally known as the great fire. It broke out in Mr. Nathan Renfroe's carriage shop, on the western side of the town, and, driven by a strong wind, it swept across the town, burning court-house, jail, hotel and dwellings. In less than two hours only five structures remained standing. Major Brookins, the Ordinary, left his own house in flames, in order to secure the public records. It was on Saturday afternoon, and at the hotel great preparations were in progress for the

*Capt. P. R. Taliaferro, a former resident of Sandersville.

Sabbath, which was to usher in court week. Mrs. Brantley was baking cake in her old-fashioned iron oven. The wooden house burned down, but when the ashes cooled and the lid was lifted from the oven the cakes were found beautifully baked.

From an old copy of the *Central Georgian* on file in the court-house, it seems that the editor of this paper, Mr. P. C. Pendleton, lost office, press, type and everything else, but in less than five weeks the paper was again afloat. At great expense, Mr. Pendleton purchased the printing office of the *Eatonton Independent Press,* removed the outfit to Sandersville and began work in his kitchen. For several months Eatonton maintained a column of news in this paper, the name of which was changed to the *Georgian and Press,* but J. E. Turner, Esq., because of some political disagreement, gave up this column, after which the former name was resumed.

So great was the suffering caused by the fire that contributions for relief poured into Sandersville from every part of the State. Savannah gave $500, a sum duplicated by the Central of Georgia, and, in the aggregate, $3,439 was raised. But, while fire consumes dross, it only refines pure gold, and in time handsomer buildings replaced the ones destroyed. Mr. R. L. Warthen introduced a bill in the Legislature authorizing a tax levy to build a handsome new court-house. This building was erected, but was burned by Sherman in 1864.

Gen. Sherman's Visit. Sandersville lay in the path of Sherman's fiery march to the sea, but the town was saved from complete destruction through the importunities of Rev. J. D. Anthony, who, as a Mason, appealed to General Sherman on behalf of the citizens. However, there was much loss of property incident to the passage through Sandersville of so large a body of troops, and most of the public buildings were fired by the torch. The monument to Governor Irwin on the court-house square bears the mark of a ball which defaced it in 1864. Dr. M. R. Freeman, a young physician, who came to Sandersville from Macon, organized the first military company in the town, known as the Washington Rifles. Afterwards, under Captain S. A. H. Jones, it was one of the first companies to enlist for the war, forming a part of the First Georgia Regiment. Washington County furnished quite a number of companies to the Southern army during the war. Colonel Thomas J. Warthen, who commanded the gallant Twenty-eighth Georgia, laid down his life at Malvern Hill, and there were few homes in Sandersville which were not bereaved by the tragic losses of this period; but, when the war was over, the town began to awake to her possibilities and to reach out for greater things. In the cemetery at Sandersville stands a handsome monument to the Confederate dead, reared by the patriotic women.

Some of the Pioneers. Governor Jared Irwin was one of the earliest pioneers of the County of Washington. He located in the neighborhood of Sandersville soon after the Revolution, and with the prestige of his career as a soldier became at once the foremost citizen: a distinction which he never ceased to retain until the hour of his death. It was the privilege of Governor Irwin, who twice occupied the executive chair, to sign the famous rescinding act, by which the iniquitous Yazoo Fraud was wiped from the statute books of Georgia. His home near Sandersville was known as Union Hill.

With a party of engineers under Moses Wadley, who surveyed the line of the Central of Georgia, came Major Joseph Bangs from Springfield, Mass. He located at Sandersville, in 1838, where he established a prosperous mercantile business and became an influential citizen. Mark Newman, a Hebrew, came from Poland in 1842, when only a lad, and made for himself a large place in the service of the county and in the hearts of the people. He went to the war from Sandersville and became a major in the Forty-ninth Georgia. For upwards of thirty years until his death he was Ordinary of Washington. In 1853, Colonel Beverly D. Evans, of Marion, S. C., formed a partnership with Colonel Ed. Langmade for the practice of law. One of his sons, bearing the same name, is today an Associate Justice of the Supreme Court of Georgia. Four other sons, George, Willis, Louis and Julian, have likewise become men of mark, the last named a physician.

Dr. H. N. Hollifield came from Philadelphia in 1855. He afterwards edited a magazine in Sandersville called the Georgia Medical and Surgical Encyclopaedia. In 1858 came three other men who were destined to leave a lasting impress upon the community: Dr. W. H. H. Whitaker, of Philadelphia; William Gallaher, of Maryland, and Captain P. R. Taliaferro, of Virginia. In 1860, Drs. J. R. Smith and E. B. Hook opened the Sandersville Infirmary, but the institution was forced to suspend on the call to arms.

One of the wealthiest families of the county in pioneer days were the Skrines, including four brothers: William, Quintillian, Virgil and Benjamin. William built the first modern house in the County of Washington. It stood a mile from Sandersville and was known as the White House, on account of its novel coat of white paint. Later it was owned and occupied as a summer home by Noble A. Hardee, of Savannah.

Samuel O. Franklin and James U. Floyd were pioneer merchants, at one time partners, in the dry-goods business.

Colonel Thomas J. Warthen was a wealthy pioneer planter and man of affairs, whose prominence in the State militia before the war gave him the title of "General." He lost his life at Malvern Hill, while commanding the Twenty-eighth Georgia Regiment. Colonel Warthen reared a family of girls, who added much to the culture and social life of Sandersville. Nathan Renfroe was a substantial carriage-maker, whose son, Hon. J. W. Renfroe, was Treasurer of Georgia after the war.

Major Heywood Brookins was the first mayor of the town, and afterwards for more than a generation was Ordinary of the County of Washington. Pinkus Happ, a Jew, became a prosperous merchant, who devoted his large means to the alleviation of distress during the war and endeared himself to every one by his manifold acts of kindness. David Solomon, likewise a Jew, accumulated a snug fortune, married one of the county girls, and became a good Methodist.

Dr. Nathaniel Harris, quite a noted ante-bellum physician, came from Massachusetts and built the first handsome house within the town limits. Dr. William P. Haynes, a local Methodist preacher and a high degree Mason, was complimented by having the first local Masonic lodge named in his honor. Captain S. A. H. Jones commanded a company in one of the Indian campaigns, and was also made captain of the Washington Rifles, one of the first companies to enlist in 1861. Captain Ike Nerrman, a native of France, made Sandersville his home in the late fifties. At the outbreak of the war he organized a company, at the head of which he proved himself a gallant soldier. Harris Brantley was a wealthy pioneer planter, whose only daughter married Hon. Coleman R. Pringle, known as the father of Prohibition in Georgia.

Rev. Daniel Hook, in the year 1860, organized in Sandersville a church of the Disciples of Christ. His son, Judge James S. Hook, was afterwards State School Commissioner of Georgia. Captain Evan P. Howell, late editor and part owner of the *Atlanta Constitution*, lived in Sandersville at the outbreak of the war. Pressly Hyman, one of the promising young men of Sandersville in the early seventies, removed to the West and became Lieutenant-Governor of Nevada.

To mention by name only a few more of the early pioneers of Washington, the list includes: William Hardwick, John Rutherford, George Franklin, Zachariah Brantley, William A. Tennille, Dr. John B. Turner, General Lewis A. Jernigan, a noted educator, afterwards Ordinary of Washington; Colonel Morgan Brown, Nathan Haynes, William Smith, better known as "Uncle Billy," a wealthy planter; William Hodges, Daniel Ainsworth, Colonel E. S. Langmade, Dr. A. A. Cullens, Dr. Eldridge Williamson, Benjamin Tarbutton, Captain Henry C. Lang, Thomas E. Brown, Henry Brown, John Langmade, and Robert Hyman. Most of the original settlers of Washington were Revolutionary soldiers, but they sleep in unmarked graves.

Tomb of   On a plantation three miles west of
John Rutherford. Sandersville, just off the Milledge-
                    ville road, is an old weather-beaten
tombstone, on which the following epitaph is inscribed:

> "To the memory of JOHN RUTHERFORD, a soldier
> of the Revolution, who lived long afterward to share the
> honors of his countrymen. He retired for many years
> from public life and died in the affection of his country,
> on the 31st of October, 1833, in the seventy-fourth year
> of his age. He is buried at his request by the side of
> his first wife, Polly Hubert."

Recently the graves of two Revolutionary soldiers have been located in the neighborhood of Sandersville: William Ganier and John Sparks, and just as soon as markers can be obtained from the Federal government these graves will be marked by Jared Irwin Chapter, D. A. R. On the old Jordan place, near Davisboro, the last resting place of John Jordan has been located. He was a soldier of the Revolution, under General Elbert. His grave at present is marked only by white hyacinths. Likewise within a short distance of Davisboro, two other burial places of Revolutionary patriots have been discovered. These are the graves of William Hardwick and Moses Newton. Samuel Elbert Chapter, D. A. R., of

Tennille, has undertaken the marking of these graves, and is at the same time intent upon locating other historic spots.

Thomas W. Hard- Sandersville is the home of the gifted
wick: Senator- Thomas W. Hardwick, who—at the
Elect. youthful age of forty-two—is Georgia's
new Senator-elect. His service of twelve years in the popular branch of Congress was rewarded with the Senatorial toga at a recent primary election, and in December next Mr. Hardwick will take his seat as Major Bacon's successor in the American House of Peers.

Fort Irwin. General Jared Irwin, with his three brothers, John Lawson, William and Alexander, all of whom were Revolutionary soldiers, built a fort near Union Hill to protect this section of Georgia from the Indians, and it became known as Fort Irwin. Nothing is positively known concerning the character of this stronghold. But it was doubtless securely built, and, occupying a strategic point, it was instrumental in keeping the savages at a safe distance from the settlement.

Tennille. Three miles distant from Sandersville, on the main line of the Central of Georgia, is one of the most important commercial centers in this part of the State: Tennille. Without rehearsing the facts previously set forth in Volume I, some additional items may be cited. On March 4, 1875, the town received its first charter of incorporation and at this time the corporate limits were fixed at one-quarter of a mile in every direction from the depot of the Central Railroad. Provision was made in this charter for an election, to be held on the first Saturday in May, 1875, for an intendant and four aldermen, each to hold office for one year.* During the next few years the growth of the town was so rapid that, on October 24, 1887, an Act was approved granting Tennille a new charter and extending its corporate limits to a distance of one thousand yards in every direction

*Acts, 1875, p. 187.

from the warehouse of the Central Railroad. Hon. John C. Harman was designated as the first Mayor, with Messrs. W. J. Joiner, Jr., J. E. Murchison, H. S. Hatch, W. P. Davis, James W. Smith and H. E. Hyman as Aldermen.[1] In 1900 the style of the corporation was changed from the "town of Tennille" to the "city of Tennille." On September 19, 1881, the Tennille and Wrightsville Railroad was chartered, with the following incorporators: Messrs. W. C. Matthews, B. D. Smith, G. L. Mason, G. B. Harrison, H. N. Hollifield, G. W. Peacock and Z. Peacock, of the County of Washington, A. T. Hanas, of the County of Washington, and W. B. Bales, W. A. Tompkins, W. L. Johnson, J. A. McAfee, T. W. Kent and W. W. Mixon, of the County of Johnson.[2] Tennille is well supplied with strong banking establishments, with excellent school facilities, splendid water and light plants and with a wide-awake and progressive body of citizens.

WAYNE

Waynesville. Wayne County was organized in 1803 out of lands acquired from the Creeks under the treaty of Fort Wilkinson; and by an Act approved December 8, 1806, the following commissioners were named to choose a site for public buildings: Solomon Gross, Francis Smallwood, John Mundon, William Clement and William Knight.[3] But the county was slow in finding settlers, and it was not until December 4, 1829, that a site was finally fixed on land donated by William Clement, one mile from the village of Waynesville.[4] Both the town and the county were named for General Anthony Wayne, of the Revolution, who aided in Georgia's redemption from the British.

Jesup. But when the County of Charlton was formed from Wayne in 1855 it left Wayneville on the extreme lower edge of the county, making a new site for public buildings necessary, and in the course of time the

---

[1] Acts, 1887, p. 618.
[2] Acts, 1881, p. 268.
[3] Clayton's Compendium, p. 326.
[4] Acts, 1829, p. 193.

county seat was removed to Jesup, a town named for General Jesup, of the United States army, who rendered important service to the State in the Creek Indian war of 1836. The town of Jesup was incorporated on October 24, 1870, with the following commissioners, to-wit.: William Clarey, W. H. Whaley, G. H. Cameron, T. P. Littlefield and W. C. Remshart.[1]

Fort James. This stronghold, built to defend the frontier during the Indian wars, was located on the west bank of the Altamaha River, fifty miles above Darien and twelve miles below the mouth of the Ohoopee. There was also a fortification by this name built in Colonial times, to defend the old settlement of Dartmouth, above Augusta, in what is now Elbert County, Ga.[2]

WEBSTER

Preston. Webster County was formed out of Randolph and was first known as Kinchafoonee, from a well-known creek of this name, but Kinchafoonee provoked a ripple of laughter over the State, and on February 21, 1856, the name was changed to Webster, in honor of the great orator of New England. At the same time the name of the county-seat was changed from McIntosh to Preston. The town was incorporated by an Act approved December 22, 1857, with the following commissioners, to-wit.: George M. Hay, John W. Easters, William H. Hallen, James·G. M. Ball and Henry W. Spears.[3]

WHEELER

Alamo. On August 14, an Act was approved creating by Constitutional amendment the new County of Wheeler from a part of the County of Montgomery.

[1] Acts, 1870, p. 207.
[2] Vol. I, p. 537.
[3] Acts, 1857, p. 187.

This Act was ratified at the polls on November 5, 1912, after which the new county was formally created by proclamation of the Governor, on November 14, 1912. Alamo, a town on the Seaboard Air Line, was made the county-seat. Some of the oldest families resident in the county are the Kents, the Gillises, the Calhouns, the Mc-Lennans, the Clementses, the McRaes, the Morrisons, the Curries, the Clarkes, the Adamses, the Ryalses and the McArthurs.

Where Governor Troup Died. Governor George M. Troup, while on a visit to the Mitchell place, one of the numerous plantations owned by him in this section of Georgia, in 1856, was seized with a violent illness, which here ended his days. William Bridges was the overseer in charge of the Mitchell place at the time of Governor Troup's death. In another part of this work will be found a picture of the pioneer cabin in which the great apostle of State Rights breathed his last. The Mitchell plantation was settled by Hartwell Mitchell in 1814. It was located on the west side of the Oconee River. This fine old plantation is now the property of the Kent family of Wheeler. Still another plantation owned by Governor Troup in this county was the Horseshoe Place. But the old Governor is buried on the banks of the Oconee River, in Montgomery County, at Rosemont, still another plantation which he owned, where a beloved brother, Robert L. Troup, was already buried.

WHITE

Cleveland. In 1857 the County of White was organized out of Habersham and named for Colonel John White, an officer of the Continental Army, whose brilliant exploit on the Great Ogeechee was unsurpassed in the annals of the Revolution. The county-seat was first called Mount Yonah, but the name was afterwards changed to Cleveland. It has never been quite settled for whom the town was named, but presumably it was for Colonel Benjamin Cleaveland, the hero of King's Mountain, notwithstanding a slight variation in the spelling of his name. Cleveland was chartered by an Act ap-

OVERSEER'S CABIN ON THE MITCHELL PLACE, IN WHEELER COUNTY,

Where Gov. George M. Troup Breathed His Last.

proved October 18, 1870, with the following town commissioners, to-wit.: William B. Bell, Virgil Robertson, A. J. Comer and William G. Goodman.*

———

Nacoochee: Relics of a Forgotten Race. At the foot of Yonah Mountain, in the picturesque upper part of White County, lies one of the most beautiful valleys in the world—far-famed Nacoochee. Neither the Yosemite nor the Shenandoah can match it in some respects. There are lineaments of loveliness which it shares in common with no other spot on earth. It matters not how extensively one has traveled, he cannot visit this Lost Paradise of the Cherokee Indians without feeling the spell of enchantment which the scene here throws around him, and though he may not quote the language he will at least voice the sentiment of Tom Moore's apt lines:

> "There's not in the wide world a valley so sweet
> As this vale in whose bosom the bright waters meet."

The cradle of the Chattahoochee—it has been described in the wondrous witchery of Lanier's song; but the power to do it justice lies neither in the poet's pen nor in the artist's brush. The task of recalling some of the historic memories in which this romantic region of the State abounds is a much simpler one. There is a wealth of legendary lore connected with Nacoochee; and from the mellow recollections of an old gentleman—now gone to his reward—who knew the valley like a book, every page of which was dear to him, and who in childhood explored its hidden mysteries, and listened to its weird fairy tales, and wandered to the utmost verge of its green meadows, the following brief account has been condensed. Says Mr. George W. Williams:

"Nacoochee has a history as thrilling in interest as the tales of the Arabian Nights. This valley was doubtless for ages one vast lake. The

———

*Acts, 1870, p. 182.

fretful waters at last cut a channel through the rocks at the east end of the valley and the great basin was drained, leaving a fertile area of landscape some seven miles in length, with the Chattahoochee River winding through the verdant prospect. The Cherokees selected this quiet and safe retreat for the capital of a populous nation, and Nacoochee Old Town, the name by which the settlement here was first known, became the chief town of the Cherokees. At one time, it must have been the center of an ancient civilization. The original occupants of the valley were a warlike race of people. They surrounded themselves with long lines of fortifications, leveled the tops of the hills, and raised huge mounds. On the high places resided the chiefs of the nation, surrounded by knights as brave as ever drew a lance. During the past seventy-five years many relics have been found in the valley, furnishing proof most positive of hard-fought battles, in which shot and shell were used. When the writer was a boy, his father, who was one of the original settlers in the valley, taught his sons the science of farming; and from time to time they plowed up many, many rare and curious specimens, including gunlocks, swords, broken shells, tomahawks, arrows and human skeletons.

"In 1834, when the miners were digging a canal for the purpose of washing the beds of the streams for gold, a subterranean village was discovered, containing some forty houses in number. These were buried ten feet deep. The logs were hewn and notched as at the present day. This village was covered by a heavy growth of timber; and near it, under a tree, fifteen feet in circumference, which must have been at least five hundred years old, there was found a double mortar, ten inches in diameter, perfectly polished. It was made of transparent quartz. This village was doubtless built by DeSoto in 1539. More recently a discovery was made here which interested me very much. A plough-share, near an Indian mound, struck a hard substance. On examination it proved to be part of a walled sepulchre. The bottom was paved with polished stones, and the tomb contained many skeletons, one of immense size, also conch shells, pipes, and other curious specimens of handiwork, besides a piece of inwrought copper. As the natives were ignorant of the art of working in this metal and never buried in walled sepulchres, the question naturally arises: When did these huge men live? A learned historian of Copenhagen says that America was discovered in the year 985 by Biaske Horjeufsen. It is also said that a colony from Wales settled in this country at the same time. Doubtless these early European adventurers were exterminated by the vast tribes of Indians. It is mainly by way of tradition that we hear of them. The walled sepulchre may have been built by the Welsh colony in the tenth century of the Christian era.''

Nacoochee Old Town was undoubtedly one of the places at which DeSoto stopped in his quest of the yellow metal. Signs of a somewhat lengthy sojourn by the Span-

iards in this locality are still numerous. Colonel Charles
C. Jones, Jr., identifies the Xualla of the old Spanish
narrative with an Indian settlement somewhere in this
region, a surmise which is more than justified by the
monumental remains and which furthermore tallies with
the description. According to Mr. Williams, the Indian
Queen of the tribe here settled, at the time of DeSoto's
visit, was Echoee. Nacoochee and Eola were her daughters, both beautiful, dark-eyed Indian maidens. Lorenzo,
a companion of the bold knight, having acquired knowledge of the fact that certain treasures of priceless value
were concealed in a cavern under Mount Yonah, cun-
ningly sought to possess them. He partially succeeded
by artful blandishments in fascinating Queen Echoee.
But in the end he was killed by old Wahoo, the chief of
the tribe. Echoee, with her daughter Eola, was drowned,
but Nacoochee was saved by Sautee, the young sixteen-
year-old son of a Choctaw chief. As a sequel to the rescue, there developed quite naturally a love affair. But
the marriage of Nacoochee to Sautee was forbidden. The
pair resolved upon flight, and when pursued and overtaken hurled themselves from an overhanging cliff of
Mount Yonah into the vale beneath. They were buried
in a common grave. The large mound in front of the
summer home of Dr. L. G. Hardman, formerly the Nichols place, marks the traditional spot in which the lovers
are supposed to be interred. Nacoochee and Sautee valleys, uniting, perpetuate the names of the ill-fated pair,
while the grave in which they sleep is kept perennially
green with cypress, ivy and rhododendron.

WHITFIELD

Dalton. Dalton, the county-seat of Whitfield, was first
       known as Cross Plains. But in 1847, when the
State road was built the name was changed to Dalton,
in compliment to a civil engineer, John Dalton, who, real-

izing the possibilities of this locality as the site for a future town, made a survey of the land and divided the same into lots.* His judgment was subsequently confirmed by General Joseph E. Johnston, who made Dalton his base of operations during the Civil War. The town was incorporated by an Act approved December 28, 1853. Two schools, the Dalton Female College and the Southern Central Baptist University of Georgia, were chartered in 1850, each with a strong board of trustees. But for additional particulars in regard to Dalton the reader is referred to Volume I of this work.

Red Clay: The Cherokee Council Ground   Red Clay, famous in history and legend as the Cherokee Indian Council Ground, lies a short distance north of the town of Dalton. Nearly a century has passed since this historic spot, stamped forever with the agony of a noble race, witnessed the signing of the famous treaty between those of the Cherokees who favored and those who opposed the United States Government. To this council of the two factions came the Indian chiefs and head men of the Cherokee Nation.

In the deliberations which ensued, the treaty party, headed by Ridge, declared ''that the Cherokees could not exist amidst a white people; that while they loved the land of their fathers, they considered the fate of the exile far better than submission to the laws of a State.'' At the head of the party opposed to removal was John Ross, principal chief of the Cherokees. The Committee of Conference met at Red Clay in October, 1835. To relieve the Cherokee Nation from its distressed condition, George M. Waters, John Martin, Richard Taylor, John Baldridge and John Benge, acting under the instructions of John Ross, principal chief, on the one part, and George Chambers, John Gunter, John Ridge, Charles Vann and Elias Boudinot, on the other, acting under instructions of Major Ridge and others of the treaty party, ''agreed to bury in oblivion all unfriendly feelings and act unitedly in treaty with the United States for the relief of the nation.''

This agreement was signed at Red Clay, October 24th, 1835. The treaty party met at New Echota, the capital of the Cherokee Nation, near the present town of Calhoun, and on the 29th of December, 1835, concluded the treaty with the United States Commissioner. The chiefs of the anti-treaty party did not attend this convention, and made every effort to

---

*White says that the town was named for Tristram Dalton, an Englishman, but on the authority of Hon. Paul B. Trammell, it was named for John Dalton, as above credited.

negotiate a new treaty, more favorable, but without success. By its terms the Indians were permitted two years' grace in which to leave their beloved lands, but the time expired and they still repudiated the treaty. The United States government decided that the only possible way to make them move would be at the bayonet's point.

John Ross, who made the most zealous efforts to save his people from expulsion, was born at Rossville, Georgia, October 3rd, 1790. His father was a full-blooded Scotchman and his mother a half-breed; he was therefore one-fourth Indian, as the Indians say, ''a quateroon.'' He lived for a number of years at the home built by his grandfather, John McDonald, at Rossville, Ga., but he enlarged it, adding a council chamber twenty-three feet long, which for years had only one door. As a precaution, he later added two more doors, one opening into his bed-room in the center of the house. The house is now owned by John McNair McFarland, a descendant of the McFarlands, into whose hands the Ross place passed, and in its exterior and interior has been little changed.

Chief Ross, about two years before the exile, built a home at Flint Springs, Tenn., some five miles north of Red Clay. It was a two-story log house, a part of which still stands, though it has been improved and much changed. Nearby, on the Ross land, Dr. Butler, a missionary to the Indians, taught a school. It has been said that Ross moved to his Tennessee home for protection, as the Government had troops stationed near there; certain it is that with his Indian wife, his children and negro servants, he was living at Flint Springs about 1837.

Tradition says that he had a daughter famed throughout the Cherokee land for her beauty, her grace of manner and modesty; in truth an irresistibly charming maiden. A young Indian chief was her suitor and gained the favor and approval of Ross, but not the love of the girl, for she had already given her heart to another, whom she frequently met in a sequestered trysting place. The young man vowed that he could no longer endure life without her, and she yielded to his pleadings; in the dark and silent hours of the night she met her lover at the appointed place, mounted the horse behind him, rode away and married the man of her choice.

Near the Georgia-Tennessee line there still stands an ancient, two-story brick house built by Chief McEntyre. This quaint old mansion stands guard over an Indian burying-ground. In the corner of an old-fashioned garden, in a tangle of briers and vines, are several time-worn tombstones bearing names and dates still legible and interesting to the romantic passerby. A few years ago there came from the West several of the descendants of these Indians to visit the home and graves of their forefathers, made precious by tradition. Rev. A. R. T. Hambright, a gentleman eighty-five years old, still living near Red Clay, gives an interesting account of a visit made by him when a child in company with a trader and his uncle, to the McEntyre home. The men had a large amount of silver, which they had secured from the Indians in trade and barter. This silver they carried in saddle bags across an Indian pony, which the little six-year-old boy rode. This was done to divert suspicion, as at that time the Cherokee Nation was in a state of disorder. This silver was exchanged for paper money at McEntyre's, where they spent the night.

In the years previous to the Red Clay convention, the Ross and Ridge parties indulged in bitter and relentless hostilities, out of which grew the tragic death of Chief Jack Walker. The Chief became infatuated with a young white girl of fifteen summers, by name Emily. Her family opposed the suit, but watching her opportunity she eloped with her lover. Taking the girl on the horse with him he swam the Tennessee River, pursued by her infuriated brothers, but untouched by their bullets. After their marriage they returned and lived in Walker Valley, near the present town of Cleveland, Tenn., on what is now called the Pryor Lea farm. Tradition says that he had two wives, the other an Indian, and that the two lived in the same house in a most friendly manner until the chief was called away for a short time, when the Indian wife invariably whipped the white one. The squaw, however, got her whipping when the chief returned.

At a meeting of the Council at the Old Fort, between Cleveland and Spring Place, Walker was accused of treason. He left for home with a friend, and when about nine miles away, at Muskrat Springs, was waylaid and shot by an assassin hidden in the top of a tree. Old men still living remember the exact spot, for often as children it was pointed out to them.

Tradition says that his wife, Emily, told several of her friends that she felt very uneasy about him during his absence on that memorable day, as she knew the Indians were angry, and that she felt relieved when looking out she saw him riding up the road on his gray horse. She sent a servant to take his horse and stood waiting for him to come to her. As no one came, she went out to learn the cause of the delay, finding only the servant, who said with trembling voice, "Mr. Walker is not here." She said she saw him as clearly as she ever saw anything in her life. A little later, at nightfall, he was brought home fatally wounded, living only a short time.

It was at this period of the strife that John Howard Payne arrived in the Nation of the Cherokees, resolved to study the Indian problem on the spot. Payne sympathized deeply with the red man, and when arrested by Colonel Bishop at the home of Chief Ross at Flint Springs, he found papers which contained bitter criticisms concerning the treatment of the Cherokee Indians. Payne was carried to Spring Place, where a short time he was imprisoned in the Vann house.

At Kenan Spring, not far from Red Clay, dwelt "Chief Rattling Gourd," renowned as a counselor. The home where he dwelt is no more, only a few foundation stones remain, but the land surrounding still bears his name, and is called the "old Rattling Gourd field." He did not die in this country, as stated, but went West with his tribe, educated himself and became an officer of some importance. In this section dwelt also old "Deer-in-the-Water," "Sleeping Rabbit," "Otter Lifter" and "Seven Nose," whose very names have reference to stirring accounts of legendary adventure, and who were renowned in their day as leading men in their tribe. South of where the town of Dalton now stands dwelt Chief Red Bird near the beautiful Hamilton Spring. He was a devotee of the race-track and met an untimely death, for while drunk he was thrown from his horse. He was buried directly west of the spring, and his grave is now covered by a railroad embankment. Two miles south of the town lived "Drowning Bear," a mighty hunter. His feats are still recalled, and a creek which flows through the place bears the name of Drowning Bear Creek. Near the center of the town was the ball ground, a beautiful level spot shaded by forest trees, where the contending parties, with faces painted in the brightest of colors, headed by their chiefs, met and engaged in ball playing. A monument to the Confederate dead now marks this place.

The Council Ground of the Cherokee Indians was ideally located. On the east and west it was protected by the hills, through which roamed game in abundance, deer, turkeys, foxes, wolves and bears, and which the Indians never killed unnecessarily. Four immense springs in a radius of two miles were included in the Council Ground which extended north and south for some distance, its exact size is now a matter of conjecture. As the Indians burned the leaves every year no undergrowth marred the beauty of the forest, which resembled a park.

On Georgia soil stood the council house, very near the center of the Council Ground, and less than 100 feet from the Tennessee line. This council house was later renowned as the treaty cabin, for it was occupied, so says tradition, by General Winfield Scott and General Twiggs, who were sent to Red Clay to remove the Indians. About 1850 it was moved to a spot a few feet northwest, and a large rambling dwelling now stands on the original site of the council house. In 1911 it was demolished.

East of the council house was a large grove of oaks, where the chiefs and counselors smoked their pipes and deliberated upon the affairs of their nation. Not far distant was the grave of Sleeping Rabbit, a famous chief and warrior. A mound of rocks overgrown with bushes and vines, still marks his resting place. The famous Indian cure-all, Tuc-a-le-chee-chee-wah-wah (drink and live spring), is nearby. To this spring the Indians brought their sick, believing they could be cured by drinking the water. This failing, they immersed the patients in the water, and if a cure was not effected, other remedies were deemed fruitless, and they were left to die. About a mile north of the old council house was Deep Spring. Tradition tells us that the Indians held this beautiful dark blue spring in greatest awe, for they believed it bottomless. A ledge of rock projects itself across the upper east side and falls sharply back, and at this spot no bottom has ever been found, either by the red or white man. Tradition says that when the edict of banishment came that many Indians gathered from the tribes and cast their treasures into its depths, happier to bury them in the sacred waters than to leave them to the paleface.

When the dusky warriors and maidens were gathered together for removal westward, the assembled chiefs and counselors met at the Council Ground under the spreading oaks and murmuring pines, and after smoking the pipe of peace, in imploring attitudes turned their dark eyes to heaven, pulled the swinging limbs to them, and in their wild devotion bedewed the sprigs and branches with their tears. When the final departure drew near all arms were taken from the Indians and they were marched between files of soldiers. Tradition says that a chief known as "Big Bear" had but a short time before buried his wife and only child, and that in his deep grief he implored that he be spared the life of an exile. His prayers were unheeded and he was forced to take up the march. He secured a bayonet and hiding it under his blanket, as he passed by the graves of his loved ones, broke from his companions and threw himself across the mound, and, falling upon the sharp bayonet, he was pierced to the heart, thus dying by those he loved dearer than life. And today, "side by side, in their nameless graves the lovers are sleeping," for General Twiggs, in sympathy, ordered a Christian burial. The Indians turned their faces westward, journeying hundreds of miles, through forest and over desert, sometimes drenched with rain, sometimes consumed with thirst, thousands dying on the long march of months, and thus began the "exile without an end and without an example in story."*

March, 1913.   WILLIE S. WHITE.

WILCOX

Abbeville. Wilcox County was organized in 1857 from Dooly, Irwin and Pulaski, and was named for General Mark Wilcox, a distinguished officer of the State

---

*Authorities consulted: White's Statistics, Rev. A. R. T. Hambright and Mr. F. T. Hardwick.

militia and a dominant figure in ante-bellum State politics. Abbeville was made the new county-seat. Some of the more prominent of the early pioneer citizens of the county were: G. R. Reid, D. Reid, J. L. Wilcox, M. G. Fortner, Thomas Warren and James Holt. On September 5, 1883, the town was incorporated, with Stephen Bowen as mayor and Messrs. W. A. McLane, Robert J. Fitzgerald, L. M. Gunn, S. N. Mitchell, James A. Stubbs and E. V. Johnson as councilmen. Abbeville is located on the Ocmulgee River, and when a part of the county was taken to form Dodge, in 1870, it left Abbeville near the extreme eastern edge of Wilcox.

WILKES

Washington. On the site of Heard's Fort, in 1780, arose the present town of Washington, the first town in the United States to be named for the great commander-in-chief. Its charter of incorporation was granted by the Legislature on December 7, 1805, in an Act providing for its better regulation. The commissioners named at this time were: Francis Willis, James Corbett, Felix H. Gilbert, Thomas Terrell and William Sanson.* In the neighborhood of Washington, there were two pioneer schools of wide note, one of them taught by Rev. Hope Hull, who was probably the first Methodist preacher in Upper Georgia; the other taught by Rev. John Springer, the first Presbyterian minister ever ordained in the State. Among the pupils of Dr. Springer were Jesse Mercer and John Forsyth, both of whom were destined to the highest honors. When Josiah Penfield left at his death a sum of money with which to found a school, Jesse Mercer sought by every means within his power to secure this school for Washington; and his failure to do so was one of the keenest regrets of his life. But he nevertheless made this school the object of his

*Clayton's Compendium, p. 278.

most devoted interest, and today it bears the name of Mercer University. One of the first plants ever established in Georgia for the manufacture of cotton and woollen goods was located near Washington, where likewise the first cotton gin was erected. The name of this pioneer industrial enterprise was the Wilkes Manufacturing Company, as appears from an Act approved December 13, 1810; and, included among the stockholders were: Matthew Talbot, Bolling Anthony, Benjamin Sherrod, John Bolton, Frederick Ball, Gilbert Hay and Joel Abbott.* In the old Heard House, in Washington, a landmark which formerly faced the town square, was held the last meeting of the Confederate Cabinet. Some of Georgia's most distinguished sons have been residents of this historic town; but since these have already been mentioned in Volume I, it is needless to repeat them here. The reader is also referred to the preceding volume of this work for additional facts in regard to Washington.

Wilkes in the Revolution. With respect to the part which the County of Wilkes played in the drama of the Revolution, it is enough **to say that the name by** which the Tories called it was the Hornet's Nest. The expression is most apposite. For nowhere was the spirit of independence so characteristic of the rugged frontiersman, more defiant of tyranny or more eager to accept the gage of battle than in the forest stretches of upper Georgia. The most wanton acts of brutality known to the reign of terror under Toryism were perpetrated in Wilkes upon defenceless women and children by Tory bands who respected neither age nor sex—who felt neither pity nor remorse. The wild carnivals of slaughter which occurred in Wilkes, where the torch and the bludgeon alternately flashed in the eyes of helpless victims, doomed to an ignominious death, shamed even the savage orgies of the ancient Aztecs. But it was not until the fall of Savannah into the hands of the British, exposing the up-country to the perils of invasion, that scenes of unbridled license like these transpired. Then it was that Elijah Clarke began to ride night and day through the wilderness, gathering his faithful dragoons. It is estimated that not less than 300 frontiersmen were enlisted—first and last—under his standard, though he never seems to have commanded more than 100 men in any engagement.

------

*Clayton's Compendium, p. 667.

It is not a little singular that a county like Wilkes, which bore so dramatic and prominent a part in the struggle for independence, should possess a dearth of unmarked graves. Few of the last resting places of the Revolutionary veterans of Wilkes are known, though the whole region fairly bristled with steel, when the crimson tide of invasion reached the foothills. The explanation is doubtless to be found in the unsettled conditions of pioneer life on the exposed frontier. Elsewhere will be found a partial and incomplete, but somewhat lengthy, list of the officers and privates who took part in the battle of Kettle Creek. Where these brave men lie, who supported the arms of Washington, beside what streams, or in what hidden nooks and corners of the forest, will be known only when the sea and the land alike shall give up their dust, but with the light before us it may be gravely doubted if there is a belt of woods on the American continent which is richer in heroic ashes or represented by brighter or prouder names on the muster rolls of the Revolution.

Heroic Women of the Reign of Terror under Toryism. Nor were the women of Wilkes cast in less heroic molds. Hannah Clarke—though little is said of her by the historian—was one of the bravest heroines of the Revolution. Due to the exploits of her husband as a leader of the Whigs in upper Georgia, it fell to her lot to endure many hardships and indignities at the hands of the Tories. The ordeals which she experienced during these troublous times were manifold. On one occasion, when Colonel Clarke was absent from home, the roof over her head was burned, and, with a family of several children, she was driven shelterless into the forest. Later she was robbed of a horse on which she was riding to meet her husband, near the border line between North Carolina and Georgia; and, at still another time, when accompanying her husband on one of his campaigns, a horse was shot from under her, and it was only by a miracle that she escaped instant and violent death. The mishap occurred on the outskirts of a field where a skirmish was in progress. Two children were with her in the saddle, both of whom likewise escaped without harm. It was not unusual for this fearless woman to attend her husband in his campaigns, in order to be near at hand in the event he should happen to be wounded or fall a prey to the malaria of the swamps. She was present at the siege of Augusta, when Colonel Brown surrendered; and, notwithstanding the numerous insults and outrages heaped upon her by the Tories, she counseled humanity in the treatment of prisoners. Mrs. Clarke attained to a ripe old age and lived to see the State of Georgia prosperous and contented under the Federal Constitution. She survived General Clarke by twenty-eight years. According to White, she was buried beside her illustrious husband at Woodburn. But no trace of either grave can be found within the present borders of Wilkes. Testimony at this day points conclusively to the burial-place of General Clarke in what is now the County of Lincoln.

Nancy Hart, at the time of her celebrated encounter with the Tories, was a resident of Wilkes, living near the Beaver Dam ford, on the Broad River, in a section afterwards formed into Elbert.

Sarah Williamson, if somewhat more cultured, was not a whit less courageous than either of the above-named heroines of Wilkes. She came of an excellent old Huguenot family, and, before her marriage to Micajah Williamson, was Sarah Gilliam, of Henrico County, Va., a niece of the distinguished Dr. Deveraux Jarratt, an Episcopal clergyman. It is said that Colonel Williamson, who was then a man of large means, gave sixty negroes for the fertile upland plantation, over which he installed his fair bride as the young mistress. She proved to be an expert manager; and, when her husband was at the front, she not only ran the plantation, but also kept the looms and the ovens busy, furnishing supplies to the army as well as to her own household. Nor did she escape the perils incident to frontier life during the reign of terror in upper Georgia. The Tories, incensed by the activities of her husband, took peculiar delight in annoying Mrs. Williamson. One day they made a raid upon her home, and, after gorging themselves with plunder, applied the torch. It is said that the Tories also hanged her eldest son in her presence, compelling her by force to witness the murder of her own offspring. Colonel Williamson received a number of severe wounds, from the effects of each of which his devoted wife nursed him back to health. When the home place was burned by the Tories, she refugeed with her slaves to North Carolina, where she remained until hostilities ceased.

The family of children reared by this extraordinary woman was patriarchal in size and distinguished in character. Five sons lived to complete useful careers. Her daughters—six in number—became famous belles of the up-country, during the era of peace which followed the Revolution, and they each married husbands who attained to high eminence in public affairs. Nancy married John Clarke, who afterwards became Governor of Georgia. Sarah married first Judge Griffin and, after his death, Judge Tait, the latter of whom served for ten years in the United States Senate from Georgia. Susan married Dr. Thompson Bird. Her daughter Sarah became the wife of Judge L. Q. C. Lamar, Sr., and the mother of the great jurist and statesman of the same name, who served on the Supreme Bench of the United States, in the national Senate, and in the Cabinet of President Cleveland. Mary married Duncan G. Campbell, for whom Campbell County was named, and who signed the famous treaty of Indian Springs. He was also the pioneer champion of female education in Georgia. His son, John A. Campbell, occupied a seat on the Supreme Bench of the United States and took part as a commissioner in the celebrated conference at Hampton Roads. Martha married a Fitch and Elizabeth a Thweat, both men of fine business and social connections. Thus it will be seen that, besides landing for her daughters the capital prizes in the matrimonial lottery, Sarah Williamson also furnished from among her descendants, two illustrious judges to wear the ermine of the nation's highest court of appeals.

How a Great Christian School was Financed by a Colonial Jew. It is not generally known that the handsome fortune upon which Mercer University was built came from the coffers of a Colonial Jew, whose grave is still to be found by the wayside, near his old home, on the Augusta road, some eight miles from Washington, Ga., where, according to his express wishes, he was buried in an upright position. There is no lack of evidence to support the statement that the original endowment of the great Baptist school—barring, of course, the Penfield legacy—was derived in this manner. The facts are well known to the people of Washington. But to give them the proper attestation, Dr. H. R. Bernard, auditor of the Mission Board of the Georgia Baptist Church, may be cited as authority for the story which is here told. In a communication, dated October 12, 1911, and addressed to Dr. Joseph Jacobs, of Atlanta, a former pupil, this well-known Baptist minister, narrates the story as follows: Says he:

"Dear Friend: In 1798 a Mr. Simons, a resident at the time, I suppose, of Wilkes County, Georgia, married a Miss Nancy Mills. Mr. Simons was an Israelite. He was a man of considerable means and very active and very popular in business circles; and in the course of time accumulated a handsome property. In his day we would have said that he was rich. The date of his death I do not find recorded, but it was some time previous to 1827. His large estate was heired by his widow, Mrs. Nancy Simon. Jesse Mercer, a very devout and worthy Baptist minister, a man of very high standing in his denomination and in this county, who had lost his wife some time before, married Mrs. Simons and came into possession and into control of large means.

"During the lifetime of Mrs. Simons, after her second marriage, which covered a period of less than fourteen years, she readily entered into the benevolent enterprises suggested by her husband, Mr. Mercer. Mr. Mercer, in his own right, was not worth property, but he was a man of thrift and fine business judgment, and was benevolently inclined, and conceived that the very best thing he could do for after generations was to found a college. Mercer University was the result, a very flourishing institution in Georgia at this time, with many years of useful service back of it, and with a prospect of useful service for years to come. It numbers now about 400 students.

"Mr. Mercer lived fourteen years after his second marriage, and he and his wife, agreeing always, contributed continuously to the enterprise of founding Mercer University. At his death he willed, with advice from his wife, formerly given, all the residue of his estate, after his honest debts were paid, to the endowment of Mercer University. I have tried to ascertain from our records the exact amount of his benefactions to the university, but have not been able to do so. It is safe, however, to estimate from $40,000 to $400,000. So you see that Mercer University is largely indebted to the skill and enterprise of a Jewish financier, for much the larger part of its life and power.

"A copious Providence this, which founds a Christian college on Jewish corner-stones.

"By the way, Mr. Simons—or Captain Simons, as he is sometimes referred to—is down in our history as a remarkably kind and faithful husband. His wife, while not a professed religionist of any faith, was fond of going to church and entertaining ministers at her home. In all this she was warmly supported by her good husband. In fact, he frequently attended religious services with her. She, too, was—in the lifetime of both her husbands—a most estimable wife, fulfilling every obligation that came to her as a married woman. She was devoted to the interests of her home and did her part at every point.

"Sincerely your friend,

(Signed)   "H. R. BERNARD."

Eccentric Captain Simons. To quote a local historian:* "The old brick academy, in which Jesse Mercer preached before the church was built, stood near the home of a young widow, a very charming "sister Baptist"—Mrs. Nancy Simons, daughter of John Mills, and widow of Captain Abram Simons. Mr. Mercer admired her very much, and on the 11th day of December, 1827, they were married. As Mr. Mercer got the greater part of the money which founded Mercer University from this wife it is interesting to know something of Captain Simons, the man who made the money. He lived six miles east of Washington, Ga., on the Augusta road; his old home is standing yet; upstairs in it is a very large room built for dancing, and is today called the 'ball-room.' Abram Simons was a colonial Jew, of strong plain sense, though uneducated; he made a large fortune and was sent to the Legislature.

"Mr. Mercer, in writing his wife's obituary, said Simons was a man of the world, who loved to surround himself with men of high standing and 'big names.' In short, he was a sporting man, was a member of the Augusta Jockey Club, and entertained lavishly. However, this was not very much to the taste of the refined little woman, whose veins were filled with the aristocratic blood of the Mills. Yet, it is said she loved her husband, and he was extravagantly proud of her.

---

*Miss Annie M. Lane, Regent, Kettle Creek Chapter, D. A. R., Washington, Ga.

"Not long ago I visited the grave of Captain Simons. It is on the roadside in a rock enclosure. No monument or stone tells who is buried there, though he was a Revolutionary soldier, and a man of wealth.

Buried in an Up-right Position. "When he came to die he had his grave prepared and walled up with solid rock. He left orders that they bury him standing on his feet with his musket beside him to fight the devil with. His orders were carried out. His coffin was placed on the end, and this necessitated the digging of a grave twice the usual depth.

The Widow Simons. "Nancy Simons Mercer made Jesse Mercer an excellent wife. With refined and cultured manners she entertain his friends in a manner which was to his taste. She was a beautiful little dark-eyed woman, who always dressed faultlessly.

"In the book called 'The Story of Wilkes County,' by Miss Bowen, I find the following: 'It is said that when Mr. Mercer went to the tailor for new clothes, Mrs. Mercer always went with him and was always very particular to order that the backs of his waistcoats should be made of yellow satin. Yellow was her favorite color, and always graced the ribbons of her best bonnets and caps.' ''

"Mercer's Cluster." "Mr. Mercer's life was now greatly to his taste, with a fortune at his disposal and a relaxation from the hard frontier life. His pen was employed in writing for the press, and his fame went abroad. About this time he had published 'Mercer's Cluster,' a book of poems, later converted into hymns.

The Christian Index. "In 1833 the *Christian Index,* which had been edited for several years at Philadelphia, with the approval of the Baptist Board of Foreign Missions, under whose auspices the paper was first commenced at Washington, D. C., the management was transferred to Jesse Mercer. He bought at his own expense new press and type, costing $3,000, and removed the *Index* to Washington, Ga. It was published (that and a temperance paper) in a two-story dwelling at the corner of Main and Depot Streets. Some years after the *Index* was moved to Penfield, Ga. My father, Dr. James H. Lane, bought the house and had it remodeled, and when the old mantels and wainscotings were taken down old manuscripts of interest were found. I was born in that house. We have an old writing desk at which Jesse Mercer did his editorial work.

Mr. Mercer's Great Disappointment. "On account of failing health, Mr. Mercer gave up the editorship of the paper, and in 1840 he gave it to the State Baptist Convention, with all its appendages. Mr. Mercer had purchased the old brick school-house near his home, on 'Mercer Hill,' and it was the dream of his life to establish a college there. A man by the name of Josiah Penfield, of Savannah, left $2,500, on the condition that they raise the same amount to build a school for the education of young preachers. In 1833 the legacy was turned over to the convention, and Mr. Mercer made a hard fight to have the school located at Washington, Ga., and it was the disappointment of his life that the school was located at Penfield. However, he made donations of large sums of money at different times to maintain the college. In 1838 the name of Mercer University was given it.

"In May, 1833, Nancy Mercer was stricken with paralysis while walking in her flower garden and lingered just one year, never being able to utter a word or walk a step, and on the following May passed away, when all nature was beautiful. They covered her grave with the flowers from her own garden, those which she had so tenderly cared for. Some of these flowers are to be seen now in the garden tended by the gentle Sisters of St. Joseph, who walk where the feet of Mrs. Mercer once trod. Mr. Mercer's letters about her, to be found in 'Mallary's History,' are truly touching.

"Mr. Mercer died September the 6th, 1841, near Indian Springs, while on a visit to a friend. He was buried at Penfield."

The Hills and the Popes. Two of Georgia's most distinguished and honored families were planted in Wilkes at the close of the Revolution: the Hills and the Popes. These families have frequently intermarried; and there is scarcely a Southern State in which they are not today represented. Abraham Hill settled in Wilkes County, Ga., in 1780 or 1781. By tradition he was of Scotch-Irish extraction. His grandparents removed from Nansemond County, Virginia, to Chowan, now Gates County, North Carolina, in 1770; and here he was born in 1730. There were four brothers, Abraham, Henry, Isaac and Theophilus. Abraham Hill, in 1756, married Christian Walton, a daughter of Thomas Walton, who, in 1757, was a member from Chowan County in the North Carolina General Assembly. During the latter part of the seventeen-sixties he settled in what was afterwards Wake County, and became a Justice of the Peace and member of the first Court of Pleas and Quarter Sessions for Wake County, in 1771. He was re-elected to this office in December, 1778, by the Provincial Congress of North Carolina, and there is strong presumptive evidence that he had served in this capacity during the intermediate period. On removing to Wilkes County, Ga., at the time above mentioned, he acquired lands on both sides of Long Creek, about three miles above its confluence with Dry Fork and about twenty miles northwest of Washington.

His home must have been very near the Indian line. For, in 1790 the Cherokee border was only twenty miles west of Washington. During this same year it was removed twenty miles further west, but there was still little security, either to life or to property, in this exposed neighborhood. Abraham Hill died in 1792; his wife in 1808. Here they lie buried on the old estate. In the same area sleeps their son, Thomas, and his wife, Sarah McGhee, and their grandson, James A. Hill, and his wife, Amelia Hill. These two last were first cousins. In the late seventeen-eighties Abraham Hill erected a large, commodious frame homestead, esteemed in those days as truly palatial. It was probably the first plastered house in this part of Georgia. Completed in 1790, it remained practically unaltered as late as the eighteen-seventies, when it passed into alien hands.

Burwell, Willis, John, Henry Augustine, and Wiley Pope, five brothers, were born in North Carolina. Burwell, the eldest, was born in 1751 and was only twelve years old when his father died. He married in 1792 Priscilla Wootten, a sister of Thomas Wootten, a pioneer immigrant to Wilkes; at some during the Revolution he was a Justice of the Peace and a member of the Court of Pleas and Quarter Sessions for Wake County, N. C., and was a member of the Provincial Congress of North Carolina at Halifax, in 1781-1782. He removed to Wilkes County, Ga., probably in 1787, as in July of that year he obtained from the State 1,300 acres of land in Wilkes. He was a member of the State Senate from Oglethorpe County, in 1794-1795, and a member from the same county in the Constitutional Convention of 1798. He strenuously opposed and voted against the Yazoo Fraud, and with indignation and wrath repulsed and denounced a tentative step to bribe him. His death occurred in 1800. At this time he was in his forty-ninth year. His wife died in 1806. Both are buried at the old homestead near Pope's Chapel, in Oglethorpe County, Ga.

Besides four daughters, Abraham and Christian (Walton) Hill had eight sons, only one of whom failed to reach adult years. Burwell and Priscilla (Wootten) Pope had three sons and four daughters. Now begins the intermarriage of these families. Three of Abraham Hill's sons married daughters of Burwell Pope, while two of his daughters married Burwell Pope's brothers, viz., Henry Augustus and Wiley. It seems that the men of the latter family made reprisals for the capture of their sisters by the men of the former, or, to quote the late Judge Pope Barrow, "the Hills and the Popes intermarried backwards and forwards, right and left."

Two of Abraham Hill's sons married daughters, and two of his grand- daughters married sons, of Micajah McGehee. One son married a daugh- ter of Benjamin Andrew, of Liberty County, Ga., a member of the Council of Safety during the Revolution, and an uncle of Bishop Andrew. Another son married Miss Polly Jordan. One daughter married Josiah Jordan, and another Benjamin Blake. Burwell Pope's fourth daughter married a Holmes. His eldest son died unmarried. One married Miss Sallie Davis, and Burwell, Jr., married Sallie K. Strong. This Burwell was commissioned a brigadier-general in 1828, and commanded a brigade in the Florida In- dian War. He died in Athens in 1840. Henry Augustine Pope, by his first wife, had only one daughter and a son, Middleton, to reach mature years. From this son, who married Lucy Lumpkin, are descended the Barrows of Athens. Henry Augustine Pope, by his second wife, had a daughter and two sons. One of the latter was twice married. His first wife was Sarah Toombs, sister of Hon. Robert Toombs, and his second wife, Miss Addie Davis. Colonel Wiley and Polly (Hill) Pope had three sons and a daughter. The latter married a Huling. One son married a Callaway, and their son Wiley became the father of 22 children, only five of whom reached mature years. Another son died at Scull Shoals, on the Oconee River, while a third son, Wiley Hill Pope, died near Independence, in Wilkes County, in 1868, leaving two sons who lived with their mother in Coweta, or Meriwether, County, near Hogansville. John Pope married a Miss Smith, and died in 1821, leaving six daughters and two sons.

Henry Hill, a brother of Abraham, married Sarah Cotten. They came from North Carolina to Wilkes about 1787. He died about 1800, and his wife in 1812-1814. They had four sons, viz., John, Abraham, Theophilus and Henry—these names are the same as those of the four sons of Abraham. There were also four daughters, one of whom married Colonel William Johnson, for many years the sheriff of Wilkes. Another married a Josey, and from them is descended Mrs. J. C. C. Black, of Augusta. Another married Josiah Woods, and a fourth daughter married Henry Pope.

Burwell Pope Hill and Lodowick Meriwether Hill, sons of Wiley, and grandsons of Abraham Hill, married daughters of Colonel William Johnson, their second cousins. After Burwell Hill's death, his widow married Rev. William D. Martin, of Meriwether County, Ga. She was the grand- mother of Justice Warner Hill, Mrs. Justice Samuel Atkinson, Governor John M. Slaton and Hon. W. M. Slaton, Superintendent of the Public Schools of Atlanta. The wife of Judge Benjamin H. Hill is a granddaughter of Colonel Lodowick Meriwether Hill.

Isaac Hill, a brother of Abraham, came from North Carolina to Wilkes about 1787, but later in life, resided either in Clarke or in Franklin.

Abraham Hill's progeny, though not as numerous as the stars of heaven, yet are sufficient in numbers to attest the appropriateness of his name, scripturally defined as "the father of a great multitude." The descend- ants of the Hills, Popes, and McGehees, will be found in almost every section of Georgia, Alabama, Mississippi, and Texas. Impelled by the adventurous spirit of the Anglo-Saxon, so strikingly manifested in their forefathers, whenever the population became dense or crowded or the soil failed to respond in abundant fruitfulness to their labors, they severed all family and local ties and migrated westward. They wanted broader acres, with greater opportunities for acquiring wealth and for obtaining advancement in professional and political life. To this day, they are a sturdy, industrious, law-abiding, peace-loving and God-fearing people. They have striven arduously to acquire not only a competence but a liberal supply of worldly goods, the possession of which gives power, influence, and the ability to do good. They are proud of their ancestry and love their kindred, but their neighbor no less. They illustrate and exemplify in their lives an abiding faith in the proverb that ''a good name is rather to be chosen than great riches, and loving favor rather than silver and gold.'' In agricultural, commercial, and industrial lines, many have become wealthy; while not a few have won distinction in political and professional life and have filled with credit to themselves and with profit to their country, positions of great honor and trust.

Historic Homes of Wilkes. Eleven miles northwest of Washington, on the south side of the road to Danielsville, stood the old home of Gen. John Clark, afterwards Governor of Georgia. Gen. Clark was for years one of the most commanding characters in the early history of the State. On one of the tombs in the old burial-ground is lettered this inscription: ''George Walton Clark, son of John and Nancy Clark, born January 11, 1797; died, October 27, 1798.'' Here, on the night preceding the battle of Kettle Creek, the Revolutionary troops were encamped. In the year 1800, this fine old estate became the property of Col. Wiley Hill. The original building was a large, commodious frame structure, of the best type then prevalent, but in the eighteen-fifties, after the death of Mrs. Hill, it became the property of their youngest daughter, Mrs. William M. Jordan. She razed the old building and erected in its stead what was probably the handsomest home in the county, but, unfortunately, within a year after its completion, this magnificent dwelling was destroyed by fire. It was replaced by a roomy cottage, but this has since been removed and there now remains nothing except the burial-ground to mark the site. Col. Wiley Hill, his wife, and a number of their family are here interred.

The homestead of Col. Lodowick Meriwether Hill, one of the most stately, imposing, and beautiful in the county, is situated fifteen miles northwest of Washington on the road to Danielsville and one and a half miles from the line of Oglethorpe. It was originally a large two-story frame building, erected during the first quarter of the last century, with eleven rooms, and a wide veranda. In the eighteen-fifties, it was remodeled on the Colonial style, with fourteen rooms, four of which were 20 by

20 feet each. There were wide halls running through from east to west, opening upon wide porches, and still wider halls running north and south from the front to the center of the building; besides a wide, long colonnade, with massive fluted columns, three feet in diameter, supporting the parapet roof. The upper front hall opened upon a balcony. This handsome old home is still in a perfect state of preservation and, save an addition of two rooms in the rear, is just as it was in the fifties. The various buildings on the place, such as barns, gin houses, etc., were large and imposing. All were substantially built and kept in splendid repair. There were so many of them that the place appeared more like a town than a country-seat. Mr. A. P. Anthony, who married Miss Lucy Hill, is the present owner and occupant.

The homestead of Col. Wiley Pope Hill is situated eight miles northwest of Washington on the Danielsville road. It is a large two-story frame building with a wide veranda. It stands in a beautiful grove of forest trees and, save an addition of some two or more rooms made in recent years, looks just as it did when built. His widow, Mrs. Jane (Austin) Hill, died last year in her eighty-ninth year. One daughter and two sons now own and occupy the old homestead.

Washington! There is not a town in the State around whose majestic old homes there clusters more of architectural beauty, of social charm, of intellectual culture, or of historic renown. Most of these homes are built on the stately pattern peculiar to the spacious days of the old South; and while the spirit of modern enterprise is everywhere apparent in this wideawake community it is still fragrant with the memories of a gentler time. "Haywood," the splendid old home of Judge Garnett Andrews, was built in 1798, by Gilbert Hay, Esq., a gentleman of wealth, well known to the people of the State a hundred years ago. He was John Clark's second, in his famous duel with William H. Crawford. "Haywood" is today owned by Mrs. T. M. Green, a daughter of Judge Andrews. The home of Gen. Toombs is still one of the chief centers of attraction in Washington. This fine old Colonial mansion was built by Dr. Joel Abbott, in 1815. It was subsequently remodeled by Gen. Toombs, who here, during the ante-bellum period, dispensed a hospitality characteristic of this princely Georgian. Col. F. H. Colley, who married Miss Kate Toombs, a niece of the General, now owns and occupies the mansion. The Alexander home, built by Felix Gilbert, great grandfather of Mr. Charles Alexander, is now the home of the Misses Alexander. It dates back to the year 1808. In the rear of this home stands the famous Presbyterian poplar, one of the largest trees in the State. The handsome old Lane home was built in 1798. It was the old home of Garland Wingfield, and was moved from Walnut Hill, where the Rev. John Springer taught his noted school. This property now belongs to Misses Annie and Emmie

MOUNT PLEASANT:
The Old Home of the Talbots, Near Washington, Ga.

Lane, great nieces of Garland Wingfield. The Cleveland house, built by Albert Semmes, and owned by A. Cleveland, is now the property of J. T. Lindsay. The Jesse House, built as a Methodist parsonage, in 1815, was the home of the Semmes family for years. It is now owned by Col. J. M. Pitner. The Tupper home, built in 1804, by Albert Semmes, was remodeled in after years by the Rev. H. A. Tupper, D. D., who occupied it for some time. It is now the home of Mr. E. A. Barnett, a former mayor of Washington. The old Fielding place, built in 1819, on a lot bought in 1794, for years the home of Dr. Fielding Ficklin. It is now owned by Dr. Lynden. The Alexander Pope place, built in 1814 and afterwards remodeled by Mr. Pope, is now the home of Dr. Simpson. The Gabriel Toombs place, built by the father of Gabriel Toombs, was once the home of Merrell Callaway, father of James Callaway, Esq., of Macon. It is now owned by Mr. Augustus Toombs.

Mt. Pleasant: The Old Talbot Home. In Volume I of this work will be found a brief reference to this historic old landmark, a part of which is still standing, near Smyrna church, on the old road to Lincolnton. While it reaches back to the days of John Talbot, the Virginia immigrant, and was also the home of Matthew Talbot, an honored chief-magistrate of Georgia, it was known for years prior to the Civil War, as the home of Thomas Talbot, an elder brother of the Governor. This revered old patriarch lived to celebrate his eighty-sixth birthday. Distinguished for his great piety there is a current anecdote which will illustrate his reputation in this respect. It was customary, in the early days, to hold court near the cross-roads. One day the Bible was missing, and there was nothing on which to swear witnesses. Whereupon a man walked up to Thomas Talbot, and, slapping him on the shoulder, said: "Swear by Talbot, he's next to the Bible."

Thomas Talbot's father, John Talbot, was the wealthiest land-owner in Wilkes. Just after the Revolution, or just before—there is some doubt on this point—he acquired a large body of land in this part of the State, containing some 50,000 acres. He settled on these lands in 1783. John Talbot served in the Legislature and was also a delegate to the Convention in Augusta, called to ratify the Federal Constitution. He gave five acres of land to Smyrna church, part of it to be used as a burial-ground; and here, within a walled enclosure, just to the rear of the church, this revered old pioneer today sleeps. Whitney, the inventor of the cotton gin, sometime in the seventeen-nineties, lived on a small farm of eighty acres, adjoining Mr. Talbot's plantation, on which he set up one of his gins— probably the first ever erected. Later, the old gin house became appurtenant to the Talbot estate.* But for years rice and tobacco were the chief crops raised in Georgia, especially by the Virginia planters.

---

*See Vol. I, p. 1052.

Major-General W. H. T. Walker, a gallant Confederate officer, who lost his life in the battle of Atlanta, on July 22, 1864, was a descendant of Thomas Talbot. Madam Octavia Walton LeVert, perhaps the most celebrated Southern woman of her day, belonged to this same family connection. Mrs. Elizabeth Talbot Belt, the last member of the Talbot family born at Mount Pleasant—the old Talbot home in Wilkes—is now living in her eighty-sixth year at Millen, Ga. She is a gentle lady of rare intellectual gifts, with a vigor of mind marvelous for her years; and she is never more delightfully reminiscent than in telling of her girlhood days in Wilkes. Mrs. Belt is connected also with the famous Washington family of Virginia, as the following record made in her grandfather's Bible will attest:

"Thomas Talbot and Elizabeth Creswell, married August 22, 1790, Laurens District, S. C., by the Rev. John Springer. Elizabeth Creswell was the only daughter of Mary Garlington and the Rev. James Creswell. Mary Garlington was the grand-daughter of Annie Ball, fourth daughter of Col. Richard Ball, and half-sister of Mary Ball, the mother of George Washington."

———

WILKINSON

Irwinton. In 1905 Wilkinson County was organized out of a part of the lands acquired from the Creek Indians, under the treaty at Fort Wilkinson, and was named for General James Wilkinson, of Revolutionary fame, one of the commissioners on the part of the United States to treat with the Creeks, at Fort Wilkinson. The town was incorporated by an Act approved December 4, 1816, with the following-named commissioners, to-wit.: Solomon Worrell, David Roland, Adam Hunter, Peter McArthur and William Beck.[1] When the town was re-incorporated in 1854, the commissioners named at this time were: Elbert J. Gilbert, Nathaniel A. Carswell, William Taylor, Wade F. Sanford and William O. Beall.[2] During this same year a charter was granted for the Talmage Normal Institute, with the following board of trustees: Green B. Burney, Thomas N. Beall, William Fisher, Eleazer Cumming, E. J. Gilbert, N. C. Hughes,

---

[1] Lamar's Compendium, p. 1024.
[2] Acts, 1853-1854, p. 254.

Leroy Fleetwood, F. D. Ross, James Jackson, Joel Deese,
R. L. Story, R. I. Cochran, N. A. Carswell and William
Taylor.[1] Some of the early representatives of Irwin
County in the General Assembly were—Senators: John
Ball, Robert Jackson, John Hatcher, William Beck,
Samuel Beall, Daniel M. Hall, W. G. Little and Joel
Rivers; Representatives: John T. Fairchilds, Matthew
Carswell, Daniel Hicks, Charles Culpepper, Morton N.
Burch, Osborn Higgins, Benjamin Mitchell, Benjamin
Exum, James Neal, Joel Rivers, William G. Little and
John Hatcher.

WORTH

Sylvester. On December 20, 1853, portions of two older
counties, Dooly and Irwin, were organized
into a new county called Worth, in honor of a distinguished officer of the Mexican War, General William J.
Worth, a son-in-law of General Zachary Taylor. This
same Act authorized the Inferior Court judges to locate
a site for public buildings and to make a purchase of
whatever land was necessary, and out of this legislation
grew the present town of Sylvester, one of the most enterprising communities of South Georgia. Its charter
of incorporation was granted December 21, 1898, with
W. H. McPhane as mayor and Messrs. C. W. Hilhouse,[2]
W. A. Jones, J. G. Polhill and W. L. Sikes as councilmen.
Sylvester's present public school system was established
in 1900. Some of the pioneers who represented Worth
County in the Legislature were: Daniel Henderson. M.
Simmons, G. G. Ford, Royal R. Jenkins, W. J. Ford, J.
M. Summer, David H. Champion and D. McClellan.

---

[1] Acts, 1853-1854, p. 146.
[2] Acts, 1898, p. 269.

Pindartown.   On the banks of the Flint River, called by the Indians "Thronateeska," has been located the site of an old Indian village, known as Pindartown.   In after years there was a white settlement of some importance at this place.   Pindartown was for a long time the only post-office in this part of the State, and when Newton and Palmyra arose it was for years a recognized rival of these towns.   It was even the post-office for Albany, until 1836, when the latter town received its first charter.   Its location at the head of navigation on the Flint gave it fine prospects at one time, but with the rise of Albany, its glories began to fade.   There are numerous local traditions to the effect that Oglethorpe himself here made a treaty with the Indians.

ADDENDUM

WHITFIELD

History of Dalton. The city of Dalton, formerly Cross Plains, was incorporated in 1847. Captain Edward White, a Northern man, was at the head of a syndicate who bought the land on which the city was built.

In selecting the location, he planned for a great city, surveying the streets, and setting aside sites for parks, school houses, churches and public buildings. Dalton's three principal streets are a mile in length by a hundred feet in width. As there was no large town between Knoxville, Tenn., and Augusta, Ga., he believed that Dalton would become the metropolis of North Georgia. At that time Ross' Station (Chattanooga) and Marthasville (Atlanta) were only clusters of cabins.

Captain White was a man of great public spirit and donated many sites for public buildings to the city.

Associated with him in the syndicate were a number of men prominently identified with the building of the town. Many of the Dalton streets were named for these men. The main business street was named for Colonel John Hamilton, and the beautiful residence street, Thornton Avenue, was named for Colonel Mark Thornton; Pentz Street was named for Mr. Frederick Pentz, and Morris Street for James and Franklin B. Morris.

The city was named for the wife of Captain White, whose maiden name was Miss Emma Dalton. She was a daughter of General Tristram Dalton, who was at one time speaker of the House of Representatives of Massachusetts.

Until the beginning of the war, Captain Whites' dream of a great future for Dalton seemed about to be realized, for it was a busy, prosperous place, with handsome churches and business houses, two banks, three hotels and many beautiful homes, with a cultured, refined people, of whom their descendants are justly proud.

The war changed all this, and Dalton was left in ashes, with only a few houses standing, to show where the town had once been. One of the few homes that was not burned was the home of Captain White. It was torn down a few years ago, and a handsome residence erected on the site by Mr. Lynn Denton.

Many of the early settlers were from South Carolina, Virginia and South Georgia.

The first Mayor was A. E. Blount, and the one serving during the time of the war was Judge Elbert Sevier Byrd.

The first Ordinary of the county was William Gordon. The first Sheriff was Captain Fred Cox, and the first Clerk of the Court was John Anderson, and the first will probated was that of Thomas Wylie.

In 1844 a German colony, under the leadership of Count Frederick Charles, settled in North Dalton. Some of the names of men comprising this colony were: Peter and Adam Kriescher, Herman and Augustus Yeager, A. Lippman, Charles Knorr, A. Bolander, Henry Rauchenberg, Augustus Guntz, Adam Pfanakhche, John Setzefant and numbers of others.

A list of pioneer citizens of Whitfield County:*

Captain Ed White
Franklin B. Morris
Major James Morris
Dr. F. T. Black
Thomas Cook
Dr. John Harris
John Anderson
Garland Jefferson
C. C. McCrary
Wick Earnest
Charles Adams
Charles Barry
Dr. J. Bailey
Jabez Pitman
R. S. Rushton
James Buchanan
Jack Oliver
Prof. John Tyler
Judge William P. Chester
Col. J. A. R. Hanks
Col. J. A. W. Johnson
Judge Leander Crook
Dr. B. B. Brown
Rev. Levi Brotherton
Rev. George Selvidge
T. S. Swift
Col. Patrick McCowan
Col. J. T. Whitman
John Norris
Andrew Norris
Major James Bard
Mark Thornton
Col. I. E. Shumate
Dr. John Allen
Lewis Bender
Dr. M. R. Banner
Dr. Foute

Dr. Waugh
Frank Jackson
Robert O'Neill
John Hill
Bob Hill
Ralph Ellison
John Beaty
Judge Dawson Walker
Wiley Farnsworth
Anderson Farnsworth
Robert Burner
John Henry King
Rev. H. C. Carter
C. B. Welborn
Dickson Taliaferro
James Longly
Captain Fred Cox
Judge Jesse Freeman
Col. W. K. Moore
J. F. Denton
Richard Tarver
Dr. Winston Gordon
Col. Jesse Glenn
Judge Ebert S. Bird
John Hamilton
Judge Underwood
Wilson Green
Joseph Lynan
J. N. B. Cobb
Jack Cobb
Thomas Henderson, Sr.
Captain A. P. Roberts
Henry Davis
Warren R. Davis
Col. Charles E. Broyles
Amos Sutherland
Rev. A. Fitzgerald

---

*Authority: Mrs. Warren Davis, historian John Milledge Chapter, D. A. R. Information received too late to be inserted in the proper connection.

A. E. Blunt
Mr. Holt
Nathaniel Harben
Dr. Groves
John and Nick **Bitting**
Major Harden
Jesse Trotter
J. M. Crute
J. W. Sitton
William Nichols
John P. Love
James Fields
Mr. Cuyler
Mr. Crawford
David Ware
Mr. Hawthorn
Mr. Spencer
Mr. Thompson
John Reynolds
Mr. Wright
Jacob Wrinkle

William Hammond
Lawrence Barrett
Ed Craigmiles
Mr. Sims
Duff Green
Thomas Jolly
Albert Senter
Mr. Lother
Mr. Fincher
George Williamson
Tim Ford
John Hackney
Mr. Emory
Mr. Franklin
Mr. Bishop
Frederick Pentz
Mr. Paxton
Mr. Sasseen
Henry Wrench
Mr. Cate
J. B. Nichols

INDEX

VOLUME ONE

INDEX

VOLUME TWO